Leading Edge
Internal Auditing

Leading Edge Internal Auditing

JEFFREY RIDLEY
ANDREW CHAMBERS

ICSA Publishing
*The Official Publishing Company of
The Institute of Chartered Secretaries and Administrators*

In association with

Prentice Hall Europe
London New York Toronto Sydney Tokyo Singapore
Madrid Mexico City Munich Paris

First published 1998 by
ICSA Publishing Limited
Campus 400, Maylands Avenue
Hemel Hempstead
Hertfordshire, HP2 7EZ

© Andrew Chambers and Jeffrey Ridley 1998

All rights reserved. No part of this publication may be reproduced, stored in a retrieval system, or transmitted, in any form, or by any means, electronic, mechanical, photocopying, recording or otherwise, without prior permission, in writing, from the publisher.

Typset in 9.25/12pt Sabon
by Keyword Typesetting Services Ltd

Printed and bound in Great Britain by MPG Books Ltd, Bodmin, Cornwall

British Library Cataloguing in Publication Data

A catalogue record for this book is available from
the British Library

ISBN 1-860720-3-58

1 2 3 4 5   02 01 00 99 98

*Dedicated to the profession
of internal auditing*

Contents

Preface	page xix
Foreword	xxiii
Acknowledgements	xxv

INTRODUCTION
What is modern internal auditing?   xxix

Be a proactive small internal audit unit	xxix
Understand modern internal auditing principles and practices	xxix
Understand modern management principles and practices	xxx
Understanding technology is core to best practice internal auditing	xxxi
Achieve best-practice internal auditing services	xxxi
Recruit and develop appropriate internal audit staff	xxxii
Develop leading edge internal auditing	xxxii
Summary	xxxiii
Bibliography	xxxiv

PART I
Establishing internal auditing in an organisation   1

CHAPTER 1
Achieving added value from leading edge internal auditing   3

Understand the history and development of professional internal auditing	3
Seek evidence of internal auditing practices	5
Analyse internal auditing practices: traditional, new and leading edge activities	7
Relate the internal auditing concerns and issues of others to your own vision	11
Benchmark for success in internal auditing	12
Achieve leading edge values in the smaller internal audit unit	13
Add leading edge value through professionalism	16

viii   Contents

Add leading edge value through talented people — 19
Add leading edge value through independence and objectivity — 21
Add leading edge value through innovation — 23
Chapter summary — 24
Principia — 25
Bibliography — 26
Cases — 28

CHAPTER 2
Leading edge internal auditing as part of the management control framework — 52

Add leading edge value by being an expert on management control — 52
Define management, control and governance — 57
Create a framework of control objectives for your own organisation — 65
Link management, control and governance to performance — 72
Think like a criminal — 74
Understand the importance of time and the future — 75
Teach managers to self-assess and report on their responsibility for control — 77
Chapter summary — 79
Principia — 80
Bibliography — 80
Cases — 82

CHAPTER 3
Market the success of modern internal auditing — 111

Market modern internal auditing — 111
Lead an innovative and imaginative service — 115
Create a vision of future internal auditing — 115
Market internal auditing as objective and independent — 117
Establish and market an internal audit charter based on professional standards — 119
Design job specifications to meet your customers' needs — 121
Maintain an internal audit manual — 123
Market exciting internal auditing pictures — 123
Link your vision, charter, job specifications and manual into marketing quality — 125
Compete in the internal auditing market place — 129
Chapter summary — 132
Principia — 132
Bibliography — 133
Cases — 134

CHAPTER 4
Design quality into internal audit teams — 153

Add value through teamwork	153
Use technology to make teams more effective	157
Interlock all teams in a web of common objectives	157
Create interlocking internal audit teams	158
Establish features of excellence in internal auditing teams	162
Seek value from innovative internal auditing teams	163
Avoid conflict in internal auditor/specialist/auditee teams	164
Chapter summary	165
Principia	165
Bibliography	166
Cases	166

PART II
Internal auditing procedures — 183

CHAPTER 5
Audit planning — 185

Applying risk assessment to the development of audit plans at all levels	185
Part A: Planning and conducting an audit assignment	185
Understanding the audit as a project	186
The psychology of the audit project	186
Understanding the activities of an audit	188
Preparing for the audit	189
Making introductions	189
Finding and documenting facts	190
Testing for compliance	190
Completing the assessment of internal control	190
Assessing the impact of control weaknesses	190
Reporting audit results	191
Concluding the audit	191
Following up	191
Facilitating activities of an audit	192
Part B: Making an audit needs assessment	192
Audit views of risk	192
Internal audit risk	193
Modelling internal audit risk	194
Components of internal audit risk	195
Reducing to a formula	200
Subjective judgements in audit needs assessment	201
Mechanics of formula design	202

x Contents

Weighting factors	208
Seeking consensus	210
Chapter summary	210
Principia	211
Case	212

CHAPTER 6
Measuring internal audit performance — 214

Placing internal audit in context	215
Market testing internal audit	215
Understanding what internal auditing Standards require	217
Categorising internal audit performance measures	218
Measuring inputs	221
Measuring processes	222
Measuring outputs	223
Interpreting performance measures	226
Integrating performance measures with good management practice	226
Evaluating value for money from internal audit, using performance measures	228
Chapter summary	230
Principia	230
Notes	231
Cases	232

CHAPTER 7
Reporting and progressing audit findings — 237

Understand the types of internal audit report	238
Tailor for the reader	243
Understand the objectives of audit reports	244
Understand there are other ways to achieve the objectives of audit reports	245
Use the Audit Summary Working Paper (ASWP) form	246
Develop a draft report for discussion	248
Know which auditors should be involved	250
Ensure appropriate circulation	252
Achieve appropriate timing	253
Write balanced reports	254
Draft reports effectively	256
Use an acceptable presentation style	256
Use English well	259
Write clearly	259
Make sure structure and content are right	261
Present audit reports orally	266
Follow up	266

Measure reporting success	270
Retain audit reports	270
Review audit reports	270
Chapter summary	271
Principia	271
Notes	272
Case	273

CHAPTER 8
Impact of information technology on internal auditing — 275

Using IT to improve audit service	275
Matching audit technology to management's technology	275
Being constructive as well as objective	276
Auditing the systems development process	278
Auditing IT facilities	284
Auditing individual IT applications	286
Using audit software	287
Using software for audit administration	289
Chapter summary	289
Principia	290
Notes	291
Cases	291

CHAPTER 9
Internal auditing working with the board — 303

Understanding responsibility for internal control	303
Defining internal control	305
Reporting publicly on internal control	305
Deciding the scope of the directors' internal control report	307
Understanding the mission of the audit committee	307
Interfacing internal audit with the audit committee	309
Assisting in developing an internal control report for publication	313
Assessing the effectiveness of internal control	315
Chapter summary	319
Principia	319
References	320
Notes	320
Cases	321

APPENDICES
A Glossary of terms	337
B The Institute of Internal Auditors: Code of Ethics	346

xii Contents

C The Institute of Internal Auditors: Statement of Responsibilities
of Internal Auditing348
D The Institute of Internal Auditors: Summary of General and Specific
Standards for the Professional Practice of Internal Auditing351
E Sample charter for small internal auditing departments354
F Sample code of business conduct357
G Key issues in common business activities366
H Principia for leading edge internal auditing380
I List of organisations that can be contacted385

INDEX 391

List of Figures

1.1	1997 Spectrum snapshot of UK internal auditing	page 9
1.2	Mautz and Sharaf's eight postulates of auditing	10
1.3	A vision of internal auditing	11
1.4	Ten key attributes of world-class internal auditing in the year 2000	15
1.5	Nine key strategies for internal auditing to achieve by the year 2000	16
1.6	Twelve actions for your internal audit unit	17
1.7	The auditor's code: fundamental principles of independent auditing	18
1.8	The IIA framework for the professional practice of internal auditing	19
1.9	A common body of knowledge for internal auditing	20
1.10	Most frequent terms describing internal auditors in job vacancies	23
1.11	Examples of audit services provided by internal audit units	24
2.1	Ten key attributes of world-class internal auditing in the year 2000	53
2.2	Average time spent on types of internal audit work	56
2.3	Management perceptions of internal audit value	56
2.4	Seven S framework – a new view of organisation	57
2.5	Definitions of control pre-1990s	60
2.6	Definitions of control 1990 onwards	61
2.7	CIPFA governance definitions	63
2.8	Nolan standards in public life	64
2.9	Standards of corporate governance in the public services	65
2.10	Guidance on control (CoCo)	66
2.11	The code of best practice	68
2.12	Nolan elements of best practice	70
2.13	A framework for control and governance	71
2.14	Russell fraud check-list	75
2.15	The control time span	76
3.1	Rules for promoting quality	113
3.2	Deming's 14 quality points	114
3.3	Promotion of internal auditing by others	114
3.4	ACT – a motif for all internal audit units	115

3.5	Examples of vision statements	116
3.6	Theory underlying audit committee status	118
3.7	Descriptions most often used in internal audit job vacancy notices	121
3.8	The TQM framework	126
3.9	Quality measures for the internal audit unit	126
3.10	Internal auditing reasons for ISO 9000 registration	129
3.11	Internal auditing benefits from ISO 9000 registration	130
3.12	Advantages and disadvantages of outsourcing internal auditing	131
4.1	Eastman Kodak Company: characteristics of an effective team	155
4.2	The NSQT team training structure	156
4.3	Examples of internal audit teams	160
4.4	Importance of internal audit features of excellence in teams	163
5.1	Synonyms of risk components	194
5.2	Formula for a retail stores company	195
5.3	A Training and Enterprise Council internal audit risk formula	196
5.4	A Training and Enterprise Council scoring scale for the 'size' factors in the internal audit risk formula	197
5.5	A Training and Enterprise Council scoring scale for the 'control' factors in the internal audit risk formula	198
5.6	A Training and Enterprise Council scoring scale for the 'audit' factors in the internal audit risk formula	199
5.7	Formula for a UK privately owned company, manufacturing packaging and other products	203
5.8	Formula for a specialised lubricants and chemicals marketing company	204
5.9	Formula for a manufacturer and distributor of brands of alcoholic beverages	205
5.10	Formula for a privately owned, diversified health care company, in diagnostics, orthopaedics, molecular medicine, therapeutics and biochemistry	206
5.11	Formula for a personal finance subsidiary of a UK clearing bank	207
5.12	Matrix method of arriving at relative weights for factors	209
6.1	Potential advantages of contracting out internal auditing	216
6.2	Potential advantages of in-house internal auditing provision	216
6.3	Standard on Planning (IIA)	217
6.4	Specific Standard 560 Quality Assurance (IIA)	218
6.5	A model of input, process and output	219
6.6	Management satisfaction survey	220
6.7	*Input* performance measures	221
6.8	*Process* performance measures	223
6.9	Implicit or explicit objectives of internal audit	224
6.10	*Output* performance measures	224

List of figures   xv

6.11	Internal audit reporting success	225
6.12	Factors affecting internal audit independence	227
6.13	CIPFA's 'four fundamental questions' to be addressed by the audit committee, by management, by the head of internal audit, and by external audit	228
6.14	Economy (*inputs*) measures in the context of a value for money approach	228
6.15	Efficiency (*process*) measures in the context of a value for money approach	229
6.16	Effectiveness (*outputs*) measures in the context of a value for money approach	229
7.1	Guidance on communicating results (IIA)	238
7.2	Internal audit organisational status and communication with the board (IIA)	240
7.3	Internal audit purpose, authority and responsibilities (IIA)	241
7.4	Internal audit quality assurance (IIA)	242
7.5	Requirements of internal audit reports (IIA)	243
7.6	Audit summary working paper	247
7.7	Discussion of internal audit conclusions and recommendations (IIA)	249
7.8	Inclusion in reports of auditee's views (IIA)	249
7.9	Signing internal audit reports (IIA)	251
7.10	Reviewing internal audit reports (IIA)	251
7.11	Authorised report signatories (IIA)	252
7.12	Circulation of audit reports	253
7.13	Audit report distribution (IIA)	254
7.14	Getting audit reports out promptly	255
7.15	Balance in audit reports (IIA)	256
7.16	Rules for writing reports	257
7.17	Essential attributes of audit reports (IIA)	260
7.18	Summary reports (IIA)	262
7.19	Content of audit reports (IIA)	263
7.20	Recommendations in audit reports (IIA)	266
7.21	Follow-up (IIA)	267
7.22	Monitoring the status of audit recommendations	270
8.1	Internal audit objectivity and involvement during systems development	278
9.1	The spirit of external control	304
9.2	COSO's 1992 definition of internal control	304
9.3	The Rutteman 1994 definition of internal control and internal financial control	305
9.4	The Institute of Internal Auditors' definition of internal control	306

9.5	Public reporting on internal control – minimum Rutteman requirements for the content of the report	308
9.6	The four duties of an audit committee	308
9.7	Data on audit committees	309
9.8	Audit committees formally reporting on internal control	314
9.9	Internal audit's overall summary opinion on internal control effectiveness	316
9.10	Letter of representation on internal control	317
9.11	Criteria for assessing internal control effectiveness	318

List of cases

1.1	Internal auditing 1997: new and leading edge	page 28
1.2	Use a Delphi study to develop best practice internal auditing	30
1.3	Internal auditing 1987	37
1.4	Internal auditing professional examinations	40
1.5	Developing new offerings	47
2.1	A control overview: internal control is like a well-lit Christmas tree	82
2.2	Management and control in a large retail company	83
2.3	Easycall Ltd: a top-down review of a control environment	85
2.4	Do charters make a control difference?	91
2.5	The world is no riskier a place	99
2.6	Internal control and internal auditing in Network Housing Association (NHA)	100
3.1	Our 1993 vision and mission	134
3.2	Helping ensure the public purse is protected	136
3.3	Using job descriptions to market internal audit	138
3.4	Internal auditing is an exciting art	142
3.5	Total quality management and the internal auditor	144
3.6	Marketing	150
4.1	Teams and workgroups – working across networks	166
4.2	The team is everything	168
4.3	Is success what you do, or what the team does?	172
4.4	Post Office Counters Ltd: the quality journey	177
5.1	Supervising	212
6.1	Determination of appropriate internal audit resources	232
6.2	Benchmarking	233
6.3	Measuring customer satisfaction	234

xviii List of cases

7.1	Some rules for written communication	273
8.1	Use of interrogation software	291
8.2	Effective audit use of portable computers	292
8.3	Best practice internal audit involvement with information technology	292
8.4	Information Technology glossary	299
9.1	Terms of reference for the audit committee	321
9.2	Timing and content of audit committee meetings	325
9.3	Implementing a control and risk self-assessment programme	327
9.4	Control risk assessment – defining a new vision	331
9.5	Tomorrow's company: the role of business in a changing world	334

Preface

> Let us not take it for granted that life exists more fully in what is commonly thought big than in what is commonly thought small. (Virginia Woolf, 'The Common Reader', *Modern Fiction* (1925))

There is increasing management interest in the values which internal auditing can add to an organisation's internal control framework. These values have been appreciated and encouraged by operational management for some time, in all sectors: they are values for many organisations at both national and international levels. Internal auditors provide a mixture of benefits, from quality in the performance of internal auditing work and associated other services, to contributions to the achievement of organisation objectives; from experience, training and development gained by internal auditors, to future contributions to their organisation's management and specialist careers.

More recently, values from internal auditing have been attracting attention from regulators, non-executive directors in listed and private companies, governing members of many public sector and voluntary organisations, and even the public. This attention arises from an increasing focus on governance and codes of conduct issues by all types of organisation, not only in the UK but worldwide. This focus is not new. There has always been concern over how organisations are managed and controlled. Concern not only by management and internal auditing, but also by many outside regulators – all with an interest in good management practices, meeting legal requirements, and success. Even survival.

What is new, is that many of these outside regulators are now starting to influence the development of internal auditing practices. Over the next few years this influence will change the way many internal auditing units now operate.

Competition amongst audit providers is now a key issue in many organisations and this will spread across sectors as audit committees continue to grow in number and experience. This competition will also change many of the current practices by internal auditors and increase the use of technology in their audit work.

This book targets small internal auditing units, serving all sizes of organisation – small, medium or large. It is written with internal auditing practitioners in mind. Its guidance is also intended to be of use to all those who have an interest in internal auditing best practice – management, directors and governors. Its contents describe how internal audit can provide value from services that will satisfy, if not delight, its customers.

Small internal auditing units account for most activity in the worldwide internal auditing market-place. Drawing a dividing line between small and large internal auditing units is not easy. Deciding what is a small internal auditing unit can be relative to the size of an organisation. Many units have only a single internal auditor, full- or only part-time. Others have more than 100, serving organisations varying in size, from less than 100 to more than 100,000 staff. Throughout this book we examine cases which we believe apply to small internal auditing units of five or less staff, serving varieties of organisation staff sizes, both small and large, across all sectors.

The strengths, weaknesses, opportunities and threats that affect small internal auditing units may be different in larger organisations, but many of the concerns and issues of internal auditing are the same in internal audit units regardless of size.

At the end of each chapter, we have set out principles for the small internal auditing unit. We have called these principles 'principia', and show the complete set at Appendix H. We believe Sir Isaac Newton's use of the scientific term 'principia' for his *Mathematical Principles of Natural Philosophy* to be appropriate also for the science of internal auditing: its use for rules requiring reasoning and rationality is well established. It also dates auditing as an old science with well-established principles, all of which remain still in use today and will be tomorrow. We believe our 'principia for internal auditing' are an essential guide for any small internal auditing unit committed to achieving excellence in all the services it provides.

Part I of the book provides guidance on how to establish an internal auditing unit. Part II describes each of the internal auditing processes needed to develop a strategic plan, audit tactics and agree objectives for each audit assignment: how to conduct an audit to achieve and communicate results. We do not forget the importance of action by internal auditors and management to follow up audit recommendations to ensure that appropriate changes are made to improve control. Follow-up is an essential part of the care internal auditors need to take to ensure their customer's satisfaction, if not delight.

The cases and 'principia' in each chapter provide guidance, whether the reader is establishing a new internal audit unit or reviewing an existing unit to seek improvements in the services it provides. In each chapter, the discussion provides leading edge practices for the strategic direction and planning needed to create the best internal auditing processes, products and services: best not just for the internal auditor, but also best for internal auditing customers throughout the organisation being served.

Finally, we believe our 'principia' to be of importance to all internal auditing units with professional aims, whether small, medium or large. This book is therefore a useful guide for all internal auditors whose aim is to be best.

Jeffrey Ridley
Andrew D. Chambers
July 1997

Foreword

In the last decade, and more especially during the last five to six years, enterprises both in the private and public sectors have experienced many new challenges and demands. The combination of a harsh economic climate and rapid developments in technology, market conditions, internationalisation and cost-awareness have demonstrated the need for solutions. All sectors have experienced increased expectations as regards the achievement of defined objectives, efficient use of resources, improved quality in products and services and, in addition, attention to significant risks such as environmental awareness.

In recent years, corporate governance has been the subject of critically important discussions in many countries around the globe. In this context, the term 'corporate governance' encompasses the proper management of corporations and public sector enterprises. Important elements are ethics, accountability to owners, creditors, workers, authorities and the public-at-large, who demand sound financial and operational control over the activities of the enterprise.

The only way of addressing these issues is an effective system of internal control put in place by management, with oversight from a board of directors. Such a system represents the only effective way of preventing problems as opposed to reacting to them only after loss has occurred. Establishing and maintaining an effective system of internal control calls for skills that can only be provided through a competent and professionally qualified internal auditing function.

Internal auditing is a mature profession whose practitioners are experts in internal control, fraud detection and prevention, and other areas of the corporate governance structure. The audit objective includes promoting effective control at reasonable cost.

Strong corporate governance is an essential ingredient in public trust and reliability for private and public organisations. Auditing is a key factor in this process. In addition to statutory auditor attestations on financial reports, internal auditing is an essential linkage in assuring an adequate system of internal control.

The authors of this book, Jeffrey Ridley and Andrew Chambers, belong to the few people I consider as the European grandfathers of internal auditing. In their never ending efforts to promote the profession, as academics and practitioners, both of them have influenced tremendously the modern practice of internal auditing. 'Leading Edge Internal Auditing' is another successful milestone in their passion for our profession.

Jean-Pierre Garitte, CIA
Senior Vice Chairman of the Board
The Institute of Internal Auditors
October 1997

Acknowledgements

The following are copyright of and reprinted with permission from The Institute of Internal Auditors, Inc., 249 Maitland Avenue, Altamonte Springs, Florida 32701 USA:

Framework for the Standards for the Professional Practice of Internal Auditing
Glossary of Internal Auditing Terms
Code of Ethics
Statement of Responsibilities of Internal Auditing
Summary of General and Specific Standards for the Professional Practice of Internal Auditing
Certified Internal Auditor (CIA®) examination programme

All references into internal auditing research by The IIA Research Foundation (IIARF) are reprinted with permission from The Institute of Internal Auditors, Inc., 249 Maitland Avenue, Altamonte Springs, Florida 32701 USA. These references include the following major projects:

Wood, Wilson and Holub (1989): Professionalism in Internal Auditing
Albrecht, Howe, Schueler and Stocks (1988): Evaluating the Effectiveness of Internal Audit Departments
Systems Auditability and Control© (SAC). (1991)
Albrecht, Stice and Stocks (1992): A Common Body of Knowledge for the Practice of Internal Auditing
Ziegenfuss (1994): Challenges and Opportunities of Small Internal Audit Organisations
Gupta and Ray (1995): Total Quality Improvement Process and the Internal Auditing Function
Ridley and Stephens (1996): International Quality Standards: Implications for Internal Auditing
Gray and Gray (1996): Enhancing Internal Auditing through Innovative Practices

References to The IIA-UK, including details of its professional internal auditing examinations in Chapter 1, sample code of business conduct at Appendix F, and

xxvi Acknowledgements

Case 2.3 Easycall Ltd: A top down review of a control environment, are reproduced with permission from the Institute of Internal Auditors - UK, 13 Abbeville Mews, 88 Clapham Park Road, London SW4 7BX, UK.

References and use of case material from the publications *In Business: The Essential Factfile* (1997), and *Manual of Internal Audit Practice* (1990), are reproduced with permission from ICSA Publishing Ltd., Campus 400, Maylands Avenue, Hemel Hempstead, Hertfordshire, HP2 7EZ, UK.

We are grateful to Graham Rand for his inspiration on several matters, and in particular for his development work which underpins most of the issues addressed in Appendix G: Key issues in common business activities.

The material used for Case 1.1: Internal auditing 1997 – new and leading edge, is reprinted with permission from the May/June 1997 issue of *IIA Today*, published by The Institute of Internal Auditors, Inc., 249 Maitland Avenue, Altamonte Springs, Florida 32701, USA.

The material used for Case 1.3: Internal Auditing 1987 is reprinted with permission from the Report of the National Commission on Fraudulent Financial Reporting, Copyright © 1987, by the American Institute of Certified Public Accountants, Harborside Financial Center, 201 Plaza Three, Jersey City, NJ 07311-3881, USA.

The Auditors' Code in Figure 1.7, is reproduced with permission from The Auditing Practices Board, PO Box 433, Moorgate Place, London EC2P 2BJ, UK.

References to the 7-S Framework diagram – A New View of Organisation, at Figure 2.4 and the Business Horizons' June 1980 article, *Structure is not Organisation*, are reproduced with permission from JAI Press Inc., 55 Old Post Road – No. 2, PO Box 1678, Greenwich, Connecticut, USA.

The material used for Case 2.6 Internal Control and Internal Auditing in Network Housing Association Limited is reproduced with permission from its chief executive, Mr Richard Smillie, and internal audit manager, Mrs Kelsey Beswick.

References into the publication *Corporate Governance. A Framework for Public Service Bodies* (1995) and standards/definitions of corporate governance in Figures 2.7 and 2.9, are reproduced with permission from The Chartered Institute of Public Finance and Accountancy, 16 Park Crescent, London W1N 4AH, UK.

Extracts from The Citizen's Charter (1991), The Citizen's Charter – Five Years On (1996), and the Committee of Standards in Public Life – First Report (1995) and Second Report (1996), used in Chapter 2, Case 2.4: Do charters make a difference?, and the material reprinted in Figure 2.8, are Crown copyright and reproduced with the permission of the Controller of Her Majesty's Stationery Office.

The material used for Figure 2.10 Guidance Control (CoCo) is reprinted with permission from Guidance on Control, 1995, The Canadian Institute of Chartered Accountants, Toronto, Canada. Any changes to the original material are the sole responsibility of the authors and have not been reviewed by or endorsed by the CICA.

Extracts from the Inland Revenue internal audit charter in Chapter 3, are reproduced with permission from Mr Norman Buckley, Controller of the Inland Revenue Audit Office, UK.

References to the Eastman Kodak Company and Kodak Limited material quality, teamwork and internal auditing material in Chapters 3 and 4, and Cases 3.1 and 4.2, are reproduced with permission from both these companies.

The material for Case 4.4: Post Office Counters Ltd: The Quality Journey, is reproduced with permission from its author Mr George Hooper and Carfax Publishing Limited, PO Box 25, Abingdon, Oxfordshire OX14 3UE, UK. This case was presented at the proceedings of the 2nd World Congress for Total Quality Management, 1997. It is reprinted from the journal, *Total Quality Management* Volume 8 Number 2 & 3, pp S187–S190.

The team training structure reproduced at Figures 4.2 and details of The National Society for Quality through Teamwork (NSQT) are used with permission from that society.

Sir Winston S. Churchill's Speech in the House of Commons, 18 June 1940, reproduced in Chapter 7 with permission of Curtis Brown Ltd, London on behalf of The Estate of Sir Winston S. Churchill. Copyright Winston S. Churchill.

The material for Case 8.3: Best Practice Internal Audit Involvement with Information Technology, is reproduced with permission from the Housing Association Internal Audit Forum, UK. Ms Jane V. Davies Bloodworth, Chairman, c/o Sovereign Housing Association, Berkshire House, 17–24 Bartholomew Street, Newbury, Berkshire RG14 5LL, UK.

The material used for Case 9.4: Control Risk Assessment – Defining A New Vision, is reproduced with permission from Mr Tim J. Leech, FCA, MCS Control Training & Design Inc., 3 Robert Speck Parkway, Suite 1010, Mississauga, Ontario L4Z 2G5, Canada.

INTRODUCTION

What is modern internal auditing?

> ... the comprehensive review and appraisal of the diverse operations of an organisation as a service to management ...
>
> (Lawrence B. Sawyer (1973) *Modern Internal Auditing*)

Be a proactive small internal audit unit

Most current random sample research into internal audit units demonstrates a high percentage employing five or fewer staff, and not all on a full-time basis. This book addresses the challenges and opportunities facing small internal audit units in organisations across all sectors. Many of these challenges and opportunities apply to all sizes of internal audit unit, but for those with fewer resources they are sometimes more difficult to respond to. Yet, this should not be so. With the right support from its management and organisation, even the smallest internal audit unit should be able to provide a proactive and modern professional service. Application of the principles described in each chapter can only change any internal audit unit for the better.

Understand modern internal auditing principles and practices

Internal auditing is a young, modern profession. It is one of the first professions, if not the first, to establish international standards and a code of ethics for its professional practices. These standards and the code were developed in the 1970s and subsequently published worldwide for adoption by the profession. Today, they have been enriched by research and successive interpreting guidelines and statements, outlining in detail how professional internal auditing should be practised. The standards and code are now in use in thousands of organisations in more than 100 countries, across all business and public sectors. They embrace many traditional auditing principles and management standards. They are published by a number of professional authorities and are used to establish best internal auditing practices by regulators, organisations and all types of auditors. They make internal auditing modern. Appendices B, C and D reproduce these statements and standards; Appendix A provides a glossary of terms used in their content.

All who practise internal auditing need to understand what these standards recommend, and to adopt or modify them to suit their own auditing environment: 'compliance with the concepts enunciated by the standards is essential before the responsibilities of internal auditing can be met' (The IIA Standards for the Professional Practice of Internal Auditing (1995) p. 4).

This book draws significantly on recent research by the Institute of Internal Auditors Research Foundation into current challenges and opportunities that exist in small internal audit units in North America. This research and its results apply equally well to small internal audit units outside of North America.

Modern internal auditing embraces many sciences. As mentioned in the preface, the development of principia is also appropriate for internal auditing principles. Scientific thought and discovery are never far from auditing techniques. In particular, understanding the science of management is core to best practice internal auditing. Auditing is a fundamental part of management control, regardless of the size of an organisation, or the sector in which it operates. Control is the primary responsibility of an organisation's management, regardless of why it is required, or by whom. Reasonable control and effective auditing are therefore primary responsibilities of management. This maxim applies in all organisations and in all auditing. Auditing responsibilities are seen in the established principles and standards for all levels of management, from senior to supervisory. Auditing exists in all management cultures; even those based on empowerment and interlocking teams.

Understand modern management principles and practices

An understanding of management responsibilities is therefore fundamental to the establishment and development of any internal auditing unit, whatever its objectives or size. This applies whether the internal auditing provider is a member of an organisation's staff, or the activity is outsourced, partly or wholly, to a contractor. Internal auditing practices always require an understanding and application of the science of management, including all its principles of planning, assessing, doing and verifying. The importance of management principles and standards applies in all aspects of internal auditing and in all our cases; the best internal auditors are also the best managers.

All internal auditors should be aware of current thinking and good practice concerning management and managing. This means knowing about how businesses are established, and how they work, grow with success and survive. This rule applies across all sectors and in every organisation, regardless of size. Most organisations have their own specific sector or industry issues, but all have common management and managing issues. Each chapter of the book is referenced into a factfile of management information published in 1997. This emphasises the need for all internal auditors to relate internal auditing to management issues and to understand the common concerns which affect both today.

Understanding technology is core to best practice internal auditing

Internal auditors need to understand the challenges and impact of technology on management and organisations; these challenges and impacts are rarely only internal. They span across organisations and their supply chains at national and international levels. Technology embraces the use of all applied sciences and technical methods in an industry and its sector. Information systems and communications are an important area using technology, but there are many other areas. Technology is also fundamental to control in all operations and their success.

Information technology means much more than the present-day use of computers to process information. In many textbooks and research projects, it is now given a much wider definition, covering the present and future use of technology in information systems, telecommunications, office and operational automation. In this book, IT is defined as the combination of computers, telecommunications and information resources in an organisation and its sector to achieve objectives.

Achieve best-practice internal auditing services

Internal auditing has been defined as 'an independent appraisal function established within an organisation to examine and evaluate its activities' (The IIA Statement of Responsibilities of Internal Auditing (1990)). Since the 1940s, internal auditing has been developed and promoted internationally by accounting and auditing institutes as an independent professional service, to serve all levels of management, in all sectors. Internal auditing is now promoted not only as a service to management, but also as a service to the organisation.

This wider promotion of internal auditing is built into a 1981 revised statement of responsibilities of internal auditing, published by The Institute of Internal Auditors in the USA, and adopted worldwide by many organisations, audit committees and internal auditing units in their work. We use this wider 'organisation' interpretation of internal auditing in our cases. This widens the internal auditing customer base to include all who work in an organisation.

Achieving best practices requires a continuous search for internal audit benchmarks, and development of measures with which to verify improvements. This book and its cases, together with The IIA standards and related principia, form an excellent pathway for the benchmarking enthusiast. Appendix I lists organisations which can provide information for internal auditors in their benchmarking practices.

Recruit and develop appropriate internal audit staff

Maintaining appropriate levels of trained internal auditors and specialists in an internal audit unit can be difficult. For many organisations, meeting internal audit needs is not seen as core to their success or survival. Sometimes these needs are met by employing contracted staff from an external provider of internal auditing services. The practice of outsourcing internal auditing, in part or whole, has increased over recent years, and there is a growing and competitive market-place for providers of internal auditing services and associated specialisms.

As well as knowledge and skills, internal auditors need to be imaginative and confident. Many of the situations and control issues that face internal auditors require an ability to think both laterally and with certainty that their views are correct. In developing audit recommendations there can be many influences which might persuade internal auditors to change their views, reducing the quality of their service to the organisation.

Many of the cases consider the relationship between audit needs and maintaining appropriate trained staff resources, emphasising that best internal audit performance needs best trained and qualified staff.

Develop leading edge internal auditing

All competitive market-places have examples of products and services seen to be at the leading edge of innovation. These products and services rarely emerge by accident. They are carefully designed to meet studied customer expectations, have clear specifications, are well packaged, and have a high level of quality and customer after-service. Internal auditing is no exception to this rule.

Many professional internal auditors have developed leading edge activities in the audit and management services market-places, both to stretch their own competencies and to continuously improve the services they provide to their customers. These are internal auditors who have developed a critical understanding of the science of management and the use of technology. They are at the forefront of implementing that understanding into the products and services they provide to their organisations and are often seen as pioneers in their organisations and across sectors, with many adventures, achievements, some failures and much satisfaction!

Current developments in the market-places for auditing and management services which are encouraging leading edge internal audit activities are:

- the appointment of new non-executive board members and new auditing committees;
- management interest in internal control frameworks, public statements on governance and compliance with externally imposed codes of conduct;
- management interest in risk assessment and risk management;
- recognition of the importance of strong supply chains within and across organisations;
- new organisation alliances, associations and joint ventures;
- the use of consultants to facilitate organisation change and improvement;
- the use of technology to process and store increased information with speed, flexibility and accuracy;
- increased auditing and regulatory activities;
- new global market-places.

Some of these developments have been taking place internationally for many years; others are more recent. All are stimulating new and leading edge internal auditing in the control market-place. It is important that all internal auditors and management should understand and recognise their impact on internal auditing. Each case adopts a leading edge vision. By doing so, it demonstrates that marketing internal auditing services requires vision.

Summary

Best internal auditors:

- understand management principles and standards;
- consider everyone in their organisation;
- personally adopt and comply with professional standards;
- have appropriate levels of knowledge and experience, and maintain their competence;
- continuously strive to improve quality in the services they provide in the auditing and management market-places;
- are confident and have imagination;
- are proactive and visionary.

The above qualities should be apparent in the cases described in each chapter.

Bibliography

Bailey-Scudamore, I. and Van Vlijmen, J.R. (1997) *In Business: The Essential Factfile*, ICSA Publishing, Hemel Hempstead, UK.

Sawyer, Lawrence B. (1973) *The Practice of Modern Internal Auditing*, The Institute of Internal Auditors Inc., Altamonte Springs, USA.

The Institute of Internal Auditors Inc. (1993) *Codification of Standards for The Professional Practice of Internal Auditing*, IIA, Altamonte Springs, USA.

Ziegenfuss, Douglas E. (1994) *Challenges and Opportunities of Small Internal Audit Organisations*, The IIA Research Foundation, Altamonte Springs, USA.

PART I

Establishing internal auditing in an organisation

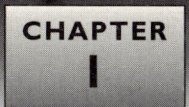

CHAPTER 1

Achieving added value from leading edge internal auditing

> The scope of internal audit requirements has increased tremendously.
>
> (*First Statement on Internal Auditing*, The IIA Inc., 1942)

Understand the history and development of professional internal auditing

The nature and practice of internal auditing have undergone significant change in the last decade. However, many organisations have experienced little change to their internal auditing practices over the past 30 years. True, there are now more internal audit units; yet most of their practices are still based on fundamental auditing principles, as developed in the early years of the twentieth century. These auditing principles remain as true today as they were when first used by both internal and external auditors.

Of course, some may disagree with these statements. Indeed, some internal and external audit practitioners will argue that their auditing practices use new techniques, continuously improving and better today than the principles of yesteryear. Many will claim to have added new values to their auditing practices in order to satisfy today's more complex control requirements. There is certainly evidence to support these beliefs in some organisations and sectors. But equally there is evidence which shows there are other areas of little real change, in terms of basic auditing principles and practices, in many internal audit units. Despite a 1990s focus on rapid change within many organisations, in some internal audit units technology has still not penetrated deeply into auditing practices, while in others internal auditors are still not seen as part of the management team.

During the past 50 years, organisations worldwide in the private and public sectors have established internal audit units and promoted their services as part of management control and the development of key staff. Often, this has been an aspect of internal management strategy – sometimes in response to external influences such as government legislation, stakeholder interests and external audit.

The development of professional internal auditing goes back to the formation of The Institute of Internal Auditors (IIA) in the USA in 1941. The IIA introduced a worldwide image for internal auditing as an 'added-value' professional service, using the challenging statement:

> Today's happenings pose new and perplexing problems to internal auditors. The requests and regulations of the several branches and agencies of Government demand a complete knowledge by internal auditors of their effect on the normal units of the companies they represent. The scope of internal audit requirements has increased tremendously.

Shortly after this 1942 statement, chapters of The IIA were established across the USA and worldwide, including the UK. The growing UK membership of The IIA eventually merged the five existing chapters into an affiliated national institute in 1975. This institute is now named The IIA-UK, and is the largest affiliated organisation to The IIA. The IIA-UK is one of a number of affiliated national institutes worldwide, with a commitment to a common:

- statement of responsibilities;
- code of ethics;
- set of general and specific standards;
- body of knowledge and a requirement for continuing education;
- body of theoretical (and empirical research) literature on best internal auditing;
- requirement for quality assurance to be designed into internal audit work;
- set of benchmarking practices.

Other UK professional bodies or institutes, especially professional accounting institutes, have also promoted standards and guidelines for best-practice internal audit. Prominent among such publications has been the Auditing Practices Board Statement (SAS 500) 'Considering the work of internal audit', which views internal audit as an element of the overall control system established by management. This statement gives guidance on the extent to which the external auditor may rely on the work of the internal auditor. It describes internal audit as:

> An appraisal or monitoring activity, established by management and the directors for the review of the accounting and internal control systems as a service to the entity. It functions by, amongst other things, examining, evaluating, and reporting to management and the directors on the adequacy and effectiveness of components of the accounting and internal control systems.

Both The IIA and APB statements describe internal audit as an independent appraisal unit, established by management, for the review of control as a service to the organisation. Both envisage a wide role for internal audit in terms of reviewing and assessing the adequacy of control, emphasising control objectives of reliability, integrity, compliance, protection, economy, efficiency and effectiveness. This focus on control objectives, when assessing the reasonableness of control, is an essential part of the development of internal auditing.

The Institute of Chartered Accountants in England and Wales (ICAEW) and The IIA use similar frameworks as the structure for their internal auditing guidelines. Both include independence, proficiency, scope, performance and management. In 1976, The IIA developed hypotheses, through research, that demonstrated the importance of auditee perceptions of internal audit work. Auditor/auditee participative teamwork relationships are considered by researchers to be the best way forward for the achievement of audit and organisational goals. A related statement in the research recommends constructive working relationships, but with the proviso that internal audit should not allow its objectivity to be impaired. The message being clearly signalled at that time is that working with management is best for all audit work, but that this should not impair internal audit objectivity and independence. Within organisational constraints, objectivity and independence must be paramount.

Internal audit is now widely seen as a highly professional and skilled task. While there have been influences on the growth of internal auditing in organisations, much of this development has occurred primarily as an extension of management's responsibility for control. This responsibility still rests with all managers, but is now, more than ever before, also associated with all staff in an organisation, and many outside the organisation with interests in its success. Quality programmes, environmental issues and codes of good conduct now place greater responsibilities for control on everyone in an organisation, and all those associated with its products and services, including its suppliers and customers.

Seek evidence of internal auditing practices

There is ample written evidence to show that governments, regulators, professional institutes and accounting firms have all been playing an active part in recent years to shape internal audit services in organisations. There is also evidence that other stakeholders are becoming more aware of the value of internal audit through management communications, both inside the organisation and to the public. A continuing catalogue of organisation failures and litigation highlight the importance and degree of effectiveness of internal audit.

There have been two recent research reports on the status of internal audit in the UK, and its value, as perceived by senior management. Both illustrate a changing service with demands that are stretching the services it can and should provide. The first is by The Chartered Institute of Public Finance and Accountancy (CIPFA) (1990) and the second by Ernst & Young (1995). Both are studies involving organisations across all sectors. Both have appropriate titles:

- CIPFA: *The Client's View of Internal Audit*
- Ernst & Young: *Is your organisation in a position to monitor internal control?*

The CIPFA report places importance on the previously mentioned APB guidelines for internal audit and sees these as a 'code' for promoting effective internal auditing. Conclusions include positive perceptions of value from internal audit and recommendations concerning development of internal audit and its promotion. Ernst & Young's report reveals the following three areas of concern for management and internal audit:

- almost 40 per cent of top companies have no internal audit service;
- under 50 per cent of companies with an internal audit service are confident that their monitoring will be adequate input to any directors' public statement on internal control;
- 66 per cent of finance directors believe that the skills of their internal audit service need to be strengthened.

Many of the messages and related advice in both of these research reports, and in other internal audit literature, provide useful directions for monitoring internal control and developing effective internal audit units for the future. There is still little evidence that the public is showing any real interest in the aims and values of internal audit. To the public at large, internal audit is not yet an active consideration when viewing the performance of organisations. This may not always be so. The future development of internal auditing will probably see more active public interest in its quality of service and reporting.

That internal audit has a future there can be no doubt. The processes of organisational development, management theory, technological revolution, global marketing, competition and regulation at national and international levels, are all now making an impact on that future. They will continue to do so, regardless of the size of internal audit units, affecting all organisations today, and all internal audit units, both small and large.

Case 1.1 shows how leaders in the internal auditing market place are currently addressing present and future internal auditing practices in their own organisations. Their views will affect the development of internal auditing professional practices across the world. Personal statements, like those in the case, can provide internal auditors with directions and confidence for the development of their own internal auditing practices. Show these statements to your management and discuss their implications for your own internal auditing practices. Write your own personal statements on the present and future internal auditing practices in your organisation and sector.

Analyse internal auditing practices: traditional, new and leading edge activities

A worldwide spectrum of traditional, new and leading edge internal audit best practices is evolving, in response to various concerns, issues and the quality and competence of staff involved in its work and management. This spectrum covers present and emerging control issues. Its practices and professionalism are international – UK internal audit staff travel the world. Internal audit is now established in organisations of all sizes in the UK, spanning all the main sectors of the economy – private, public and third. Some internal audit services are provided by an organisation's own staff, some by contract staff, and some a mixture of both. A dynamic competitive market for internal audit providers now exists, influenced by audit cost, quality, regulatory and re-engineering processes. There is a growing use of the services of internal audit agencies and consortiums, mainly in the public and third sectors. The scope of internal audit resources is usually related to audit need assessments and size of the organisation served. There is evidence that increased regulation of organisations is increasing the number of internal audit units. There is no evidence that the size of internal audit units is increasing. Few internal audit units, once established, cease to operate, though some do change hands between organisation and contract staff. Sometimes internal audit is a requirement of one or more of an organisation's stakeholders. There is evidence that some organisation regulators are now setting standards for internal audit practices, and that internal audit is receiving more public recognition in governance and conduct issues.

This internal auditing spectrum now spans worldwide activities and services, driven by market forces, internal and external to the organisations served. Although every internal audit unit is different in size, shape and the variety of its work, there are many common features in all units. Literature and other internal audit research show that the best internal audit units operate today as part of a strong culture of control by management. That culture embraces risk assessment, and educates all organisation staff to expect a high level of internal audit contribution to the objectives of the organisation. How this involvement in risk and organisation objectives is achieved involves proactive players in both internal audit and management.

All internal audit practices are based on principles of management and auditing. Yet, services provided by internal auditors can and do vary significantly across organisations and sectors worldwide – even sometimes across units in the same organisation. These variations reflect who requires internal audit, organisations' control environments, client needs and the competence of those marketing and providing the service. Each of these factors separately and collectively influences the values internal audit can contribute to an organisation.

ICAEW Audit Faculty (1996) research revealed a wide variety of different types of work being undertaken by internal audit, in both the private and public sectors.

On a time basis, the average of the different types of work undertaken by internal audit units is split as follows:

- operations and business processes, 30 per cent;
- financial audits, 24 per cent;
- information systems audits, 13 per cent;
- special investigations/fraud-related, 10 per cent;
- regulatory compliance work, 7 per cent.

The remaining areas, which all came at in at 4 per cent each, were: value for money reviews, control self assessment, assistance to the external auditors, and other. 'Other' included audits of: environmental issues, contracts, joint ventures, and new products. These categories of internal auditing influence many of the values currently perceived from internal audit work. Behind each category is a variety of practices, some traditional, some new and some at a proactive leading edge, competing with other services, both internal and external to the organisation being served. Figure 1.1 provides a snapshot of this spectrum in 1997.

Traditional audit work is fundamental to all services provided by an internal audit unit. Such audit work is based on researched methods of planning, verification and reporting. Audit theory has been evolving for traditional auditing for most of this century. External audit theory is restated in Mautz and Sharaf's (1961) eight postulates of auditing; see Figure 1.2. These same postulates apply to the traditional auditing practices of the internal auditor. They represent the financial, compliance and verification audits which make up much of the testing that takes place during an internal audit.

New internal audit activities are now practised worldwide to meet changing control requirements and career expectations of professional internal auditors. Many are established in some internal audit units, being developments from traditional auditing. For others, the term 'new' means they have only recently been adopted. Each requires learning, practice and benchmarking.

Leading edge internal audit activities are usually more pioneering and controversial, offering new challenges for the internal auditor. Being leading edge, these activities demand a re-engineered and imaginative internal audit, focused on future control and regulation, and involve both the science and technology of internal auditing. Significant investment of time and resources by management and internal audit practitioners are required. Leading edge internal audit can come into conflict with traditional auditing principles. Some leading edge activities will eventually come into the category of new, creating new internal audit products and services and changing the course of future internal audit development. Others will fail to meet the expectations of both internal audit and its clients. These will not survive or be adopted by other more successful competitors in the auditing and management market places. Such is the story of all development and experiment. Leading edge internal auditing is challenging.

Figure 1.1 1997 Spectrum snapshot of UK internal auditing

	Traditional	New	Leading edge
Why internal audit?	Management Owner	Regulator Governing body	Mandatory Public
Provided by:	In-house Parent body	Audit firm Agency Consortium	
Reporting lines:	Finance External audit	Audit committee Chief executive	Chairman Stakeholders
Objectivity/ independence:	Charter	Partnerships External	Regulated
Professional qualifications:	Accounting	Internal audit Computing	Management Specialisms
Scope of work:	Accounting Financial Compliance Stock check	Risk assessment Business objectives Consultancy Conduct/ethics Whistleblowing Computers Systems	Risk management Quality management Environmental management
Skills:	Written Oral Behavioural	Computing Teamwork Integrated	Expert systems Virtual reality
Performance:	Critic Detector Protector Checker	Assurer Comforter Assessor Assistant Teacher Partner	Change agent Innovator Leader Value adder
Management:	Hierarchical	Empowered team Quality measures Customer surveys	Visionary
Auditor co-ordination:	External	Environmental Quality Regulator	Integrated
Other audits:	Operational Management Value for money Systems Computer	Self-assessment	Quality Environmental Health and safety Due diligence Joint ventures

Figure 1.2 Mautz and Sharaf's eight postulates of auditing

- Financial statements and financial data are verifiable.
- There is no necessary conflict of interest between the auditor and the management of the enterprise under audit.
- The financial statements and other information submitted for verification are free from collusive and other unusual irregularities.
- The existence of a satisfactory system of internal control eliminates the probability of irregularities.
- Consistent application of generally accepted principles of accounting results in the fair presentation of financial position and the results of operations.
- In the absence of clear evidence to the contrary, what has held true in the past for the enterprise under examination will hold true in the future.
- When examining financial data for the purpose of expressing an independent opinion thereon, the auditor acts exclusively in the capacity of an auditor.
- The professional status of the independent auditor imposes commensurate professional obligations.

The IIA has identified the following emerging best and successful internal auditing practices, many of which can be seen in the Figure 1.1 spectrum as new and leading edge activities:

- developing a partnering role with audit clients;
- participating in corporate task forces;
- aligning corporate goals, department plans and performance evaluations;
- educating management on their internal control responsibilities;
- carrying out customer satisfaction surveys;
- utilising self-directed, integrated work teams;
- providing training to audit committee members;
- utilising integrated auditing;
- external quality assurance reviews of internal auditing practices;
- emphasising TQM principles and applying them aggressively;
- utilising computer-assisted techniques;
- including audits of environment, health and safety;
- developing a formal risk assessment system involving management;
- empowering staff to experiment with a variety of approaches in developing innovative solutions to problems;
- providing internal consulting services, such as focusing on problem-solving rather than problem-finding.

All these trends are encouraging internal audit experiment and development of leading edge practices.

Relate the internal auditing concerns and issues of others to your own vision

Using the developed spectrum shown in Figure 1.1, create a vision of internal auditing in your own organisation. Seek views from your management and auditees concerning their control needs. Relate these to concerns over the development of your internal auditing practices. Make sure your description is forward-looking. Given the significant and rapid changes being experienced within internal auditing, as evidenced by current literature, it is important that your description applies to the future as well as the present.

Use the description of internal auditing in Figure 1.3 to benchmark how you and your management see the development of your professional practices in the future. This description was developed during research in 1997, from input by academics and leading internal audit practitioners in the UK.

Case 1.2 shows how the description in Figure 1.2 can be used to focus on current and future concerns and issues for development of internal auditing in

Figure 1.3   A vision of internal auditing

- Internal auditing should be seen to be objective and independent in all its services, even though some of its work may facilitate management decisions and involve internal auditors in organisation developments. It should be accountable for its services in an organisation to the full board or governing body.
- All internal audit staff should have a commitment to continuously improve their professional knowledge and experience, act with integrity and be competent in the performance of their work, in all their organisation's risks and controls.
- Internal audit should have appropriate resources and provide value to their organisations, by applying professional judgement with rigour, in unrestricted appraisals, which include prevention, detection and performance objectives.
- Internal audit work should be planned, proactive, formal and clearly communicated to appropriate levels of management; and followed up to ensure all auditees are satisfied with the quality of its processes and action is taken to reduce risk and improve unreasonable control.
- All internal auditing should be co-ordinated with other audit work in an organisation, when such association adds value to the audit environment and audit results. Co-ordination should be at all levels of audit activity – strategic, tactical and operating.
- Internal auditing requires good management skills, both to develop all its products and services and to carry out its appraisal activities, at the right levels of measured quality and assurance: as such, it is an excellent training ground for future operational managers.

organisations. Concerns and issues identified by participants developing the description are used to create internal auditing best-practice benchmarks and guidelines. Internal auditors in units of any size can measure their own concerns and issues against those in the case.

Benchmark for success in internal auditing

The IIA benchmarking service is now well established. Called GAIN – Global Auditing Information Network – it is marketed as:

- a tool for reassuring priorities and direction;
- a benchmark for comparing best practices;
- an instrument for evaluating auditing issues;
- a window for viewing auditing practices of successful organisations.

GAIN offers global, national and industry group benchmarks. Its methods are based on benchmarking practices which now exist in most organisations. Best practice benchmarking (BPB) is a continuous discovery process. It means continuously comparing practices to seek the best and change. The UK Department of Trade and Industry, in its publication *Best Practice Benchmarking*, defined what is involved as:

- establishing what makes the difference, in customers' eyes, between an ordinary supplier and an excellent supplier;
- setting standards in each of those things, according to the best practice that can be found;
- finding out how the best companies meet their challenging standards;
- applying other people's experience to meet new standards, and exceed them.

BPB is not a new technique. What is new is the way that many organisations worldwide, across all sectors, have adopted BPB to drive continuous improvement, as they structure to meet competition, with excellent products and superior services. The importance of customers during BPB is paramount. It is what customers think that defines excellence and superiority. Leading customers to that belief is an essential part of promoting products and services as best.

Benchmarks can be both internal and external to the organisation. They can be structures, practices, technology, equipment and people; they can be a mixture of any or all of these. They can be standards, codes of practice, regulations and even the law. They can be social, environmental, economic, financial and religious. They are what people, as customers, see as being best for them at a given time. They are created by innovation, research, development and above all, competition. They are constantly changing, because competition drives improvement.

A good approach to benchmarking is to establish a team from those with interest and/or responsibility for internal audit in an organisation. The team should include at least one main internal audit customer. Then take the following five steps:

1. Determine the features of your internal audit unit to be benchmarked. Do not choose too many – no more than five at first. Use Case 1.2 as a guide.
2. Agree what influences there are on your features: consider both internal and external influences. Use these influences to establish your benchmarks.

Before proceeding, create a framework to identify what you need to measure. Select the key features you wish to benchmark: these are the most important actions you believe you and your organisation need to develop, to improve regulation, audit, control and excellence in your organisation. Having agreed the features, identify the internal and external influences which impact how they perform: see these influences as levels, which can and do interact one with the other. Study how these levels impact your organisation's control and your internal audit service.

Agree measures for each of your benchmarks. The right measures are important. Test how appropriate they are by trying to link them into your team's vision of excellent and superior internal audit. If the link is not strong, change your measure.

3. Use your measures to identify and agree 'current gaps' between your practices and benchmarks.
4. Analyse your 'current gaps'. Look for reasons why you do not already meet your benchmark's level of service. Consider structure, processes, delegated responsibilities, competencies, resources, etc. Agree what actions need to be taken to achieve best practice; over what time span and how it will be measured. Promote and publish your key measures throughout your organisation.
5. Continuously follow up achievement of your benchmarks. Celebrate success.

Achieve leading edge values in the smaller internal audit unit

Albrecht, Howe, Schueler and Stocks' (1988) study evaluating the effectiveness of internal audit units determined the five characteristics that create effectiveness as:

- talented people;
- good career advancement;
- capable leadership;
- top management support;
- high visibility.

In determining the most important characteristics which appear to play a significant role in the perception of internal audit effectiveness, the same research identified the following attributes:

- team player concept;
- training;
- professionalism;
- independence, objectivity and fairness;
- approach to auditing;
- relationship with external auditors.

These characteristics and perceptions of attributes are important for all internal audit units, whatever their size. The research concluded that audit directors can enhance the effectiveness of their internal audit departments by developing four areas within their organisation: corporate environment, top management support, quality of internal auditors and quality of audit work.

That was 1988. In the previous year, the USA Treadway Commission (National Commission on Fraudulent Financial Reporting) had recommended that all public companies should maintain an effective internal audit unit, staffed with adequate resources. Its recommendations for internal auditing underlie and support all the conclusions from the study.

Case 1.3 provides detail of the Treadway recommendations for internal audit. Use this detail to measure your own internal auditing today and for the future. Consider how the Albrecht *et al.* conclusions relate to the same recommendations. During the past 10 years, each of these studies has guided developments in internal auditing, in organisations of all sizes. They will continue to do so into the twenty-first century.

In recent years, politics, economics and technology have quickened the pace of change at national and international levels, creating new types of organisational structure. Regulation and audit are now respected, with many new auditing activities and supervisory bodies emerging. Control has been provided with new definitions, embracing all aspects of good governance.

Brink (1991) summed up The IIA's first 50 years in his editorial celebration issue of its *Internal Auditor* journal, as follows:

Where do we go from here?
Our first 50 years can be a base for viewing the future. At the centre of our forward evaluation is the question of what we think the world will be like in the future, and what we think the needs of organisations will be then. No one can give absolute answers to those questions, but some projections are possible:

Continuing Focus of Controls
Organisations will almost certainly continue to grow in terms of size and range of operations, and managers will need to establish new objectives, strategies, and policies. More than ever, organisations will need to have effective controls. There will be an increasing need for the protective services provided by the internal

auditor, such as preservation, custody, and compliance, all with new dimensions that reflect the complexities of the new technologies. This expanded range of services will continue to emerge from the internal auditor's review and evaluation of operational controls.

Management: The Major Client
The client focus of the internal auditor has expanded enormously, from the accounting director in the early days, to all segments and levels of the organisation. I believe internal audit's major client will continue to be management; and that while there will also be certain responsibilities to boards of directors, stockholders, and the general public, the latter responsibilities will be secondary, never undermining or overriding the basic service role to management. The internal auditor will be viewed primarily as a member of the management team, dedicated to serving the long-run, overall welfare of the organisation. That long-run welfare must be the standard by which all conflicting factors are evaluated.

Over recent years the Big Six accounting firms have all been addressing values of current and future internal audit practices in the UK and internationally. Arthur Andersen, in its practical research document 'Internal Audit 2000: An Overview' (1994), published consensus results of a series of symposiums with 100 senior internal auditors, representing internal audit units in the UK, across all sectors. The results created a vision of internal audit for the year 2000 and identified ten attributes to be key to the internal audit unit of the next century. These are shown in Figure 1.4. To achieve the key attributes, the report recommends nine key strategies, shown in Figure 1.5.

The Office of the Auditor General of Canada published a survey (1992) of heads of internal audit in 40 public and private sector organisations in Canada and the United States. This research focused on the future direction for internal auditing stating, 'the shift is toward more pro-active, preventive auditing rather than after-the-fact detective auditing. The intention is to identify risks, trends or breakdowns before problems occur.'

Figure 1.4   Ten key attributes of world-class internal auditing in the year 2000 (ranked in order of perceived importance)

1. Professional.	6. Change agents.
2. Close to the business.	7. Customer-focused.
3. Provide solutions.	8. Expert in controls.
4. Independent.	9. Cost-effective.
5. High profile.	10. Multi-skilled.

16 Leading edge internal auditing

Figure 1.5 Nine key strategies for internal auditing to achieve by the year 2000 (ranked in order of perceived importance)

1. Recruit and retain good people.
2. Establish and communicate a clear vision and strategy.
3. Demonstrate the value of internal audit.
4. Understand customer needs.
5. Focus on risk.
6. Improve the communication of results.
7. Improve the audit process.
8. Educate management on risks and controls.
9. Is your organisation in a position to monitor internal control?

Strategies recommended to achieve this goal included:

- greater use of technology in carrying out audits;
- audit involvement at the design and implementation stages of systems and programmes;
- attention to trend and risk analysis in planning, carrying audits and reporting.

This research also predicted that the co-operative, collaborative approach between auditor and auditee would continue. It alerted its readers to the fact that several groups believe that internal auditors must develop the methodology and expertise to audit environmental issues.

All these comments on internal auditing in the early and mid-1990s provide a useful guide to developing actions for the small internal audit unit. Figure 1.6 shows actions that can be reviewed by the small internal audit team and adapted to its size and organisation needs. Creating such action lists, based on research and literature, is an important part of improving internal auditing services in any organisation.

Add leading edge value through professionalism

Many of the professional attributes demonstrated by internal auditors, and valued by senior management, are the same as attributes recommended in audit codes of practice for external auditors. The UK Auditing Practices Board (APB) has published (1996) its own code of practice for external auditors. See Figure 1.7.

The Auditors' Code is published for the information of all those who have an interest in financial reports on which an opinion has been expressed by independent auditors. The code sets out the fundamental principles which APB expects to guide the conduct of auditors and which underlie its Auditing Standards and the ethical standards of professional bodies whose members

Figure 1.6 Twelve actions for your internal audit unit

1. Be expert in governance and maintain that expertise.
2. Teach management how to control.
3. Promote use of self-assessment techniques for management to evaluate risks and establish the right level of resources for reasonable control.
4. Understand and use your organisation's objectives when planning internal audits.
5. Relate objectives for each audit test to your organisation's objectives.
6. Establish management commitment to all the elements of governance, at each level of audit planning.
7. Learn to recognise the influence and effect of change.
8. Focus auditing into the future.
9. Consider revolution as well as evolution in your internal auditing practices.
10. Use teamwork in all of your audit work.
11. Measure, measure and measure again. If it cannot be measured, it cannot be improved.
12. Build the five characteristics of internal auditing and these 12 actions into your vision. Without them it will be difficult for any internal audit unit to survive.

undertake the role of independent auditors. The APB expects that auditors, in complying with its standards, will follow the spirit of the code.

Many internal auditors will recognise the importance of this code in their own audit work. Most senior management and audit committees see professional care to be a key value of internal auditing and will also look for this code in the services provided by internal auditors. Even though many internal audit units are a mixture of professionally qualified and unqualified staff, it is important that professional codes are recognised by all internal audit staff. Wood, Wilson and Holub (1989) studied professionalism in internal auditing, introducing their findings as follows:

> Professionalism has long been of concern to internal auditors. Indeed, in common usage, professionalism is equated with many of the hallmarks of good auditing, such as integrity, objectivity, and independent judgement.
>
> But the word 'profession' has a second, more specific meaning, denoting occupations that share certain identifiable characteristics. Because of their important social functions, and their internal structure, such occupations have earned a heightened position in society's hierarchy.
>
> The traditional professions of law, medicine, and theology have been joined by those of architecture, diplomacy, academia, psychology, dentistry, teaching and others. Many more occupations, such as nursing, library science, engineering and accountancy, have moved towards professional status.
>
> Internal auditors have every reason to think of themselves as professionals in the sense of caring about what they do and bringing to their jobs the best skills

Figure 1.7 The auditor's code: fundamental principles of independent auditing

Accountability

Auditors act in the interests of primary stakeholders, whilst having regard to the wider public interest. The identity of primary stakeholders is determined by reference to the statute or agreement requiring an audit: in the case of companies, the primary stakeholder is the general body of shareholders.

Integrity

Auditors act with integrity, fulfilling their responsibilities with honesty, fairness and truthfulness. Confidential information obtained in the course of the audit is disclosed only when required in the public interest, or by operation of law.

Objectivity and independence

Auditors are objective. They express opinions independently of the entity and its directors.

Competence

Auditors act with professional skill, derived from their qualification, training and practical experience. This demands an understanding of financial reporting and business issues, together with expertise in accumulating and assessing the evidence necessary to form an opinion.

Rigour

Auditors approach their work with thoroughness and with the attitude of professional scepticism. They assess critically the information and explanations obtained in the due course of their work and such additional evidence as they consider necessary for the purposes of their audit.

Judgement

Auditors apply professional judgement taking account of materiality in the context of the matters on which they are reporting.

Clear communication

Auditors' reports contain clear expressions of opinion and set out information necessary for a proper understanding of that opinion.

Association

Auditors allow their reports to be included in documents containing other information only if they consider that the additional information is not in conflict with the matters covered by their report and they have no cause to believe it to be misleading.

Providing value

Auditors add to the reliability and quality of financial reporting: they provide to directors and officers constructive observations arising from the audit process; and thereby contribute to the effective operation of business, capital markets and the public sector.

Figure 1.8 The IIA framework for the professional practice of internal auditing

- Statement of Responsibilities of Internal Auditing
- Code of Ethics
- Standards for the Professional Practice Internal Auditing: General, Specific and Guidelines
- Statements on Internal Auditing Standards
- Professional Standards Practice Release

and energies they can muster. Through their association, The Institute of Internal Auditors, internal audit practitioners have been reaching for formal recognition of their occupation as a profession in the classical, specific sense.

One path towards professionalism in an internal audit unit is for the unit to publicise commitment to a professional framework. The IIA has created its own framework, which can be adopted by internal audit units of any size. See Figure 1.8 and appendices. Each part of The IIA framework references into the others, thus forming clear objectives for professional recognition. Despite the importance of such a framework, there are many internal audit units without such a guide for their professional practices.

Add leading edge value through talented people

As mentioned earlier in the Albrecht *et al.* study, keys to development of professional practices are talented people with career prospects. Achievement of professional qualifications by internal auditors is an important part of their value. The IIA has researched and promoted a common body of knowledge for internal auditors since the 1970s. Its current certified internal auditor examinations are based on a common body of knowledge, researched by Albrecht, Stice and Stocks (1992). See Figure 1.9.

The 20 disciplines identified by the researchers cover 344 detailed competencies. The same research predicts that the following four areas within internal auditing will call for attention in the future:

- impact of technology;
- quality revolutions;
- globalisation of business;
- increased importance of non-technical skills.

While clarifying the last of the above four issues, the research refers to non-technical skills in the following words:

Figure 1.9 A common body of knowledge for internal auditing

Ranking of disciplines	Number of competencies
Reasoning	4
Ethics	6
Auditing	43
Communication	18
Organisations	17
Computers	39
Sociology	11
Fraud	17
Financial accounting	35
Data gathering	13
Legal	14
Marketing	14
Managerial accounting	16
Statistics	10
Finance	23
Economics	17
Quantitative methods	12
International	12
Government	9
Taxes	4
Total	334

It is noteworthy that three of the top four areas of knowledge rated as most important were not typical auditing or technical areas. Reasoning, communications and ethics were amongst the highest rated areas in the survey data. Practitioners suggest that the success of internal auditing in the future will be the ability to be part of the decision-making process. Technical specialists will be needed, but success will come with the ability to analyse, interact with and communicate audit findings.

More recently, The IIA has started a new research project into a competency framework for internal auditors (CFIA). This project is currently being sponsored by The Institute of Internal Auditors Research Foundation. The *IIA Educator*, Summer 1997 issue, reports this research as greatly affecting the future of the internal auditing profession:

> It will determine programmes and forums, continuing educational criteria, and the content, structure, and format of future research and training programmes in internal auditing, CFIA will establish a platform for:

- the conditions for competent/best internal auditing practice;
- the set of role performances required to realise competent/best internal auditing practice;
- the cognitive and behavioural skills entailed by the various roles involved in realising competent/best practice;
- the forms of practical knowledge entailed by these roles, particularly the role characterised as a 'competent internal auditing practitioner';
- the criteria and processes appropriate for assessing competent practice, role performance, and the possession of requisite skills and knowledge;
- assessment structures appropriate for determining the competence of internal auditors internationally.

Such research is essential in a profession growing globally at a significant rate, with international standards and work. The questions being asked and studies by the research team will apply to internal auditing in units of all sizes. The study outline above provides useful guidance for any framework of professionalism established by internal auditors to measure the competence they need for their services, now and in the future.

Talented people continue learning throughout their professional career. They plan their experience to develop knowledge and skills. Continuing education must be structured and formal. It should be used by management to promote the professionalism of the internal audit unit, both internally and externally. Good benchmarks for all internal audit staff are The IIA's education programmes of certificates and professional examinations. In the USA, The IIA offers a worldwide Certified Internal Auditor qualification. The IIA-UK offers a programme of examinations at practitioner and professional levels, with a separate qualification in computer auditing.

Case 1.4 provides the reader with details of these examination programmes and examples of questions asked in recent CIA examinations, which refer to new and leading edge developments appropriate to small internal audit units.

Add leading edge value through independence and objectivity

Internal audit objectivity and independence are seen by many as its most important values. Yet, in some organisations, neither are established formally by statements of audit conduct and direct reporting lines to senior board or governing body members. Nor does internal audit objectivity and independence always mean that its services are unrestricted, communicated formally across the organisation, or assessed regularly by senior management and board members.

Ziegenfuss (1994) places importance on reporting lines for establishing independence and recognises most respondents with a direct line to their audit committee and board of directors. Such reporting lines are now common for most internal audit units. What remains less common in small internal audit units, are:

- a formal charter recognising a commitment to external standards;
- a requirement for all internal audit restrictions to be documented and reported.

The framework of external professional internal auditing can be an important part of its objectivity and independence. Surprisingly, very few internal auditors and their management link compliance to external standards with independence and objectivity. Yet, compliance to external standards is often seen to be essential in other functions, such as accounting, external auditing, legal, environmental, quality, etc. Internal auditors in all internal audit units should test out this statement with their management! Recognition of the importance of external standards can be key to the quality of internal audit objectivity and independence.

Within his committee's study of corporate governance, Cadbury (1992) focused on unrestricted reporting lines for internal audit, stating that 'it is essential that heads of internal audit should have unrestricted access to the chairperson of the audit committee in order to ensure the independence of their position'.

Scope of work for internal audit should relate to all control environments in which an organisation operates, past, present and future. Control environments are always dynamic. All controls are subject to many internal and external influences, particularly time and changing organisation objectives. Technology, global markets, costs, stakeholder expectations, government requirements, public concerns over governance, fraud and deception can also strongly influence levels of control. These and other influences will always exist. Change should be recognised as an important influence on an internal audit unit's objectivity and independence.

All internal audit units should guard their objectivity and independence with care. The values of internal audit objectivity and independence can be, and probably frequently are, jeopardised by conflicts of interest, as some internal auditors become involved in management team decision-making and non-audit activities. Recognising this as a concern and issue is an important part of internal audit planning and associated audit work.

One other test of the quality of internal audit objectivity and independence is to establish the freedom internal audit has to report to and work with other monitoring units, internal and external to the organisation. Examples of other audit work are:

- external audit;
- government audit;
- regulatory audit;
- quality audit;
- environmental audit.

Most audit committees and senior management see value from co-ordination of internal and external audit work. There are some signs that this view is widening to include quality and environmental audit. Yet, current research into co-ordination of internal audit and external audit shows that this relationship can be improved in many organisations, across all sectors.

The Audit Faculty and The IIA both support co-ordination of internal and external audit, but neither yet go so far as to recommend 'audit partnerships'. Audit committees are likely to influence how relationships develop between internal and external audit, but those guiding both professions have a role to play. In 1996, The IIA addressed the value of internal audit co-ordination with other auditors and review agencies, promoting improved working relationships between internal audit and other auditors. The various approaches recommended are for multi-disciplinary teams, co-working, co-ordination, joint work and combining of resources. The value and meaning behind each of these practices for internal audit objectivity and independence are likely to become more clear in the future. The driver for co-ordination of all audit is likely to be the audit committee. As the learning curves of these committees grow it is likely that all audit work in their organisations will become more co-ordinated.

Add leading edge value through innovation

Those who recruit internal audit staff in the public sector tend to use emotive imagery to attract the best experienced and qualified staff, thus enhancing the value of internal audit. The most frequently used descriptions for internal auditors in job vacancy notices are 'rigorous', 'astute', 'a self-starter', 'innovative', 'outstanding', 'leader' and 'honest', ranked in that order! See Figure 1.10.

Innovation in internal audit can also mean development of auditing techniques and practices to meet new customer specifications. During its development over the past 50 years, professional internal audit has widened its traditional financial audit service into other audit and review activities, partly at the request of management, but often as part of a drive to improve its services. Figure 1.11 lists some of the new and leading edge internal auditing practices that have developed in some organisations during the past 10 years.

Figure 1.10 Most frequent terms describing internal auditing in job vacancies

Rigorous	aggressive	positive	strong drive
Astute	willing	flexible	diplomatic
Self-starter	motivated	enthusiastic	
Innovative	pro-active	creative	
Outstanding	excellent		
Leader	persuasive		
Honest			

Figure 1.11   Examples of audit services provided by internal audit units

- computer audits
- value for money audits
- forensic audits
- contract audits
- joint venture audits
- pension fund audits
- quality assurance audits
- due diligence audits
- financial status of suppliers
- quality self-assessments
- environmental audits
- internal performance reviews
- reviews of external statutory audit work
- customer satisfaction surveys
- employee attitude surveys

Gray and Gray's (1996) research in North America recognises a growing interest by internal audit and its clients in innovative roles for internal auditors and innovation in internal audit functions. The following five needs for innovation are common to most internal audit units:

- a need for a change process to improve quality of internal audit practices;
- a need to increase efficiency;
- a need to expand internal audit resources;
- a need to increase the value added of internal auditing;
- a need to boost staff skills, performance and morale.

Consider offering your customers a changed or new innovative service by your internal audit unit. See Case 1.5 for an example of what process to use to identify and develop such a service.

Chapter summary

A spectrum of traditional, new and leading edge professional internal audit best practices has evolved worldwide. This spectrum of internal audit is now well established in many UK organisations, across all sectors. Some internal audit units operate internationally. Internal audit is resourced by an organisation's staff, contract staff, or a mixture of both. It is seen by senior management as an important partner in their organisation's control

▶

framework, with opportunities to develop its services. Sometimes it is a requirement of one or more of an organisation's stakeholders. Its practices are sometimes required and guided by an organisation's regulator. Professional standards are an essential guide for ensuring that internal audit adds value through the services it provides. It is essential that those standards and guidelines that exist are kept up to date and satisfy both the needs of internal audit and the organisations it serves. Most organisations place a high value on internal audit objectivity and independence. Best-practice charters and terms of reference for internal audit emphasise the importance of its objectivity and independence. Internal audit is now seen by management as a participant in many activities outside of its traditional audit role. The value of internal audit objectivity and independence can be jeopardised by conflicts of interest. As internal auditors become more involved in management team decision-making and non-audit activities, their participation in decision-making may influence their auditing judgement.

Many of the attributes demonstrated by internal auditors, and valued by management, are the same as attributes recommended in audit codes of practice for external auditors. Management expect value from internal audit in a wide variety of audit and performance review activities. Most expect traditional audit work, associated with finance, accounts, security and business objectives. Some now see values from other types of monitoring, associated with quality, customers, the environment, due diligence and joint ventures. Management currently sees little value in co-ordination of internal audit with other auditors, internal or external to the organisation. The exception is external audit, though in all sectors there is little evidence that value from such co-ordination is seen as significant or even measured. There are some signs of interest that there is value from co-ordination with quality and environmental audit.

Principia

1. Understanding the history and development of internal auditing is the foundation for creating a vision for its future.

2. Internal auditing is developing as a spectrum of unrestricted traditional, new and leading edge activities across all organisations of all sizes, in all sectors.

3. Best practice internal auditing and good management practices use the same quality measures of planning, doing, checking and action.

▶

4. Many of the attributes demonstrated by internal auditors, and valued most by management, are the same attributes recommended in codes of best practice for external auditors.

5. Seeking best practice internal auditing is a continuous learning process.

6. Professional internal auditors critically understand today's and tomorrow's management principles and practices.

7. To be successful, internal auditing must attract and satisfy talented people.

8. Internal auditing objectivity and independence are its most important assets.

9. Co-ordination of all audit work in an organisation strengthens its objectivity and independence.

10. Imagination and confidence are the keys to innovative internal auditing.

Bibliography

ICAEW Audit Faculty (1996) *Internal Audit and its Value*, The Institute of Chartered Accountants in England and Wales, London.

ICAEW Audit Faculty (1996) *Towards Better Auditing*, The Institute of Chartered Accountants in England and Wales, London.

Aid to Industry (1985) *Survey of Internal Auditing in UK Companies*, Touche Ross, London.

Albrecht, W., Stice, J. and Stocks, K. (1992) *A Common Body of Knowledge for the Practice of Internal Auditing*, The Institute of Internal Auditors Research Foundation, Altamonte Springs, USA.

Albrecht, W., Howe, K., Schueler, D. and Stocks, K. (1988) *Evaluating the Effectiveness of Internal Audit Departments*, The Institute of Internal Auditors Research Foundation, Altamonte Springs, USA.

APA, HM Treasury (1996) 'Benchmarking government internal audit departments', *Auditorium*, Autumn.

APB (Auditing Practices Board) (1995) *Considering the work of internal audit*, Statement of Auditing Standards (SAS) 500, London.

APB (Auditing Practices Board) (1996) *The Auditors' Code*, APB, London.

APB (Auditing Practices Board) (1996) *The Audit Agenda – Next Steps*, Accountancy Books, Milton Keynes.

Arthur Andersen (1994) *Internal Audit 2000: An overview*, Arthur Andersen & Co., London.

Audit Commission (1996) *It Takes Two – A good practice guide to co-operation between internal and external auditors*, The Audit Commission, London.

Bain, E. and Band, D. (1996) *Winning Ways Through Corporate Governance*, Macmillan Press, London.
Barclay Simpson (1996) *1996 Market Report*, Barclay Simpson, London.
Binder Hamlyn (1996) *Internal Audit in the Public Sector*, Survey conducted by Binder Hamlyn with *Internal Auditing* magazine, Andersen Worldwide, London.
Brink, V. (1977) *Foundations For Unlimited Horizons: The IIA 1941–1976*, The Institute of Internal Auditors Inc., Altamonte Springs, USA.
Cadbury, A. (1992) *The Financial Aspects of Corporate Governance*, Gee & Co. Ltd, London.
Conference Board and KPMG (1992) *New Directions in Internal Auditing*, Research Report No. 946, The Conference Board Inc., New York.
ECIIA (1996) *Position Paper on Internal Auditing in Europe*, European Confederation of Institutes of Internal Auditing, Brussels.
Ernst & Young (1995) *Is your organisation in a position to monitor internal control?*, Ernst & Young, London.
European Commission (1996) *Green Paper on the Role, Position and Liability of Statutory Auditors*, EC Spokesman's Service, Brussels.
Gray, G. and Gray, M. (1996) *Enhancing Internal Auditing Through Innovative Practices*, The Institute of Internal Auditors Research Foundation, Altamonte Springs, USA.
HM Treasury (1993) *Government Information Systems Audit Manual*, HMSO, London.
HM Treasury (1996) *Government Internal Audit Manual*, HMSO, London.
ICAEW (1990) *Guidance for internal auditors – Auditing Guideline 308*, The Institute of Chartered Accountants in England & Wales, London.
ICAEW (1997) *Added-value professionals: Chartered Accountants in 2005: A consultation document*, The Institute of Chartered Accountants in England & Wales, London.
ICAS (1993) *Auditing into the Twenty-First Century*, The Institute of Chartered Accountants of Scotland, Edinburgh.
IIA-UK (1976) *A Survey of Internal Auditing in the United Kingdom*, Institute of Internal Auditors – UK, London.
IIA Inc. (1978) *Standards for the Professional Practice of Internal Auditing* (revised 1993), The Institute of Internal Auditors Inc., Altamonte Springs, USA.
IIA Inc. (1994) *The IIA's Perspective on Outsourcing Internal Auditing, A Professional Briefing for Chief Audit Executives*, The Institute of Internal Auditors Inc., Altamonte Springs, USA.
Lampe, J. and Sutton, S. (1994) 'Evaluating the Work of Internal Audit: A Comparison of Standards and Empirical Evidence', *Accounting and Business Research*, vol. 24 (96): 335–348.
Marcella, Jr, A. J. (1995) *Outsourcing, Downsizing, and Reengineering: Internal Control Implications*, The Institute of Internal Auditors Inc., Altamonte Springs, USA.
Mints, F. (1972) *Behavioral patterns in internal audit relationships*, The Institute of Internal Auditors Research Foundation, Altamonte Springs, USA.
Office of the Auditor General of Canada (1992) *Internal Auditing – in a changing management culture*, Office of the Auditor General of Canada, Ottawa, Ontario.
Palmer, P. (1992) *Internal Audit and Control in Charities*, Moores Rowland, London.
Ridley, J. (1996) *BRACE 1 – Benchmarking Internal Audit in Housing Associations*, Housing Association Internal Audit Forum, London.
RSA (1995) *Tomorrow's Company: The Role of Business in a Changing World*, Royal Society of Arts, London.

Stoner, J. and Werner, F. (1995) *Internal Audit and Innovation*, Financial Executives Research Foundation, Morristown, New Jersey, USA.

Wade, K. and Birchall, D. (1996) *Environmental Auditing Survey*, The Henley Research Centre, Henley.

Wilson, J. and Wood, D. (1989) *Managing the Behavioral Dynamics of Internal Auditing*, The Institute of Internal Auditing Research Foundation, Altamonte Springs, USA.

Wood, D. and Wilson, J. (1989) *Roles and Relationships in Internal Auditing*, The Institute of Internal Auditing Research Foundation, Altamonte Springs, USA.

Wood, D., Wilson, J. and Holub, E. (1989) *Professionalism in Internal Auditing*, The Institute of Internal Auditors Research Foundation, Altamonte Springs, USA.

Ziegenfuss, Douglas E. (1994) *Challenges and Opportunities of Small Internal Audit Organizations*, The IIA Research Foundation, USA.

Case 1.1 Internal auditing 1997: new and leading edge

(Reprinted with permission from the May/June issue of *The IIA Today*, published by The Institute of Internal Auditors, Inc., USA.)

The case

The following interviews with 1997–8 nominees for The Institute of Internal Auditors International Board of Directors are included in the May/June 1997 issue of *Auditing News*. *Auditing News* is published to all IIA members bi-monthly, communicating news, ideas, events affecting the profession of internal auditing. Each of the interviewees has a long and distinguished record of service to The IIA and is an experienced internal auditor.

You should refer to Appendix C, The IIA Statement of Responsibilities of Internal Auditing.

Chairman of the Board Nominee
Michael P. Fabrizius, CIA
Vice-President of Internal Audit, Bon Secours Health System Inc., USA

The challenges healthcare will face are many and diverse: increase cost effectiveness; implement and improve use of technology; manage the increase in alliances, partnerships, and joint ventures; and focus on regulatory issues. Audit departments in all industries will face many of these same problems, and The IIA needs to be a leader as new audit issues arise. The IIA will create the framework to improve the internal audit practice model by providing the guidance, tools, and techniques we need to excel at our jobs. In turn, the perception of internal audit as value-adding partner will increase.

Senior Vice-Chairman of the Board Nominee
Jean-Pierre Garitte, CIA
Director of Internal Audit, J. Van Breda & Co., Antwerp, Belgium

The 21st century will begin with a drastic redesign of corporate governance not only in banking and insurance, but in other industries which deal with public trust, such as investments, insurance policies, and savings bonds. Management will no longer deal solely with investors, but with employees, suppliers, customers, banks, the government, and with the public at large. Internal Auditors will have a key role to play in that process. Currently, they are in a position to provide these outside stakeholders, with reasonable assurance. However, if they don't pay attention, in the future others may take that role away.

Vice-Chairman Professional Development Nominee
Thomas A. Johnson, CIA
General Auditor, The CIT Group, Livingston, New Jersey, USA

A more effective and efficient internal audit department is going to be the key to success in the financial services industry in the next millennium, and technology is going to have a two-pronged impact on that success: (1) How will technology change the risk profile of a financial services organisation? The challenge will be to keep people on board who are up-to-date with changes in technology, and to manage risks by keeping pace with the changes rather than hanging one step behind. And (2) how can we use technology as an enabler for the internal audit department? Of course we'll have to program the key indicators into the system, but then technology can search 100 per cent of the transactions for any abnormalities as we perform the audit. I see technology as the key to the 21st century.

Vice-Chairman Professional Practices Nominee
Robert W. Rudloff Jr, CIA
Director of Internal Audit, Trump Taj Mahal Casino Resort, Atlantic City, New Jersey, USA

The rapid growth explosion the gaming industry is experiencing will eventually deplete its pool of talented people with industry experience. Ultimately, this will trigger the most significant challenge to the industry and its auditors, as businesses face the risks associated with less experienced management.

Vice-Chairman Professional Services Nominee
Richard M. Serafini, CIA
Director Internal Audit Services, Deloitte & Touche LLP, Jacksonville, Florida, USA

The most significant issue for outside consultants will be the same for the entire internal audit profession. As business challenges become more complex, the internal audit director will need to maintain credibility as a value-added partner to management and the audit committee. Internal audit directors need to be very, very creative so that the audit profession doesn't fall behind; unfortunately, this is not typically one of the internal audit's strengths. Internal auditors will have to learn to keep up with the times, and one day training sessions will not be the answer. If internal audit directors lose their credibility, then outside auditing firms will need to be ready to prove their worth as value-added business partners.

International Secretary Nominee
Howard J. Johnson, CIA
Vice-President and Director of Internal Auditing, JCPenney Company Inc., Dallas, Texas, USA

The retail industry's biggest challenge in the years ahead will be getting our arms around all the information that's available to us when performing an audit. Retailers' operations tend to be quite dispersed and as transactions occur around the world the best way to gather and analyse great quantity of information will be technology. We'll need to use technology to identify where the opportunities are, be they problems or best practice type situations, so that we can perform on a proactive rather than a reactive basis.

International Treasurer Nominee
Anne Merethe Bellamy, CIA
Assistant Director General, Kredittilsynet, Oslo, Norway

In the financial sector, it will be very important to make a transition from a fundamentally financial audit to more operational oriented audits. We will need to meet the increased demand for more proactive, management-oriented, and multi-disciplinary internal audits. Hopefully, if we take these steps it will help us meet the most significant challenge I see for the entire profession – increasing the recognition and promoting the image of internal auditing.

Consider

1. The comments of each of the nominees and analyse these into those that concern your own organisation, and those that concern your sector. Decide which are the most important to you and discuss these with your management. Seek solutions to any problems that your analysis reveals.
2. How the visions of the nominees are reflected in your own and your organisation's vision for internal auditing.

Case 1.2 Use a Delphi study to develop best practice internal auditing

The case

As the name suggests (with its allusion to the Oracle at Delphi), a Delphi study is essentially future-focused. It is used to probe the future when it is difficult or not appropriate to extrapolate the future from the past. Given the significant and rapid changes being experienced within internal audit, as evidenced by current literature, it is appropriate to use a future-orientated study focusing on concerns/issues of today and tomorrow. Such a study requires the participants not to meet each other as they consider their benchmarks of best practice and guidelines. They can be guided by the internal audit unit, but not led. Participants should be at all levels in the organisation. Each should identify their own internal auditing concerns and issues. Results are analysed by the internal audit unit and presented to management for consideration during internal audit planning processes at strategic, tactical and operational levels.

As a guide for the development of an internal auditing Delphi study, the following results came from the study supporting Figure 1.2.

1. Internal audit objectivity and independence guide

Internal auditors should be independent of the activities they audit.

Benchmark

Internal audit should be required and openly encouraged to be objective in all the services and recommendations it provides: independent reporting lines should be clearly established in the organisation structure in which it works, to establish and maintain this objectivity. Internal audit should be accountable for its services in an organisation to the full board or governing body. Internal audit should report to an appropriate level of management and be sufficiently professional in its work and independent of its organisation's day-to-day operating structure, processes and systems, to be able to provide objective advice, assurance and review of the organisation's controls and help to achieve the strategic goals and safeguard the interests of the organisation. The appropriate level should be an executive director or equivalent.

Concerns/issues

- Dependence on control environment structure in place.
- Objectivity of internal audit must be maintained, despite increasing new non-audit tasks.
- Can the audit committee be confident that executive management has not influenced internal audit independence and objectivity?
- Reporting on top management.
- Computing competence.
- Conflict in their role as servants and independent auditors.
- Involvement in risk assessment and business process re-engineering can impinge on independence.

- Balance between independence and need to be part of organisation structure.
- Visibility of internal audit.
- Many internal audit units still do not have an appropriate level of independence.
- Will the evolving new roles of internal audit jeopardise traditional ideas of independence?
- In a downsized, re-engineered enterprise, traditional notions become less compelling.
- Involvement in value-for-money audit work.
- Replacement of independence concept with concepts of integrity and objectivity.
- Retaining independence and objectivity.
- Internal audit should be portrayed as a diagnostic unit which interfaces with organisational development departments to assist in business planning and development.
- Internal audit is moving to more of a 'preventative' rather than 'cure' role. This means being active at the outset of development projects and an integral member of the development team. This can place a strain on independence, but if handled with care can easily demonstrate a considerable improvement in the perceived added value of internal audit.
- Internal audit can be independent at various sub-levels but cannot be wholly independent of senior management.
- Problems with management audits and increased reliance on internal audit by external audit.

2. Internal audit professionalism

Guide

Internal audits should be performed with proficiency and due professional care.

Benchmark

All internal audit staff should have a commitment to continuously improve their professional knowledge and experience, act with integrity and be competent in the performance of their work, in all their organisation's risks and controls. Appropriate specialist resources should be available to ensure all internal audit work achieves a high level of professional competence. An internal audit unit should be resourced by competent staff and appropriate level in number and qualifications, for the size, diversities, complexity, uses of technology and pace of change of its organisation's activities. An internal auditor is committed to being professional when continuously learning through knowledge and skill programmes, based on personal and organisation needs. An internal auditor's understanding of control makes a significant contribution to an organisation's risk assessment processes.

Concerns/issues

- Increasing use of specialist internal auditors drives outsourcing of audit needs.
- How are levels and competencies of internal audit established?
- Are internal auditors specialists in auditing and/or specialists in control?
- Do the current definitions of control embrace all management processes?
- Can internal auditors claim to understand all aspects of control?
- Status on internal audit in some organisations and breadth of their education and experience.
- Computer competence.
- Most internal auditors are accountants; internal audit work requires the expertise of other professionals, as well as accountants.
- Internal audit staff need to have a multi-skilled approach to their work.
- How do internal audit staff audit ethical issues?
- High-calibre staff are very hard to find; when you do, they don't stay long!
- The dilemma is to what extent internal audit should attempt to mirror the organisation's skills.
- All internal audit staff should have basic financial skills and be capable of auditing computer applications.
- Will automated auditing impact on levels and competencies of internal audit staff?
- Might virtual auditing techniques, applied by virtual auditors, be the means of auditing virtual enterprises?
- Do we live in an 'audit' society?
- Is there an end to the growth of auditing?
- How much of GDP can a society spend on (invest in) auditing?
- Professions other than accountants must be attracted to internal audit.
- In future, internal audit will be a core group of generalists using specialists as appropriate.
- Much more use needs to be made of secondments from and into line units.
- Internal auditors should be at the forefront of technology use in their organisations.
- A broader range of skills should fit them better for other roles in the organisation.
- Remuneration will need to be enhanced if internal auditors of the future are to be retained.

3. Internal audit scope of work

Guide

The scope of internal auditing should encompass:

- examination and evaluation of the adequacy and effectiveness of all the organisation's system of internal control;
- quality of performance in carrying out assigned responsibilities.

Benchmark

Internal audit should have appropriate resources for its scope of work and provide value to their organisation's objectives. Internal audit should focus on high-risk operations and include prevention, detection and performance objectives in all its services. Internal audit should be authorised to carry out a rolling programme of compliance and operational auditing covering all managers in the organisation it serves, and their responsibilities for control environments, risk assessments, control activities, monitoring, information and communication. This should include a right of access to all policies, objectives, structures, premises, systems, people and performance measures, and proactive involvement with all other monitoring activities in the organisation being served.

Concerns/issues

- Do control assessments review all senior management activities?
- How able are internal auditors to assess risk?
- How well is risk assessment by internal auditors communicated across and up the organisation?
- Will control self-assessment by managers reduce the need for internal audit?
- Should A be considered more important than B?
- Need to consider value of qualitative as well as quantitative data.
- Increasingly, one-to-one interviews used to evaluate performance centres.
- This happens now, but in multinationals we are only fooling ourselves – the companies and cost of a wide scope are simply too large.
- Many internal audit units have a limited scope, e.g. only financial controls or few 'prevention' roles.
- Should internal audit review all board activities, where most can be at stake?
- Will external audit staff influence the direction of internal audit work too much towards financial control?
- Measurement of ethical performance/control as a part of risk management (particularly reputation risk) strategy.

- Compliance testing has to go to the line units under a structured programme designed by internal audit.
- Internal audit will do much more focused, substantive work in the future.
- Those listed companies without internal audit might put one in place.

4. Internal audit performance

Guide

Audit work should include planning the audit, examining and evaluating information, communicating results and following up.

Benchmark

Internal audit work should be planned, formal, clearly communicated to appropriate levels of management, and followed up to ensure all auditees are satisfied with the quality of its processes and action is taken to reduce risk and improve unreasonable control. Internal audit work should be co-ordinated with other types of audit work when such association adds value to the audit environment and audit results. Internal audit work should be planned through structured and formal risk assessment, audit programmes and followed-up reports. All internal audit work should be appropriately documented. All internal auditors should strive continuously to improve the quality of their work. Internal audit work should be co-ordinated with the work of other auditors and management monitoring activities.

Concerns/issues

- Little co-ordination with other auditors.
- Are planned audit programmes flexible enough to meet auditees' needs?
- Must be an integral part of risk management strategy.
- Some organisations are giving internal audit other auditing roles, which are not about control.
- More reliance by management on automated monitoring.
- Insufficient use of information technology by internal audit.
- The theory of auditing is changing.
- More emphasis on working with areas of organisation which can influence business development/planning strategy.
- Become more involved in decision-making processes.
- Much closer liaison with risk managers.
- There will be pressure on internal audit to carry out a wider range of specialist audits – OK, providing the focus continues to be achievement of the organisation's objectives, including a high compliance content.
- Too structured an approach may stifle creativity.

5. Internal audit management

Guide
The head of internal audit should properly manage the internal audit unit.

Benchmark
Internal audit requires good management skills, both to develop all its products and services and to carry out its appraisal activities, at the right levels of measured quality and assurance: as such, it is an excellent training ground for future operational managers. Internal audit should be managed and promoted as a proactive service, anticipating required levels of control across all supply chains and processes needed, to provide superior practices and services for all its organisation's customers and protect all its stakeholders. An effective internal audit service will provide committee and management assurance, aid decision-making, improve business performance and reduce the risk of undetected fraud. All internal audit activities will be measured for their quality and client satisfaction.

Concerns/issues
- How does internal audit achieve an understanding of the business and executive management?
- Is the background experience of internal audit sufficiently business orientated?
- Are performance measures for internal audit sufficiently quantitative?
- Does internal audit have sufficient information to understand the business?
- It is difficult to discriminate rigorously between management responsibility for internal audit at head of internal audit, senior management and audit committee levels.
- Usefulness of motherhood statements, like the above guides.
- Impact of cost savings on internal audit resources.
- Outsourcing of internal audit activities/responsibilities.
- Is it the role of internal audit to contribute to external customer satisfaction and protect all stakeholders' interests?
- Many organisations do not yet give appropriate status to the head of internal audit, or expect a proactive, preventative service.
- If a job is worth doing, is it worth doing even badly?
- Who audits the auditors?
- There are many opportunities for a well-managed, value-adding, internal audit unit.
- Stakeholder approach will increasingly be adopted by organisations wishing to demonstrate a commitment to meeting their needs and expectations:

internal audit will need to adjust to this and develop linkages with all areas of the organisation which have a direct interface with stakeholders, to ensure a consistent and objective approach.
- Internal audit should be developed as a training ground for future managers (a huge opportunity).
- How do you measure the quality of internal audit work?
- Who are the clients of internal audit?
- Has internal audit management a clear focus for the future?

Consider

1. How the concerns and issues of participants in the Delphi study impact your own internal audit unit.
2. How they influence your internal auditing status and future development.
3. Sharing your concerns and issues with your management.
4. Seeking further support and advice from your professional institute and current internal auditing literature.
5. Other concerns and issues not observed in the Delphi study; share these with other internal auditors in the UK, through your professional institute and at training seminars and conferences.

Case 1.3   Internal auditing 1987

(Report of The National Commission on Fraudulent Financial Reporting, 1987. Chairman: James C. Treadway, Jr, formerly a Commissioner of the Securities and Exchange Commission (SEC), USA.) You should also refer to Appendix C, The IIA Statement of Responsibilities of Internal Auditing.

The case

Extract from Section III B: Internal audit function and chief internal auditor

Recommendation: Public companies should maintain an effective internal audit function staffed with an adequate number of qualified personnel appropriate to the size and the nature of the company.

Properly organised and effectively operated, internal auditing gives management and the audit committee a way to monitor the reliability and the integrity of financial and operating information. The internal audit function thus is an important element in preventing and detecting fraudulent financial reporting.

Support of top management

To be effective, internal auditors must have the acknowledged support of top management and the board of directors through its audit committee. The company should set forth in writing the scope of responsibilities for the internal audit function. The scope of responsibilities as well as any change in role or function should be the subject of review by the audit committee. The optimal size of the internal audit function and the composition of its staff depend on the company's size and nature and the scope of responsibilities assigned to the function.

The education, experience, and professionalism of the internal auditors help determine the effectiveness of the internal audit function. The company should encourage the development of its internal auditors by providing continuing professional education programs and offering attractive career paths.

The Commission recognises that some smaller companies could experience a significant hardship if compelled to employ persons to serve exclusively as internal auditors. Thus, the Commission's use of the term 'internal auditor' includes, where appropriate, persons who do not function exclusively in that capacity.

IIA standards

The professionalism of internal auditors has been enhanced in recent years by the efforts of The Institute of Internal Auditors (IIA), the professional organisation for internal auditors. Standards of The IIA offer excellent guidance for effective internal auditing and reflect some of the most advanced thinking on fraud prevention and detection. The Commission encourages public companies who have not done so to consider adopting The IIA standards.

The IIA's standards call for a quality assurance program to evaluate the operations of the internal audit function. The standards provide guidelines that describe, as suitable means of meeting the quality assurance standard, a program that includes the following elements: supervision, internal reviews, and external reviews. The Commission endorses these concepts as ways to enhance the effectiveness of the internal audit function. Confidentiality and other issues associated with external reviews are important in management's decisions as to who should conduct such reviews, how they should be conducted, and with what frequency they should be conducted.

Objectivity of the internal audit function

Recommendation: Public companies should ensure that their internal audit functions are objective.

The effectiveness of a company's internal audit function depends a great deal on the objectivity of the chief internal auditor and his staff. Public companies should ensure that their internal auditors are free to perform their functions in an objective manner, without interference and able to report findings to the appropriate parties for corrective action. Three principal factors contribute to independence and objectivity: the organisational positioning of the function, the

Figure 2.6　Definitions of control 1990 onwards

1990 Auditing Practices Committee of CCAB Limited, UK: Auditing Guideline, Guidance for Internal Auditors:

The regulation of activities in an organisation through systems designed and implemented to facilitate the achievement of management objectives. The main objectives of the internal control system are:

- to ensure adherence to management policies and directives in order to achieve the organisation's objectives;
- to safeguard assets;
- to secure the relevance, reliability and integrity of information, so ensuring as far as possible the completeness and accuracy of records; and
- to ensure compliance with statutory requirements.

1992 Committee of Sponsoring Organisations of the Treadway Commission (COSO), USA: Internal Control – Integrated Framework:

Internal control is a process, effected by an entity's board of directors, management and other personnel, designed to provide reasonable assurance regarding the achievement of objectives in the following categories:

- effectiveness and efficiency of operations;
- reliability of financial reporting;
- compliance with applicable laws and regulations.

1994 The Institute of Internal Auditors – UK: Professional Briefing Note Six, Internal Control:

Internal control is part of the management process. It is through the actions taken by management to plan, organise and direct the performance of sufficient actions to provide reasonable assurance that the following objectives will be achieved:

- accomplishment of established objectives and goals for operations and programmes;
- the economical and efficient use of resources;
- the safeguarding of resources;
- the reliability and integrity of information;
- compliance with policies, plans, procedures, laws and regulations.

ICAEW 1994 Committee on the Financial Aspects of Corporate Governance (Cadbury Committee), UK: Internal Control and Financial Reporting:

Internal control is the whole system of controls, financial and otherwise, established in order to provide reasonable assurance of:

- effective and efficient operations;
- internal financial control;
- compliance with laws and regulations.

▶

Figure 2.6 Contd

1994 The Institute of Chartered Accountants in England and Wales, UK: Internal Control and Financial Reporting – Guidance for Directors of Listed Companies Registered in the UK (the Rutteman Report):

Internal financial control is all the internal controls established in order to provide reasonable assurance of:

- the safeguarding of assets against unauthorised use or disposition;
- the maintenance of proper accounting records and the reliability of financial information used within the business or for publication.

1995 The Canadian Institute of Chartered Accountants, Canada: Guidance on Control:

Control comprises those elements of an organisation (including its resources, systems, processes, culture, structure and tasks) that, taken together, support people in the achievement of the organisation's objectives. These objectives may fall into one or more of the following categories:

- effectiveness and efficiency of operations;
- reliability of internal and external reporting;
- compliance with applicable laws and regulations and internal policies.

CIPFA (1995) interpreted the Cadbury and Nolan reports into a framework of structure, process, financial reporting, internal controls and standards of behaviour; see Figure 2.9.

The most recent interpretations of control and governance are those by The Canadian Institute of Chartered Accountants (1996), following a study (CoCo) into the COSO integrated control framework and its application in Canada. CoCo creates its own framework and links this to COSO and the USA Malcolm Baldrige Quality Award criteria. This search for relationships between control definitions is an important part of the understanding and application of control principles. Figure 2.10 shows the CoCo control framework criteria. CoCo links to COSO are also shown. Internal auditors should test their own understanding of these links before reading those in the CoCo study.

Publicly declared compliance with codes of best practice, to assure all stakeholders and the public, is required by many industries in all sectors. The London Stock Exchange now requires all listed companies to state in their annual report whether they are in compliance with a published code of best practice (Cadbury 1992). This requirement has also been adopted by unlisted companies and organisations across all UK sectors, sometimes enforced by regulation but more often on a voluntary basis. Figures 2.11 and 2.12 show the Cadbury (1992) recommended code of practice and those proposed by Lord Nolan (1996) for parts of the public service.

Another example of a code of practice is given by The IIA-UK in *Reporting on*

Figure 2.7 CIPFA governance definitions

Governance

Governance is currently defined as being the structures, systems and policies in an organisation, designed and established to direct and control all operations and relationships on a continuing basis, in an honest and caring manner, taking into account the interests of all stakeholders and compliance with all applicable laws and regulatory requirements. Governance is based on the following principles of openness, integrity and accountability.

Openness

Openness is required to ensure that stakeholders can have confidence in the decision-making processes and actions of public service bodies, in the management of their activities, and in the individuals within them. Being open through meaningful consultation with stakeholders and communication of full, accurate and clear information leads to effective and timely action and lends itself to necessary scrutiny.

Integrity

Integrity comprises both straightforward dealing and completeness. It is based upon honesty, selflessness and objectivity, and high standards of propriety and probity in the stewardship of public funds and management of a body's affairs. It is dependent on the effectiveness of the control framework and on the personal standards and professionalism of the individuals within the body. It is reflected both in the body's decision-making procedures and in the quality of its financial and performance reporting.

Accountability

Accountability is the process whereby public service bodies, and the individuals within them are responsible for their decisions and actions, including their stewardship of public funds and all aspects of performance, and submit themselves to appropriate scrutiny. It is achieved by all parties having a clear understanding of those responsibilities, and having clearly defined roles through a robust structure.

Internal Control (1994; Appendix F). This code is worth studying in full. Link its use of control and governance to the definitions already mentioned. The code summarises the definitions of control discussed earlier, and integrates these into a framework of best practices for all control objectives.

An awareness and understanding of all the management, control and governance definitions are important when addressing levels of control in an organisation. Case 2.3 takes a top-down approach to studying control in an organisation. Part of one of the case study questions in The IIA-UK MIIA

Figure 2.8 Nolan standards in public life

First Report of the Committee on Standards in Public Life. Chairman: Lord Nolan. Presented to Parliament by the Prime Minister by Command of Her Majesty, May 1995

The seven principles of public life

Selflessness

Holders of public office should take decisions solely in terms of the public interest. They should not do so in order to gain financial or other material benefits for themselves, their families, or their friends.

Integrity

Holders of public office should not place themselves under any financial or other obligation to outside individuals or organisations that might influence them in the performance of their official duties.

Objectivity

In carrying out public business, including making public appointments, awarding contracts, or recommending individuals for rewards and benefits, holders of public office should make choices on merit.

Accountability

Holders of public office are accountable for their decisions and actions to the public and must submit themselves to whatever scrutiny is appropriate to their office.

Openness

Holders of public office should be as open as possible about all the decisions and actions they take. They should give reasons for their decisions and restrict information only when the wider public interest clearly demands.

Honesty

Holders of public office have a duty to declare any private interests relating to their public duties and to take steps to resolve any conflicts arising in a way that protects the public interest.

Leadership

Holders of public office should promote and support these principles by leadership and example.

Figure 2.9 Standards of corporate governance in the public services

(The Chartered Institute of Public Finance and Accountancy, UK: Corporate Governance: A Framework for Public Service Bodies (1995) – Diagram 2)

Organisational structures and processes
- statutory accountability
- accountability for public money
- communication with stakeholders
- roles and responsibilities
- balance of power
- the board
- the chairman
- non-executive board members
- executive management

Financial reporting and internal controls
- annual reporting
- internal controls
- risk management
- internal audit
- audit committees
- external auditors

Standards of behaviour
- leadership
- codes of conduct
- selflessness
- objectivity
- honesty

professional examinations, it represents a common scenario in organisations across all sectors.

Create a framework of control objectives for your own organisation

A test for expertise in management, control and governance is for an internal auditor to create a framework of how external and internal controls integrate to achieve all their organisation's control objectives. Figure 2.13 provides structure for such a framework.

Figure 2.10 Guidance on control (CoCo)

The Canadian Institute of Chartered Accountants, Canada: 1995

Control frameworks: the criteria

Purpose

A1 Objectives should be established and communicated.
A2 The significant internal and external risks faced by an organisation in the achievement of its objectives should be identified and assessed.
A3 Policies designed to support the achievement of an organisation's objectives and the management of its risks should be established, communicated and practised so that people understand what is expected of them and the scope of their freedom to act.
A4 Plans to guide efforts in achieving the organisation's objectives should be established and communicated.
A5 Objectives and related plans should include measurable performance targets and indicators.

Commitment

B1 Shared ethical values, including integrity, should be established, communicated and practised throughout the organisation.
B2 Human resource policies and practices should be consistent with an organisation's ethical values and with the achievement of its objectives.
B3 Authority, responsibility and accountability should be clearly defined and consistent with an organisation's objectives so that decisions and actions are taken by the appropriate people.
B4 An atmosphere of mutual trust should be fostered to support the flow of information between people and their effective performance towards achieving the organisation's objectives.

Capability

C1 People should have the necessary knowledge, skills and tools to support the achievement of the organisation's objectives.
C2 Communication processes should support the organisation's values and the achievement of its objectives.
C3 Sufficient and relevant information should be identified and communicated in a timely manner to enable people to perform their assigned responsibilities.
C4 The decisions and actions of different parts of the organisation should be co-ordinated.
C5 Control activities should be designed as an integral part of the organisation, taking into consideration its objectives, the risks to their achievement, and the inter-relatedness of control elements.

▶

Figure 2.10 Contd

Monitoring and learning

D1 External and internal environments should be monitored to obtain information that may signal a need to re-evaluate the organisation's objectives or control.

D2 Performance should be monitored against the targets and indicators identified in the organisation's objectives and plans.

D3 The assumptions behind an organisation's objectives should be periodically challenged.

D4 Information needs and related information systems should be reassessed as objectives change or as reporting deficiencies are identified.

D5 Follow-up procedures should be established and performed to ensure appropriate change or action occurs.

D6 Management should periodically assess the effectiveness of control in its organisation and communicate the results to those to whom it is accountable.

CoCo links to COSO integrated framework model

Control environment	B1,2,3,4, C1
Risk assessment	A1,2,5, D1
Control activities	A3, C4,5
Information and communication	A4, C2,3, D4
Monitoring	D2,3,5,6

Each of the following five elements in the framework can be researched to provide detail of their impact and influence on an organisation's management and performance.

1. Societal interests and values concern ethics and public attitudes to the organisation's existence and performance – not just locally or nationally, but also in relation to the wider impacts an organisation might have on global issues.
2. Stakeholders are all those interests, financial or otherwise, in an organisation's performance. Rarely are these interests exclusive to one type of stakeholder. More often, interests are networked amongst groups of stakeholders. Some stakeholders are passive, others can be active, with strong influences on an organisation's management, control and governance objectives.
3. Rules and regulations are all the directives which establish mandatory and voluntary directions for an organisation's behaviour, and those who are associated with its performance. These can be international, national, local

Figure 2.11 The code of best practice

(As recommended by Cadbury (1992) *The Financial Aspects of Corporate Governance*.)

1. The board of directors

1.1 The board should meet regularly, retain full and effective control over the company and monitor the executive management.

1.2 There should be a clearly accepted division of responsibilities at the head of a company, which will ensure a balance of power and authority, such that no one individual has unfettered powers of decision. Where the chairman is also the chief executive, it is essential that there should be a strong and independent element on the board, with a recognised senior member.

1.3 The board should include non-executive directors of sufficient calibre and number for their views to carry significant weight in the board's decisions.

1.4 The board should have a formal schedule of matters specifically reserved to it for decision to ensure that the direction and control of the company are firmly in its hands.

1.5 There should be an agreed procedure for directors in the furtherance of their duties to take independent professional advice if necessary, at the company's expense.

1.6 All directors should have access to the advice and services of the company secretary, who is responsible to the board for ensuring that board procedures are followed and that applicable rules and regulations are complied with. Any question of the removal of the company secretary should be a matter for the board as a whole.

2. Non-executive directors

2.1 Non-executive directors should bring an independent judgement to bear on issues of strategy, performance, resources, including key appointments and standards of conduct.

2.2 The majority should be independent of management and free from any business or other relationship which could materially interfere with the exercise of their independent judgement, apart from their fees and shareholding. Their fees should reflect the time which they commit to the company.

2.3 Non-executive directors should be appointed for specified terms and re-appointment should not be automatic.

2.4 Non-executive directors should be selected through a formal process and both this process and their appointment should be a matter for the board as a whole.

3. Executive directors

3.1 Directors' service contracts should not exceed three years without shareholders' approval.

3.2 There should be full and clear disclosure of directors' total emoluments and

▶

Figure 2.11   Contd

> those of the chairman and highest-paid UK director, including pension contributions and stock options. Separate figures should be given for salary and performance-related elements and the basis on which performance is measured and explained.
> 3.3   Executive directors' pay should be subject to the recommendations of a remuneration committee made up wholly or mainly of non-executive directors.
>
> **4.   Reporting and controls**
> 4.1   It is the board's duty to present a balanced and understandable assessment of the company's position.
> 4.2   The board should ensure that an objective and professional relationship is maintained with the auditors.
> 4.3   The board should establish an audit committee of at least three non-executive directors with written terms of reference which deal clearly with its authority and duties.
> 4.4   The directors should explain their responsibility for preparing the accounts next to a statement by the auditors about their reporting responsibilities.
> 4.5   The directors should report on the effectiveness of the company's system of internal control.
> 4.6   The directors should report that the business is a going concern, with supporting assumptions or qualifications as necessary.
>
> *Note*: The company's statement of compliance should be reviewed by the auditors in so far as it relates to paragraphs 1.4, 1.5, 2.3, 2.4, 3.1 to 3.3, and 4.3 to 4.6 of the code.

    or issued by other bodies with which an organisation is associated, through its operations and those participating in its performance.
4. Control concepts are the developed theory and principles underlying all control and monitoring activities.
5. External monitoring covers all the independent groups who are involved in regulation, review and investigation of an organisation's activities. Some of these groups have contractual relationships with an organisation, some have legal status, some are voluntary. Many have stakeholder interests.

When an internal auditor has prepared a management, control and governance framework, it should be evident that each of the five elements integrates into all the others. This integration is a good test of how well the framework has been structured. Case 2.4 looks at such a framework through the promotion of a UK national charter for public service organisations. When reading its content, note how the case constantly returns to all five of the elements in Figure 2.13.

Figure 2.12   Nolan elements of best practice

(As recommended by Lord Nolan's Committee on Standards in Public Life, a second 1996 report on standards in public life, addressed to education bodies, training and enterprise councils and housing associations.)

Best practice, subject always to proportionality for smaller organisations, includes:

Appointments
- A publicly available written appointments process.
- Job descriptions and person specification.
- The use of advertisement and/or consultation with interested bodies and other forms of canvassing.
- The encouragement of nominations (including self-nominations).
- The sifting of candidates by a nominations committee.
- Defined terms of appointment after which reappointment should not be automatic.

Openness
- Making the agendas and minutes of governing body meetings widely available, together with board papers, where this will not inhibit frankness and clarity.
- Publicising forthcoming meetings and summarising decisions in a newsletter or through some other user-friendly method.
- Holding an open annual meeting at which board members can be questioned by the public and press.
- Setting up more specialised consultation bodies for important interest groups.
- Publishing an annual report which includes information on the role and remit of the body, its plans or strategy; the membership of the board; and where further information can be obtained.
- Publishing audit reports.
- Making publications available as widely as possible, for example by sending them to interested parties and putting them in local public libraries.

Codes of conduct
- A statement of the aims and values of the body.
- Statements of the obligations of the body towards its customers, staff, community, and other interested parties.
- Information about the body's approach to openness and arrangements for acquiring information about its activities.
- Procedures for handling enquiries and complaints.
- Procedures for raising complaints with an independent body.

Whistleblowing
- A clear statement that malpractice is taken seriously in the organisation and an indication of the sorts of matters regarded as malpractice.
- Respect for the confidentiality of staff raising concerns if they wish, and the opportunity to raise concerns outside the line management structure.
- Penalties for making false and malicious allegations.
- An indication of the proper way in which concerns may be raised outside the organisation if necessary.

Figure 2.13 A framework for control and governance

Societal interests and values

Stakeholders
European/international/UK parliament
executive councils/bodies
local authorities
investors
customers
funding bodies
employees
suppliers
professional institutions
universities
advisory groups
religious bodies
employer associations

Rules and regulations
charters
awards
cultures
codes
standards
laws
regulations

Control concepts
integrated control = control environment; risk assessment; control activities; monitoring
information systems = communications
governance = openness; integrity; accountability
management = superordinate goals; strategy; structure; systems; style; staff; skills

External monitoring
police
external auditors
inspectors
regulators
ombudsmen
watchdogs
action groups
public opinion
media

Link management, control and governance to performance

Cadbury did not relate directors' responsibilities for control over finance with performance. More recently, an inquiry by The Royal Society of Arts (*Tomorrow's Company*, 1995) concluded that the nature of competition is changing as the level of interdependence between companies and the community increases. That interdependence requires organisations to take an 'inclusive approach' with customers, suppliers, employees, investors and the communities in which they operate, locally, nationally and globally.

Recognising governance as fundamental to performance is not new. Good governance has evolved from social and altruistic management principles developed over this century. More recently Humble (*Social Responsibility Audit*, 1973) preached social responsibility as an important area in which every business must set objectives and secure results. However, his basic concept for company survival was not only social responsibility, but also profitability:

> Since business is the wealth-producing institution of our society it must be profitable. The greatest social irresponsibility would be to so manage business that wealth was not produced for the community's fabric of schools, homes, roads and so on. This is recognised even in countries where the word 'profit' is not acceptable. 'Surplus' or 'maximum value added to minimum materials and money put in', or similar phrases are preferred. What is done with the profit or surplus is another argument ... which can't start if there's nothing to divide. Responsibility and profitability are inseparable.

Other management pioneers at that time, both practitioners and academics, supported Humble's belief in the 'profit motive' in private enterprise systems. In the same year as Humble's social responsibility audit was published, The CBI published *The Responsibilities of the British Public Company*, a report by a committee under the chairmanship of Lord Watkinson. This report also reflects the belief that profit is fundamental, defining the growing influence of different groups and institutions on profit and the behaviour of the company itself.

One of the earliest UK recognitions of governance as an economic issue came in 1979. In that year, The Institute of Chartered Secretaries and Administrators published a series of papers on corporate governance and accountability, by distinguished contributors from industry and academia, introducing these thus:

> In recent years, public debate has ranged over industrial democracy, audit committees, the duties and responsibilities of company directors, disclosure of information, accounting standards and other subjects but there has been little new thought about more fundamental aspects – the 'why'; and 'how' of corporate governance.

Two of the contributors, Sir Arthur Knight and Dr K. Midgley (as he then was), examined boardroom responsibilities, listing the claims of various groups that management need to take into account in their decision-making. These lists included most of the groups currently referred to as the organisation's 'stakeholders'. In ranking these groups they identified consumers as 'Customers [, who] come first; . . .'. They did not at that time see other groups (stakeholders) as customers too! In listing groups with claims on an organisation they both predated the current wide definition of 'stakeholder'. Conclusions reached by both contributors placed accountability clearly at the door of directors, and profitability as still the most reliable guide to management efficiency.

Corporate concerns and public disenchantment with behaviour in some major businesses world-wide during the 1980s led to a growing demand for improved ethical standards to be adopted publicly by many organisations. These demands have not abated; if anything, they have increased, extending also to governments and their supporting administrations. Many organisations now publicly declare codes of ethics to their stakeholders, linking these to some, if not all, of their other objectives. The Institute of Business Ethics' report on *Current Best Ethical Practice in the United Kingdom*, published in 1992, included the following statement in a proposed code:

> We will provide products and services of good value and consistent quality, reliability and safety. . . . We will avoid practices which seek to increase sales by any means other than fair merchandising efforts based on quality, design features, productivity, price and product support. . . . We will provide a high standard of service in our efforts to maintain customer satisfaction and co-operation.

Achieving quality in products and services is now a well-studied and -researched road to success and even survival in today's government and business operations. There is ample evidence in developed theory and principles that quality is associated with competition, performance and profitability; yet there is little evidence that control or governance has been a focus in any of this research. Use of control for quality is not new. Omachonu and Ross (1994) use 'conformance to requirements' as a current universal definition of quality; emphasising the importance of design, deviation and standards. They also recognise that control for quality is different to the use of traditional control concepts for financial statements:

> The classical control process will require significant change if TQM is to be successful. Traditionally, control systems have been directed to the end use of preparation of financial statements. Focus has been on the components of the profit-and-loss statement. Quality control has historically followed a three-step process consisting of (1) setting standards, (2) reporting variances and (3) correcting deviations. . . . In an organisation that perceives control systems in this way, there is the danger that the system will become the end rather than the means. This is not to say that classical control does not have a place in quality management.

What place classical control has in quality management activities at strategic, tactical and operational levels is explored by the authors, but not as an integrated approach to organisation success. Nor is classic control defined to include the wider aspects of governance or external controls over an organisation's activities.

Think like a criminal

Preventing fraud is one of management's responsibilities in any organisation. Using an integrated control framework to prevent and detect fraud can be an important part of the internal auditor's and manager's activities. Understanding what fraud is and how it can be carried out in any organisation, at all levels, and from both inside and outside, is key to its prevention and detection. Control and governance as fraud deterrents are essential for the success of all organisations.

The risk of fraud is always present. Approaches to its investigation and disclosure vary. Almost without exception it can impact all of society and an organisation's stakeholders. It can cause considerable damage, far beyond the value of the immediate loss, leading sometimes to significant performance failures and even closure of operations and whole businesses. In the public sector it can lead to political unrest and loss of power.

Russell (1977) studied fraud cases across the world and drew the following conclusions for the internal auditor:

> Fraud in the marketplace, embezzlement in positions of trust, bribery in public life, theft of securities, check kiting [failing to honour a cheque], illegal political donations, mail frauds, overloaded expense accounts, manipulation of payrolls, issuance of false financial statements, credit-card swindles, illegal competition, kickbacks and payoffs, bankruptcy frauds, and arson are a few of today's challenges.
>
> The outside criminal – the burglar or robber – usually visits his victim but once and leaves telltale evidence of his entry. But the inside criminal is a different story. How is he tracked down? The inside criminal may be the owner, the manager, or the lowest employee. All are in a position to steal on a continuing basis.
>
> Here are four ways by which fraudulent activities are uncovered:
> - the reduction of the resource to a noticeable level of depletion;
> - the accidental discovery of the fraud;
> - the revelation by an informer;
> - the diligence of an inquisitive ... member of the accounting or internal audit staff who can concentrate on the problems of balances, of checks, and eliminations ..., as Brad Cadmus said:
>
> > It appears that the internal auditor can make the best contribution to the control of fraud when:
> > - management clearly assigns the responsibility for handling cases;
> > - the internal audit program is designed not only for operational audits but also provides for an imaginative approach to the possibilities of controlling fraudulent activity;
> > - the internal auditor fully understands the legal implication of fraud;
> > - the auditor acquires the attitude that not every foozle is a fraud and has the keen perception of fraud when he comes in contact with it;
> > - the auditor gains training and experiences in interrogation of suspects;

Figure 2.14 Russell fraud check-list

- When something does not look right, be persistent in running it down.
- To obtain the best results, establish proper relationships with the people you audit.
- Recognise improper actions, entries and figures when you see them.
- Develop your ability to remember bits of information and, by association, place them in an overall pattern.
- Dishonest people are poor liars – listen for their double-talk.
- Learn to ask open-ended questions – but only the right kind.
- Don't trust an informer's allegations, but never ignore them.
- Be alert to the possibility of false documentation.
- Don't rely on evidence that cannot be fully supported.
- Make sure that audit sampling is not only scientific, but sensible too.
- Do not be misled by appearances.
- Do not be satisfied with unreasonable answers to audit questions.
- Don't ignore unrecorded funds for which the organisation has a legal or moral responsibility.
- Learn as much about the auditees as you possibly can.
- Keep audit programmes from becoming too limited or stereotyped.

- the audit staff recognises that recent disclosures of widespread payola have been made (whether the payola was necessary or not, a serious loss of control over substantial funds occurs when such disbursements are made from off-the-books funds and from laundered money moved from country to country without records);
- the internal auditor is assured by public accountants and outside directors that his responsibility runs to them as well as to management when fraud by top management is suspected;
- the auditor does not place unlimited dependence on internal control (the internal control system that can't be penetrated has not yet been invented).

Russell created a fraud check-list for internal auditors which is as useful today as it was when first designed. See Figure 2.14.

Understand the importance of time and the future

Understanding the above definitions of control, governance and management science leads the internal auditor into understanding how these are interpreted and applied in the areas that they audit. The definitions provide a wide international acceptance of control and governance as being designed and effected

Figure 2.15 The control time span

Control objectives	Time span		
	Past	Present	Future
■ efficiency	?	?	?
■ economy	?	?	?
■ effectiveness	?	?	?
■ ethics	?	?	?
■ environmental	?	?	?
■ empowerment	?	?	?
■ enlightenment	?	?	?
■ equality	?	?	?

by people, to achieve specific separate and overlapping objectives, always related to yesterday, today and the future. This time span can be used with any of the key objectives in the definitions to create a useful matrix for development of 'questions' and 'check lists' in any internal audit assignment. Such a matrix is a useful guide during the audit planning, reviews, testing, reporting and follow-up. Using the three Es, expressed in The IIA definition of efficiency, economy and effectiveness, and example, an internal auditor's questions on control can always be designed around time. How efficient were you yesterday? How efficient are you today? How efficient will you be tomorrow?

Most leading edge internal auditing goes beyond the three Es objectives to other important objectives of control. Using the definitions for management, control and governance, the leading edge internal auditor can add more objectives to the matrix. *Ethics* and *environmental issues* are two obvious objectives. More recently, *empowerment* and *enlightenment* have impacted the control environment: empowerment as part of process re-engineering and quality management, enlightenment through technology and a growing pursuit of knowledge and innovation, by both organisations and the people they employ. *Equality* is now a control issue in many organisations. Discrimination, as part of an organisation's culture, can be a significant control weakness.

From three Es, we now have eight. The development can go on. Eight control objectives creates 24 question 'boxes' – see Figure 2.15 – all to be addressed during every internal audit assignment. Understanding the right questions to ask and the relationship of answers reveals organisation strengths and weaknesses for future management control and governance.

Teach managers to self-assess and report on their responsibility for control

Recent years have seen a growth in the number of statements on internal control in organisations, addressed both internally and externally, prepared by management, auditors and sometimes stakeholders. All require an understanding of how control objectives are achieved. All require a formal process of consideration and design, if they are to have value in the organisation and for outside observers of an organisation's operations. In many cases these statements also form part of the internal audit charter and may even be written by internal auditors as part of their service to the organisation.

Current literature shows the pattern of management perceptions of value from internal audit contribution to writing statements on control. Some managers see a growing value from internal audit in this area of reporting. Some see a growth in internal audit contributing to the preparation of reports to regulators and reports on the environment. Yet others see growth in internal audit contributing to external statements on internal control in annual reports. The contribution which internal audit can make to reliability and integrity of reports and statements on control should be seen by management and internal auditors as one of its highest values.

All control statements are based on a risk assessment process. Such assessment processes have in the past frequently been based on letters of comfort, often called representation letters. These letters are signed by managers across organisations at time intervals, sometimes linked to financial reporting, expressing an opinion on control and commenting on any absence of or weakness in control. In many cases representation letters are used by external audit, particularly when an organisation has many locations, not all letters for different control objectives. They are used for environmental, quality and business conduct statements. The main weakness underlying the signing of representation letters is the risk assessment process used to establish the level of control before they are signed.

In recent years control self-assessment techniques have developed in North America and spread across the world. Many of these techniques are linked to the growth of interest in control definitions, models and external control statement requirements. Initially promoted by external consultants, more and more internal auditors have adopted facilitation of control self-assessments to promote their own internal consultancy services and improve audit planning. This link into internal auditing performance is important. Control self-assessment by managers should never be seen in isolation from managing and monitoring. It is a fundamental part of all aspects of management and auditing. What the good internal auditor brings to control self-assessment is control expertise.

There can be a danger that unless risk assessment is formalised and monitored, its practices can be too narrow. The most important risks can be overlooked! For this reason it can be an advantage to have risk assessed through a team approach, using internal audit as a facilitator. Members of the team span all levels in the activity being assessed. Some teams can include an activity's suppliers and customers, both internal and external. Consider Case 2.5 and question whether risk assessment processes should cover the changes and influences described.

The IIA established a Control Self-Assessment Centre in 1997, which now offers a CSA Qualification, based on a programme of study and practice. This centre brings together guidance on self-assessment and training internal auditors. How internal auditors sell CSA in their organisations is addressed by Jordan (1997), in the first issue of The IIA's *CSA Sentinel*:

> Internal auditors can help raise awareness of CSA by conducting training classes or by amending the traditional audit approach to include at least some CSA participative concepts. Explain to audit customers that you can come back and help them with a full CSA approach later if they're interested. You use the techniques you have, including formal training, to raise their awareness with regard to what's available, what CSA is, and how they can use it. Then you allow the interested individual groups to ask for CSA.

In the same issue Leech (1997) discusses his developed process for identifying control and quality management requirements in organisations (see also the case in Chapter 9). His new vision and environment have the following attributes:

- empowered, accountable employees;
- culture of continuous improvement and learning;
- extensive employee participation and training;
- broad stakeholder focus;
- staff at all levels, in all functions, are the primary control analysts and reporters;
- management and staff are accountable for designing and maintaining control systems that provide the desired level of assurance regarding the achievement of business and quality objectives;
- management and staff are provided with control assessment and design skills that are adequate for proper fulfilment of their responsibility to assess and report to officers of the board and others on the current status of control, quality and risk;
- consensus at all levels on relevant business and quality objectives is a primary goal;
- candid disclosure of the state of control and the risks being accepted by the unit or organisation is encouraged and rewarded;
- accountability for business and quality objectives exists and is accepted by staff at all levels and in all functions;
- employees at all levels are responsible for finding new and better ways to improve and optimise control portfolios so that achievement of organisational goals is advanced;
- employees at all levels and in all functions continually reassess the adequacy and appropriateness of control choices and make adjustments when new

information emerges regarding risk status, prioritisation of objectives and the control options available;
- control and quality management are considered to be synonymous and are fully integrated programmes/concepts.

These statements offer leading edge opportunities for all internal auditors, whatever the size of their internal audit units. Case 2.6 shows how in one small internal audit unit these opportunities have been taken. They have provided a growth in status and scope of work in the unit described which will continue to develop their internal auditing services into the future.

Chapter summary

Leading edge internal auditors are management, control and governance experts. This requires a critical understanding of control frameworks and the ability to design a framework for their own organisations. Management value internal audit having an unrestricted scope of work in their current control frameworks; yet, many do not see internal audit currently adding value to all aspects of governance and the objectives of all control activities: some doubt whether their internal audit has the strength to contribute to all governance issues. The value of internal audit's contribution to development and monitoring compliance with organisation codes of conduct and codes of best practice is not yet seen in many organisations. Internal auditors should develop the ability to think like criminals if they are to prevent and detect fraud. All control objectives are in a time span of the past, present and future. Audit of control objective requirements and achievements requires the internal auditor to consider each aspect of time in all audit objectives and work. Management control self-assessment is an important part of all control statements and reporting. The pattern of management perceptions of value from internal audit contribution to assessments and statements on control is mixed, both in sectors and between managers. Many see a growing value from internal audit contributions in the assessment and reporting of control status. The contribution internal audit can make to reliability and integrity of external reports and statements should be seen by management as one of its highest values. Internal audit and management should address the links between quality and governance. All sizes of internal audit unit can service all governance issues if appropriately resourced, with professional qualifications and management support. Internal audit staff and senior management should ensure that the quality of internal audit services meets all their organisation's governance requirements.

▶

Principia

1. Internal auditors should always be seen as control experts.
2. Planning, organising, directing and monitoring are essential parts of all control activities.
3. Divisions of responsibilities are a key control mechanism.
4. Financial, social, quality and environmental control objectives are international issues, across all supply chains, in all sectors.
5. Control embraces all aspects of governance, including ethics, equality, honesty, caring and sustaining.
6. Creating integrated control frameworks in an organisation provides an understanding of their strengths and weaknesses.
7. Understanding how fraud is perpetrated is key to its prevention and detection.
8. The best internal auditors review control in the past and present, and accurately forecast the future.
9. Internal auditing should contribute to the reliability and integrity of all management reports and statements on control.
10. Control self-assessment by managers is essential for all aspects of management, and auditing.

Bibliography

Bain, Neville and Band, David (1996) *Winning Ways Through Corporate Governance*, Macmillan Press, London.
Cadbury, A. (1992) *The Financial Aspects of Corporate Governance*, Gee, London.
Coopers & Lybrand (1993) *Effective Business Control – a guide for directors*, London.
Coopers & Lybrand (1996) *Cadbury compliance – a survey of published accounts*, London.
COSO (1992) *Internal Control – Integrated Framework*, Committee of Sponsoring Organizations of the Treadway Commission, USA.
Ernst & Young (1995) *Is your organisation in a position to monitor internal control?*, London.
Humble, J. (1973) *Social Responsibility Audit – a management tool for survival*, Foundation for Business Responsibilities, London.
Jordan, Glenda S. (1997) *Control Self-Assessment: Making the Choice*, The Institute of Internal Auditors Inc., Altamonte Springs, USA.
Leech, Tim J. (1997) 'Control and Risk Assessment', *CSA Sentinel*, The Institute of Internal Auditors Inc., Altamonte Springs, USA.

Omachuno, J. Vincent, K. and Ross, Joel, E. (1994) *Principles of Total Quality*, St Lucie Press, Delray Beach, Florida, USA.
Peters, Thomas J. and Waterman, Robert H. Jr (1982) *In Search of Excellence*, Harper & Row, London.
Richard, Ratliff L., Wallace, Wanda, A., Sumners, Glenn E., McFarland, William G. and Leobbecke James K. (1996) *Internal Auditing Principles and Techniques – Second Edition*, The Institute of Internal Auditors Inc., Altamonte Springs, USA.
Ridley, Jeffrey and D'Silva, Kenneth (1997) *A Question of Values: Internal Auditing June 1997*, The IIA-UK, London.
Russell, Harold F. (1977) *Foozles & Fraud*, The Institute of Internal Auditors Inc., USA.
Schiff, Jonathan B., Miller, JoAnn and May, Claire B. (1989) *Issues Paper: Guidance on Internal Control*, National Association of Accountants, New Jersey, USA.
Sheridan, T. and Kendall, N. (1992) *Corporate Governance – An Action Plan for Profitability and Business Success*, Financial Times/Pitman, London.
Simon, Robert (1995) 'Control in an Age of Empowerment', *Harvard Business Review* – March/April, USA.
Stearn, H. J. and Impey, K. W. (1990) *Manual of Internal Audit Practice*, ICSA Publishing Ltd, Hemel Hempstead.
The Canadian Institute of Chartered Accountants (1996) *Guidance on Control*, Toronto.
The Chartered Institute of Management Accountants (1992) *A Framework for Internal Control*, London.
The Chartered Institute of Public Finance and Accountancy (1995) *Corporate Governance: A Framework for Public Service Bodies*, CIPFA, London.
The Institute of Chartered Secretaries and Administrators (1979) *Corporate Governance and Accountability*, ICSA, London.
The Institute of Chartered Accountants in England and Wales (1994) *Internal Control and Financial Reporting*, London.
The Institute of Internal Auditors (1994) *Professional Briefing Note Six – Internal Control*, London.
The Institute of Internal Auditors (1995) *Professional Briefing Note Eight – Reporting on Internal Control*, London.
The Institute of Business Ethics (1992) *Business Ethics and Company Codes*, IBE, London.
The Nolan Committee (1995) *Standards in Public Life*, HMSO, London.
The Nolan Committee (1996) *Standards in Public Life – Second Report*, HMSO, London.
The Royal Society for the Encouragement of Arts, Manufactures and Commerce (1995) *Tomorrow's Company*, RSA, London.
Treadway Commission (1987) *Report of the National Commission on Fraudulent Financial Reporting*, USA.
Tricker, Robert I. (1994) *International Corporate Governance*, Simon & Schuster, Singapore.
UK Government White Paper (1982) *Standards: Quality and International Competitiveness* (Cmnd 8621), HMSO, London.
Waterman, Robert H. Jr, Peters, Thomas, J. and Phillips, Julien R. (1980) *Structure is not Organization*, Business Horizons, USA.
Ziegenfuss, Douglas E. (1994) *Challenges and Opportunities of Small Internal Audit Organizations*, The IIA Research Foundation, USA.

Case 2.1 A control overview: internal control is like a well-lit Christmas tree

The case

December is the time of year when all internal auditors and managers can remind themselves of the important characteristics of control, as they prepare and admire their traditional Christmas tree. The IIA standards set out the environment for adequate control in an organisation as the 'design of structures and systems, the setting of objectives, goals and interrelationships all operating together to achieve ... expected results' (guideline 300.02.4).

There are three important qualities for the festive Christmas tree. It must be:

- attractive in shape;
- decorated colourfully;
- positioned as a focal point for celebration.

The tree that achieves these qualities – whether large or small, in home, street or workplace – creates an environment which will influence the actions of those who are in its presence.

Shape, colour and celebration are also very important characteristics of internal control. Each plays an important part in establishing the 'adequate' and 'reasonable' levels of control which are essential if 'expected results' are to be achieved.

Shape is the result of good design. In control, this design is in the planning and direction of all management and work practices. The required shapes of control must be thought out carefully, with the purpose clearly in mind. There needs to be a vision of the shape that the organisation requires if it is to achieve its objectives. Attractive shapes promote effectiveness, efficiency and economy. Unattractive shapes create weaknesses in control.

Colour brightens the shape. It arouses emotions. In the same way colourful controls encourage compliance. The relationships and connections between all the visions, strategies, policies and operational rules in an organisation need to be carefully coloured, if reasonable control is to exist. Motivation is the brightest colour in control. It makes relations and links work well in the many supply chains in and across organisations. It sets the tones in the control environments. An understanding of how motivation influences control is an important part of control planning.

Celebration around a well-positioned tree is a highlight of the festive season. It is also important that good control generates celebration for those participating in its success. Awards and positive reinforcements when control contributes to success and achievement is an important part of management at all levels in the organisation. Linking control to success and celebration should be a part of the reporting of all audit results.

Consider

1. Are the messages in the above imaginative story seen in your organisation's control framework? Do shape, colour and celebration encourage compliance with your organisation's control frameworks? Look for evidence of each and ask questions if it is absent.
2. As you gather around Christmas trees every year, reflect on its control qualities of shape, colour and celebration. Think of the control that went into providing the desired results! Keep your tree in mind as you plan every internal audit.

Case 2.2 Management and control in a large retail company

(This is a CIA essay question from The IIA November 1996 professional examinations.)

The case

Management of a large retail company with over 125 stores has become concerned about the increasing customer complaints. Customers reported that electronic scanners are not charging proper prices in the stores in the Southeast region. While there has been some decline in profitability in the Southeast region, the company has not experienced unusual fluctuations in profitability. Although the company has strong central management, each region controls its own prices and, within limits, an individual store manager can change prices in a store to compete locally.

The internal audit department has just completed an audit of the Southeast region. Following are excerpts from the auditor's notes.

1. Each store operates in a client/server computing environment. All prices are stored in the regional database. The database is downloaded daily to each store to run the computer check-out system. Because the database is administered in a client/server environment, there is no need to reconcile the downloaded database with the master database. Further, there is no need to use control totals or other similar totals, because the company does not operate in a batch mode.
2. All price changes are approved by the buyer responsible for procuring the goods.
3. Buyers are evaluated on the profitability of items which they purchase.
4. Each buyer has access to the database for price changes. Access to the overall database is limited by passwords. However, a buyer will often delegate access to an assistant to perform the mechanical duties of keypunching in the data and updating the database.

5. Each buyer has the responsibility to develop promotional campaigns and advertising for each store in the region. However, within limits, a local store manager can place an ad for some special close-outs.
6. Each store manager has the ability to change the price table on the store's price database. However, those changes are not uploaded and thus cannot affect other stores.
7. In order to maintain the integrity of the price database, the full database is downloaded from the regional database each morning prior to the start of business.
8. Close-out items are specially marked and are required to be entered at the cash register, rather than scanned in. In order to expedite customer service, the cashier enters only the price of the product, not its number. The price entered does not affect the selling price recorded in the store's database.
9. The stores have been complaining about inventory shrinkage on certain products, that is, the stores do not have inventory on hand when the perpetual inventory indicates goods are present.
10. The price table database is reconciled with the authorised price list kept by each buyer on a quarterly basis. The reconciliation is performed by an assistant to the merchandising manager, who is separate from the buyers making changes to the database.
11. The company prepares daily reports of sales per store and per department within each store.
12. Before any new product can be input into the price database, its product number and purchase approval must first be entered into the database. Approval is required from the merchandise manager, and data are input by an assistant separate from the buyer. The merchandise manager has a separate password to access the database.
13. Any new product entry must conform to the company's existing product numbering scheme. An edit check is run to determine that the product number is valid.

Consider

Given the description of the company's system and the audit findings, identify:

(a) five control strengths;
(b) five control weaknesses;
(c) for each weakness identified, state the potential impact of the weakness on the company.

Organise your answer as follows:

- control strengths;
- control weaknesses;
- potential impact on the organisation.

(See page 108 for solution.)

Case 2.3 Easycall Ltd: a top-down review of a control environment

(This is part of a case extracted from 1997 study texts, published by The Institute of Internal Auditors-UK, for its MIIA professional examinations: Paper 10 – Advanced Internal Auditing.)

The case

Introduction

Easycall Ltd is a large £2 billion mobile phone operation. Its head office is located in the South of England and Easycall has good road and rail links to London. The company employs approximately two hundred people at this location. These people work principally in direct sales, marketing and finance. The majority of its non-core activities, such as information technology, have been outsourced to external contractors. The direct sales force at head office is supplemented by a number of dealers contracted by the company to sell mobile phones and air time contracts through their retail outlets.

Shareholders

Easycall is owned jointly by two telecommunication companies who have an equal number of shares in the company. They are based in continental Europe and allow the chief executive of Easycall complete autonomy in the running of the business, as long as its objectives are being achieved.

Objectives of Easycall

Easycall is one of the four operators in the mobile phone sector. The principal objective of the company, as stated by the chief executive, Geraldine Powell, is to become a major player in the mobile phone industry. She intends to achieve this by increasing market share through an aggressive marketing campaign, selling innovative products and providing the customer with good value for money.

Market

The overall mobile phone market in the UK is worth £16 billion per annum. Easycall has a 12 per cent share of this market. There are three major competitors, two of whom were launched in 1985 and the other in 1992. Easycall, launched in 1994, is therefore a relative newcomer to the sector. It is also the only one of the four major players who does not have a stock exchange listing. As the last of the four big networks Easycall had a massive challenge – how to make a mark and become known as a major mobile phone manufacturer. It did this through a well-known and innovative advertising campaign. When it launched in 1994 Easycall had the most rapid expansion plans of any mobile operator in the UK – from an initial 50 per cent of the population to 70 per cent at the end of 1994 (covering the places where over 40 million people live and work), to 90 per cent during 1995.

Strengths and weaknesses

Following a major review of Easycall by external consultants all executive managers were advised of the main conclusions relating to the strengths and weaknesses of the company. These can be briefly stated as:

Strengths

- It has a high public profile through innovative advertising;
- it has a reputation for excellent customer service;
- the telephone it markets outsells all other handsets;
- it deals direct with its dealers and does not use service providers.

Weaknesses

The company's main weaknesses can be described asf follows:

- While it is gaining market share, it does not have the strength in subscriber base of its two main rivals;
- its innovations are quickly copied by its rivals, therefore providing a limited opportunity to capitalise on customer interest;
- it is losing money through the fraudulent use of mobile phones and bad debts;
- it can currently service only 45 per cent of the UK population and in a recent press survey was highlighted as the company with the worst record in connections;
- it has difficulty in retaining customers;
- the company has grown quickly and does not have a firmly developed culture of corporate governance.

The chief executive is keen to capitalise on the strengths and reduce the weaknesses of the company, particularly those relating to governance, fraud, and the servicing and retention of its customer base. The deputy chief executive, John Wood, has, on the instructions of the chief executive, prepared an overview of the current status of the company relating to the perceived problem areas – see Appendix A.

Future plans

The major item on the agenda of the executive board of Easycall is the planned flotation on the stock exchange, within the next year, as a public limited company. Experts value the company, the fastest-growing mobile phone network in the UK, at around £2.1 billion now and expect this figure to rise to £2.7 billion after the float.

The move is expected to raise enough capital to pay off existing debts to shareholders of around £650 million. Easycall already has enough money in the bank to finance its national network coverage and the flotation will leave the company with just £450 million of debt.

The shares are to be sold through a global offering to institutional investors in the UK, Europe, North America and Asia, and to retail investors in the UK. Existing Easycall customers will be given the opportunity to purchase shares but there will be no special incentives or preferences.

The chief executive is insistent that the flotation of the company is successful. In the light of the external consultant's report she is particularly concerned about the image of the company in terms of its level of internal control. This concern has been further heightened by reports in the press that certain pension fund trustees are requiring that their fund managers only invest in organisations with a reputation for good corporate governance.

Apart from the flotation plans, the company is developing a more aggressive advertising campaign to promote the new loyalty scheme for continuing customers, which gives a 10 per cent discount on all calls made and the cheque back scheme for customers who both purchase a new mobile phone and are connected to the service.

After the flotation the chief executive is also keen for the company to review its policy on outsourcing. She is not convinced that the group are getting value for money from their information systems function, which has been outsourced to an external provider.

Appendix A: Extract from memorandum to Geraldine Power, chief executive Easycall from John Wood, deputy chief executive Easycall

Subject: Overview of issues of concern following the external review

Corporate governance issues

The organisation has grown rapidly since its inception two years ago and there is no culture of 'internal control'. The structure of the organisation is flat with only three positions between the lowest graded member of staff and the chief executive. There is an emphasis on employee empowerment and business process reviews. This means that the majority of staff work in integrated business teams of between five and eight people.

The board of directors do not have a formal control strategy nor do they report on the effectiveness of the organisation's internal controls in the annual accounts.

An Audit Committee has recently been formed in recognition of the requirement of the Cadbury Code of Best Practice. The members of the audit committee are the chief executive of the organisation and three non-executive directors, one of whom has extensive experience of the telecommunications industry.

Internal audit

The group has an internal audit function which was set up two years ago when the company was first launched. The internal audit function numbers five in total including the director of internal audit. The director of internal audit has the authority to buy in specific technical skills as required.

There is no formal internal audit charter but the appointment and dismissal of the director of internal audit are the responsibility of the chief executive. The director of internal audit reports administratively to the finance director and functionally to the chief executive. Audit reports are received by the relevant business unit director, team manager and the finance director. A management summary of the key issues arising from each audit is prepared for the chief executive. In addition an annual summary of audit work undertaken and the audit conclusion on the level of control within the organisation is required by the chief executive.

It is noted that the director of internal audit has no direct reporting line with the audit committee, although it would appear that he is keen to develop a more formal relationship.

The director of internal audit has recently carried out a risk assessment exercise across the whole organisation to determine the strategic audit plan for the next three years. This plan includes a mixture of compliance, systems-based, consultancy and business process reviews. The two latter were included following an interview with the chief executive, who saw these as adding value to the work internal audit did within the organisation.

Internal audit is responsible for the audit of all head office operations and the functions outsourced by the company.

Fraud

Easycall has a dedicated security and investigations department using state-of-the-art fraud prevention and detection systems and computerised criminal intelligence systems. Its task is to look at all elements of the networks operations looking for any loopholes that could result in loss of revenue to the company and probing for potential problems for legitimate subscribers to the network. In 1995 Easycall was also involved in a government study group looking at the area of mobile phone fraud. Despite this, the costs relating to fraudulent use of mobile phones are increasing.

'Subscription fraud' is a particular problem. This occurs where information is fraudulently used to allow a thief to sign up for a mobile phone and then charge the calls to an innocent party. The fraudulent use of the phones themselves is also common. Easycall protect their customers by instigating such controls as:

- programmable security code;
- smart card pin to stop unauthorised calls;
- digital encoding to prevent eavesdropping; and
- review of abnormal telephone activity.

However, as technology moves on, this task becomes increasingly more difficult – the recent introduction of the Subscriber Identity Module, a phone card that can be used with any compatible phone set, is an indication of this.

Retention of customers

The retention of customers is a problem and the number of subscribers cancelling their subscription is higher than Easycall would like. In 1996 the figure was 20 per cent, with most of these cancelling after one year's subscription. Some experts blame this problem on the gaps in coverage and on the fact that the network providers grossly underestimated the speed at which the market would grow. 'It was simply not anticipated in the late 1970s that everyone would aspire to have a mobile phone or that those who had them would use them all the time', said Simon Rockman, editor of *What Mobile Phone* magazine.

At the present time, despite its ambitious plans, Easycall can service only 45 per cent of the British population. The main transmitters are based around London, Southampton, Birmingham, Sheffield, Manchester and Glasgow. There are plans to construct transmitters in the areas around Dover, East Anglia and Cardiff by the end of December 1996 and the remainder of the country by the end of December 1997. By December 1997 the company is planning to be able to service 95 per cent of the British population.

The solution may lie in new satellite systems that will not be affected by proximity to ground transmitters. The first of these will be launched into orbit next summer, with service expected to start in 1998. Easycall is not involved with the satellite project, and there is a question mark over the use of satellites as they are likely to pose environmental problems in space and may not be the long-term answer.

Another reason for the poor retention rates are the problems with bad debts. Most Easycall customers are in the 18–25-year age bracket, and this is a group who are most prone to bad debts. A significant number of new subscribers fail to pay their phone bill, which leads to automatic disconnection. If the contract is less than one year old they have to repay the full retail cost of the phone and a high proportion are unable to do this, which has led to mounting bad debts which have to be written off.

The 18–25-year age group include a significant number of potential customers who have failed credit clearance or who do not wish to be tied to a conventional air time contract. The market has therefore not yet been fully exploited.

Consider

Following the external consultant's review and his own work, the deputy chief executive has recommended to the chief executive that internal audit undertake a comprehensive top-down review of the control environment of the organisation. The chief executive has agreed to this request but is also anxious to be brought up to date on the issues relating to corporate governance particularly the implementation of an internal control strategy within the organisation. She is also interested in what internal audit can tell her about the risks faced by the company in respect of fraud, outsourcing and the corporate strategy for gaining market share through aggressive advertising.

Part A

You are the director of internal audit. Prepare a formal report to the chief executive covering the following issues.

- A brief overview of the background and importance of the concept of corporate governance, with reference to specific control models, such as Cadbury or COSO.
- An overview of what is meant by a risk and control strategy and how modern internal audit techniques can help the business to implement such a strategy. (Your answer should include details of the role of the chief executive, business units and internal audit in the implementation of such a strategy and should also take due note of the way in which staff are organised within Easycall.)
- The benefits of internal audit working closely with the audit committee specifically stating the ways in which internal audit and the audit committee can provide mutual support to each other.

Part B

- From the perspective of the director of internal audit, discuss your approach to a top-down review of the control environment of the organisation.
- Given the information in the case study, indicate which areas of the business pose the most significant risks to the continued success of Easycall, and outline how these risks can be most effectively managed.

- The chief executive has indicated that she has concerns about the outsourcing of the information technology function. Explain the risks involved in outsourcing a non-core activity generally. Discuss how these risks can be managed with specific reference to the information technology function within Easycall.

Case 2.4   Do charters make a control difference?

The Citizen's Charter: raising the standard

Presented to Parliament by the Prime Minister by command of Her Majesty, 1991. (This White Paper sets out the mechanics for improving choice, quality, value and accountability. Not all apply to every service. But all have a common objective to raise the standard of public services, up to and beyond the best at present available. There is a well-spring of talent, energy, care and commitment in our public services. The aim of the Citizen's Charter is to release these qualities. Then we will have services in which the citizen can have confidence, and all public servants can have pride. (Crown copyright material in this case is reproduced with the permission of the Controller of Her Majesty's Stationery Office.)

The case

Introduction

All public services are paid for by individual citizens, either directly or through their taxes. They are entitled to expect high-quality services, responsive to their needs, provided efficiently at a reasonable cost. Where the state is engaged in regulating, taxing or administering justice, these functions too must be carried out fairly, effectively and courteously.

This Government continues to uphold the central principle that essential services – such as education and health – must be available to all, irrespective of means. And its consistent aim has been to increase choice, extend competition and thereby improve quality in all services.

In a free market, competing firms must strive to satisfy their customers, or they will not prosper. Where choice and competition are limited, consumers cannot as easily or effectively make their views count. In many public services, therefore, we need to increase both choice and competition where we can; but also to develop other ways of ensuring good standards of service.

Many of Britain's key industries and public services have been privatised in the last decade. This has been done in a way which promotes direct competition between providers as far as possible. Where elements of monopoly remain, regulation protects the consumer.

92 Leading edge internal auditing

Choice can also be extended, within the public sector. When the public sector remains responsible for a function it can introduce competition and pressure for efficiency by contracting with the private sector for its provision.

Finally, choice can be restored by introducing alternative forms of provision, and creating a wider range of options wherever that is cost-effective. This has been a key objective, for example, of reforms in housing and education.

Through the Citizen's Charter the Government is now determined to drive reforms further into the core of the public services, extending the benefits of choice, competition, and commitment to service more widely.

The Citizen's Charter is the most comprehensive programme ever to raise quality, increase choice, secure better value, and extend accountability. We believe that it will set a pattern, not only for Britain, but for other countries of the world.

The Charter programme will be pursued in a number of ways. The approach will vary from service to service in different parts of the United Kingdom. The Citizen's Charter is not a blueprint which imposes a drab and uniform pattern on every service. It is a toolkit of initiatives and ideas to raise standards in the way most appropriate to each service.

The Charter programme will be at the heart of government policy in the 1990s. Quality of service to the public, and the new pride that it will give to the public servants who provide it, will be a central theme.

There are four main themes in the White paper:

- *Quality* A sustained new programme for improving the quality of public services;
- *Choice* Choice, wherever possible between competing providers, is the best spur to quality improvement;
- *Standards* The citizen must be told what service standards are and be able to act where service is unacceptable;
- *Value* The citizen is also a taxpayer; public services must give value for money within a tax bill the nation can afford.

The range of mechanisms in the Charter covers:

- more privatisation;
- wider competition;
- further contracting-out;
- more performance-related pay;
- published performance targets – local and national;
- comprehensive publication of information on standards achieved;
- more effective complaints procedures;
- tougher and more independent inspectorates;
- better redress for the citizen when services go badly wrong.

Every citizen is entitled to expect:

- *Standards* Explicit standards, published and prominently displayed at the point of delivery. These standards should invariably include courtesy and helpfulness from staff, accuracy in accordance with statutory entitlements, and a commitment to prompt action, which might be expressed in terms of a target response or waiting time. If targets are to be stretched, it may not be possible to guarantee them in every case; minimum, as well as average, standards may be necessary. There should be a clear presumption that standards will be progressively improved as services become more efficient.
- *Openness* There should be no secrecy about how public services are run, how much they cost, who is in charge, and whether or not they are meeting their standards. Public servants should not be anonymous. Save only where there is a real threat to their safety, all those who deal directly with the public should wear name badges and give their name on the telephone and in letters.
- *Information* Full, accurate information should be readily available, in plain language, about what services are being provided. Targets should be published, together with full and audited information about the results achieved. Wherever possible, information should be in comparable form, so that there is a pressure to emulate the best.
- *Choice* The public sector should provide choice wherever practicable. The people affected by services should be consulted. Their views about the services they use should be sought regularly and systematically to inform decisions about what services should be provided.
- *Non-discrimination* Services should be available regardless of race or sex. Leaflets are being printed in minority languages where there is a need. In Wales public bodies are aware of the needs of Welsh speakers.
- *Accessibility* Services should be run to suit the convenience of customers, not staff. This means flexible opening hours, and telephone inquiry points that direct callers quickly to someone who can help them.

And if things go wrong? At the very least, the citizen is entitled to a good explanation, or an apology. He or she should be told why the train is late, or why the doctor could not keep the appointment. There should be a well-publicised and readily available complaints procedure. If there is a serious problem, it should be put right. And lessons must be learnt so that mistakes are not repeated. Nobody wants to see money diverted from service improvement into large-scale compensation for indifferent services. But the Government intends to introduce new forms of redress where these can be made to stimulate rather than distract from efficiency.

Scope

The Citizen's Charter applies to all public services. These include government departments and agencies, nationalised industries, local authorities, the NHS, the courts, police and emergency services. In the private sector, it covers the key utilities; it does not encompass wider consumer protection law.

Audit – how it works

The National Audit Office audits central government and a number of organisations which receive government funding. The Audit Commission is the principal auditor for local government and, with the National Audit Office, for the NHS.

Both these organisations provide a financial audit. But they also do important work in improving value for money. The National Audit Office, in its value-for-money studies, tends to examine aspects of individual departments in depth. The Audit Commission has specialised in comparative studies which examine value for money in the services provided by a large number of local authorities.

We want to see informed, hard-hitting and imaginative audit applied as widely and openly as possible. This would help the public to understand better how good and how efficient local services are. Much of the comparative information produced by the Audit Commission has helped to do this. It has given a powerful incentive to many authorities to improve performance.

Local authority audit – a programme for reform

In the best authorities, good services are provided to a high standard. But the present disparity in standards between different local authorities means that too many people in Britain are still ill-served by their authorities, forced to accept sub-standard service. Inefficiency and waste go hand in hand with poor financial control and too little concern for the cost of services to those who pay for them.

Under the Charter programme, we want to help the auditors do an even better job in their work for the public. The Government therefore proposes to introduce legislation to remove obstacles which stop the Audit Commission exposing to the public details of how their council is doing. This would force local authorities to respond, in detail and in public, to the recommendations made by their auditors. The changes would enhance the role of the Audit Commission and increase the impact of its work.

Holding councils to account in public

At present, when local authorities receive a report from their auditor, they do not have to respond to it in any way. The proposed legislation would require authorities to publish a formal response to their auditor's reports. They would have to set out what action they propose to take. This response will have to be debated and approved by the full council in open session. There would be safeguards to protect genuinely confidential matters where these are raised by the auditor.

Better information

At present there is a wide gap in quality between the best local authority services and the worst. The legislation would require all authorities to publish – not only in committee agendas but in ways more accessible to the public – information which shows what standard of service they are providing at what cost. The standards would be on a common basis, to be prescribed following consultation, so the standards and costs in one authority can be easily compared with another. This information would be subject to checking by the auditor.

League tables of performance

At present there is no easy way of comparing one authority's performance with another. The Audit Commission publishes comparisons, but these do not identify individual authorities by name. Legislation will be introduced to permit the Commission to identify individual authorities. There would be safeguards to protect genuinely confidential information. Public debate about the efficiency and quality of services would as a result be much better informed. In cases of extreme inefficiency the Government would not hesitate to use its powers to close down inefficient direct-labour organisations.

NHS audit

We shall also invite the Audit Commission to publish similar comparative tables for the NHS as a stimulus to improvement. These will supplement standard information for patients which health authorities are expected to provide. We would expect relatively weak health authorities take action to bring about management improvements.

The main inspectorates cover key areas of public service – police, prisons, schools, social services. The inspectorates are concerned with value for money and standards of output and performance. However, their central responsibility is to check that the professional services that the public receives are delivered in the most effective way possible and genuinely meet the needs of those whom they serve. In the past, inspectorates have often been staffed exclusively by members of the profession they oversee. Under the Citizen's Charter programme, the Government will change this balance.

The case for change

It is important that there should be a professional element to inspection. However, we believe that it is essential also that inspectors reflect the interests of the public receiving a service as well as the profession providing it. If an inspectorate is too close to the profession it is supervising, there is a risk that it will lose touch with the interests of the people who use the service. It may be captured by fashionable theories and lose the independence and objectivity that the public needs. Professional inspectorates can easily become part of a closed professional world.

The Citizen's Charter will therefore begin to open up inspectorates to the outside world. It will make them much more responsive to public concerns. To this end, we will appoint lay members to more inspectorates to work closely with professional colleagues. The lay members' job will be to ensure that the judgement of what represents good practice is not left just to the professionals – professional views will be balanced by the sound common sense of other members of the public. New insights can also be brought to inspection from the experience of those whose professional lives have taken them into other fields.

We shall encourage all the inspectorates to make a point of inviting the views of the public and to publish signed reports which show the evidence and approach that they have used, but which are free of jargon. A good report should raise public awareness and inform policy, as well as bring pressure to bear on management. Reports with a local relevance should be made widely available locally. And we will look to national inspectorates to produce comparative studies and draw together the results of local experience.

Prisons

The Prisons Inspectorate was reconstituted in 1981. It is headed by a distinguished and independent figure, who is assisted by experienced professional advisers. It has right of access to all prisons, and to the Home Secretary, to whom it reports its conclusions and recommendations. Its reports are published and available to Parliament. The Government will ensure that the Prisons Inspectorate remains strong and independent in the future.

Police

The Inspectorate of Constabulary plays a particular role in management and in setting national standards across local police forces. HM Inspectors report to the Home Secretary. But they also advise both local police authorities and chief constables on the management of forces, and on best policing practice. Each force is inspected annually; the inspector's report is given to the local police authority, and is published.

HM Inspectors are presently appointed from the ranks of chief constables. As an initial step, the Home Secretary will appoint more lay experts to the Inspectorate later this year. They will be experienced people able to support the Inspectorate in its work to improve efficiency. The Government will also encourage continuing close co-operation between the Audit Commission and the Inspectorate to identify scope for improved efficiency and quality of service.

Schools

We attach particular importance to raising standards in schools. Parents need better information to be able to exercise their rights to wider choice. This will enable more to exercise more pressure for higher standards in schools. In addition we want to see rigorous and independent inspection based on the widest possible range of evidence. That, too, will contribute significantly to raising quality in education.

Decisions following the review of Her Majesty's Inspectorate of Schools will be announced shortly. However, in line with the Citizen's Charter, the changes which result from this review will reflect these principles:

- the need for independent judgement about schools, teaching and learning based on objective inspection and analysis of performance measures;
- the need for the inspection process to involve lay members with a range of expertise and experience other than in teaching or educational administration;
- the need to ensure that inspection is carried out independently of the producer interest;
- the need for those who audit professional standards to see their work as an integral part of promoting value for money.

There will be a statutory requirement for the regular inspection of schools. We envisage that a specific grant will be paid directly to schools to enable them to buy inspections, with a corresponding reduction in revenue support grant to LEAs. The choice of inspectors will be left to governing bodies. There will be a requirement to distribute the results of inspections to all parents at a school, plus a follow-up report a year later on the action taken. The Schools Inspectorate in Wales is also under review. We will bring forward conclusions later this summer.

Social services

The day-to-day responsibility for social services rests with local authorities who are required to set up arm's-length inspection units. But the national role of the Social Services Inspectorate provides an important reinforcement of those local inspection arrangements in England and an assurance that they are working properly. The Government is committed to a strong and effective Inspectorate which is fully sensitive to public concerns. We are therefore reviewing the Inspectorate's role to see how it could be further strengthened. It will introduce an independent lay element into the Inspectorate's work. Proposals on how best to achieve this will be published for consultation later this year.

Although internal auditing is not mentioned specifically in the White Paper, the Prime Minister in a message to The IIA in June 1991, on the occasion of its Fifty Years anniversary, recognises its importance:

Internal audit has a vital role to play throughout the public and private sectors in the United Kingdom, a role enhanced by the sterling efforts of your organisation over the years to improve the quality of service provided.

I wish you continued success in the development of the profession.

Five years on . . .

The following message from the Prime Minister is extracted from a follow-up White Paper, published in 1996 to mark five years of the Citizen's Charter:

I set up the Citizen's Charter five years ago with a simple aim: to continually improve the quality of public services for the people of this country and to make them first class. I wanted to ensure that, first and foremost, public services respond to the needs and wishes of their users. For too long too many people have felt powerless when using public services. That had to change, and it has. Thanks to the Citizen's Charter.

I have never accepted that public services should be run for the convenience of those who work in them. They exist to serve the needs of individual people, be they customers or patients, parents or passengers. This ethic has always motivated the best of our public servants and we all owe a huge debt of gratitude to those people who dedicate their lives to public service: the nurses, the police, the teachers and many others.

But good intentions are not enough. Any organisation must continually question whether it can perform its role more effectively; whether the way things have always been done is really what its customers need or want. Moreover, the users of a service should know what they can expect from it. Too often this has not happened and services have become distant, unresponsive or overbearing.

That is why, through the Citizen's Charter we have set new standards and new targets. It is why we have given people more information than ever before, with performance tables for schools, hospitals, local authorities and police and fire services, to help them make choices and question the way things are run. It is why we have reviewed complaints procedures and encouraged services to consult users. They are at the sharp end. It is their views that can make a difference.

Five years on, the Charter is making a real impact on the whole range of public services. There are now forty-two national charters setting out minimum standards and targets as diverse as ambulance response times to the time it takes the Inland revenue to deal with your tax demands. Locally there are now more than 10,000 charters setting service standards at a level that has a direct impact on the quality of individuals' lives – for example, what an elderly person can expect from his or her local social services department.

Five years ago there were many doubters who said that the performance of public services could never be measured. This White Paper sets out the evidence that across the public services, by setting and measuring targets, the Government is delivering concrete improvements in the quality and efficiency of services. It also contains more than a hundred new commitments.

Consider

1. The monitoring and measuring control principles underlying the Citizen's Charter aims. Are these evident in your own organisations?
2. Why is internal auditing not mentioned in either White Paper?
3. How does the Charter influence levels of control in the organisations that own, supply and are served by your organisation? And, how do those influences impact control in your own organisation?
4. How are the same principles used by you and your management to develop professional internal auditing, whether you are in the public service, or another sector?

Case 2.5 The world is no riskier a place

(Extracted from *In Business* (1997) B 25.2, ICSA Publishing, Hemel Hempstead.)

The case

The world is no riskier a place now than it has been at any time in the past. However, the issues confronting business are more diverse and potentially more complex than ever before. As existing markets expand and new ones open up, the successful company will be the one which looks beyond the obvious to anticipate the unexpected risks. Even by the standards of this century of progress, the past 10 or 15 years have seen exceptional change. This change has been largely driven by two ostensibly separate forces – the collapse of Communism and the take-off of high technology.

The demise of the Soviet Bloc altered international geopolitics almost overnight. As the USSR disintegrated, so too did the bipolar system which – while flawed and often uneasy – left most nations knowing roughly where they stood. In five short years, the shifting sands of world relations seem more uncertain than ever before. No longer does the developed world have things all its own way. Its economic and political pre-eminence is being challenged at every turn – by the tigers of the Pacific Rim, by revitalised Latin American countries such as Brazil and Chile, and by the massive potential markets of China and India.

It is little coincidence that such challenges have often been mounted on the back of high technology. As the world becomes smaller, so industrialised countries begin to lose the monopolies that kept the rest of the world at bay. Lower labour costs allow some Pacific Rim countries to produce computer chips more cheaply and more effectively than their counterparts in the West. Satellite TV has penetrated to even the remotest Indian village. On the Internet, an African villager is equal to a Canadian executive. The developing world is taking Western consumer values and throwing them right back in our faces – with interest.

In this brave new world, commercial muscle is more important than military might. Capitalism has broken out all over the world, with many countries now actively seeking foreign investment for the first time. However, the widespread persistence of insurgency, criminal violence, corruption and inadequate legislation means that this expanded zone of access may not grow substantially over the next 10 or 15 years. Indeed, investment opportunities may even be curtailed if electorates or governments reject the free market experiment: former communists have already returned to power in Poland and Lithuania, and foreign investment can meet stiff opposition not only in the former Soviet bloc but also in Asia.

The race therefore goes not necessarily to the strong but to the quick – those who see the opportunities and exploit them before anyone else. The rule book is not so much being constantly rewritten as actually torn up. After the collapse of the USSR, one of Gorbachev's aides memorably told a group of Western journalists: 'Gentlemen, there are no rules any more'. While opportunities continue to outstrip legislation – which they do in many parts of the world – so business will face threats coming from all angles. Only once these risks have been identified and assessed can they be reduced.

Consider

1. How do the widest implications of risk impact control in your organisation?
2. Do you think worldwide, when contributing to statements on control in your organisation?

Case 2.6 Internal control and internal auditing in Network Housing Association (NHA)

Mission

Network Housing Association's mission is to:

- provide good-quality housing and services for people in need;
- see housing as part of the wider area of social policy and considers it appropriate to work in partnership with statutory bodies, voluntary agencies and the private sector to combat disadvantage and social deprivation;
- participate in partnerships acting as a provider, facilitator or agent with others working towards the same objectives.

Turnover: £36 million
Staff: 349
Internal audit staff: 2 full-time.

The case

What are housing associations (HAs) and where do they work?

Information published in November 1995, by The National Federation of Housing Associations (NFHA) – now National Housing Federation (NHF) identified the fact that 'well over half of all housing association homes are in areas of greatest housing stress, in the metropolitan districts and in Greater London'. There are HAs in every local authority area in the UK.

The NFHA is the representative organisation for HAs in England, with a membership total of 1,465 at November 1995. Its members continuously emphasise the core values of housing associations through meetings, training, guidelines, codes of practice, publications and influence. Its 1996 objectives relate to success, the future role of HAs, support for members and achievement of excellence and value for money in all its work areas. Representative organisations with similar aims exist in Wales and Scotland.

To receive government funding, HAs must formally register with a housing corporation. There are four housing corporations, one in each of England, Wales, Scotland and Northern Ireland: they are government executive agencies with powers of regulation and audit over housing associations.

HAs exist as either charities, industrial and provident societies or registered companies: they can be any one of these or a mixture of two or all. As such entities, they are also regulated by the laws governing their legal status.

HAs vary considerably in size and the geographic area in which they provide homes. The largest 200 HAs in England own and manage three-quarters of the total number of rented units.

During recent years there have been significant changes to the organisation structures in many HAs, as they have focused their services in the housing and care markets and customer needs. Quality of service is paramount. Most have created visions and missions with quality and care aims. The market they serve is competitive, growing and attracting substantial public and private funding. As in all markets, funding and competition drive innovation, quality and change, continuously creating new risks and increasing the importance of control.

Internal control in HAs

HAs have been strongly influenced during recent years by government regulation, with mandatory requirements for audit practices, codes of conduct and reporting on internal financial control. This influence is ongoing and increasing. There are published guidelines for HAs on governance, covering audit practices, codes of conduct, internal financial control and risk assessment. Each of these publications has been guided by the others and national debate.

There are internal audit units in many housing associations, some resourced by their own staff and some by outsourced staff, mainly provided by consortiums, agencies and professional accounting firms. Most are guided by professional internal auditing standards. Some are members of The Housing Association Internal Audit Forum (HAIAF).

Benchmarking research by The HAIAF in 1996 shows an interesting perception of internal auditing by the HA respondents, heads of internal audit (HIA), chairpersons of audit committees (AC), chief executives (CE). All were asked to compare their perception of internal audit to a selection of other professional services. One hundred and nine responded to this question (HIA – 42, AC – 30, CE – 37). Perceptions of professionalism can have a significant impact on everything associated with developing and promoting internal control and an internal audit service, amongst its staff and customers.

The following shows how perceptions of internal audit professionalism vary between HIAs, ACs and CEs in 1996, with a perceived emphasis on the policeman, consultant and accountant roles for internal auditors. The other perceived roles are probably associated with the new and developing nature of internal audit in housing associations. Of particular interest is the 'doctor' perception by many CEs.

Perceptions of professionalism

Other professions	HIA %	AC %	CE %
Solicitor		3	
Priest			3
Doctor	5	7	28
Teacher	7	3	
Policeman	7	17	16
Consultant	62	47	40
Accountant	12	20	10
Manager	7	3	3

Public focus on internal control and internal audit in NHA

In its 1995/96 annual accounts, NHA included the following statements on governance and control:

Governance

The Cadbury Report on the Financial Aspects of Corporate Governance (1992) reflected a climate of opinion in the private sector which accepted that changes were needed in the standards of financial reporting and accountability. The public sector also accepted the principles of corporate governance as relevant and in response to the recommendations in the Code of Best Practice of the Cadbury Report, The National Federation of Housing Associations published a Code of Governance (1995) to support the associations in implementing best-practice corporate governance through their systems of openness, integrity and accountability.

Statement on the system of internal financial control

The Committee of Management is responsible for establishing and maintaining systems of internal financial control.

The internal controls are established in order to provide reasonable assurance of:

- the safeguarding of assets against unauthorised use or disposition;
- the maintenance of proper accounting records and the reliability of financial information used within the Association or for publication.

Such systems can provide only reasonable and not absolute assurance against any material financial misstatement or loss. Key elements are:

- formal policies and procedures are in place, including the documentation of key systems and rules relating to the delegation of authorities, which allow the monitoring of controls and restrict the unauthorised use of the association's assets;
- experienced and suitably qualified staff take responsibility for important business functions. Annual appraisal procedures have been established to maintain standards of performance;
- budgets are prepared which allow the Committee of management and management to monitor the key business and financial objectives and the progress towards financial objectives set for the year and the medium term;
- all planned major property developments and any new initiatives are subjected to a risk assessment process, the results of which are reported to the Finance Sub-Committee;
- the Audit Committee reviews reports from management, the internal auditors and the external auditors to provide reasonable assurance that control procedures are in place and being followed.

On behalf of the Committee of Management, the Audit Committee has reviewed the effectiveness of the system of internal financial control in existence in the association for the year ended 31 March 1996. Areas for improvement were identified and appropriate actions have been agreed.

Signed by the Chairman of the Committee of Management

Development of internal audit in NHA

Internal audit was established in NHA in 1992. First by the appointment of one full-time internal auditor, and two and a half years later by the appointment of an additional full-time internal auditor. An audit committee was established in 1995, consisting of five non-executive voluntary governors, with the internal audit manager as secretary. In 1997, the internal audit manager was appointed to a group manager role of internal audit and consultancy, embracing responsibility for internal audit, quality management and systems development, with a full-time staff total of four and one staff part-time. The following is a profile of the group manager:

Age 30, she is deeply involved in activities associated with audit and control with two professional institutes and in her sector's representative bodies. She is studying for an MBA qualification. She is supported by NHA in these continuous learning activities. Her internal auditing responsibilities are outlined in the following charter, published in 1993 and currently being updated.

Internal audit charter

Internal audit has a formal charter approved by the Chief Executive and Audit Committee. Apart from the reporting structure already covered, this charter contains the following statements:

- the Management Committee requires the internal audit service to function professionally, adhering to the Code of Ethics, Standards and Guidelines of The Institute of Internal Auditors;
- the internal audit service is not relieved of responsibility in areas of the association's business which are subject to review by others (e.g., external audit). but should always assess the extent to which reliance can be placed upon the work of others and co-ordinate the internal audit planning with those other review agencies.

Marketing internal audit in NHA

Since 1995 a brochure as been used by internal audit to promote its services in NHA. It contains the following material:

- Internal audit is an independent appraisal function established within the organisation to examine and evaluate its activities, as a service to the organisation. Its objective is to assist members of the organisation to discharge their responsibilities effectively.
- Our principal objective is to provide a professional opinion on the adequacy, application and effectiveness of the internal controls within NHA. Through this we contribute to NHA's objectives by ensuring the proper, economic, efficient and effective use of resources.

- Our aims are to provide managers with assurance on the adequacy, application and effectiveness of their systems of control; to alert managers to weaknesses in control which may result in errors or losses; to provide managers with practical and constructive advice on how particular problems may be resolved and controls improved to minimise the chances of further problems: to provide value for money in the service we deliver to management.
- The authority and responsibilities of the Internal Audit Service are set out in an internal audit charter approved by the Board. We have the authority to ask for whatever information and explanations we need to undertake our duties. We also have the duty to use it in strictest confidence and to carry out our work with the least possible disruption to the normal activities of the unit or section we are auditing. Our remit covers the whole of NHA.
- Internal audit ultimately reports to the Audit Committee and has a direct line of reporting, on an as need basis, to the Chair of the Association. This is to achieve the strongest possible degree of independence, so that audit reports can be as objective as is possible. On a day-to-day basis we report to the Chief Executive.
- The internal audit plan, updated every year, is approved by the Audit Committee. Audit effort is focused on the areas of highest risk to the business. 'Risk' means possible loss or misstatement. Therefore sections working in areas of NHA where the risk is relatively high will be audited annually. Departments where the possibility of financial or operational loss is low will be audited less frequently or may receive a less comprehensive audit visit. In addition to the annual plan there are also ad-hoc audits or reviews undertaken following a request by management.
- Internal audit visits begin with a planning meeting where the areas to be covered by the audit are discussed. The manager has the opportunity to highlight any areas they may wish to see covered as part of the review. Visits are undertaken to strict deadlines in accordance with the Audit Plan. Visits aim to determine solutions to particular problems. Visits end with an audit report covering the areas reviewed.
- We are committed to working in partnership with the service departments to secure the maximum benefit to the Association's customers. We provide quality, value-for-money services to our clients in a positive, flexible and professional manner. We assist managers in the achievement of their objectives. We provide advice on internal control systems and the application of the Association's financial regulations.
- Internal audit reports are originally produced in draft which will be discussed with the relevant managers. When the content of the draft report has been agreed and a timetable for the implementation of the recommendations set out, the report will be finalised and issued. An executive summary of audit activity is produced on a regular basis and submitted to the Audit Committee.

- We also undertake value-for-money reviews, special investigations and advice on new systems and controls.
- We are specialists in internal audit and offer experience backed by financial and management qualifications.

Internal audit participates in control presentations to all new staff. Currently there is a focus by management on control self-assessment and internal audit is involved in and facilitating this development.

The following mission statement for her new group role has been developed in 1997.

Partners in business achievement

- Internal Audit and Consultancy is committed to achieving a match between NHA's internal systems capabilities and its business activities, to contribute to NHA's goal of sustained growth and achievement.
- Internal Audit and Consultancy offers a unique service/delivery package of systems development, quality improvement and internal control review. We aim to achieve excellence in the design and operation of secure, reliable and efficient business systems, utilising the benefit of new and existing technologies in partnership with all levels of management.
- Using the combination of specialist and professional skills and expertise and by continuous development of our staff, we will provide support and advice throughout the entire project life cycle.
- We believe that the quality and integrity of information available for decision-making have a direct impact on the association's competitiveness, image and delivery of promises.
- Supporting NHA's business achievements by ensuring robust internal systems, Internal Audit and Consultancy is helping to achieve ongoing success.

Internal audit benchmarking in 1996

Asked to comment on the results of a benchmarking exercise in 1996, using BRACE 1, the internal audit manager stated:

> There was one area of general weakness which I had to tackle, that is co-ordination with external audit. I instituted formal opening meetings with external audit to discuss plans, give feedback on significant internal audit findings which may affect their work, and provide copies of audit reports. At each meeting of the Audit Committee, confirmation of internal and external co-ordination is now discussed. A methodology for the review of internal and external audit co-ordination is being developed. I feel this year has produced great benefits from closer co-ordination. BRACE 1 was particularly informative on other areas, such as the impact of technology on internal audit and perceptions of management, all of which have created actions for improvement.

Consider

1. The approach of NHA and its internal audit manager to the regulatory and reasonableness requirements for control, governance and internal audit in housing associations. How do the actions they have taken compare with your own sector, organisation and internal audit resources? Draw conclusions from your comparisons and share these with your management.
2. Are the links between control objectives for quality and governance clearly established in the NHA annual report and internal audit group mission?
3. Can you identify any other actions NHA and its internal audit manager could, or should, have taken to establish controls and improve its audit services?
4. What are your views on the wider role the internal audit manager now has, which includes other non-audit service activities? Can internal audit independence and objectivity be maintained in the areas serviced by these other activities, If so, how would you do this?

Case 2.2 Solution

Reference

Ratliff, Richard L., Wallace, Wanda A., Sumners, Glenn E., McFarland, William G. and Loebbecke, James K. (1996) *Internal Auditing Principles and Techniques*, 2nd edn, The Institute of Internal Auditors, Altamonte Springs, FL, pp. 99–120.

Control strengths

1. Scanners are used. The use of scanners reduces the number of input errors and can be considered a control strength, even if the advantages might not be realised in this case.
2. A centralised price table is used. If well controlled, centralised price tables provide an efficient way by which to ensure that prices are uniform and that sales are recorded in accordance with approved pricing.
3. Supervisory approval of price changes is required. All price changes are supposed to be approved by the buyer. If implemented correctly, this would be a strong control.
4. Buyers are evaluated on the basis of the profitability of the items they acquire. This is a broad managerial control to emphasise the responsibilities of the buyers and to help ensure goal congruence within the organisation. Controls are designed to influence behaviour; therefore, a compensation system needs to be recognised as a control.
5. Access to the regional database is restricted to buyers. This should ensure the implementation of authorised price changes only.
6. Passwords are required to access the database. Passwords can be effective in controlling access to data.
7. Local changes to price tables are not uploaded to the master price database. The master database, therefore, is not corrupted by local changes.
8. The full database is downloaded each morning. This control ensures the uniformity and accuracy of prices.
9. Reconciliation of the price table with the authorised price lists is performed by the merchandising manager's assistant. This provides an independent reconciliation control by someone outside of the buyer's area.
10. Daily reports on store profitability are prepared. This is part of management's monitoring controls and should alert management to important changes or trends.
11. Approval is required for new additions to the price database. Products are added to the database only with the approval of the merchandising manager. This ensures that only authorised products are added.
12. A validity (edit) check is performed on product numbers. All items must

conform to the company's list of valid product numbers. This helps ensure that incorrect items are not entered into the price table.

Control weaknesses and potential impact on the organisation

Weakness: There is no evidence of a verification of the completeness of the download to the individual stores each day.
Impact: This could result in incomplete downloading or incorrect downloading of data. Some reconciliation or the use of control totals would help ensure the complete downloading of the records to the individual stores.

Weakness: Each buyer has access to the full database, not just to the portion for which that buyer is responsible.
Impact: An individual buyer may either inadvertently or deliberately change prices without proper authorisation.

Weakness: The buyer occasionally delegates password access to an assistant.
Impact: The assistant has complete access to the database and may inadvertently or deliberately change authorised prices. Further, there is no accountability as to who made changes.

Weakness: Review of price changes to the database is not performed in a timely manner by someone independent of the buyer. The reconciliation is done quarterly, which is not frequent enough to catch problems.
Impact: Since the database is critical to the organisation, a timely review of changes should be performed by someone independent of those making the changes. This should lessen the number of errors that customers are encountering.

Weakness: The store managers have broad authority to make price changes.
Impact: This broad authority may weaken management's evaluation system which holds the buyers responsible for the profitability of items.

Weakness: The full database is downloaded every day, instead of only downloading changes. The volume of items downloaded can be a potential cause of error, especially if there is no reconciliation of the downloaded database with the master database.
Impact: Downloading the entire database takes more time and effort than downloading only the changes, and is therefore less efficient. Also, there are more opportunities for errors to occur.

Weakness: Price changes made by store managers are effective only for a day, since the regional database is downloaded again each morning.
Impact: If a store manager forgets to update local price changes each day, customers may be charged incorrect prices for goods. This weakness may explain some of the customer complaints regarding pricing.

Weakness: Special-offer items that are entered at the cash registers do not require individual product identification.
Impact: Lack of identification of items sold may cause a loss of control over perpetual inventory because these items are not removed from inventory as they are sold. This could be the cause of the inventory shrinkage problems.

Weakness: Inventory shrinkage is occurring.
Impact: Occurrence of inventory shrinkage indicates an internal control weakness.

Weakness: Daily sales reports reflect performance by store and by department only. The reports do not furnish information about product movement.
Impact: The value of the reports is limited; they would be more useful if they contained data on overall product performance.

Weakness: The merchandising manager's assistant has access to the database to enter new products. If this also provides access to the price table, this would be a weakness since this individual also reconciles the price table to the authorised price lists.
Impact: Unauthorised price changes could be entered by the assistant.

CHAPTER 3

Market the success of modern internal auditing

> There is a strong need for internal audit to promote its services to its clients more effectively, but, perhaps equally importantly, internal audit must first develop the services it is promoting. (CIPFA (1990) *The Client's View of Internal Audit*)

Market modern internal auditing

Like any product or service, the success of modern internal auditing lies in the way it is promoted, sold and serviced in the organisation market-place. Sawyer (1973) saw this when he summarised the first chapter of his book:

> Modern internal auditing, to be successful, must be grounded on management support and acceptance and on imaginative service to management. Also, it must have a reporting status in the company that ensures proper consideration of the findings and recommendations developed by the auditor. To this end, the internal auditor's charter must set forth explicitly his (her) broad authority and correlative responsibility; the management directive must spell out clearly the requirement for prompt and responsive replies to his (her) audit reports; and the auditor's job description must call for the efforts of superior people, not average ones. Audit manuals should supply standards and guidelines, not detailed instructions. The auditor must mount a continuing campaign to sell his (her) product to executive management; and the product he (she) sells must be of the quality that will capture and keep management's interest.

Compare this summary with the marketing of any high-quality product or service today. Internal auditors should study the promotion programmes of their own organisation's products and services, and promotion programmes of other organisations marketing internal auditing services. There are many lessons to be learnt from each.

Consider the following promotion criteria common for most products and services:

- focus on specifications that satisfy customer's needs;
- excellent leadership;
- team learning;
- measured quality;
- continuous innovation and improvement.

These criteria can be interpreted in terms of the set of principles and rules summarised in Figure 3.1. Compare this set of principles with those of Deming in Figure 3.2, developed over his many years of promoting quality in Japan, North America and throughout the world.

Deming himself saw his famous 14 key points as the basis for transformation of American industry. They were also the basis for the lessons for top management in Japan in the 1950s. He emphasised that adoption and action on the 14 points is a signal that management intends to stay in business, with aims to protect investors and jobs. They apply to small organisations as well as large, to service industries as well as to manufacturing. They apply to all units within an organisation.

Many internal audit providers use the criteria in Figures 3.1 and 3.2 to market their internal auditing products and services. Some link their internal auditing products and services into other consultancy products and services, associated with control, risk and governance. Some have developed benchmarking data bases of internal audit organisations and practices. Most will provide health checks and quality assurance reviews of existing internal audit departments. All state that their internal audit staff are highly qualified, experts in control, have extensive experience and access to audit methodologies and specialist support. All claim to be flexible with resources and emphasise the international character of their firms. Figure 3.3 shows some of the statements currently used by accounting firms to market their internal audit services.

This chapter will deal with the following key words and phrases, seen as promotion criteria in Sawyer's summary, advertising of internal audit by others and quality rules:

- Lead an innovative and imaginative service.
- Create a vision of future internal auditing.
- Market internal auditing as objective and independent.
- Establish and market an internal audit charter based on professional standards.
- Design job specifications to meet your customers' needs.
- Maintain an internal audit manual.
- Link your vision, charter, job specifications and manual into marketing quality.
- Market exciting internal auditing pictures.

Figure 3.1 Rules for promoting quality

1. **Customer focus** – all customers are different; their satisfaction is paramount
   - Focus on both internal and external customers, primary and secondary.
   - View all customers as partners in your supply chains.
   - Understand all your customers' needs.
   - Aim for customer delight at all times, not just satisfaction.
   - Do not ignore customer complaints.

2. **management leadership** – organise for quality
   - Establish a clear and motivating vision understood by everyone.
   - Identify your key success factors and build these into a clear mission statement.
   - Provide the right structures, methods and resources for quality achievement.
   - Communicate well at all levels, both in clarity and timeliness.
   - Give high visibility to your quality policy.

3. **Teamwork** – recognise and encourage the power of teams
   - Develop teams across the whole supply chain, internal and external.
   - Interlock all teams at operation, function and cross-function levels.
   - Reinforce and reward teams for success.
   - Teach teams to focus on your vision and mission statements.
   - Delegate responsibility to teams to take action.

4. **Analytical approach** – if it cannot be measured, it cannot be improved
   - Measure by statistics – do not inspect.
   - Establish measures in all processes, across all supply chains, with high visibility.
   - Relate all measures to your vision and mission statements.
   - Focus measures on customers, both internal and external.
   - Take prompt corrective action on all measurements.

5. **Continuous improvement** – look for problems, develop solutions and train
   - Create a learning organisation with a constant commitment to improve.
   - Encourage a constant and continuous search for excellence.
   - Be creative – look for paradigm shifts.
   - Benchmark – internally and externally.
   - Verify the success of change.

Figure 3.2 Deming's 14 quality points

1. Create constancy of purpose to improve product and service.
2. Adopt new philosophy for new economic age by management learning responsibilities and taking leadership for change.
3. Cease dependence on inspection to achieve quality; eliminate the need for mass inspection by building quality into the product.
4. End awarding business on price; instead minimise total cost and move towards single suppliers for items.
5. Improve constantly and for ever the system of production and service to improve quality and productivity and to decrease costs.
6. Institute training on the job.
7. Institute leadership; supervision should be to help do a better job; overhaul supervision of management and production workers.
8. Drive out fear so that all may work effectively for the organisation.
9. Break down barriers between departments; research, design, sales and production must work together to foresee problems in production and use.
10. Eliminate slogans, exhortations and numerical targets for the workforce, such as 'zero defects' or new productivity levels. Such exhortations are divisive as the bulk of the problems belong to the system and are beyond the power of the workforce.
11. Eliminate quotas or work standards, and management by objectives or numerical goals; substitute leadership.
12. Remove barriers that rob people of their right to pride of workmanship; hourly workers, management and engineering; eliminate annual or merit ratings and management by objective.
13. Institute a vigorous education and self-improvement programme.
14. Put everyone in the company to work to accomplish the transformation.

Figure 3.3 Promotion of internal auditing by others

A positive contribution to business objectives:
- provides practical recommendations and advice;
- offers effective solutions to business problems;
- acts as an advisor and facilitator;
- provides people with the right training and experience;
- uses specialists;
- is a source of revenue enhancement and cost reduction;
- recommends cost-effective controls;
- uses risk assessment for audit planning;
- facilitates control self-assessment.

Figure 3.4 ACT – a motif for all internal audit units

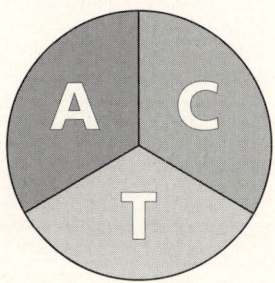

Lead an innovative and imaginative service

Imagination in internal auditing is key to its success. It uses vision to create innovative auditing (A), consultancy (C) and teaching (T) products and services. It continuously improves these to meet anticipated new and increasing expectations by both internal auditors and all its customers. Figure 3.4 provides an excellent motif for all internal audit units, of whatever size. Each of the letters provides a reminder of the direction for internal audit missions. Together, the letters stimulate ACTion to make innovation happen.

Create a vision of future internal auditing

Imagination needs direction – not in a controlled sense, but in a creative sense. It is the art of forming mental images and constructively channelling these into visions for the future. It is not easy to find examples of internal auditing vision statements. Not all internal auditors are committed to the value of vision statements. Yet, in their organisations they are often prominent as management statements or team statements, and always associated with their organisation's products and services. So why not for internal audit? Vision statements now generally aim to promote a vivid picture of an ambitious, desirable state that is connected to the customer and better in some important way than the current state.

Vision statements need to be exciting, even emotional. They need a total commitment to succeed. They need to be measured and updated as time improves the vision. They need to be short and simple. Examples of vision statements used by some internal audit departments and internal auditing providers are shown in Figure 3.5.

In each of the internal audit units from which the examples have been taken there is a clear link, with appropriate measures, between their visions, their missions and the results of their audit work.

Figure 3.5 Examples of vision statements

- 'Our audits are plaudits.'
- 'Partnership in practice.'
- 'Internal audit – supporting management.'
- 'Taking a different view.'
- 'Adding value through internal audit.'

The vision statement 'Our audits are plaudits' was created by a small internal audit unit to sell the wider corporate internal auditing vision statement shown in Case 3.1. This use of a vision statement to motivate both internal audit staff and management towards developing and accepting a less punishing, more reinforcing type of internal audit reporting, encouraged new internal auditing leading edge services:

> The internal audit staff is highly qualified and capable, displaying sound business judgement and strong auditing and consultancy abilities. A diversity of backgrounds and work experiences exists and is shared among the staff. Auditors are viewed as having significant potential for holding key positions in the corporation, including career path opportunities within internal audit. Auditing provides unique developmental opportunities through broad exposure across the corporation. There is an active programme of ongoing training for auditors worldwide to recognise business evolution, technology advances and state of the art audit techniques.
>
> Management and supervision at all levels within the internal audit function are known for their excellence in personnel and quality management. Visible leadership, active personnel development, effective listening and a strong sensitivity to customer needs are among the traits for which audit management and supervision are most noted.

The vision statement 'Partnership in practice' introduced the following quality-associated missions:

- Our purpose.
- Our services.
- Our team.
- Working together.
- Our commitment to quality.
- The challenge of change.

The vision statement 'Internal audit – supporting management' introduced similar quality-related missions:

- Our role.
- Adding value.

- Our key objectives.
- Our team.
- Our staff.
- Our commitment to quality.
- Our commitment to our customers.
- Our management team.

The vision statement 'Taking a different view' introduced value as an internal auditing product, measures and a customer focus:

- Providing value to our clients.
- Why we make a difference.
- What this means to you.

The vision statement 'Adding value through internal audit' introduced proactive missions focused on improving performance and value:

> In the world's top companies internal audit is changing rapidly. Internal auditors are using new technology and management techniques to deliver services more efficiently and effectively. Many are becoming far more proactive, helping to spread best practice ideas and identify opportunities for improving productivity.

A number of internal auditing groups now provide advice and support for internal audit units in specific industries. Some of these advisory groups have developed vision and mission statements which are influencing internal audit unit growth and direction in their areas. One example of such a group is in the public sector. The Audit Policy and Advice team in H.M. Treasury has recently published its own charter, which is shown in full in Case 3.2. All internal audit units in the public sector should be aware of this charter and its implications on internal auditing in their organisations.

Market internal auditing as objective and independent

Use reports to your audit committee to strengthen and market your objectivity and independence. Audit committees are now well established, across all sectors, and in their organisations are usually one of the sources of approval for internal audit responsibilities and work. Where audit committees exist there are reporting relationships with internal audit. Use these reporting relationships to sell internal auditing as a leading edge service. Link internal auditing responsibilities and standards into all aspects of the audit committee's work. If an audit committee has not been established an internal audit unit should always have reporting access to its organisation's board or governing body. Use this access to market new and leading edge internal auditing.

For internal audit units to be objective and independent, in all control and governance issues, their work should always be reviewed and supported by an audit committee or a similar group of senior non-executive management.

Figure 3.6 Theory underlying audit committee status

1. Independence at board level.
2. A rotating membership and chair.
3. Unrestricted reviews.
4. Monitoring all control activities.
5. Co-ordinating all auditing activities.
6. Advisory only.
7. Reports to full board.
8. Recognised externally.

Audit committees, boards and governing bodies are now guided by the UK nationally developed governance and conduct codes of best practice mentioned in Chapter 2. These all have underlying theory based on international experience and research; see Figure 3.6. Link this theory and research into your own internal auditing services. Strengthen your auditing authority and power with the control requirements now demanded from your organisation. Audit committees and senior management do see value in internal audit involvement in their control needs. Use this need to market your services.

The long learning curves that audit committees have in some parts of the private sector contrast with the short learning curves in other sectors. It will take some time for audit committees to establish themselves across organisations in all UK sectors. What we do know from research into the longer learning curves of some audit committees is that the seven characteristics shown in Figure 3.6 exist in the best audit committees.

Summarised, an audit committee is a halfway house between the full board and all monitoring in an organisation. It is independent of all executive authority. Others attending audit committee meetings are seen to be 'in attendance' only. Membership of the audit committee, including the secretary, is independent from all other monitoring responsibilities. Audit committee members meet alone for at least part of each meeting. Membership of an audit committee, including the chair, rotates. Over time most non-executive members of the full board are trained to serve a term on its audit committee.

This freedom should not be taken for granted. It is stated in the audit committee charter and restated in every report it issues to the full board. Sufficient resources are provided for an audit committee to carry out its review responsibilities. Any restriction or lack of resources is made known immediately by the audit committee, to the full board. The scope of audit committee interest in control is as wide as the responsibilities of the full board:

- control for economy, efficiency and effectiveness;

- financial and government regulation;
- the co-ordination, planning and results of all internal audit, external audit and regulatory activity;
- all fraud;
- conflicts of interest and other ethical issues;
- customer complaints;
- the effect of change on control.

An audit committee only advises, it does not make executive decisions. Recommendations are made to those with executive authority and the full board. Results of all reviews by an audit committee are reported to and discussed by the full board. The audit committee's existence is seen outside an organisation: it is mentioned in the organisation's annual report. That report includes an activity statement signed by the audit committee chairman.

This status will take some time to become established practice in all organisations. However, the theory can be used now to measure the effectiveness of an audit committee, by member self-assessment or by internal audit. Each of these characteristics should be referred to in an audit committee's charter and be visible in the marketing of internal auditing.

Current 'top of the organisation' interests lie in control frameworks and risk analysis, both for external reporting reasons and for increasing the value from audit processes. Use these interests to develop appropriate internal auditing services. There is less audit committee and senior management interest in value from internal audit being part of quality assessment and improvement programmes. Audit committees and senior management see little current value from internal audit involvement in environmental management, though some in senior management see this as a value in the future. There is little evidence of internal audit adding value in organisation health and safety programmes. Few in senior management see value from internal audit involvement in whistleblowing. Use this lack of interest in your marketing, to demonstrate the importance of each to the organisation. Cultivate management interest in each and market internal auditing as a solution.

Establish and market an internal audit charter based on professional standards

The IIA standards require an internal audit unit to have a statement of purpose, authority and responsibility. How this statement is prepared and communicated is left to the organisation. Many, but not all, internal audit units use an internal audit charter to communicate their internal audit scope and responsibilities. Despite the importance of this communication not all organisations take the opportunity of using it to sell all the values of their services in a visionary or promotional style.

Ziegenfuss (1994) reported that 33 per cent of his respondents in small internal audit units did not have a charter. He considered a charter 'is important because it provides the internal auditing department with legitimacy and a sense of mission'. Ziegenfuss's sample charter, reprinted at Appendix E, contains the following sections:

- Introduction.
- Nature of internal auditing.
- Objective of internal auditing.
- Scope of internal auditing.
- Responsibilities and authority of internal auditing.
- Fraud.
- Performance standards.

It concludes with the statement: 'internal audits will be performed according to organisational policy, the Standards as issued by The IIA and good business sense'.

Compare these contents with the contents of one of the charters mentioned in Figure 3.5 published by a public sector internal audit unit in the UK:

- *Our purpose* We are an Executive Office of the organisation, responsible to the Chairman.
- *Our services* We provide independent assurance that control systems are adequate and effective.
- *Our team* We have a wide skills base, business expertise and internal controls expertise. We are committed to continuing professional education and development, and are professionally qualified.
- *Working together* We understand the pressures which managers encounter.
- *Our commitment to quality* Our reputation depends upon the quality of our work and in meeting our customer's needs in every assignment we undertake.
- *The challenge of change* The climate of our working world is changing.

The charter concludes with the statement:

Adding value

As a catalyst for change, we add value to the organisation by identifying and recommending improvements so that:

- processes and records protect the organisation and its staff from error or malpractice;
- control systems are effective in delivering core results;
- financial probity is maintained;
- resources are used to achieve value for money;
- processes are as efficient as possible.

Both charters highlight the professional status of internal auditing. Both imply a requirement for internal audit staff to comply with external professional standards and codes of ethics. These statements support and strengthen the objectivity and independence of internal auditing.

There can be valid objections to using a charter to promote internal auditing in an organisation, particularly, if internal audit resources are limited. Yet, the process of developing a charter, and its publication, can encourage management support for internal audit resources, and lead the services being provided into leading edge values. For that reason, if for no other, a charter is of significant value for any internal audit unit, regardless of its size.

Design job specifications to meet your customers' needs

Barclay Simpson (1996) publishes an annual overview of the internal auditing job market in the private and public sectors. Its report recognises a changing market in 1997:

> Over the last decade, and particularly over the last five years, the internal audit recruitment market has undergone profound changes. It is easy to miss how the numerous incremental changes have resulted in totally different picture. Internal auditors in all areas of the economy are better represented and undertake more broadly based roles. They are fewer in number, younger and better qualified. The distinction between public and private sector has become blurred. The accounting profession, particularly the Big Six firms, are increasingly involved in internal auditing. Internal auditing has become internationalised and more specialised. The use of contract staff, a tiny market five years ago, continues to grow. Overall, internal auditing in terms of the value of its output has grown substantially and in terms of breadth, it is becoming a larger and more diverse market. These trends are likely to continue.

Figure 3.7 lists the phrases concerning scope of work most often used in internal audit job vacancy notices.

Figure 3.7   Descriptions most often used in internal audit job vacancy notices

'Variety of challenging non-routine assignments.'
'Consulting and adding value.'
'A diverse range of audits.'
'Minimise business risks and exposure.'
'Involvement in special project investigations.'
'Training for future management role.'

Two recently advertised positions for Heads of Internal Audit describe the values management can receive from internal audit independence and a broad scope of work in today's control environment in the following terms:

Advertisement 1

> The prime function of this position is to provide an effective independent review of each business strategy, operations and day to day activities. The audit team are responsible for far more than simply compliance issues and the Head of Internal Audit must be capable of understanding the specifics of a business quickly in order to deliver an incisive appraisal of areas such as the strategic plan, threats and opportunities facing the company, management strengths and development areas and so on.

Advertisement 2

> Working closely with the Managing Director and senior Board Members you will be required to provide an independent appraisal of the company's internal control framework and to facilitate its continuous improvement in support of the strategic and operational objectives of the group.
>
> You will need not less than 5 years' post qualification experience in an internal audit role. Totally familiar with the design and implementation of modern audit techniques and the creation of centres of excellence for internal controls, you will also be skilled at risk assessment and successful in contributing strongly to efficiency and effectiveness. You will have integrity, exceptional interpersonal, influencing and communication skills and ability to work equally well as a member of a team or independently is crucial.

Internal audit job titles vary considerably. Most have the words 'internal' and 'audit/or'. Many use global 'flags' like 'international' and 'European'. A few use words like 'operational', 'business', 'management', 'consultant', 'control'. Job titles for managers of internal audit units vary, using 'general', 'head', 'group' and 'chief'. In the UK, the title 'director' (common in North American usage) is used only rarely. Audit is clearly still seen by those employing internal audit staff as being the most appropriate description of their work.

Job titles and descriptions are an important part of marketing internal auditing, to both internal audit staff and to those they report, during audit work and any other services that they provide. They are often the weakest part of control over staff in an organisation and in the internal audit unit. All staff in an internal audit unit should have an up-to-date job description, which has been agreed, and is used to review their performance. Job descriptions take on a new meaning if they are used to design a job, specify responsibilities for the holder and organisation, promote its value, evaluate performance and motivate staff.

Case 3.3 reviews internal audit job descriptions recommended by Ziegenfuss (1994), and suggests the addition of some exciting words for marketing the positions described.

Maintain an internal audit manual

Documentation of internal auditing procedures is an essential part of quality control in an internal audit unit. A manual provides both instruction and advice for internal audit staff, and all those who are involved with their work, the audit committee, management and external audit. Appendix E is a sample internal audit manual recommended by Ziegenfuss (1994) for the small internal audit unit. He introduces the manual as:

> ... extremely helpful in documenting the policies and procedures needed to efficiently carry out the performance of the department's work. If an auditor were to go into a department (such as the purchasing department) and find no policy and procedures manual, chances are he or she would comment about this lack of managerial control in the audit report. So why don't we practice what we preach? Probably for the same reasons our auditees give us: It takes too much time to develop and maintain a manual, or we feel it is not needed because we already know what is expected of the department and ourselves.
>
> The fact is you do need one. Why? First, to document the understanding between yourself and the management of your organization concerning your responsibilities (audit charter) as the lead auditor. Second, to provide a trail for your successor should you leave your present position. Third, a manual provides a reference to guide you in performing your audit. Auditing is a systematic process. This means that certain steps should be performed during every audit to ensure consistency and objectivity. Lastly, a manual can ensure compliance with The IIA's Standards. This is important because the Standards have been developed by expert practitioners and have proven to be the optimal manner in which to operate an internal auditing department.

The manual in Appendix E is developed with the following four principles in mind:

1. Lead auditors of a small internal auditing department of 10 or less do not have time to develop and maintain an audit manual. (For purposes of this report, the term 'lead auditor' refers to the highest-ranking internal auditor in the department.)
2. An audit manual is a necessary requirement for ensuring that an effective internal auditing programme is in operation.
3. An audit manual should allow practitioners to comply with The IIA's Standards.
4. The lead auditor should periodically review the contents of the manual to ensure that the manual reflects both current and optimal practice.

Market exciting internal auditing pictures

Albrecht *et al.* (1992) started the executive summary of their report into a common body of knowledge for internal auditing with the following statement: 'Internal auditing is an exciting and challenging profession'.

Excitement in internal auditing starts with its management and should be developed at each stage of the audit process, from planning through to communication of results. The setting of audit objectives which meet the organisation's needs, the evaluation of audit tests and drawing of conclusions can all be times in the audit cycle when the qualities of excitement – elation, appeal, agitation, disquiet, interest, motivation, fascination and exhilaration – can be used by the professional internal auditor to improve audit results. Yet, excitement in an audit needs to be controlled. This requires a studied understanding of human relations and the ability to maintain satisfactory relationships with everyone involved in audit work. Understanding people is a recognised requirement for internal auditing professional proficiency – The IIA Standard 260.

Creating excitement in the performance of audit work is an important part of the development of every internal auditor. The professional common body of knowledge for internal auditors recognises importance in the key disciplines needed for excitement – reasoning, problem-solving, communication and organisation skills. The following four rules for generating excitement apply in internal auditing. They are not difficult to learn. Applying the rules to each level of audit management and during the performance of audit work can be more difficult.

Rule 1: Do not restrict the scope of any audit

When developing audit objectives and plans, always consider all aspects of internal control, from reliability and integrity, through compliance and safeguarding to economy, efficiency and effectiveness. Do not miss any. Consider each as it relates to the audit assignment and to the organisation's objectives.

Rule 2: Audit deeply

Analyse, compare and contrast. Establish 'what should be' and measure this against 'what is'. Consider the relationships between financial and non-financial information. If necessary, use technical support to understand the operations being audited.

Rule 3: Look into the future

Consider the importance of control for the future. Be aware of possible changes in risk at strategic, tactical and operational levels. Remember that organisations, procedures and people change. Forecast possible effects and bring these into your audit conclusions.

Rule 4: Focus on quality

View every system as a supply chain. Consider the needs of the suppliers, the system owners and their customers. Review the specifications and measures used by each to ensure quality exists in all the products and services. (Do the same for the audit process being used – continuously improve the process and make sure your customers are delighted.)

Applied with due professional care, these four rules can change any internal auditing assignment into an exciting picture of consultancy, shared knowledge, risk management and best practices: adding value to the organisation and development of those performing the audit work. Case 3.4 compares the work of internal auditors with that of artists, drawing on similarities between the skills of each. These similarities identify many features which most internal audit units could improve in their search for best practices.

Link your vision, charter, job specifications and manual into marketing quality

Getting to grips with quality is the title of a booklet produced by the Department of Trade and Industry for its 'Managing in the '90s' programme, part of the DTI's Enterprise Initiative. This programme is supported by literature, practical advice and an excellent selection of videos on free loan, dealing with quality improvement policies, ISO 9000 quality systems and the concept of total quality management (TQM).

The DTI estimates that about one-third of all effort expended in British businesses (not just industry!) is wasted on correction, rectification and rework: TQM is defined as a way of managing to improve the effectiveness, flexibility and competitiveness of a business operation or function. Reading and viewing this material provide a guide to how everyone in an organisation should be controlling their processes, to be efficient, effective and economic. It is essential reading for all professional internal auditors. A knowledge and experience of TQM, even if only within the internal audit department, can only improve the audit service provided and enrich all the internal audit staff, both by job satisfaction and career development.

Figures 3.8 and 3.9 show the quality management framework for an organisation and how quality measurements based on the framework can be developed for an internal audit unit.

The TQM concept requires all supplier and operating process relationships to create excellent products and services, which satisfy all customers' needs. Developing supplier partnerships and knowing customer needs become paramount in the quality environment of team-building and continuous improvement, which develop between groups within the organisation and between other organisations. Identifying the 'customer' is not that easy, particularly in large and international organisations.

In TQM everyone is involved, in every way, in everything they do, the

126 Leading edge internal auditing

Figure 3.8 The TQM framework

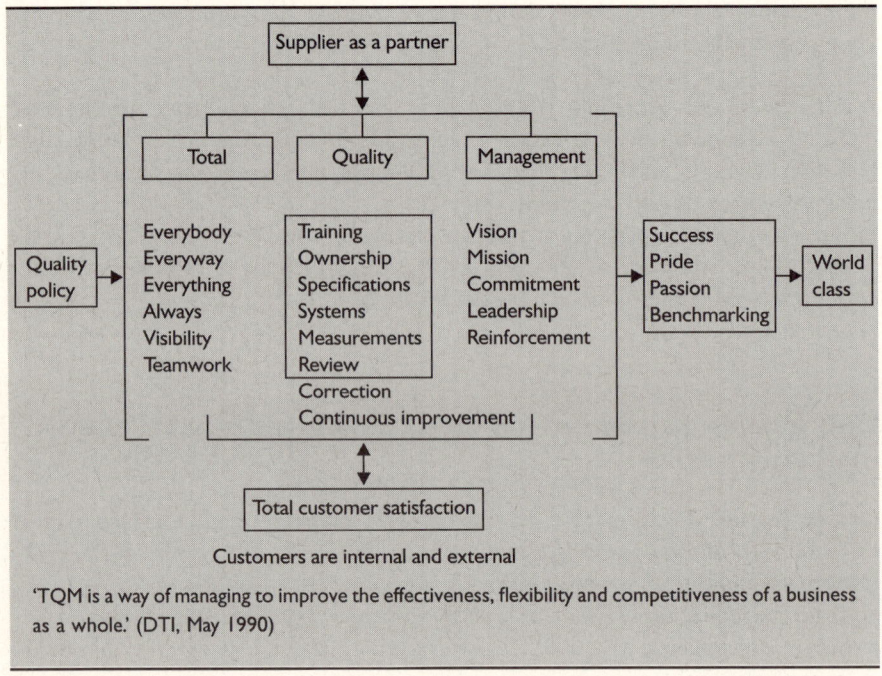

Figure 3.9 Quality measures for the internal audit unit

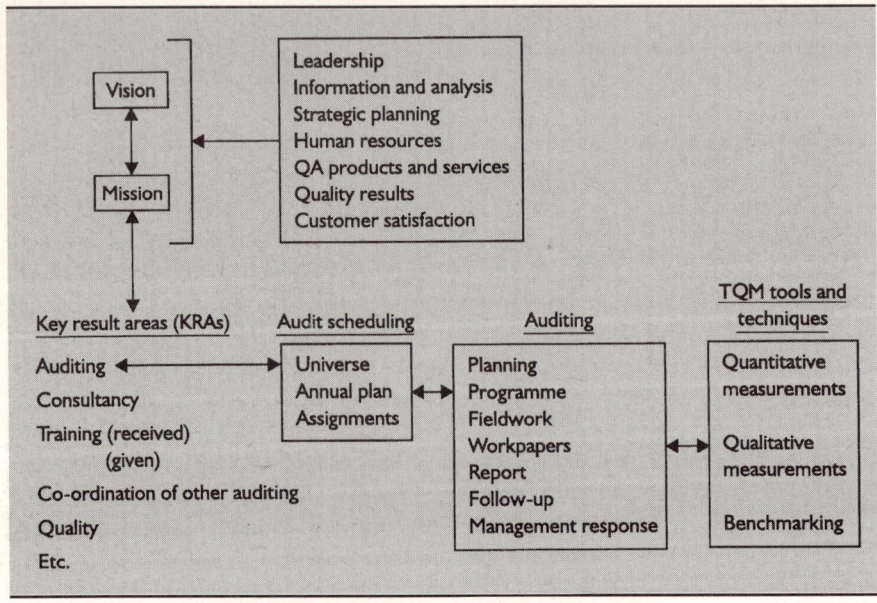

involvement is total – all management and all staff. The internal supplier and customer become just as important as the external supplier and customer. It is the excellence of these working relationships, and all the processes, that guarantees the high quality of the product or service and satisfies the customer. Reliance is not placed on quality checks after the service has been completed or product made. The TQM environment develops teams and monitoring activities which are always 'customer' orientated. The customer becomes paramount.

Many organisations already provide internal TQM training and all internal audit managers should take advantage of this for themselves and their staff. If your organisation does not do so – in whatever sector – then ask why. Do not wait for your organisation to adopt TQM, seek the training and use the knowledge gained in the scope of all your audits.

What are some of the gains to be achieved?

- Recognition of the *supplier-process-customer chain* for the audit process drives the audit programme into the heart of business activity and highlights the key controls needed for business success.
- Establishing who is the customer and what are *customer needs* helps focus audit tests into the most important areas and issues.
- The concept of *auditor/auditee* teamwork during the audit process is achieved, and 'participative auditing' becomes a reality.
- *Audit results* and *recommendations* concentrate on prevention rather than detection, looking to the control of quality in the future, rather than the past.
- *Quality assurance* requirements to meet The IIA Standards take on a wider meaning, linking the quality aims of the internal audit unit into those of the organisation.
- Emphasis on *continuous improvement* in the TQM environment encourages internal audit staff to continually seek improvements in the audit process.
- The audit process becomes a *quality system*, which can lead to recognition under the international accreditation standard ISO 9000.
- TQM requires *quality measures* in all processes, to monitor quality and highlight non-conformance with standards.
- *Quality successes* are more easily recognised and rewarded at team and individual levels.

Total quality management in an organisation (even if only in the internal audit unit) requires the total commitment of management. However, it is not a journey's end, just the beginning. It is the start of a road which requires a continuing quality commitment by everyone, every day, in every way, in everything. The enthusiasm it generates can lead to the highest accolades of excellence and the achievement of world-class status. Gupta and Ray (1995) researched national quality award-winning organisations in the USA, to review the emerging involvement of internal auditing in quality management environments. A summary of some of their results is shown in Case 3.5. They ask the following questions:

In such an environment, where does the internal auditor fit in? Is the quality revolution going to pass by internal auditors? Are internal auditors going to be mere spectators? Are they going to react to the process of quality improvement rather than be involved in it? Are they going to see the quality movement as one more management fad and stick to their traditional roles?

Ridley and Stephens (1996) researched the impact of the international quality standard ISO 9000 on internal auditing. They identified internal audit units in 1996 with registrations to this standard. All of the units had been established for some time: all had some form of internal auditing charter, procedures and a wide scope of audit work before they considered ISO 9000: all had some form of quality assurance designed into their processes, but only a few had previously experienced any formal external review, mainly by a professional accounting firm. One unit had been reviewed in 1991 by The IIA's own voluntary quality assurance review service.

The most significant impact is their use of ISO 9000 to develop and register audit documentation, records and auditing systems. In all cases the process of registration required changes and improvements to satisfy the Standard's 20 quality requirements. Some are using ISO 9000 as a framework for implementing quality assurance into their internal auditing practices. Some used their certification to promote quality consulting and auditing as an internal auditing service. Reasons for registration varied in order of importance across each of the functions. Analysed, they form the pattern in Figure 3.10.

In each of the functions there is a mix of reasons for registration, that changed as the process of registration proceeded and ISO 9000 experience increased. In most cases the initial intention was not to seek improvements in professional practices, but to document the current practices more clearly and uniformly. However, addressing ISO 9000 quality requirements focused attention on the structure needed to achieve and maintain a quality organisation and system. This focus emphasised responsibilities for quality at all levels. Continuous cycles of monitoring and correction, driven by the quality system and its required reviews, also encouraged staff to strive for new methods and responsibilities.

Benefits during registration were mainly in the quality vision and mission, which required management leadership, teamwork and good communication to mould existing internal auditing practices into compliance with ISO 9000. Changes required training and a writing or rewriting of audit procedures.

Each of the internal audit units taking part in the case study identifies the four main benefits from ISO 9000 shown in Figure 3.11.

Conclusions reached in 1995 from this research evidence indicate that the impact of ISO 9000 on internal auditing will continue to grow worldwide. This growth will be fuelled by growth in registrations by organisations in all supply chains and a growing interest on the part of The IIA and internal auditors in the development and marketing of their services. ISO 9000 will continue to influence how quality and control is achieved in many organisations across the world. This

Figure 3.10 Internal auditing reasons for ISO 9000 registration

Procedural
- need to update procedures
- need to improve procedures
- need to motivate internal auditing staff to comply with procedures
- need for more uniform procedures

Strategic
- requirement by organisation to pursue ISO 9000
- requirement by organisation to demonstrate quality in services provided

Organisational
- need to change structure of global/national service
- need to improve supervision
- improve team building

Marketing
- part of programme to market test internal auditing services in competition with other bids
- part of a programme to market internal auditing services within the organisation

influence will span organisational structures, strategies and learning. Internal auditing can use ISO 9000 to:

- support and strengthen compliance with the IIA Standards;
- promote quality in internal audit work;
- establish quality assurance in internal auditing functions;
- establish quality as a leading edge in the audit market-place;
- require quality learning programmes for internal auditors;
- improve links with quality auditors;
- forge links between quality objectives and governance;
- sell quality consultancy by internal auditors.

Compete in the internal auditing market place

Competition in the internal auditing market place is a recent development influenced by growth of organisation interest in internal auditing services across

Figure 3.11 Internal auditing benefits from ISO 9000 registration

Quality policy

Like The IIA standards, ISO 9000 requires a declaration of quality purpose. For ISO 9000 this is the publication of a quality policy. Each of the internal auditing functions had incorporated such a statement in its charter.

Standard of conduct

The IIA standards require internal auditors to take due professional care in their audit work. Compliance to ISO 9000 quality requirements promoted diligence in audit work and established an environment that embraced many of the principles in The IIA Code of Ethics.

Documentation

The IIA standards require written policies and procedures for all audit work. Such evidence was reinforced by the ISO 9000 quality requirements for controlled documentation and records.

Quality assurance

The IIA standards requires evidence of supervision and quality assurance in all audit work. The ISO 9000 quality assurance and quality audits requirements provided a framework for the supervision and management of all internal auditing practices.

---

all sectors in the UK and worldwide. This competition has been driven mainly by the Big Six professional accounting firms, though other internal auditing consultancies and consortiums are involved. The UK government policy of competing for quality in the provision of services in the public sector has also been a strong influence on who provides internal auditing services.

What started in the early 1990s as outsourcing of internal auditing, has developed into a mixture of total outsourcing, strategic partnerships and the supply of contract staff. Contracting staff into internal audit functions and teams is not new. The IIA recognise a need for some contracted-out internal audit work in its standards for professional internal audit. Evidence from literature clearly indicates the practice of using consultants for computer, systems, security and fraud is established in internal audit work in many organisations. Many internal audit units now use outsourced resources at strategic, tactical and operational levels.

Recent research in North America into outsourced internal audit predicts:

- the entry of new internal audit providers other than professional accounting firms;

Figure 3.12 Advantages and disadvantages of outsourcing internal auditing

For
- cost/quality
- availability of trained/specialist staff
- auditing flexibility
- independence
- qualifications/knowledge/languages/skills/professionalism

Against
- cost probably higher
- lack of organisation knowledge
- loss of control over internal audit work
- too external auditing focused
- loss of in-house experience
- conflict of interest with two masters
- speed of response
- continuity of staff

- new and different career orientations for some internal audit staff;
- changes in internal audit practices;
- contention over liability and responsibility for internal audit work.

These predictions are not narrow and can span not only internal audit, but the whole audit environment, including external, internal, environmental and quality audit. Current literature in the UK identifies the advantages and disadvantages of outsourcing shown in Figure 3.12.

These results can be a guide for all internal audit units planning to market their internal audit services. Consider each one carefully, particularly its implications for future internal auditing. Outsourcing internal audit is likely to continue and grow, with its value now being measured by audit committees. Its far-reaching effects are still to be fully researched and analysed. One immediate impact in many in-house internal audit functions has been to address quality assurance in their services and introduce more formal quality systems in internal audit work. Another is to research and develop new services for the organisations being served. These are common reactions in all market places where there is increasing competition from the providers of products and services.

Finally, when marketing internal auditing be guided by the experiences of marketing management in your organisation. Consider the theory as well as the practice of marketing shown in Case 3.6. And measure your marketing success with your charter/objectives.

Chapter summary

Few internal audit functions currently market their services, promote values for their services or a vision for their future, although most communicate their responsibilities. Market modern internal auditing services that meet today's and tomorrow's control needs. Create a vision which is better than the service you provide today and use it to measure your progress towards its achievement. Lead an imaginative and innovative internal auditing service that delights its customers. Use your objective and independent status to strengthen your reporting lines. Improve this status by using external professional standards and codes of ethics to market for all aspects of your work. Use a charter agreed with management to sell internal auditing. Those that recruit internal audit staff in the public job market-place, use demanding and emotive superlatives to attract the best experienced and qualified staff, thus enhancing the value of internal audit. Use your internal audit unit's job descriptions to attract the best staff, develop their competence and sell the services it provides. Maintain an up-to-date manual which documents all internal auditing processes. Report measures that link your vision, charter, job descriptions and manual with your organisation's objectives. Contribute to your organisation's quality improvement programmes. All the indications in the UK audit market place are that competition will grow amongst internal audit providers, both from organisation staff and from those external to the organisation. Establish your internal audit unit at the leading edge of this competition.

Principia

1. Success of modern internal auditing lies in how it is researched and developed, and then promoted in the organisation market place.

2. Innovation and understanding its customers' needs are the keys to how internal auditing should be sold throughout the audit process.

3. Internal auditing vision and mission statements must be exciting.

4. Measures of internal auditing performance must be linked to its customers' and organisation's objectives.

5. Audit committees should strengthen internal auditing objectivity and independence.

6. Internal audit charters must be based on professional standards and a code of ethics.

▶

7. Use superlatives to reinforce internal audit staff and market their services.
8. Internal auditing procedures and documents are an essential part of marketing internal auditing quality.
9. Benchmark internal audit marketing with the marketing of other services, within and outside the organisation it serves.
10. Market internal auditing as a contribution to your organisation's quality improvement programmes.

Bibliography

Albrecht, W., Stice, J. and Stocks, K. (1992) *A Common Body of Knowledge for the Practice of Internal Auditing*, the Institute of Internal Auditors Research Foundation, Altamonte Springs, USA.
Barclay Simpson (1996) *1996 Market Report*, Barclay Simpson, London.
Carolus, Roger (1991), IIA 50th Anniversary issue of the *Internal Auditor*, The Institute of Internal Auditors Inc., Altamonte Springs, USA.
CIPFA (1990) *The Client's View of Internal Audit*, Research report by the Audit Panel – The Chartered Institute of Public Finance & Accountancy, London.
Gray, G. and Gray, M. (1996) *Enhancing Internal Auditing Through Innovative Practices*, The Institute of Internal Auditors Research Foundation, Altamonte Springs, USA.
Gupta, Parveen P. and Ray, Manash, R. (1995) *Total Quality Improvement Process and the Internal Auditing Function*, The IIA Research Foundation, Altamonte Springs, USA.
H.M. Treasury (1993) *Government Information Systems Audit Manual*, HMSO, London.
H.M. Treasury (1996) *Government Internal Audit Manual*, HMSO, London.
IIA (1978) *Standards for the Professional Practice of Internal Auditing* (revised 1993), The Institute of Internal Auditors Inc., Altamonte Springs, USA.
IIA (1990) *Statement of Responsibilities for Internal Auditing*, The Institute of Internal Auditors Inc., Altamonte Springs, USA.
IIA (1994) *The IIA's Perspective on Outsourcing Internal Auditing, A Professional Briefing for Chief Audit Executives*, The Institute of Internal Auditors Inc., Altamonte Springs, USA.
ISO 9000-Quality Systems and the concept of Total Quality Management (TQM) (extracted from The IIA Research Foundation report *Total Quality Improvement Process and The Internal Auditing Function*, Gupta and Ray, 1995).
Managing in the '90s, *Getting to Grips with Quality 1990*, Department of Trade and Industry, London, UK.
Ridley, Jeffrey and Stephens, Krystyna (1996) *International Quality Standards*, The IIA Research Foundation, Altamonte Springs, USA.
Sawyer, Lawrence B. (1973) *The Practice of Modern Internal Auditing*, The Institute of Internal Auditors Inc., Altamonte Springs, USA.

Sawyer, Lawrence B. (1992) 'The Creative Side of Internal Auditing', *Internal Auditor*, December, The Institute of Internal Auditors Inc., Altamonte Springs, USA.

Ziegenfuss, Douglas E. (1994) *Challenges and Opportunities of Small Internal Audit Organizations*, The IIA Research Foundation, USA.

Case 3.1 Our 1993 vision and mission

We understand customers' needs and add value as a part of the management team.

The case

Organisation

A worldwide internal audit function is directed by the Director of Corporate Audit in close co-operation with unit management. The audit staff is dispersed throughout the world with people located in areas of greatest risk. Language skills and knowledge of the local environment, a uniform mission and professional standards deliver quality audit work anywhere in the world. We understand customers' needs and add value as a part of the management team.

Environment

- Internal audit is recognised internally and externally as world class.
- Continuous improvement is a way of life.
- There is strong management ownership of the system of internal control. To maintain this, auditing interacts with line management on an ongoing basis to provide awareness of and education on the value and nature of internal controls.
- Audit work is driven by an assessment of risk and exposure in partnership with operating management.
- Auditing actively participates in the evolution of financial/operating systems and business processes to achieve a state of enhanced integration, commonality and functionality.

Personnel

The internal audit staff is highly qualified and capable, displaying sound business judgement and strong auditing and consultancy abilities. A diversity of backgrounds and work experiences exists and is shared among the staff. Auditors are viewed as having significant potential for holding key positions in the corporation, including career path opportunities within internal audit. Auditing provides unique developmental opportunities through broad exposure across the corporation. There is an active programme of ongoing training for auditors worldwide to recognise business evolution, technology advances and state-of-the-art audit techniques.

Management and supervision at all levels within the internal audit function are known for their excellence in personnel and quality management. Visible leadership, active personnel development, effective listening and a strong sensitivity to customer needs are among the traits for which audit management and supervision are most noted.

Internal audit is recognised as a great place to work.

Mission

Worldwide internal auditing

In concert with the goals and objectives of the company, the worldwide internal audit function provides an independent, objective appraisal of business activities to support management in their responsibilities to conduct operations in an environment of effective internal control. The Director of Auditing has overall accountability for auditing.

Scope of work

Accountable to senior management and the Audit Committee of the Board of Directors, internal audit's mission is to satisfy its customers' needs and add value to the business by:

- ensuring that assets are safeguarded through an effective system of internal control;
- ensuring compliance with corporate policies, government requirements, established procedures and sound business practices;
- ensuring that processes exist which will generate consistent and accurate financial and operational data;
- ensuring that processes exist to monitor the effectiveness and efficiency of operations and the achievement of business objectives;
- sharing expertise, knowledge and ideas across operating units to enhance effectiveness throughout the corporation;
- providing an awareness of risk and the value and nature of effective internal controls.

Consider

1. How each of the internal audit unit's missions relates to its vision of internal auditing.
2. Draft your own vision and mission statements using the case as a guide.

3. Prepare a plan to use your vision and mission statements to market your services.

Case 3.2 Helping ensure the public purse is protected

The case

APA's charter

Our role: helping ensure the public purse is protected by improving internal audit.

Audit Policy and Advice team is part of the Financial Management Reporting and Audit directorate in Treasury with responsibility for setting the internal audit standards and promoting best practice in internal audit. We provide assurance to the Treasury's Permanent Secretary that the standards remain in line with accepted UK and international internal auditing standards and are generally accepted by central government auditors.

Internal audit standards

The standards, which are used throughout central government as well as by some other bodies, are published in the *Government Internal Audit Manual* (GIAM). The standards support important concepts such as the constitutional position of the Accounting Officer, accountability to Parliament, propriety and value for money as set out in Government accounting and other centrally laid-down requirements. They allow scope for variation, innovation and the continuing development of the discipline.

While APA is responsible for setting standards, Accounting Officers are responsible for ensuring that they have an effective internal audit service in compliance with the standards. APA seeks to ensure that departments are clear about their responsibilities in relation to internal audit. They should inform APA if they find any problems with the application of the standards or with the interpretation of the manual. APA accepts a responsibility to give advice on matters of interpretation of the standards and on the principles involved. We therefore provide advice on the standards and their application to all central government users of the *Government Internal Audit Manual* including executive agencies and NDPBs. However we expect that agencies and NDPBs will seek guidance initially from their departments.

Best practice

APA encourages the continuing development of high-quality internal audit but is not responsible for the quality of internal audit in individual organisations –

quality is the responsibility of the management of the appropriate organisation.

Departments are responsible for ensuring that the standards are complied with and that the standard of internal audit meets their needs. We will seek feedback on the application of the standards to confirm that the standards remain appropriate.

APA promotes best practice by producing or encouraging production of guidance on major issues of concern to central government auditors where there is a clear Treasury interest and an absence of guidance from other sources.

We obtain feedback from internal auditors through seminars, conferences and other communications so as to stay in touch with the practical issues they are facing and the adequacy of GIAM in providing standards and guidance.

Our relationship with NAO is one of professional co-operation on principles, standards and best practice. We encourage co-operation between internal and external audit in the interest of safeguarding public money and avoiding duplication of audit effort. We do not pass information to NAO about specific organisations without their permission or knowledge.

By virtue of our central position we act as a point of contact for auditors and others. We provide a limited range of services to departments such as providing information on job vacancies and advice on audit appointments. We also provide information to students, researchers and foreign visitors interested in our system of internal audit. We do not provide help on issues which are properly the responsibility of audit management (e.g. pay and grading).

Treasury role

Within Treasury APA provides advice on internal audit and internal control issues. We contribute to training courses run by Treasury. We are responsible for ensuring that Treasury guidance which refers to internal audit, e.g. Government Accounting, is appropriately worded.

APA provides assistance to the Spending directorate on a basis agreed as part of our annual planning. We may provide general advice to spending teams on internal audit but we do not pass on information about weaknesses in internal audit in specific organisations which derives from our professional relationship with the auditors.

We work closely with the Treasury Officer of Accounts team (TOA) on fraud. We collect information from departments annually in order to complete an annual report on fraud in central government which is circulated within central government, placed in the House of Commons Library and issued to members of the public (plus interested parties) on request. Departments are responsible for providing us with details, as quickly as possible, of any novel or unusual frauds, or suspected frauds, affecting their departments, agencies and NDPBs. In consultation with TOA, we decide whether details of these unusual cases should be circulated confidentially to other departments.

Expectations and obligations

We will keep departments informed of central developments and other issues affecting internal audit. We expect to be informed of issues affecting the standards and their application. We welcome feedback on our work. We hope departments will respond promptly to any requests for information which we will try to keep to a minimum.

We will consult before we make any changes to the mandatory standards. We have an obligation to explain and provide interpretation on the meaning and application of the standards.

Advisory group

We have established an independent advisory group to assist our planning and to help advise on monitoring the quality of APA's work.

Consider

1. How does this charter impact you if you are in a public sector organisation?
2. Do you have a charter which links into the requirements of APA?
3. Are you required to seek and comply with APA's advice?

Case 3.3 Using job descriptions to market internal audit

The case

Job descriptions for the small internal audit unit

Job descriptions are an important part of quality control in an internal audit unit. Their content should be designed so that they link into the organisation and internal auditing objectives. They should be capable of being measured and provide motivation for improvement, by the jobholder and internal audit unit. Ziegenfuss (1994) provides the following examples of job descriptions and a performance evaluation form, for the small internal audit unit.

Job description – lead auditor

Responsibilities

Overall
The lead auditor is responsible for managing the internal auditing function.

Specific
1. Develops and maintains a charter for the internal auditing function which reflects the department's responsibilities, authority, and reporting relationships.
2. Develops and obtains proper approval for goals, audit work schedules, staffing plans, and financial budgets for the department.
3. Co-ordinates the department's work with that of the organisation's external auditor.
4. Prepares a quarterly report of the department's progress in carrying out the plans developed in (2).
5. Performs individual audits according to the Standards for the Professional Practice of Internal Auditing issued by The Institute of Internal Auditors.
6. Maintains personal proficiency and that of staff auditors by obtaining an adequate amount of continuing education.
7. Supervises staff auditors by assigning them to jobs which match their abilities, reviewing their work, and appraising their performance.

Qualifications

Education
A master's degree (either an MBA or MS in accounting) is recommended, but additional experience (five years) in a supervisory auditing position can be substituted for the master's degree.

Professional certification
Certified Internal Auditor (CIA).

Experience
Five years' experience at the in-charge auditor level or higher.

Job description – staff auditor

Responsibilities

Overall
Staff auditors are responsible for carrying out individual audit assignments according to the Standards for the Professional Practice of Internal Auditing issued by The Institute of Internal Auditors.

Specific
1. Perform individual audits according to the Standards issued by The Institute.
2. Obtain personal proficiency by obtaining the Certified Internal Auditor (CIA) designation and maintaining an adequate amount of continuing education.

Qualifications

Education
A bachelor's degree in an area of business in which auditor will be assigned (for example: an accounting degree if the staff auditor will be performing financial audits).

Professional Certification
None.

Experience
One year's experience in an area of business in which auditor will be assigned (for example: an accountant with experience in general accounting is hired to perform financial audits).

Performance evaluation form

Frequency: to be completed annually for the lead auditor and staff auditors, and for staff auditors upon completion of an assignment requiring 80 hours to complete.

Factor	Rating
I. Job performance:	
A. Effectively plans and organises work.	1 2 3 4 5
B. Meets established individual goals and contributes to the attainment of department goals.	1 2 3 4 5
C. Demonstrates initiative.	1 2 3 4 5
D. Seeks new and efficient means for performing the job.	1 2 3 4 5
E. Maintains accuracy, quality and quantity of work.	1 2 3 4 5
F. Effectively deals with unexpected or unusual demands.	1 2 3 4 5
G. Performs work independently, involving the supervisor when appropriate.	1 2 3 4 5
H. Leads other employees in performing work when required.	1 2 3 4 5
II. Job knowledge:	
A. Possesses and utilises necessary knowledge and skills to perform job.	1 2 3 4 5
B. Understands and follows department and company policies and procedures.	1 2 3 4 5
C. Quickly understands new techniques and concepts.	1 2 3 4 5
III. Communications and work relationships:	
A. Expresses information clearly and effectively through oral communication.	1 2 3 4 5
B. Expresses information clearly and effectively in writing.	1 2 3 4 5

Factor	Rating
C. Co-ordinates with others.	1 2 3 4 5
D. Assists others and encourages teamwork.	1 2 3 4 5
E. Presents a positive impression on others and commands their attention without tending to alienate them.	1 2 3 4 5

Note: 1 = extremely poor; 2 = poor; 3 = satisfactory; 4 = good; 5 = outstanding. Leave blank if not rated.

Consider

1. Your own job descriptions as compared with those in the case.
2. Identify improvements you would make to these 1994 job descriptions. Take into account the current focus on governance, codes of conduct and quality.
3. How do these job descriptions link into your own and your organisation's vision and mission statements.
4. What measures would you introduce to monitor the use of these job descriptions, at audit work, internal audit unit and audit committee levels.
5. Using the description of exciting internal auditing in Case 3.4, to add into the job descriptions new emotive words which best describe your own internal auditing. Words in current use in many job advertisements for internal audit staff are shown below.

Most frequently used	Other words used with similar meanings		
Rigorous	aggressive	positive	strong drive
Astute	willing	flexible	diplomatic
Self-starter	motivated	enthusiastic	
Innovative	proactive	creative	
Outstanding	excellent		
Leader	persuasive		
Honest			

6. The job descriptions with the APB 1996 Auditor's Code reproduced at Appendix F. Its following nine fundamental principles of independent auditing should be seen in each job description:

1. Accountability	6. Judgement
2. Integrity	7. Clear communication
3. Objectivity and independence	8. Association
4. Competence	9. Providing value
5. Rigour	

Case 3.4 Internal auditing is an exciting art

The case

Is there excitement for internal auditors?

> Internal auditing is an independent appraisal function established within an organisation to examine and evaluate its activities as a service to the organisation.

Important as this statement is, does it really inspire? Some see excitement in creativity in internal auditing. Creativity is not just reserved for the arts and sciences. In his article 'The Creative Side of Internal Auditing', published in *Internal Auditor* (December 1992), Sawyer goes on to say that creativity will never be tapped in internal auditing 'if we do not develop a divine discontent with what we see and if we fail to search for new ways of solving problems which we identify, or which management present to us'.

What Sawyer is expressing is the secret of excellent auditing. The ability to create from a structured and disciplined approach to facts, an attractive picture, which delights the observer and communicates what the 'artist' internal auditor can see.

Carolus (1991), who directed development of The IIA Standards in 1975, explained in the 1991 IIA 50th anniversary issue of the *Internal Auditor* that his team set out to establish internal auditing as an art which requires rules. He believed that the five general standards were written to represent the rules of internal auditing artistry, and that:

> ... internal auditors are artists. Like musicians with their notes, painters with their colours and writers with their arrangement of words, there are time-honoured rules within which the artist has learned to excel.

Both Sawyer and Carolus expressed what many leading edge internal auditors feel about their professional service, in terms of *line*, *tone*, *colour*, *scale*, *perspective* and *composition*. Each can guide the creative internal auditor in the following ways.

Line

Line starts with the audit survey – a time when the internal auditor can be 'fluent and expressive'; a time of high imagination. Background information about the activities to be audited starts the drawing process and links loose lines into a pattern of audit objectives to achieve the audit scope. *Lines establish plans.*

Tone

All objects are intrinsically both light and dark. There are many tones between white and black. Knowledge is the internal auditor's tone. Once the survey lines of the audit are planned, the levels of knowledge required for the audit must be set. Knowledge provides atmosphere and interest. Like tone, the right levels are those that draw the viewers into the audit. For the audit the viewers are the audit team and those who are being served by the audit. *Tone demonstrates knowledge.*

Colour

There is no colour without light. Colour is closely linked to tone. The internal auditor's choice of audit tests establishes the colour palette for the audit picture. Creative skill is needed in mixing the tests so that they focus light into all of the audit objectives and complement each other. It is very easy to end an audit with 'muddy' objectives if the selections of colours and mix are not right. *Colour is the focus of audit tests.*

Scale

Objects in themselves have no scale – they can only be small or large in relation to something else. Audit scale is size in relation to the risks for the organisation as a whole, and not just for the activities being audited. Risk assessment provides scale for the audit. To be creative during risk assessment requires the process to continue from the organisation level through the audit objectives to the selection of audit tests and review of results. *Scale is risk.*

Perspective

Perspective is the three-dimensional reality of the world created by leading all lines to viewing points. Each line in the audit must lead to a viewing point. Not all viewing points are within the activities being audited. The creative internal auditor looks for viewing points in other parts of the organisation and frequently leads lines to viewing points outside the organisation. *Perspective is reality.*

Composition

The arrangement of an audit has to attract those it is serving. A picture with poor composition will fail to find a buyer. The composition of the audit report must lead the eyes of the 'customer' into its subject matter and keep interest throughout the viewing. *Composition is the key to selling.*

Encouraging creative internal auditing using the artist's rules improves the performance of internal audit work. It develops a divine discontent with what is seen and opens new paths for problem-solving. Next time you look at a good painting, compare it with your most recent internal audit report.

Consider

What artistic techniques best represent the work of your internal audit unit?

Case 3.5 Total quality management and the internal auditor

(Extracted from The IIA Research Foundation report, *Total Quality Improvement Process and The Internal Auditing Function*, Gupta and Ray, 1995.)

The case

Internal auditors too can be quality champions

Generally, there is a myth that only the 'manufacturing folks' can start the 'quality movement'. Our findings indicated that for some organisations, this myth was effectively dispelled. Internal auditors, by virtue of their role, are in a unique position to lead and pro-actively support the quality movement in their organisations. The internal auditing function does not need to be a bystander and wait to get on the quality bandwagon only when someone else in the organisation sounds the quality horn. If the internal auditing function so desires, there is ample opportunity to lead and support the total quality movement in an organisation. There are a number of ways that an internal auditing department can become a quality champion:

- become a role model by TQMising internal auditing operations;
- while conducting routine internal audits, add on a quality audit programme to probe related quality issues on a fairly high level;
- on every audit, conduct an introspective analysis by asking questions such as:
  - How can my client improve its measurement system?
  - How can it reduce inefficiencies and non-value-added activities in the process?
  - How can it ensure better accuracy of the product that it delivers to the customer – internal or external – downstream?;
- get involved in providing quality management training and education;
- serve on a Quality Improvement Team in any one of the three roles: systems developer, systems auditor and compliance auditor;
- train organisational subunits or departments to conduct self-audits on their own product quality on a regular basis;
- get involved in the Baldrige application process.

The internal auditing department can start getting involved or even take a leadership role in any of the following functional areas:

- management for quality;

- competitive comparisons and benchmarks;
- cost of quality;
- customer satisfaction measures;
- process re-engineering;
- vendor quality;
- employee involvement;
- employee education and training;
- employee performance and recognition;
- product development costs;
- performance evaluation systems;
- activity-based costing system.

The internal auditor can ask a number of audit-related questions in the above-mentioned functional areas as a systems developer, systems auditor and compliance auditor. For example, in the area of vendor quality, the internal auditor can ask the following questions in each of the three capacities:

As a systems developer

The internal auditing function will be deemed to have played the role of a systems developer if one of the internal auditors was part of a team that developed the system of assessing (1) vendor's qualifications (i.e., who should approve which suppliers become certified vendors, what criteria should be employed to evaluate vendors); (2) inspection process (i.e., how the quality of product supplied by the vendor should be assessed once the vendor has been JIT certified); and (3) vendor monitoring (i.e., what statistics should be gathered to regularly monitor supplier's performance on account of on-time delivery, quantity delivered, etc.).

As a systems auditor

In the area of vendor evaluation, the internal auditing function will be deemed to have played the role of a systems auditor if it audited to ensure if there is a process in place in the procurement department to assess (1) vendor's qualifications; (2) inspection of vendor's product; and (3) supplier monitoring, etc.

As a compliance auditor

In the area of vendor evaluation, the internal auditing function will be deemed to have played the role of a compliance auditor if it audited whether duly authorised person or persons determine what suppliers become certified vendors and whether the criteria as established by the procurement department are being followed to evaluate a supplier (i.e., vendor qualification process); whether a vendor's product quality is assessed after a vendor becomes JIT certified and if so, how (inspection of vendor's product); and whether the relevant statistics on vendor performance in terms of on-time delivery, accuracy of quantity delivered is collected (supplier monitoring).

Emphasising that the internal auditing function can be a pro-active participant in the total quality movement, John J. McGinty, Vice-President of Management Control, Evaluation and Corporate Audit at Xerox, observed that:

> When Xerox initiated its 'Leadership Through Quality' programme several years ago, our directors of quality and audit agreed that the audit staff would be a role model for quality throughout the organisation. They would demonstrate the use of quality tools, 'speak quality language', and staff members would be participants on quality improvement teams. (*The IIA Internal Auditor*, 1992)

According to McGinty, the Xerox corporate internal audit function has not only been a participant in the corporate-wide conversion to a quality philosophy, but it has also reshaped itself accordingly. At Federal Express, quality and internal audit functions were grouped under one Senior Vice-President, Edith Kelly. These are her comments about the consolidation:

> The decision to consolidate these two functions under one senior level management position was just natural under the circumstances. The organisation had embarked on a full scale Total Quality Improvement Process and a need was sorely felt to reach to the masses on a grand scale to 'induct' everybody into the 'quality fraternity'. To spread the quality gospel you not only need the effective leadership but you also need to reach to the masses and our internal auditing teams were already out in the districts and stations doing these quality-oriented operational audits, so what better way could there be than to utilise the internal auditors, who already had a mission – to improve service level quality – to spread the quality gospel of the organisation.

On the same note, Len Wood, then the Internal Audit/QPI Director at Solectron Corporation, observed that internal auditors in general 'need to be sure that internal audit is adding solid value and support, never just sitting there and getting in the way' (*The IIA Internal Auditor*, 1992). The case studies included in this report document many interesting aspects of either internal auditing involvement in quality programmes, the application of TQM concepts and tools within the internal auditing function, or both. In all of these cases, the internal auditing function has added value to the entire organisation by getting involved in the TQM process.

Outside resistance to internal auditor involvement in quality programmes is exaggerated

Theoretically, resistance to internal auditors' involvement in the total quality programmes initiated in the organisation can come from two quarters: outsiders and internal auditors themselves. Based on the results of our survey and interviews, we found that the perception of resistance from outsiders to internal auditors' involvement in total quality programmes can sometimes be exaggerated. The results of our survey of Fortune 500 organisations indicated that more than 70 per cent of respondents who had been involved in quality initiatives faced no resistance. Less than 10 per cent of these respondents reported having faced great resistance. The lack of resistance was also reflected in the finding that approximately 67 per cent of respondents were 'somewhat' to 'highly' satisfied with their role in quality programmes.

We found that resistance, if any, can be overcome by the internal auditing function's demonstrating the value of its involvement in quality initiatives by emphasising that its involvement will result in 'esteem-based correction rather than destructive auditing'. Internal auditing involvement in total quality programmes results in greater respect and credibility.

In today's competitive environment, success depends on delivering quality products or services at competitive prices. Internal auditors can provide clients with the benefit of their expertise gained from other locations and ensure a fact-based, unbiased, independent perspective on the quality improvement team. According to Lohman V. Blue, Manager Internal Controls, Cadillac Motor Car Division, 'internal auditing [should] work like a clearing house... to help work out any problems [its] customers encounter'. Our survey responses and case studies indicated that involvement in quality programmes led to greater respect, added credibility, and increased appreciation for the work of internal auditors. This was primarily due to the fact that the internal auditors gave fact-based, unbiased opinions and used their knowledge of business processes and controls to add value to the customer, auditee, or client's business process, or all three. Ultimately, this results in enhanced credibility of findings and recommendations contained in routine auditing reports.

Compliance mind-set is a key obstacle to increased internal auditing involvement in TQM

Surprisingly, our survey findings indicated that, in some cases, the internal auditing function itself has resisted involvement in the organisation's total quality programmes. Some internal auditors responded that the traditional 'compliance only mind-set' or the 'normal policing attitude' is a stronger force to deal with than resistance from outsiders. According to Len Wood, then Internal Audit/QPI Director at Solectron Corporation, 'internal auditors have to learn to change their perspective and start redefining their role to be that of a valued business partner with management in a total quality organisation'.

Some respondents put forth arguments related to 'auditor independence', claiming that their involvement in the quality programmes in any capacity other than as 'auditor' would compromise their independence. However, the geometrical growth in the scope of the work of the internal auditor, since the inception of The Institute of Internal Auditors in 1941, has negated that argument quite convincingly. Today, a majority of internal auditing functions are adopting pro-active roles such as change analysts, alternate cost systems evaluator, and partner with management (Gupta and Ray, The Changing Roles of the Internal Auditor, *Managerial Auditing Journal* (1992): 3–8. One of the interesting scenarios, for example, found in the course of this study was that the internal auditing function at ITT Defence helped apply TQM tools such as quality function deployment and cause-and-effect diagrams to develop a proposal for high-value hardware components for a sophisticated information system.

Total quality applied to the internal auditing function is value added

This study found that tremendous benefits can be realised by applying TQM concepts and tools within the internal auditing function itself. There is a myth that total quality management is only for manufacturing industries. Corporations such as Federal Express have successfully challenged this myth by winning the Malcolm Baldrige National Quality Award. The basic TQM philosophy of 'do it right the first time' has equal applicability within the internal auditing function itself. The internal auditing departments of corporations such as ITT Defence and Electronics, Motorola and Xerox are prime examples of such an endeavour. For those who are interested in embarking on the journey, we recommend that they start by TQMising their own operations. The results can be dramatic. Our survey results and case studies indicated that some achievements will be tangible, such as reallocation of scarce internal auditing department resources, improved productivity and cost savings, and reduction in auditing cycle time. Other intangible benefits that were reported included increased staff morale and self-esteem, higher levels of customer satisfaction, higher job satisfaction, more effective audits and meaningful recommendations that are acted upon by auditees.

Specifically, internal auditing departments can take the following steps to implement TQM within their own function:

- develop a mission and a vision statement in line with the corporation's objectives;
- establish specific internal auditing department objectives;
- establish and implement performance measures for various stages of the internal auditing process, such as planning and scoping, fieldwork, and audit report;
- identify and involve customers of the internal auditing function;
- develop and implement internal auditing customer satisfaction surveys and other feedback mechanisms;
- identify a group of peer institutions and periodically benchmark with them to evaluate your own progress;
- emphasise periodic training and education of the internal auditing staff in the tools and techniques of total quality management as well as other total-quality related areas.

The tools of quality management can be applied to the internal auditing function

Unfortunately, there is a myth that the tools and techniques of total quality management can be applied only in the manufacturing setting. This is partly because of a mind-set that equates quality initiatives with control charts and defect rates and, in general, the sometimes overwhelming (for non-technical people) concept of statistical process control.

However, this study has demonstrated that many of the quality tools and techniques can be effectively utilised in implementing TQM within the internal auditing function. For example, Xerox's Corporate Audit Department has made effective use of benchmarking on its way to becoming a world-class internal auditing department. Similarly, the internal auditing function at ITT Defence has used Quality Function Deployment to eliminate a number of unnecessary auditing steps from its audit programmes to become more effective. The organisation's internal auditing function makes heavy use of brainstorming, uses flow charts and Pareto charts for problem identification, develops cause-and-effects diagrams to understand root causes, and monitors control charts pertaining to key internal auditing metrics to control the TQM process. 'At ITT Defence', observed David Kowalczyk, then Director of Internal Audit, 'we have even involved our customer in the auditing process by having them buy-in to the auditing objectives'. This really is a unique idea. Under this approach, the internal auditor plans an engagement and 'partners' with the client to ensure that the proposed audit is what the client was looking for and that it is something that will add value to the client's operations. This approach empowers the customers, auditees, or clients by having their input in the scoping, planning, and fieldwork phase of the audit, which in turn results in acceptance of the internal auditor's recommendations.

Training is a critical success factor for any quality programme

One of the major conclusions of this study, based on survey results and the case studies, was that there is no substitute for training. The effectiveness of quality programmes really depends on genuine employee conviction and participation. While empowering employees is critical, it is effective only if they are given training on how to apply the tools and techniques of quality management. For quality programmes to be effective, employees throughout the organisation need to be trained so that, at the very least, each individual recognises the impact of his or her efforts on some specific quality goals and objectives.

In the course of our study, we observed several training models. Some organisations preferred setting up centralised training facilities, often referring to them as 'universities'. Others set up a central training team that would travel to different locations. Yet another model followed a 'cascading' approach, where selected trainees took on the role of trainers after receiving appropriate training.

While we concluded that the use of the Baldrige framework adds value, we realised that training was a necessary first step in this process. At the very outset, a core group of employees have to be trained in the Baldrige assessment process to serve as examiners and help other groups initiate their own quality programmes.

Consider

1. How do attitudes to quality management in your own organisation compare with those discussed in the case?
2. Can you identify examples of internal audit involvement in your organisation's quality programmes? Are your examples by design or driven by your organisation's quality policies?
3. Are any of the following quality characteristics used by you to achieve quality in your audit work and other services you provide?

- Use of feedback from auditees.
- A working involvement with your organisation's quality auditors.
- Issue of a quality statement by internal audit.
- Clear understanding of audit objectives between auditor and auditee.
- Supervisory reviews of audit working papers.
- Use of quality teams to focus on activities that need to be improved.
- Training of internal audit staff in techniques for quality improvement.
- Use of quality measures.
- Reviews of selected audit work by internal audit staff independent of audit.
- Reviews of selected audit work by staff outside of the internal audit department.
- Use of internal audit standards/code of ethics/statements of responsibilities.
- Use of any other quality management standards, laws, regulations as a benchmark.

Case 3.6 Marketing

(Extracted from *In Business* (1997) D22.1, ICSA Publishing, Hemel Hempstead.)

The case

Marketing overview

What is marketing? We have defined marketing as 'the identification and satisfaction of demand at a profit'. This sounds absolutely thrilling as an introduction to a business studies programme, but what does it mean? There are differing perspectives and opinions. Marketeers, marketing professionals and marketing managers tend to have a very exalted opinion of themselves. Organisations are said to be 'marketing led'. This is usually 'Fantasy Island' thinking. Marketing is a vital function. Some organisations are customer led. Most UK companies are owner, shareholder or financially led. Within this, there is scope for strategic business planning. Finance and marketing departments battle to claim this as their own. Successful companies tend to think that strategic business planning is far too important to trust to one department. It becomes the property of a multi-disciplinary group of high-achieving and quality managers, each with a broad perspective of the business.

Perhaps we should refine our definition to:

> The planned management opportunities for serious and continuous wealth creation.

Academic vs. practical

Marketing has become the darling of academe. It is less rigorous than philosophy, less polarised than politics, even less conclusive than economics, and less demanding than mathematics. There are a few towering academics whose pioneering work has changed the way we work, live and think. Anything by Philip Kotler is essential reading. The *Harvard Business Review* contains some interesting articles.

A fairly safe piece of advice is that when paying for advice upon marketing, take a long, hard look at the person offering that advice. What evidence do you have of their current levels of success at marketing themselves or their organisation? Beware of the refugee from reality who can do all sorts of very exciting things very cheaply, but doesn't actually make much of a difference.

The practical marketeer is far more pragmatic. They will draw ideas from a range of sources, including academic, and from the ever growing business advice community. The difference is that they have a clearer vision of the opportunity and more bravery to do the things which create success. Not all of them have the same ethics/values, but they do have a reality about them.

Linkage to the bottom line

We tend to associate success with good business practice. In Tom Peters and Robert Waterman's *In Search of Excellence* (Harper & Row, New York, 1982), current success was taken as an evocation of best practice. A certain philosopher called Xanamiedes once said that 'Everything is in a state of flux.' Today's Paragons are tomorrow's Pariahs. Picking winners is a risky business. Who knows where Microsoft, Intel, McDonalds, Marks and Spencer and Shell will be in the future? So, organisations which are currently successful might be good at marketing. They also might be better producers of product, better at managing their assets, better at deploying their human resource. Success can breed success.

It is much easier to consolidate your position in a market-place when you are a key player. However, you become everybody's prime target.

Probably, organisations which 'get good and stay good' have something special about them. Organisations with a long-term track record to date could be:

Organisation	Comments
Guinness	A strong brand with good consumer marketing.
GEC-Marconi	Virtually zero marketing. Good engineering. Excellent financial control.
Marks and Spencer	Good marketing. Pioneers of supplier relationships and product quality.

In conclusion, it would be a dangerous assumption that all highly successful companies have excellent marketing. They have a cohesive and viable business strategy.

Consider

1. The messages in this overview of marketing management and relate these to the marketing of internal auditing in your organisation.
2. How does the marketing of your services link into your bottom line?

CHAPTER 4

Design quality into internal audit teams

> The simple fact is that if you have the right people in the right jobs and you have teamwork you can achieve anything you want. (Interview with Erroll J. Yates, Chairman and Chief Executive of Kodak Limited, England 1990)

Add value through teamwork

Respondents in the Ziegenfuss (1994) research into small internal auditing units listed most frequently the following five challenges or opportunities:

- less resources, money and staff;
- more responsibility and more work;
- time impediments;
- more visibility and direct contact with senior management;
- the need to be more of a generalist as opposed to a specialist.

Each is a problem of its own. Collectively, they can have a significant impact on the success of internal auditing – for the good as well as the bad. Each can be addressed, and in some cases satisfied, by teamworking with others in and outside the organisation.

Creating teams to carry out tasks more successfully is not a new concept. The use of teams of all sizes, in organisations and groups, has been with us for all time, and will continue to be so. Teams are used by people of all nations and at all levels of society, for a wide variety of reasons. All teams have a number of features in common: all consist of more than one person; all have objectives which are common to all the team members; all share some form of communication between each of the team members; all have results; all have individual members with personal agendas. Until recently, all would require some form of physical contact.

Informal teams in most organisations frequently exist by accident because of the bonds that common objectives establish in a workplace, the community or society. Organisation teams can also be informal. Formal teams are those that are established with an agreed formal agenda. Usually such teams have a timescale and an identifiable product or service for their customers. In recent years many organisations have used the team concept to encourage change, quality and innovation. Training for teams is now an established practice in many organisations, across all sectors. Management in the Eastman Kodak Company promote 'teamwork' as an important part of quality leadership at all of its locations:

> The company can be viewed as a team composed of many interlocking teams, each sharing, at its interfaces, key information linked to mission, vision and other elements of organisational focus. These teams take a variety of forms and are like small businesses with customers, suppliers and processes. Each must strive to continuously improve the quality of its own outputs. Everyone is involved in quality leadership.

The company is composed of a series of interlocking teams. Because the organisational structure of the company is linked in this way, process improvements made in one part of the organisation become linked to other parts of the organisation.

Teams in the Eastman Kodak Company are seen to work most effectively when they:

- have a mission and defined deliverables;
- provide all team members with the opportunity to participate fully and to demonstrate leadership characteristics;
- have trusting and open relationships – disagreement or conflict naturally occur within a team and discussion and problem-solving methods are used to resolve it;
- establish rules of conduct that guide and regulate the group's activities. For instance, teams meet regularly and follow agendas. A unit's management team agenda may include a review of key measures and meeting notes, identification of improvement opportunities, allocation of resources to address these opportunities, and commissioning of project teams. Teams also meet scheduled deadlines;
- enable team members to communicate openly and honestly through the use of listening and responding skills;
- use appropriate problem-solving and decision-making methods;
- encourage creativity through methods such as brainstorming. Members have a tolerant attitude that allows flexibility in dealing with problems and decisions;
- examine their group processes periodically to see what is working and what is not.

Figure 4.1 Eastman Kodak Company: characteristics of an effective team

- strengths complement each other
- have a clearly defined goal that motivates team members
- high self-esteem
- play together
- pitch in
- hard working
- establish key result areas
- share information
- share responsibilities
- right skills mix
- share a vision for the future
- put team before self
- trust each other
- define operating principles
- high regard for each other
- share a clear mission
- listen effectively
- each as a leader
- define processes, customers, suppliers, outputs and inputs

Under problem-solving tools, the quality leadership process encourages team brainstorming with the benefits shown in Figure 4.1.

The National Society for Quality through Teamwork (NSQT), in the UK, has developed a structured training programme based on many years' practical experience of working with leading organisations, which have succeeded in improving performance through the effective involvement of their people. Each course is designed to help participants tackle a Key stage on the path toward creating an environment which delivers continuous improvements in performance. The following modules can be taken individually or as part of a tailored package to enhance existing improvement programmes. See Figure 4.2.

The NSQT promotes teamwork as one of the most effective ways of enabling employees at all levels to use their creative abilities to improve the performance of the organisation they work for and the quality of their own working life. Teams are an integral part of any organisation's approach to quality management or plan to improve capability by involving people. Teams can be introduced to help the organisation pursue various objectives, any of which may need special emphasis at a particular time. For example:

- development of leadership skills;
- instilling quality consciousness among all employees;
- higher quality product or service;

Figure 4.2 The NSQT team training structure

Continuous improvement
Team-building and advanced leader skills
Leadership skills and team development
Team facilitation and teamwork skills
Building improvement through teamwork
Programme steering committee workshop
Management implementation workshop
Senior management strategy workshop

Establishing self-supervising teams
Management implementation workshop
Senior management strategy workshop
Beyond continuous improvement – SSTs

Company quality programme audit
Stage 3 Maturity
Stage 2 Development
Stage 1 Readiness

- more effective use of resources;
- more individual job satisfaction;
- expanding two-way communication between employees and management;
- development of interpersonal and analytical skills in individuals;
- improvement of performance within the organisation.

When resources are limited in small internal audit units, these same objectives can be used to establish an internal audit team with cross functional membership. By such an approach the members are more likely to be motivated towards their objectives for the internal audit assignment.

Senge (1990) sees mastering team learning as a need for all organisations in today's working environments:

> This is so because almost all important decisions are now made in teams, either directly or through the need for teams to translate individual decisions into action. Individual learning, at some level, is irrelevant for organisational learning. But if teams learn, they become a microcosm for learning throughout the organisation. Insights gained are put into action. Skills developed can propagate to other individuals and to other teams (although there is no guarantee that they will propagate). The teams' accomplishments can set the tone and establish a standard for learning together for the whole organisation.

Design quality into internal audit teams 157

Use technology to make teams more effective

Recent research by Ernst & Young International, in the UK, shows that technology in internal auditing teams is already taking place:

> Internal audit departments operate a structured service delivery approach, most often using small hierarchical teams. The consensus between team leaders was that team building was managed effectively and on the job coaching worked well. Communication within the departments and between teams was considered an issue that needed to be monitored closely. Regular team meetings and annual audit conferences were promoted whilst e-mail systems have proved very successful in keeping staff working at remote locations 'in touch'.

Advances in communications now mean that for some teams it is not necessary to meet physically. Communication can be by telecommunications, computer networks and video conferencing. These communication advances have increased opportunities for national, and international teamwork. The facility to create teams across functions and organisations at local, national and international levels has never been better.

Global team working is now common place in many organisations. If it does not already exist it is likely that it is being or will be planned in the future. Successful teamworking depends on individuals being motivated to work together, empowered to seek solutions to common problems and being able to communicate with each other. Three developments that have encouraged teambuilding in organisations of all sizes are change, empowerment and technology.

Change and its current speed of implementation in most organisations has encouraged development of teams to innovate and create new structures to achieve organisation objectives. Empowered individuals have brought to teambuilding a new dimension of group creativity, encouraged by management and board members. Local issues have been overshadowed by more immediate tasks of achieving corporate goals and visions.

Both change and empowerment have been made more possible by the use and speed of information technology. Not just computers, but also communications networks, both internal and external to an organisation. These networks now permit teams to achieve their objectives, often without meeting physically, or just on a few occasions. There can be few readers of this book who are not linked by technology into one or more teams across their organisations, and even outside with other organisations.

See Case 4.1 to consider teams working across networks.

Interlock all teams in a web of common objectives

Developing a master-plan of interlocking quality teams is part of the art of good quality management. See Case 4.2 to consider teams working in interlocking webs. The same principles apply for all teams in an organisation. Because all teams operate within a web of strands linking each member and the team itself to other teams and their objectives, it is important they are seen as part of an interlocking web of common unit and organisation objectives. All team actions and results should be linked into the actions of other teams, both across and up and down the organisation structure. Designing the correct web of teams to fit an organisation's structure and culture is an important part of good management.

Create interlocking internal audit teams

Most senior management see internal audit as partners in their management teams. Early research by Mints (1972) into internal audit behavioural patterns identified the following two behavioural difficulties in audit work between the client and internal auditor:

1. present auditee relationships still reflect basic conflicts and hostility:
2. unfavourable auditee attitudes limit the auditor's ability to contribute to overall organisational goals.

Mints recommended a participative teamwork relationship between internal auditors and their clients, analysing internal audit relationships into the following three patterns:

1. Traditional audit approach

- compliance;
- protection;
- inspection.

2. Current moderate approach

- constructive;
- helpful;
- solves problems.

3. Participating teamwork approach

- involves auditee;
- develops team spirit;
- relates audit aims to auditee's goals.

Since then, this approach has been practised by many internal auditors, with some successes, particularly when developing leading edge internal auditing activities. Participation was seen to be the way internal audit could help management achieve their overall organisational goals. Current literature offers many examples of values perceived from internal audit as a partner in the management team.

There are many other opportunities in internal auditing for the creation of teams to develop and improve services provided by internal auditors. These opportunities can be found in all parts of The IIA Standards. Figure 4.3 lists examples of 'teamworking' that can facilitate the use of each of the general standards.

The following four examples show how internal audit teams can operate.

Example 1: If you come to me with a problem without a solution

The reporting of findings, conclusions and recommendations following an audit is a process which requires a high level of professionalism. 'Internal auditors should be skilled in oral and written communications so that they can clearly and effectively convey such matters as audit objectives, evaluations, conclusions and recommendations' (The IIA, Guideline 260.02).

Teamwork solves problems. The final meetings of every audit provide opportunities for the internal audit team to explain the results of their work and achievement of the objectives of their audit. These meetings can also be the time for finding solutions to key control issues – a time for suggesting solutions, based on the internal audit team's deep understanding of organisational and procedural control and a test of the team's understanding of the auditee's operating objectives – a problem to be solved.

Research into problem-solving distinguishes its three major phases under the headings 'identification', 'development' and 'selection'. The three phases are related and in sequence. They can be repeated continuously through the problem-solving process. The same research shows the cause of most difficulty in agreeing a solution as being vague or ill-defined identification of the problem itself. This first phase is an opportunity for the internal audit team to demonstrate their knowledge and skills, by clearly identifying the facts and issues causing the problem and analysing the risks being taken by the auditee. It is an opportunity for making certain that the audit working papers are complete and include support for the audit conclusions reached.

Yet is this always so! The problem-solving process at the final meetings can too often demonstrate a lack of due professional care. Remembering the problem-solving phases can help the internal audit team, not only to clearly identify the problem, but also to guide the auditee during the development and selection of a solution.

Example 2: You are my customer – you are also my supplier

The theories and practices of quality management and quality systems are all based on supply chain teams. Understanding the supply chain is an important part of performing any internal audit. Supply chains link all activities and relationships in the transformation of materials and information into a product and service: they are a complex web of teams, internal and external to the organisation and mixtures of both. They have many ownerships and agendas. They can be the whole organisation or the smallest part of a process. They are dynamic, ever-changing and snap at the weak points, causing many failures.

Figure 4.3 Examples of internal audit teams

The IIA General Standard	Teamworking
100 Independence	■ vertical line of reporting team ■ audit committee team ■ management operating teams ■ consultancy teams ■ systems development teams ■ regulators team
200 Professional Proficiency	■ networking with learning groups ■ training courses/meetings ■ membership of organisation teams ■ membership of professional groups
300 Scope of Work	■ internal audit marketing teams ■ internal control learning teams
400 Performance of Audit Work	■ audit planning teams ■ audit objective planning teams ■ audit verification and testing teams ■ audit interview teams ■ audit reporting teams ■ performance measurement teams
500 Management of the Internal Auditing Department	■ risk assessment teams ■ development of audit procedures teams ■ recruitment teams ■ training programme teams ■ internal/other auditing teams ■ internal/external quality assurance teams ■ quality improvement teams ■ networking teams with other organisations

Most, if not all supply chain theories separate supplier from customer. This is a mistake. Recognising the supplier as a customer and the customer as a supplier can have a significant impact on product and service development. Developing the right specifications for both supplier and customer interfaces is the key to quality in teamworking. Recognising that these should be developed at the same time with the same person is fundamental to high-quality achievement.

Most internal auditors will recognise the persons they audit as either primary or secondary customers: primary if they are the first priority and have direct control over whether internal audit stays in business; secondary if they are receiving an internal auditing product or service and have only an indirect control over whether internal audit stays in business. Primary can be the audit committee and senior management: secondary can be operating management and the workforce being audited.

How many internal auditors see their primary and secondary customers also as suppliers? They provide time, information, materials and sometimes processes which can add significant value to internal auditing performance. Recognising this contribution as a supply switches the internal auditor's mind-set into a different quality relationship with the auditee. It is now the turn of the internal auditor to set the quality specifications, establish a contract and measure cost, delivery and reliability. It is now the internal auditor's role to be delighted or dissatisfied.

Are you satisfied with your customers' roles as suppliers?

Example 3: Learn to recognise, applaud and reward achievement by teams

Recognising achievement is an important part of the counselling of internal auditors on their performance and professional development. It is an essential characteristic of supervision of the individual and monitoring of team and organisation performance. Encouraging achievement is fundamental to a quality culture; it distinguishes quality management from quality control; it replaces inspection with trust and respect.

IIA research into the behavioural dynamics of internal auditing identifies several different aspects of the roles internal auditors occupy in their organisations: as police they must be alert to fraud; as examiners they must be objective and analytical; as consultants they must treat their auditees as clients; as communicators they must be clear in their reporting; as teachers they must be alert to the consequences of their actions on the learning potential of others; as future managers they must be alert to the development of their careers.

Recognising achievements in each of these roles is an important responsibility for all internal audit leaders. But this is not enough. Team successes should be applauded and rewarded. Celebrate the best results with the team. Ensure that team participation is discussed at all individual internal auditor career progress and development meetings. Reflect team ability in job descriptions and pay structures.

But it is not only in the counselling of internal auditors that achievements must be recognised. For internal auditors there is a requirement for the achievements of their auditees and clients to be recognised. Achievement of team and group goals is an important part of good internal control. How that achievement is measured and applauded tells the internal auditor a great deal about the feedback mechanisms and quality cultures of the area being reviewed.

Encouragement should be given to the internal auditor to comment on auditee accomplishments in the audit report. If achievements are a powerful ally of internal control, then the internal auditor should seek to recognise their significance and whenever possible reinforce their conclusions with applause. This guidance is built into The IIA's Standard 430.05.2:

> Auditee accomplishments, in terms of improvements since the last audit or the establishment of a well-controlled operation, may be included in the audit report. This information may be necessary to fairly represent the existing conditions and to provide a proper perspective and appropriate balance to the audit report.

Example 4: Have a good audit recommendation – look for a better one from the team

The concept of continuous improvement is a process-oriented team approach to continually providing the best product and service. It applies to both the quality of audit work and the recommendations included in the final audit report. Findings arising from the performance of audit work should be discussed with appropriate levels of management during the course of an audit and problem-solving methods used to seek the best recommendations.

All of the discussions on the conclusions arising from the audit work should be team driven, involving everyone participating in the audit, including those responsible for the controls being reviewed. The internal auditor should ensure that all findings and recommendations are based on a full and clear understanding of the following:

- what standards, measures and expectations have been used in making the audit conclusions;
- the clear evidence of what exists;
- the reasons for the difference between expected and actual conditions;
- the risks being taken.

This methodical approach to the process of establishing the cause and effect of audit conclusions ensures a continuous improvement in the development of audit recommendations.

Remember, audit recommendations are best when:

- they are created by a team;
- they can be clearly linked to agreed desired results;
- they correct the cause and not just the effect;
- they are accepted by management and implemented.

(IIA Guideline 430.04)

Establish features of excellence in internal auditing teams

Recent research shows that senior management attach importance to a mix of attributes leading to excellence in internal auditing. Figure 4.4 lists this mix, which can be seen in most literature published on internal auditing.

Figure 4.4 Importance of internal audit features of excellence in teams

Professional
- competence
- technical skills
- experience
- working relationships
- staff continuity
- business understanding
- knowledge of business culture
- practical recommendations
- follow-up of results

Quality
- quality of audit work
- innovation
- customer satisfaction

Standards
- accountability for responsibilities
- flexibility
- best practice transfer
- implementation of state of art audit techniques
- ethical behaviour

These features fall into three categories:

- professional (P);
- quality (Q);
- standards (S).

PQS is a useful motif for developing objectives for all internal auditors and linking these into their team performance. It can also be used to test existing team objectives to ensure they are designed to achieve excellence. Use this motif to discuss the achievement of excellence in internal audit teams, when progressing success with individual internal auditors.

See Case 4.3 to consider how to progress and developing the best teams using success as an objective.

Seek value from innovative internal auditing teams

Recent North American research recognises a growing interest by internal audit and its clients in innovative roles for internal auditors and innovation in internal audit units and teams. Stoner and Werner (1995) contend that 'Auditors are playing internal change agent roles normally reserved for organisational development departments'. Gray and Gray (1996) hold that 'many internal audit organisations are striving to improve the quality and efficiency of their audit work', one purpose of their book being to offer examples of innovative practices that have helped internal auditors respond effectively to changes.

Gray and Gray also establish four common goals for innovation. First the change process is intended to improve the quality of the internal audit unit. Second, to increase efficiency. Third, to expand the internal audit unit, thereby increasing the value-added of internal auditing. Fourth, to boost staff skills, performance and morale. The Gray and Gray classification sorts innovations into four main types:

- behavioural;
- restructuring of the internal audit unit;
- creation of new services;
- use of technology.

Again, referring to innovation and/or creativity, Stoner and Werner conclude that:

> Whether or not they recognise it, each day internal auditors choose to be reactive or proactive toward the forces for change occurring around them. Those who choose to be reactive are endangering their careers, their organisations, or both. Financial executives must encourage their internal audit functions to seize the opportunities for new roles, greater contributions, and more satisfying work. These new opportunities to contribute to corporate competitiveness are too important to leave to chance.

See Case 4.4 to consider how one organisation uses teams to promote quality and improvement in the products and services it provides.

Avoid conflict in internal auditor/specialist/auditee teams

All team members in a mixed team of internal auditors, specialists and auditees should be clear about the role of internal auditing in an organisation. This understanding is important if conflict and other concerns are to be avoided during teamwork. Sawyer and Dittenhofer (1996) refer to this in their chapter on dealing with people:

> Internal auditors find themselves torn by conflicting forces and faced by duties and responsibilities that may seem completely irreconcilable. They owe a duty to executive management, whose work they appraise and whose pay they accept; they also owe a duty to keep the audit committee of the board of directors informed of serious weaknesses that re-detected during their appraisals.
>
> Auditors are admonished to be problem-solving partners of operating managers and help the managers improve their operation; yet auditors have a duty to be

the watchdogs of the enterprise – alert for management inefficiency, ineptitude, and even fraud. They are urged to work together in participative teamwork with operating managers, yet are required to report deficiencies to the manager's superiors.

Avoid as much conflict as possible by following the three Cadbury governance principles of openness, accountability and integrity. Explain internal audit responsibilities clearly to all team members, linking these to the organisation's objectives and vision. Provide full details of all internal audit reporting lines. Act with honesty at all times. Seek similar information from other team members. This process of sharing personal agendas can improve respect amongst team members, relationships in team working and achieve better team results.

Chapter summary

Teamwork is essential for all organisations, throughout their structures and across their supply chains. Team working takes many forms and now uses sophisticated and complex technology to improve its performance and communications. All teams are interlocking because their members belong to other teams. Good managers design a web of interlocked teams to achieve organisation goals. Internal audit teams should be a proactive part of that web. All management see features of excellence in internal audit. These features should also be seen in internal audit team work. All internal audit teams should be innovative in their objectives and results. Creating audit/auditee teams does involve relationship problems, which should be solved by a proper understanding of the internal audit role in an organisation.

Principia

1. Successful internal audit teams in an organisation's web of teams are everything.
2. Look for features of excellence in internal audit team work.
3. Use team concepts to encourage change, quality and innovation in the internal audit unit and organisation it serves.
4. Learn to recognise, applaud and reward achievement by internal audit teams.
5. Audit recommendations are best when they are created by a successful team.

Bibliography

Eastman Kodak Company. (1990) *Quality Leadership Process Guidebook* (internal publication), USA.

Ernst & Young (1997) *The Structure of Internal Audit*, London.

Fountain, Greg and Yates, Erroll J. (1990) 'The Team is Everything', *The Edge, Business Innovation and Opportunity*, UK.

Gray, G. and Gray, M. (1996) *Enhancing Internal Auditing Through Innovative Practices*, The IIA Research Foundation, USA.

Mints, F. (1972) *Behavioural Patterns in Internal Audit Relationships*, The Institute of Internal Auditors Research Foundation, USA.

Sawyer, Lawrence B. and Dittenhofer, Mortimer A. (1996) *Sawyer's Internal Auditing*, The IIA Inc., USA

Senge, Peter M. (1990) *The Fifth Discipline*, Random House, London.

Stoner, J. and Werner, F. (1995) *Internal Audit and Innovation*, Financial Executives Research Foundation, Morristown, New Jersey, USA.

The IIA (1996) *Standards for the Professional Practice of Internal Auditing*, The IIA Inc., USA.

Ziegenfuss, Douglas E. (1994) *Challenges and Opportunities of Small Internal Audit Organisations*, The IIA Research Foundation, USA.

Case 4.1   Teams and work groups – working across networks

(Extracted from *In Business* (1997) A2 1.6, ICSA Publishing, Hemel Hempstead)

The case

Popularity of team working

In a survey, 79 per cent of UK respondents said that an increase in teamworking was one of the ways that their organisation was responding to current challenges. The way teams work, and the way they are understood is changing. Teams or work groups now tend to be flexible and temporary, as in a project team. Members of the team may not work in the same place, even going so far as having a 'virtual team'. People may belong to several different teams or project groups at the same time. Leadership may be rotated or shared, depending on the phase of the project being undertaken.

Many team projects require the team to learn fast, as well as to carry out a task. This needs to be acknowledged in the review process.

Working context

The context of the team affects the way it works. For example, if the task outcomes and resources available are determined from outside (as they often are)

this will mean that some or all of the members of the team need to be able to interact astutely with others outside the team. This implies:

1. connecting and networking with key players outside the; team;
2. watching out for changes in the setting, internal politics, etc.;
3. protecting the team against interference and excessive demands (often the role of the project leader).

This kind of activity is described as 'managing the boundaries'.

Teams and control

Few teams or projects have control over all the factors that contribute to their success. Increasingly, success depends on being able to understand and manage complex interrelationships, both within and outside the organisation and being able to influence people over whom you have no direct control. Occasionally deadlines need to be renegotiated; and an understanding of the knock-on effect on others is essential in this role.

The team is often working under great pressure to tight deadlines; ways of managing stress therefore need to be found as part of the overall team task.

Team composition

The make-up of the team is important; there will be variable choice in this. It is occasionally possible to choose the team. Wise project leaders choose for a variety of temperament and personal style, as well as the appropriate skills and knowledge. Where choice is not possible, finding different and appropriate ways to motivate and manage the team is essential, with the key aim of making it possible for all members to contribute in their own most effective way. The leader needs to let go of assumptions about how the team members ought to be, and reflect on how they actually are, and what they get out of working in a team or on a project. Achieving the task may be only one motivation: others may include recognition, a sense of belonging, doing something worthwhile, working to one's full potential.

The challenge to a team or project group is fourfold:

1. To maintain a picture of the overall end goal (and how it may change in response to organisational changes).
2. At the same time, focusing on the short-term tasks that will achieve the goal.
3. To attend to the process or 'soft' issues that will maintain motivation, effectiveness and commitment through the ups and downs of a project or task.
4. To notice, review and record the learning that is taking place.

This is done by having a clear picture of what is being aimed for, and being able to let people know what is required, while at the same time hearing from them what they think is needed. Collecting and sharing information on a continuing basis is essential, both 'hard' and 'soft' information about the organisational framework and about people's individual situations and preferences.

Although teamworking is becoming increasingly important in organisational life, it is noticeable that the reward system does not always match this change. It is important to find ways to ensure that the reward system is geared to support team success as well as individual achievement; otherwise, you may find the reward system sabotaging rather than encouraging good practice.

The skills of working across boundaries that are increasingly required for successful teamwork are also important in networks, and other loose but important connections. Networking can be described as actively taking steps to build relationships and contacts with people who can help you keep informed and get things done. Being able to sense what is important to other people and build on that is more useful in this respect than trying to get them to see things from one's own point of view. It is important that your network represents a win-win situation for the people involved in it, as the whole principle of networking is mutual gain.

Networks are facilitated by information technology: newsgroups, discussion groups and the Internet can provide relevant and accurate support and information which make it possible for people to be in contact at a distance.

Consider

1. Understand how the teamworking principles in the case apply in your own organisation and internal audit unit.
2. Apply the principles to the work of all your internal auditing teams.
3. How positive and well designed are your own networking teams?

Case 4.2   The team is everything

(Interview with Erroll J. Yates, Chairman and Managing Director, Kodak Limited, UK, 1990, reported by Greg Norman in *The Edge*, and reprinted with permission from Kodak Limited.)

The case

Success is all about teamwork. It makes no difference whether your company has two employees or 200,000, they're still a team, and if they fail to work together as a team then you're wasting your time and you're wasting them. Erroll J. Yates is a firm believer in the power of the team effect. It's served him well right the way down the line, and never more so than now, when his task is to head an 8,000-strong company spread out over a number of sites all around the country.

'The simple fact is that if you have the right people in the right jobs and you have teamwork you can achieve anything you want,' he says. 'I am a great believer in that – it is my philosophy in life. You can have 11 brilliant people, the very best in their fields, but if they are not a cohesive team they are not the best. It is the same principle as in sport. Often 11 less brilliant people can achieve more if they work as a team.'

When Yates took over in 1987 he set about the considerable task of finding out what his people felt at grass roots level. He had over 75 breakfast meetings all around the country with staff of all levels. 'The idea was to find out how they perceived the company,' he says. 'They were "no holds barred" meetings – people said what they thought. The problem of communication kept coming out again and again, and bad communication is a barrier to teamwork. We have identified it as a major problem.'

Developing an internal communication strategy was a clear priority, and what has emerged at Kodak is the 'Speak to Me' campaign. But it goes much further than that. 'We set up a management communication committee which met once a week and was made up of 12 people representing all areas of the company,' says Yates. 'This was a forum to communicate all the relevant major issues that had occurred since the last meeting. That committee has now become the company management committee, and meets for two-and-a-half hours every Tuesday. Gradually that cohesive team is now beginning to manage the company.' But communication is only part of the story of continuous improvement at Kodak, where complacency and a lack of attention to total quality had threatened the company position in a competitive market.

'Inside a number of us was the feeling that we had lost our way a bit,' says Yates. 'We had become arrogant. It didn't matter what the customer wanted, it was what we wanted that mattered. It was an inbuilt feeling that we had to do something. What we did in September 1987 was to get Bill Conway, the American quality guru, to take 70 people down to Eastbourne and get the quality programme rolling.

'In terms of manufacturing we were way ahead on quality but that did not permeate throughout the company. We realised that quality is not a flavour of the month – it is a relentless stream that has to flow and flow. It is a process that has to be taught – that has to start at the top and work downwards, and work the other way around as well.

'Back in 1987 we had only 120 management staff, and there was evidence that we were losing key people because we were not keeping up with key practices. We increased those 120 to 420 overnight, and introduced benefits like cars and health plans. Those 420 people come to meetings twice a year where we discuss results and accentuate the positive things we have achieved. It has worked extremely well. The quality has permeated right through the company. We have a quality council once a quarter, and quality half-days in various parts of the company, and it is amazing to see what has been achieved by making people feel part of the whole thing. I have come across people whose whole lives have literally been transformed by the new responsibilities they now have. In the quality council the customer is king. If you don't have customers you don't have a business. That is the hallmark of our quality programme.'

Yates is an enigmatic and likeable leader, a 59-year-old accountant with 33 years of service to Kodak behind him, and a total dedication to the welfare of the company. As the top man he resides in a spacious office 17 floors above Hemel Hempstead's magic roundabout, but he does not believe himself to be any more important than any one other individual in any one department of the company. Kodak is a matrixed organisation, managed by committees, councils and business divisions, and it operates on the basis of total involvement for everybody.

'You can't have a company strategy stating that people are your most important asset and then not keep them informed of what's going on,' he says. 'I do two or three videos every year to the whole company to keep them in the picture. I am as factual as possible and I do my best never to hide anything. I give them the bad news as well as the good news, and then anybody can see what are the real issues. It's too important to keep everything in perspective. Being the major subsidiary of a US corporation we can get press releases faxed to us from Eastman Kodak in the States and everybody gets to see them next day, but sometimes it's possible to misinterpret the significance of a company announcement in UK terms.'

Yates cited the example of a local newspaper in the Nottingham area – where Kodak have a 500-strong site – which picked up a US-originated press notice regarding cutbacks being made by the company. The banner headline 'Kodak to cut by X per cent' was accurate to the press release, but bore no relation to Nottingham and had nothing whatsoever to do with the UK operation as a whole. 'That sort of thing can cause problems,' he says. 'There is a clear communication gap there.'

'Everything that Kodak could hope to achieve in rectifying communications difficulties, improving standards and implementing total quality management relies on the ability of the whole company to pull in the same direction. No good intentions are worth a light without clear and concrete goals towards which to work, and with that in mind the company has initiated a system of Key Result Areas. These become the subject of heavy assessment per quarter,' says Yates. 'I have 12 KRAs for 1990, and the company looks upon mine as the company's. It creates a concrete goal, and performance management is so important. The first of the KRAs is pursuit of quality, a standard which will no doubt enjoy a permanent slot on the list for a long time to come. Customer focus, the second KRA, should likewise be set hard and strictly adhered to.'

Yates' list goes on to more specific areas of improvement, including the reorganisation of resources to meet the European challenge ('Kodak in Europe will be very different and we had better be ready,' he says), improving the working environment and completing the company pay strategy. He understands that despite the giant strides taken over the last three years, there is still, and will always be, much to do. 'We do still have a morale problem in some areas, I'd be the last one to hide that,' he says. 'Some of the people not directly involved in the restructuring may feel at the moment that they are in a bit of nomansland, but we will work very hard on that. It is very important that we provide for everyone.'

'We have something called a management succession and development council, which is as far as I'm concerned the most important of our councils because it is so vital to the future. It's all very well to work on how good you are as a manager, but if you are not going to train the next generation of managers and see that they are going to be better than you are then you are wasting your time. We are not talking about spotlighting tomorrow's whizzkids but making sure that everybody is trained and has a high level of job satisfaction.' Working towards that aim can mean every little detail, including, for example, in providing crèches for those whose main concern is not just self-advancement but caring for their children while the work gets done.

The crèche scheme at Kodak has, says Yates, been developed as part of the quality process and treated with the same level of importance as everything else. 'The point is that quality has to be part of everyday life – it encompasses every aspect and has to be a state of mind rather than something you have to consciously think about. We have spent a great deal of money to bring this building up to standard and I now believe that the facilities we offer are vastly superior to what they were, both for visitors, and, more importantly, for those who work here day in day out.'

Getting the commitment of his people to work towards the greater good has been the success story for Yates, and that must now be tempered with the provision of greater efficiency too. 'Every company has 20 to 40 per cent waste, which is a shocking thought,' he says. 'If we started out with about 40 per cent waste I believe we have got it down to 15 to 20 per cent now, but you have to keep pushing change through. I don't believe I'll ever get to the stage where I've done it all and achieve a level of perceived total quality. That's not possible. What we have set out on is a cultural change – a change in philosophy. You will always get cynics at the beginning when you try to do something new but we have had a good response and the rest will come through.

'You have to ask yourself, does everything you do add value to the company? If it doesn't, then why are you doing it? The day you can get every one of your 8,000 people to refrain from doing even a single thing that doesn't add value will be the day that quality is home and dry. That day can't ever come, but the challenge is to get as close to it it's possible to get. And then to get closer still.'

Consider

The importance placed by top management on the building of teams throughout its structures, to improve:

172 Leading edge internal auditing

- quality;
- communications;
- performance;
- motivation;
- management succession;
- commitment;
- adding value.

Case 4.3 Is success what you do, or what the team does?

The case

Success should not be the aim.

The aim should be to improve.

Improvement requires controlled change.

Change is best controlled when it is seen as a continuous process of selection, education and development opportunities.

Processes should always start with commitment to a vision.

A vision that must be right for the time.

Visions require measured strategies and tactics.

The achievements of strategies and tactics depend on the control of people.

People in the supply chain depend on each other for success.

To succeed as individuals is not enough.

All people in the supply chain need to belong to successful teams.

All people in the supply chain need the reinforcement of successful lives.

The role of all managers is to control.

Control requires an understanding of its objectives.

Each control objective impacts and influences success in people.

It's the way people succeed that controls the successful organisation.

Good managers in the best organisations select, educate and develop the best people and teams

The aim of every organisation should be to improve. This means not only the structure and processes, not only the people that make up the organisation, but also the people who surround the organisation, as part of its supply chains. It also means the community which it serves. Improvement generates success. Improvement does not happen by accident, it has to be controlled as a process of change. Continuous improvement is now a way of life in organisations across the world. It knows no national boundaries. The quality it creates is the way of business and government everywhere. It thrives on benchmarking and the search for best practices. It recognises change as a continuous cycle of selection, education and development.

The cycle of selection, education and development is at the heart of all human activity. It always has been and always will be. Best management of that cycle in others requires an understanding of how the cycle works for yourself. We all learn, from the day we are born, to the day we die. At first, the selection stage is mainly by others – we are fully controlled. We soon move into our own selection process and from thereon life is a mixture of choices by ourselves and others. Each and every day, each and every moment we are making and being subjected to a selection process. The choices we make forge our destiny. They create the opportunities and emotions we experience all our lives. They contribute to our failures and successes.

In any organisation, it is management's role to communicate clearly the choices people have and the results expected from those choices. Some may call this control, others opportunity. Perhaps, it is always a mixture of both. Selection is best if it is communicated as opportunity. The art of management is to be a good communicator: to communicate the importance of selection in the minds of people: to help choice.

But selection is not the end. Selection starts the education process. Being taught and teaching oneself are everyday experiences. This activity is often seen as the learning curve. In an organisation it starts the day people are employed and continues until the day of leaving. It is at its best when motivated by a feeling of self-selection. 'I choose to learn' is better than 'you will learn'. The good manager will encourage education self-selection. It drives the best understanding, A search for knowledge through education stimulates innovation.

'How, what, why, when, where, and who' are the six honest working men of Rudyard Kipling's *Just So* stories. They are as true today as they always have been. They are fundamental to invention and progress. They are the questions all people should ask as they learn.

But education is not the end. Education by itself is not sufficient for success. Education requires development. And development does not come by accident; it needs to be planned. Planned development is a skill in itself. All tasks require a period of training. For some tasks and people this training is brief: for other tasks and people it is a long and sometimes continuous process. Recognising the time needed for development is an important part of good management, in oneself and in others.

Committing time for development in oneself and others is not always easy. Pressure and stress, even in controlled change, can reduce the time available for development. We have all experienced reduction of staff and training costs: what follows can too often be a reduction of time spent on development, both at work and at home. Yet, development is the key to success. It always will be the key to successful change. Good managers recognise this. Those that train recognise this. Professions recognise this. Governments recognise this. Why is it then that development receives such a low priority with some managers and some people? To know the answer to this is the key to success.

But good managers and good people do not stop at development. The cycle of selection, education and development starts all over again. It is a continuous process and because of this needs direction; it needs vision.

A vision is a forecast of a future desired state at a point in time, which is attractive to the beholder. All people have visions. Visions change: they need to be appropriate to their time. Not all people use their visions to select, educate and develop themselves or others. Good managers create visions for organisations and, through the cycle of selection, education and development establish commitment for the future state. Commitment not just by people but by teams of people. Once the vision is agreed, key strategies and tactics must follow, linked and measured to the required future state.

A wish for success is part of everyone's vision, though the measure may be different for each person. Personal visions need to be built into team and group visions. All visions should stretch people and teams to improve. All visions should demand change for the better. All visions should aim for success. The art of good management is to establish and achieve visions by the cycles of selection, education and development of people and teams. Creating the wish to succeed in people makes success happen.

Establishing visions and commitment is not easy. Using measures for each strategy involves all people in the process. That involvement can be made easier and more quickly if managers follow the selection, education and development cycle for everyone participating in the associated supply chains. This means considering people who are employed by suppliers and customers. The good manager helps people in both suppliers and customers to succeed. The good manager builds suppliers and customers into their teams. This means that suppliers and customers must also help their people to select, educate and develop. Good managers recognise this.

But is success by people in an organisation sufficient reward and reinforcement for others to follow? All research and evidence shows that this is not so. People need to be successful in all parts of their lives, or at least to feel success. This is a tall order! How can managers help people to succeed in their lives outside the workplace? Such a question is not irrelevant. Many organisations and managers have recognised the importance of opportunities for their people to be successful in activities other than work. Provision of resources and time to select, educate and develop in families, hobbies, sports and pastimes is not new. What is new is the reduction of these facilities in times of change. Yet such reduction takes away opportunities for people to be successful, which is not what an organisation wants. Too often, managers are seen to be short-sighted in the opportunities they provide for selection, education and development both inside and outside the workplace. Yet the key to their own success lies in such opportunities.

The continuous cycles of selection, education and development in and around any organisation and supply chain, need to be managed. This means they need to be controlled. Many will say that they are controlled in the best organisations. But are they? Linking each of the processes to the primary objectives of control provides managers with a useful framework to test how successful they are. The objectives of control can be analysed as:

- reliability;
- compliance;
- security;
- economy;
- efficiency;
- effectiveness;
- environmental;
- ethics;
- equality.

None of the above needs explanation to any manager. They are all part of the decision making process in every organisation, whether by people or the teams they form. Some are more recent as objectives than others. All are changing shape and definition as we move into the twenty-first century. Without exception, each is becoming more demanding: each is becoming a requirement, not only of the organisation, but also of the community, nation and world. Yet few managers approach success in their people through the achievement of each. Any success which does not recognise all these control objectives, fails to make the most of people.

All control activities should require each of the nine objectives to be achieved. Every vision, strategy and tactic in an organisation can be influenced by the quality of performance of each. Penalty for failure to achieve any one of the objectives can make the difference between success or failure, survival or demise. Good managers realise this and use control objectives to influence the cycles of selection, education and development in the people they manage. Corporate history is full of organisations which ignored these relationships: full of the managers who did not link success in people to the management of control and change.

In the same way that visions and success are a moment in time, so is control. Each requires consideration of past and present when planning the future. The framework for controlling the cycles of selection, education and development takes on a multi-dimensional model. It is a clear understanding by managers of this fundamental law of success and control, which helps most people succeed. Success is the key motivation for change: controlled success breeds successful change.

Success, good, better, best, excellent and delight are the hallmarks of customer satisfaction. Each has an association with success – in organisations, their products, services and the people they employ. We all recognise these associations, but few analyse the controls that influence each, or award success the applause it so often deserves. Control is the key to success. Applause should be seen as an accolade, not an embarrassment.

How should performance in people be applauded? Is applause seen by people to be more an embarrassment than a reward? Are managers well trained to recognise success, reinforce its achievement or punish failure? There are clearly mixed good and bad reinforcement and punishment practices within and between all organisations. Few recognise the importance of relating such best practices to the control of selection, education and development. If it were otherwise, the number of people succeeding would increase many times. There would be no need for training awards and the focus on helping people to succeed would have a high profile in every organisation. Good reinforcement and punishment administered through the process of change is at the heart of all success.

Helping people to succeed through their cycles of selection, education and development is the only future for any organisation. It is also the only future for any community, nation or the world. Linking that help into personal and group visions is essential. Linking that help into the objectives of control in an organisation ensures success, both for the organisation and the people it employs and serves.

Consider

Using the case guidelines to measure success and improvements through your internal auditing team focus on the following features in Figure 4.4:

Professional

- competence
- technical skills
- experience
- working relationships
- staff continuity
- business understanding
- knowledge of business culture
- practical recommendations
- follow-up of results

Quality

- quality of audit work
- innovation
- customer satisfaction

Standards

- accountability for responsibilities
- flexibility
- best practice transfer
- implementation of state of art audit techniques
- ethical behaviour

Case 4.4 Post Office Counters Ltd: the quality journey

(Paper presented by George Hooper (1997) at the proceedings of the 2nd World Congress for Total Quality Management, reprinted from *Total Quality Management*, Volume 8 Numbers 2 & 3, pp. S187-S190.)

The case

Early years

The Post Office was split into the constituent four organisations of Royal Mail, Post Office Counters Ltd (POCL), Subscription Services Ltd and Parcel Force, in 1987 with the intention of allowing each business to concentrate more fully on its own areas of activity. The Chief Executive of the Post Office at this time was Sir Brian Nicholson, who actively promoted the need for each of the businesses to develop a total quality programme. John Roberts, then MD of POCL, led the development of the badged 'customer first' programme, which contained the following four principles: customer focus; people-based management; management by fact; and continuous improvement. This launch was accompanied by a trip to the US of several dozen senior managers within the business, in order to benchmark organisations with a long history of total quality, and drive in the importance of the message of 'leading from the top'. Simultaneously, dedicated quality support managers were appointed for each business unit with the specific objective of supporting the programme, managing the roll-out, and challenging the accepted methods of working and managing.

Prior to the roll-out, a comprehensive survey of attitudes and concerns of all sections of staff and agents was undertaken within the business, known as 'national diagnostics'. This demonstrated considerable concern and low morale within the business caused by inflexible management methods and attitude, distrust of communication and management; and little understanding of the concepts of quality, internal customers, or of the needs of external customers.

The roll-out, based around a training cascade delivered on a learn-use-lead format to all managers and staff, took over 18 months to complete, with each manager having to implement some of the programme, and participate in quality improvement project, before going on to train his/her own staff with the assistance of a quality support manager, in the principles of total quality and the use of several simple tools and techniques. Two key elements in this initial stage were leadership feedback system and quality improvement projects.

Leadership behaviour has been a comprehensive programme of identifying and continuously refining the leadership values and skills required within the organisation, and the development of a systematic process by which all managers must regularly measure their progress and behaviour with their teams and peers. This involves the use of anonymous input by a manager's team and peers against his/her performance against a range of specified behaviours, conducted at six-monthly intervals and leading to the display of a personal action plan, achievement of which is a personal objective. This is compulsory for all managers, with face-to-face feedback to managers given by quality managers.

Quality improvement projects were intended to involve as many staff and managers as possible in attempting to improve elements of their work, based on a quality improvement wheel with four elements: focus, plan, do and review. A database was set up of such activity in an attempt to identify and spread best practice.

'Customer first' steering groups were initially set up by the management teams with each business unit in order to drive the development and improvement of quality, and to specifically target issues of development.

A large programme of qualitative and quantitative research on external customer requirements, known as SMART (Salient Multi Attribute Research Technique) was developed. This allowed accurate identification of the service attributes of most concern to customers in various types of outlet, and has been consistently tracked since its inception to enable identification of trends, and changes in customer preferences.

Roll-out of 'customer first' continued into the agency network of about 19,000 outlets, necessitating a huge programme of training and communication, and accompanied in all outlets by the use of a customer questionnaire, issued annually or biannually, dependent on the size of the outlet, and leading to the identification of specific improvement opportunities in each outlet.

Difficulties

Initial progress was impressive, with significant staff involvement, and a significant development in management attitudes, as the threats of competition and the need for a more elective customer focus became more widely understood. However, difficulties were experienced as management and staff struggled to understand how to merge quality with 'business as usual', the two still being seen as separate activities by many. It also became increasingly difficult to measure effectively the success of the quality programme, or to demonstrate the value added, at a time when commercial constraints were becoming ever more evident.

Design quality into internal audit teams 179

To add to these difficulties, a significant reorganisation was undertaken in 1993/4, during which some 30 districts were re-formed into seven regions, and a clearer focus established in the centre on business development, with the establishment of two business units aimed at the development of new and existing business, and ensuring closer links with clients in the process.

Business excellence

The business excellence model was adopted in 1994, as offering a clear and usable framework with which to 'bring quality to life'. It offered not only a measurement system, enabling progress to be established, but also a clear model linking activities to the results achieved, and, as such, offered a development along the quality road from 'customer first'.

A strategic objective has been agreed upon by the CEC (Counters Executive Committee) to 'be a recognised benchmark of excellence', and to measure progress against this goal both internally and externally by reviewing against the business excellence model. The external measures come from applying for either the UK or European awards annually, with a target of scoring over 700 points by 1999 – the intention here is to keep the focus internally on using the model as a 'vehicle for change', against which progress can be measured, rather than going specifically for an award.

The decision was taken that all business units should undertake reviews against the model, and in order for this to happen, the 120 top managers in the business were trained as assessors internally. Following this initial training, in 1994/5 and again in 1995/6, all business units produced submission documents, outlining their activities and results against the model, which were assessed by teams of assessors from other units. The results from these initial reviews showed the following:

- low deployment of national approaches, or limited data on levels of deployment;
- low scoring overall (*c.* 200–300 out of 1000);
- poor links between enablers and results;
- a tendency in initial action planning resulting from review feedback to be over-ambitious;
- consistently low scores for process management;
- considerable investment of management time in training and supporting and preparing for reviews.

Business units then drew up dedicated business excellence plans to address the identified improvement areas, and commenced the integration of such plans into their normal planning process.

Following these initial reviews, the business undertook a top objective to design and implement a programme of process management, which commenced roll-out in 1996: this involved the identification and mapping of all the business's critical processes, and the design of a management process and structure by which the business could begin to manage these processes in parallel with the current functional structure.

Other methods of self-assessment used include: management team workshops; use of the Unit Excellence package; and self-assessment for small teams.

Developments

Process management

Following the indications from the initial business excellence reviews that the management of processes by POCL was very poor, a considerable amount of work has been undertaken to address this gap. The critical processes have been identified and mapped, and the business has defined a process management structure, which should complement the current functional structure in order to ensure that management by process is put in place in the business.

Team route to excellence

This is a systematic process which all teams must follow, which necessitates their identification of all customers and their requirements, and use of this information to design appropriate improvement activity, as well as display this information on a specially designed poster. This has proved a powerful tool, not only for ensuring clarity among teams as to their purpose and customers, but also for ensuring alignment of objectives at team level with both organisational and individual objectives.

Policy deployment

This is a Japanese planning process (also known as *hoshin* planning) which involves a 'catchball' process to ensure that strategic objectives are fed down the organisation quickly, and that all levels of management are involved in assessing their capabilities for delivering these objectives, agreeing how they will do so and feeding these back up. As such, it is a significant development on traditional 'top-down' planning techniques, and is currently being piloted in POCL as a way of delivering network transformation. This will involve the development of outlets' locations and appearance in order to deliver increased volume of sales.

Approach dictionary

One of the key learning points from early attempts to identify and spread best practice was the variation in understanding of national approaches against the business excellence model, leading to different interpretation and deployment within business units. Consequently, an exercise is currently being undertaken to develop a clear 'dictionary' of all national approaches: this will allow greater consistency between business units in their understanding and use of these approaches, enable better measurement and management of deployment, and facilitate the production and scoring of business unit submissions.

Future states

To understand the actions required to achieve the objective of scoring over 700 points against the business excellence model by 1999, an exercise has commenced which attempts to describe how the business will look once it has achieved this objective, and then clearly identify the steps required between now and then in order to do so. This has significant implications for the development of the vision of the organisation, which needs to be clearly aligned.

Conclusions

In summary, the benefits and difficulties experienced by POCL in its total quality journey are:

Benefits

- Motivation of staff;
- clear identification of the importance of internal and external customers;
- alignment of individual and team objectives with those of the organisation;
- culture of continuous improvement;
- greater understanding of the need for clear leadership.

Difficulties

- Continuing motivation and innovation in the face of organisational change;
- quantitative measure of progress;
- identification of financial benefit in the short term;
- maintaining the impetus of quality programmes;
- merging quality and 'business as usual'.

Consider

1. The quality environment in which the POCL teams are working and compare these with your own organisation's quality environment and teamworking.
2. Identify similarities and explore how these are successful, using the team principles discussed in this chapter.

182 Leading edge internal auditing

3. How can the experiences of the POCL be implemented in developing teams of internal auditors, specialists and their customers, to improve the professionalism, quality and standards (PQS) of your internal auditing services?

PART II

Internal auditing procedures

CHAPTER 5

Audit planning

> A man that looks on glass,
> On it may stay his eye;
> Or if he pleaseth, through it pass,
> And then the heaven espy.
>
> ('The Elixir', George Herbert (1633))

Applying risk assessment to the development of audit plans at all levels

Internal auditors should plan their work. This includes planning for the long-term development of the internal audit function, planning the future programme of audits to be conducted and planning the conduct of each internal audit assignment. The first of these three is the most long term, but the term 'strategic planning' is, as in the second part of this chapter, more commonly applied by internal auditors to the second.

This chapter has two parts. First we examine the approach to conducting individual audit assignments effectively. Then, in Part B, we turn our attention to conducting an audit needs assessment in order to determine which audit assignments should be conducted, their timing and the levels of internal audit resource to be allocated to each assignment.

Part A: Planning and conducting an audit assignment

This topic is very broad and it is only possible to highlight some of the issues and to explore them to a limited extent. Specific issues which internal auditors are likely to need to address in common audit areas are provided in Appendix G.

Understanding the audit as a project

An audit is a project with a definite beginning and end. A number of activities occur during the audit and their completion points are specific events within the project. The terms *activities* and *events* are borrowed from the principles of project management – others might use the expression 'stages of the audit'.

Being projects, audits expose auditors to the experience of project-oriented work and of project management. Audits thus equip auditors with an approach to work and to management which is very contemporary and which corresponds to a growing proportion of activity within modern businesses which are project-oriented. The auditor in charge of the fieldwork of an audit as well as the person to whom he or she reports are engaged in the management of projects, and the staff in the audit team are working in a project environment.

One of the big challenges of project work is completing projects. Completion may be delayed unnecessarily. In extreme cases, completion may be deferred indefinitely when the project team is disbanded or if its members move on to new projects before completion of the earlier projects. The managerial and administrative skills associated with constantly commencing, conducting and completing projects are very special skills and the experience of using these skills can be very demanding and stressful.

The psychology of the audit project

Later we explore the activities and events which are parts of the audit project. First we should touch on the so-called 'behavioural aspects' of audit work. Not all project work has such a pronounced interface between two different principal parties involved – which we may call the *auditor* and the *auditee*. We should only use the word *auditee* in audit circles, as it is audit jargon which is likely to fail to communicate effectively and may even offend others. Internal auditors are known to have considerable built-in formal authority – usually vested in their *charter* (or terms of reference). Effective internal audit work requires auditors to develop good working relationships with auditees for the following reasons:

- Auditors need the co-operation of auditees.
- Many of the most valuable audit findings and recommendations are likely to be suggested to auditors by helpful, forthcoming auditees.
- Auditors depend upon auditees to accept and wholeheartedly implement audit recommendations. Imposed changes have been shown to have a very high risk of failure.
- Auditors are the same as everyone else. They are social creatures who suffer in terms of esteem and work satisfaction if they are cold-shouldered by others.

The very significant levels of built-in authority which are implicit and explicit in the audit role are hard to balance by the needed, softer, co-operative qualities. Whereas auditors will endeavour to project themselves as friendly, helpful advisors, they may be stereotyped as spies and snoops sent by top management to check up on affairs and staff. Auditees may feel threatened by the audit process.

Audits conducted on a surprise basis are particularly threatening. Surprise visits should be minimised – reserved for situations where essential audit objectives depend upon an element of surprise. Frequently 'audits' conducted on a surprise basis are likely to comprise of internal check work which line management should use their own resources to undertake and which it should not be the responsibility of internal audit to perform.

Due to the tension which may sometimes exist between auditors and auditees, it is better from this viewpoint that audit fieldwork is conducted by teams of auditors rather than by sole auditors working on their own. The boundaries of the audit scope can often be specified so that more than one auditor can be assigned to the audit fieldwork. Teams of auditors can provide reassurance to each other, as well as inspiration in the conduct of audit work. Audits conducted on a team basis allow a useful division of responsibilities between the members of the audit team – especially the distinction and therefore specialisation between team leadership and some of the more detailed audit checking work. It is not easy for a sole auditor to move repeatedly between the audit fieldwork management role and the detailed audit work role. Nevertheless, downsized internal audit functions with wider terms of reference will frequently mean that audits have to be conducted by a single auditor working on his or her own.

The nub of the behavioural challenge of internal auditing is that internal auditors are both inspectors and advisors. They have these two roles which are in conflict with each other. An inspector has formal authority, vested in the office he or she holds and reinforced by coercive sanctions. An advisor has informal authority vested in his or her personal qualities and reinforced by suggestion and persuasion. If an auditor were to jettison the inspectorial role, the auditor would become an internal management consultant only and management would have lost a key element of their internal auditing function. If the auditor were to jettison the advisory role, the auditor would become merely an authoritarian inspector and much of the practical benefit which would usually result from internal auditing work would be lost.

Much of the benefit which results from internal auditing work relates to the acceptance and successful implementation of audit recommendations and this is much less likely to happen if the auditors are perceived as being threatening.

Role conflict – where people are required to discharge two or more roles which are in conflict with each other – is by no means unique to auditors. For instance, to give an obvious example, most people with a career find that their work is in conflict with their family responsibilities at times. The mature approach is to carry the conflicting roles in harness as far as possible, avoiding the worst excesses of each. The answer to internal audit role conflict invariably is *not* to drop one of the conflicting roles.

For internal auditors it is not just that they have at least these two roles which are in conflict with each other. The challenge is also that the stereotype image of the auditor invariably corresponds to one of these roles only – the inspectorial role. If internal auditors are unsuccessful in projecting a balanced image of themselves, their effectiveness will be impeded. In a very real sense we are able to act out the role (or roles) which others perceive us to have. In general terms it is therefore wise for internal auditors to soft peddle on the authoritarian side and to endeavour to emphasise that they are friendly, constructive people who have come to help. A lot of auditor energy will need to be expended on this if the authoritarian, inspectorial image of the auditor is to be countered so that internal auditing is more effective.

That is not to say that auditors should lose their authority – just that they should not emphasise it unnecessarily and *should* emphasise their helpful, constructive role. It remains important for instance that auditors should have unrestricted access to information and personnel, that they should have the authority to conduct audits at times of their choosing and of a scope determined by them, that they should have the right to refer matters of audit concern where necessary to top levels of line management and to the audit committee of the board – and so on.

Understanding the activities of an audit

Not every audit follows a standard sequence of activities. For instance, some audit assignments may be limited to confirming compliance with laid down procedures, whereas others will entail a full review of internal control. It also needs to be understood that the activities of an audit will tend to overlap with each other: our discussion of them here should not be misinterpreted to imply that each follows the previously discussed activity. Nevertheless, for simplicity we discuss them broadly in the order in which they feature during an internal audit. The main audit activities are as follows:

- preparation for the audit;
- fact finding and documentation;
- compliance testing;
- completing the assessment of internal control;
- weakness testing;
- audit reporting;
- concluding the audit;
- audit follow-up.

In addition to these main activities, other activities occur during the course of the audit to facilitate the completion of the main activities. These include, for instance:

- meetings;
- compiling audit working papers;
- supervision of auditors and review of audit work.

Preparing for the audit

Thorough preparation is important and will usually take place mainly in the internal audit department's office rather than at the location of the audit fieldwork. It includes:

- familiarisation of the audit team with the audit topic, making use of:
  - background information
  - previous audit working papers
  - the knowledge and experience of other auditors and locally available line management;
- determination of the scope and objectives of the audit, in consultation with senior line management and with internal audit management;
- design of the audit programme, in consultation with management;
- agreement with line management on the timing of the audit fieldwork and the composition of the audit team;
- opening of a set of audit working papers;
- administrative arrangements for the audit fieldwork, including travel, hotel and office arrangements and budget allocation.

Making introductions

Before the audit fieldwork commences it is desirable, when possible, that the team leader of the audit is introduced in person to the line manager who heads the activity to be audited by a more senior internal auditor who already knows that line manager.

At the commencement of the fieldwork, the audit team leader should make a point of introducing him or herself and the audit team to the senior line manager of the activity to be audited and of asking that line manager to make the appropriate introductions of the audit team to the line manager's staff.

These introductions will often be associated with a tour of the premises, which is a valuable opportunity for the audit team to further familiarise themselves with the subject of the audit.

By the conclusion of this introductory phase, line management should be fully appraised of (a) the scope and objectives of the audit, (b) its planned duration, and (c) the pattern of communication between the audit team and line management which will be followed during and at the conclusion of the audit.

Finding and documenting facts

Ascertaining the nature of the system of internal control is achieved in a variety of ways, including:

- making reference to previous audit working papers and procedures manuals, observation, and enquiry of line staff;
- recording the ascertained system of internal control in sufficient detail within the audit working papers to facilitate the later activities of the audit. Documentation may be in the form of:
  - narrative notes
  - audit flowcharts
  - completed internal control questionnaires
  - completed control matrices.

Testing for compliance

The procedures which are important from a control perspective should be tested by the audit team to ascertain the extent to which they are being followed in practice by management and staff. Non-compliance should be explored to discover the underlying causes of non-compliance.

Completing the assessment of internal control

The system of control, both as laid down and also as being complied with, should be evaluated by the audit team for its adequacy.

Assessing the impact of control weaknesses

Control weaknesses, either due to non-provision of a control procedure or due to non-compliance with required procedures, may be probed in more depth by the audit team. While external auditors would recognise the characteristics of this type of test as being similar to substantive testing, the internal auditor might be more likely to call this 'weakness testing'. The purposes of weakness testing are:

- To ascertain whether or not the control weaknesses have led to errors, losses or other unwanted consequences.
- To measure the extent (by value, volume, etc.) that these control weaknesses have been exploited.

Reporting audit results

The written audit report is a valuable 'means to an end' but it is not the end product of an internal audit. The 'end product' is reassurance to management that their systems of internal control are sound, or persuasive advice to management which will have the effect of making their systems of control sound. The audit report is a valuable way of achieving the end product of internal auditing.

A close-out meeting at the conclusion of the audit fieldwork (a) provides the audit team with the opportunity to ensure that line management is fully appraised with all the audit findings and proposed recommendations and (b) ensures that the audit team receives management's response to their audit findings and recommendations.

The final written audit report should be issued as soon as possible after the end of the audit fieldwork.

Concluding the audit

Steps to be taken after the end of the fieldwork include the following:

- finalising and issuing the audit report;
- completing the audit working paper files, and filing them away;
- concluding the administrative aspects of the audit, including submitting expense reports, etc.

Following up

A short follow-up audit visit may be necessary to confirm that management have taken the action which they agreed to take. But follow-up audit visits should be avoided where possible as they are time-consuming as well as being unpopular with auditees. The audit department should know the 'status' of each audit recommendation, namely:

- Has it been accepted by management – if so when?
- By when has management agreed to implement the recommendation?
- Has it been implemented?

'Following-up' upon receipt of an audit report is primarily the responsibility of the addressee of the report – which will usually be the boss of the head of the activity which has been audited. Many businesses require line management to respond formally to the audit report within a stipulated period (perhaps 28 days) confirming the action they will be taking on audit findings and recommendations, together with their target dates for this action.

It is, however, the internal auditing function's responsibility to ensure that line management is fully aware of its obligations with respect to following-up on receipt of the audit report. It is also the audit function's responsibility to have reasonable assurance that internal audit is fully cognizant of the status of their audit recommendations. Sometimes 'status control' of audit recommendations is entrusted to a special section within the internal auditing function. More usually it is the responsibility of the audit manager who managed the audit.

Facilitating activities of an audit

Holding meetings

Many different types of meeting occur during audit work – meetings of introduction, fact finding interviews, close-out meetings – and so on. Auditors need to be skilled at handling the preparation and conduct of these meetings.

Compiling audit working papers

The minimum requirement is that audit working papers should sufficiently support the audit findings and recommendations contained within the audit report.

Auditors need to develop a working paper orientation to the conduct of their audit work so that they control the work they do through the mechanism of their audit working papers which thus automatically provide the necessary evidence of work done.

Supervision of auditors and review of audit work

The Standards of the Institute of Internal Auditors require that audit work should be supervised and that evidence of supervision should be contained within the audit working papers.

During the progress of the audit, deviations from the planned programme of work should be approved by audit management.

Reporting progress

In general, audit findings should be communicated to line management during the course of the audit – verbally or in informal memorandum form.

Part B: Making an audit needs assessment

Audit views of risk

Planning should take account of risk. In most contexts this is the risk associated with uncertain futures – with which, if it be possible, it is likely also to be desirable to associate differing degrees of probability. Different types of auditing have differing, specialised views of risk. For the external auditor, audit risk is the risk that auditors may give an inappropriate audit opinion on financial statements. Internal auditors have a different mission. Internal auditing is an independent appraisal of the adequacy and effectiveness of the organisation's system of internal control and the quality of performance; it is a control which monitors the effectiveness of internal control. 'Risk assessment' and 'monitoring' are now formally acknowledged as two of the five essential components of internal control (see Chapter 9) which are also held to be the criteria for assessing the effectiveness of a system of internal control. Businesses may monitor internal control in a variety of ways: in 1995 only about 300 of the UK's top 500 companies had an internal audit, and a smaller proportion of smaller enterprises had internal audit.

Internal audit risk

For the internal auditor, audit risk can be described as the risk of giving an inappropriate opinion on internal control.

At the individual internal audit assignment level this is principally the risk of an inappropriate overall conclusion about internal control over the activity which has been the subject of the audit; typically this overall assignment conclusion is contained in a written internal audit report on the assignment. So internal auditors need to have regard to audit risk at, *inter alia*, the assignment level when they plan the focus of their attention for an audit assignment.

Internal auditing standards describe internal auditors as serving the organisation as a whole – not just the financial and accounting parts of the business, and not just management in general. Internal auditors report to the board, usually through its audit committee and in some cases to other parties such as regulators. As a consequence of advice that directors should report publicly on the effectiveness of their companies' systems of internal control, internal auditors are increasingly required to report their overall opinion of internal control. Usually this takes the form of an annual report, timed to coincide with the directors' own review of internal control. A key issue is how internal auditors may minimise their audit risk at the level of their overall opinion on internal control. It would be relatively easy to minimise audit risk if the internal auditors restricted the scope of their internal control reports or by qualifying their opinion. It is true that many audit committees restrict their review and report on internal control to internal *financial* control but this does not necessarily mean that the scope of internal auditors' overall opinions on internal control should be similarly limited.

Internal auditors' regard for audit risk at the *assignment* level will also contribute to reducing their risk of giving inappropriate overall opinions, to the extent that, if effective, it will reduce the risk of overlooking or wrongly assessing a control risk within an audit assignment, thus making an overall opinion on internal control more reliable. Here, matrix approaches to measuring assignment level inherent and control risk have for some time been vying with more traditional internal control questionnaire methods.

At the other extreme, internal auditors' regard for audit risk when they plan for the long-term development of the internal audit function will also contribute to the reliability of subsequent internal audit opinions.

Modelling internal audit risk

If internal audit resources can be applied to the activities of the enterprise in proportion to internal audit risk, then the likelihood of an inappropriate overall opinion on internal control is minimised. Whether or not the internal audit function is required to express an overall opinion on internal control, applying audit resources in this way may maximise the benefit which accrues from internal audit.

Each activity of the enterprise is a potential 'auditable unit' which may be the subject of an internal audit assignment. Together, the auditable units comprise the 'audit universe'. 'Business risk' is a function of 'size' and 'control'. 'Internal audit risk' is fundamentally the same as 'business risk', though with some possible fine tuning. The internal auditor looks at the business through the eyes of management. Figure 5.1 gives close synonyms of 'size' and 'control'. A simple analogy illustrates this. Assume £1,000 is habitually left on one's desk, and experience shows that it is goes missing overnight on average one time in two. If, again tonight, £1,000 is left out, then we can conclude that the business risk is £500 (£1,000 × 0.5). The probability of losing it (0.5) depends upon the quality of control – door locks, security guards, etc.

Note that the measure for 'control' can never be greater than '1', as no more can be lost than the amount that is at risk. In Figure 5.2, we show an audit risk formula used by internal auditors to allocate their resources between a large number of retail stores competing for their attention. Commendably simple, it is flawed in some respects. It does not discriminate between 'size' and 'control'

Figure 5.1 Synonyms of risk components

Size	Control
■ How much	■ How likely
■ Inherent risk	■ Probability
	■ System
	■ Process

Figure 5.2 Formula for a retail stores company

$$\text{Internal audit risk} = A + B + C$$

where:

A = Number of staff employed at the store
B = Turnover of the store
C = Shrinkage at the store (i.e. avoidable losses through e.g. pilferage by staff or public; damages, short deliveries, expired shelf life, etc.)

---

factors, so that potentially 'control' factors could have a magnifying impact upon the resulting internal audit risk score. Scoring each factor as a fraction of the group total does, however, limit the scope for 'shrinkage' as a symptom of weak control to have an excessive impact on the calculation. It is not entirely clear from this formula whether 'number of staff' and 'shrinkage' are being used as 'size' or as 'control' factors.

Internal audit resources should be allocated between auditable units broadly in proportion to business risk ('size', adjusted by 'control'), but allowing for some fine tuning to turn the measure of business risk into a more accurate measure of internal audit risk. We make this fine tuning by way of what we term 'audit' factors. This fine tuning acknowledges that there may be some special circumstances which make it reasonable for internal audit to adjust its resource allocation between auditable units from what would be suggested purely from a measure of business risk.

Components of internal audit risk

In Figure 5.3 we introduce an internal audit risk formula developed for a UK Training and Enterprise Council for their internal audit planning use. Each factor is scored on a scale 1 to 5, and the scales which were arrived at are given as Figures 5.4, 5.5 and 5.6 for the 'size', 'control' and 'audit' factors respectively. Reference to Figures 5.3 and 5.6 shows the special 'audit' adjustments that this TEC may make in order to turn what would otherwise be an assessment of business risk into a modification of this which we call 'internal audit risk': if none of these adjustments is deemed appropriate for a particular auditable unit, then no adjustment is made and the internal audit risk score for that auditable unit will equate to its business risk score (i.e. 'size' moderated by 'control').

It is now well recognised (for instance, in the identification of risk assessment

Figure 5.3 A Training and Enterprise Council internal audit risk formula

Annual turnover: £25,000,000
Total number of staff employed: 160
Scoring scales given in Figures 5.4, 5.5 and 5.6.

$$\text{Internal audit risk} = 20\,\frac{(3A + B + 5C + 6D + E)}{n_1} \times \frac{(2F + 3G + 2H + I)}{n_2}$$

$$\times \frac{(J + 2K + 4L)}{n_3}$$

where:

At least one factor must be scored within each of the three sets of brackets.
Each factor scored is scored on a scale 1 to 5.
The score given to a factor is weighted by the weight shown.
Within a set of brackets the weighted factor scores are summed.
The sum of the contents of the SIZE brackets only is multiplied by 20.
The sum of each of the brackets is divided by n_1, n_2 or n_3 respectively.
n_1 is the sum of the weights of the SIZE factors scored
n_2 is 5 × the sum of the weights of the CONTROL factors scored.
n_3 is 5 × the sum of the weights of the AUDIT factors scored.

The maximum possible score for an auditable unit using this formula is 100.00 and the minimum score is 0.16

and:

Size:
- A = Likely government office perception of importance
- B = Number of transactions (to be used for financial accounting systems)
- C = Third party and public reputation sensitivity
- D = Sensitivity to achievement of TEC objectives
- E = Size of budget (or total costs)

Control:
- F = Known quality of internal control
- G = Operational risk inherent in this type of operation
- H = Proportion of budget which represents salaries (lower risk if salary element is high)
- I = Reliability of management and staff

Audit:
- J = Degree of reliance placed on other external review agencies
- K = Degree of reliance placed upon other internal review agencies (e.g. financial appraisal and monitoring of the TEC's contractors)
- L = Potential for the TEC to benefit from an internal audit

Figure 5.4 A Training and Enterprise Council scoring scale for the 'size' factors in the internal audit risk formula (Figure 5.3)

Size factors

A Likely government office (GO) perception of importance

(Largest size)
5 = Critical level of risk: GO likely to have particular interest and/or rely on internal audit
4 = Very high level of risk: GO likely to have particular interest and/or rely on internal audit
3 = Significant level of risk: GO likely to have some interest and/or rely on internal audit
2 = Modest level of risk: GO likely to have little interest and/or rely little on internal audit
1 = Insignificant level of risk: GO unlikely to have an interest and/or rely on internal audit
(Smallest size)

B Number of transactions (for financial accounting systems)

(Largest size)
5 = >4,000 per annum
4 = 3,001–4,000 per annum
3 = 2,001–3,000 per annum
2 = 1,001–2,000 per annum
1 = <1,001 per annum
(Smallest size)

C Third party and public reputation sensitivity

(5 = Largest size)
Score on a range 1 to 5 where 1 means there are no known potentially disastrous political, legal or contractual risks. The existence either of minority interests or of contractual audit requirements under a partnership agreement should result in a score of 5.
(1 = Smallest size)

D Sensitivity to achievement of TEC objectives

(Largest size)
5 = Potentially disastrous
4 = Potentially serious
3 = Significant
2 = Small
1 = Negligible
(Smallest size)

E Size of the budget (or total costs)

(Largest size)
5 = Over £4m
4 = Between $1.5m. and £4m
3 = Between £0.5m. and £1.5m
2 = Between £50,000 and £0.5m
1 = Up to £50,000
(Smallest size)

Figure 5.5 A Training and Enterprise Council scoring scale for the 'control' factors in the internal audit risk formula (Figure 5.3)

Control factors

F   Known quality of internal control

(Largest control risk)
5 = Known or suspected to be very unsound
4 = Known or suspected to be weak
3 = No past audit experience; or confirmed as sound during the last audit visit
2 = Above average (and confirmed as such during the last audit visit) with standard TEC systems in use generally
1 = Excellent; no significant reorganisations; little scope for intentional manipulation
(Smallest control risk)

G   Operational risk inherent in this type of operation

(5 = Largest control risk)
Rate on a range 1 to 5, preferably at previous audit based on audit findings and recommendations. A score of 5 should be given if the risk inherent in the method of operations is considered to be very high *and* the authority of management and staff to commit the TEC is also very high *and* commercial circumstances are changing significantly in a potentially damaging way.
(1 = Smallest control risk)

H   Proportion of budget which represents salaries (lower risk if salary element is high)

(Largest control risk)
5 = Under 20%
4 = Between 20% and 40%
3 = Between 40% and 60%
2 = Between 60% and 80%
1 = More than 80%
(Smallest control risk)

I   Reliability of management and staff

(5 = Largest control risk)
Score on a range 1 to 5 where 1 represents top-quality management and staff with low turnover of both, in an operation which has existed within the TEC for more than three years and about which no known concerns are being expressed.
(1 = Smallest control risk)

Figure 5.6 A Training and Enterprise Council scoring scale for the 'audit' factors in the internal audit risk formula (Figure 5.3)

Audit factors

J = Degree of reliance placed on other review agencies

(5 = Maximum justification for allocation of internal audit resources)
Score on a range 1 to 5 where 1 indicates that the scope of *external* non-TEC reviews comprehensively covers accounting, financial *and* operational aspects; and complete reliance may be placed upon this work. Further factors to be considered are (a) the adequacy of the reporting lines of these external reviews, and (b) the extent to which the results of these reviews were satisfactory.
(1 = Minimum justification for allocation of internal audit resources)

K   Degree of reliance placed on other internal review agencies
      (e.g. financial appraisal and monitoring of the TEC's contractors ('FAM audit'), quality audit, etc)

(5 = Maximum justification for allocation of internal audit resources)
As J (above) but refers to reviews done *internally* within the TEC, or by third party/joint venture internal auditors.
(1 = Minimum justification for allocation of internal audit resources)

L   Potential for the TEC to benefit from an internal audit

(5 = Maximum justification for allocation of internal audit resources)
Score on a range 1 to 5 with a score of 1 if there are no significant constraints which are likely to preclude doing an effective audit. Constraints may be excessive audit cost, non-availability of specialist audit skills, or inadequate grasp of the systems involved.
(1 = Minimum justification for allocation of internal audit resources)

---

as one of the essential components of an effective system of internal control (COSO, 1992 – see Chapter 9)), that control should be proportionate to need. It matters proportionately less that the internal auditor overlooks a control system weakness where less is at stake, than that the internal auditor overlooks a similar control system weakness where more is at stake. It would not be appropriate to allocate internal audit resources to an auditable unit in a way which was disproportionate to business risk on the basis that, for instance, some low-risk auditable units take a long time to audit, and vice versa. Over time, proportionate allocation can be achieved by varying the interval between audits, varying the duration of the audit field work, varying the size of the audit team, and varying the experience of the auditors assigned to the team.

External auditors regard audit risk as having three components: inherent risk, control risk and detection risk. Some external auditors define 'inherent risk' as comprising the 'size' risk and also that part of the 'system' risk which is considered to be uncontrollable. Thus, for instance, they would say that trading in derivatives futures is inherently risky both on account of how much is at risk and also because the best designed processes to handle these trades are very vulnerable. In essence, the external auditor is subdividing the system or process into that which is uncontrollable, and that which is controllable, and bracketing the former with the size risk to provide a composite measure of inherent risk. This would be an unhelpful refinement for the internal auditor who does not wish to concede inevitable vulnerability. For the internal auditor to do this would make an attempt to model internal audit risk more difficult as it would become harder to avoid the uncontrollable aspects of the system magnifying the size risk into something bigger than it should be – and thereby distorting the amount of internal audit attention given to an area.

Reducing to a formula

It should be possible to reduce to a formula of factors the considerations which should be borne in mind when determining whether to conduct an internal audit of an auditable unit and, if so, how much audit resource should be expended on that audit – in such a way that the score computed by the formula for an auditable unit indicates relatively how much internal audit resource should be allocated to that audit over time. This has been done in Figure 5.3; Figures 5.7 and 5.11 give further examples.

Designing an effective internal audit risk formula is most easily done when the audit universe is highly homogeneous, as with the branches of a bank or the stores of a retail chain (Figure 5.2). In these cases it is more likely that it will be possible to arrive at just a small number of factors which are relevant to each auditable unit within the audit universe and which can readily be scored in a fairly objective way for each auditable unit.

The greater challenge has been to develop a formula approach for heterogeneous audit universes, as was the case in each example given in this chapter except for the example in Figure 5.2.

Examining how internal audit managers plan when they use traditional, more intuitive planning approaches, is illuminating. This leads to the suggestion that the audit risk formula should be organised so that it copes with the possibility that not every factor will be scored for every auditable unit. The rules are (a) a factor should be scored only if it is a relevant determinant of relative audit resources and if internal audit knows what the score should be, and (b) at least one factor should be scored for each audit from each of the 'size' and 'control' parts of the formula. This flexibility corresponds to the thinking processes that an internal audit manager inevitably has to go through when weighing up the rival claims for audit resources of very different auditable units. This flexibility may be applied to the 'size' part of the formula only, but on occasion it may be helpful, though not always essential, to extend the same flexibility to the other two parts of the formula.

Despite this potential flexibility, some internal audit functions prefer to apply a formula-based approach to audit planning just to the homogeneous part of their audit universe. Some apply traditional planning techniques to the heterogeneous part of their audit universe, or they may develop a different audit risk formula for that purpose.

Another approach is to design a group-level audit risk formula to determine the division of overall group internal audit resources between the group's different business units; and then a different audit risk formula for each business unit to divide the audit resources allocated to that business unit between its auditable units.

Subjective judgements in audit needs assessment

Some appropriate factors may be subjective while the values of others, especially most of the 'size' factors, are likely to be determined by direct reference to the business's database. In the interests of conciseness in this chapter we have omitted the scoring scales for most of the example internal audit risk formulae. Figures 5.4 to 5.6 give the scoring scales for the formula shown in Figure 5.3. While a majority of the 'size' factors in the formula given as Figure 5.4 are hard and objective, this is quite unusual, as can be seen by examining the other formulae given in Figures 5.7 to 5.11. Using subjective factors within the audit risk formula is not necessarily inappropriate, as not all elements of risk can be measured objectively. Strict guidance can sometimes be developed to provide greater consistency in scoring the subjective factors. For instance, Factor F ('Known quality of internal control') in the formula described in Figures 5.3 and 5.5, while in essence a soft, subjective factor, has been bolstered by some rigorous guidance on how it should be scored in given circumstances. It should not be assumed that subjectivity is eliminated by this planning tool. Subjectivity exists in the following:

- choice of factors for the formula;
- determination of the relative weights to be accorded to each factor;
- determination of the scoring scale for each factor;
- the scoring of the subjective factors;
- determination of the auditable units with the audit universe;
- determination of the absolute quantity of internal audit resource to be made available;
- interpretation of the audit risk scores computed by the formula (they are data

which the audit function should interpret, not follow slavishly: there may be relevant issues which have not been taken account of by the formula).

The approach explored in this chapter allows the enterprise to carefully agree upon the basis to be used for audit planning and then to apply the technique consistently, and to amend it knowingly from time to time. It looks professional, and appearances matter. It allows the internal audit function to explain why it is focusing on particular areas. It enables internal audit to agree with the audit committee and with management the basis to be used to determine the programme of audits to be conducted, thereby reinforcing their independence as it is more likely to be apparent when management are putting pressure upon internal audit to review relatively low-risk areas of the business or to avoid reviewing high-risk areas. It provides the means to measure trends in the degree of audit coverage over the years and it provides a basis to model the impact on audit coverage of possible future changes in risk or in internal audit resource levels.

Mechanics of formula design

Recalling the earlier analogy with the risk of loss through leaving cash on the desk overnight, it is readily apparent that the amount at risk cannot be greater than the amount left on the desk even if control is appallingly weak or non-existent, for instance:

Size   ×   Control = Commercial risk
[£1,000]   [0.6]   [600]

The implication of this is that the maximum possible score from each of the 'control' and 'audit' parts of the audit risk formula should be a score of 1. Assuming, as in the technique used in this chapter, that each factor is scored on a scale 1 to 5, if there are three factors in the 'control' part of the formula the sum of the three scores given for them should be divided by 15 (3×5, where 3 is the number of factors scored and 5 is the sum of the worst case scores). The same applies to the 'audit' part of the formula and is illustrated in the following hypothetical example. This example also shows the correct arithmetic for the 'size' part of the formula assuming that the rules are that one or more of the 'size' factors should be scored and a scale 1 to 5 is used. In this example both of the 'size' factors have been scored:

Internal audit risk = Size factors × Control factors × Audit factors

say:

$$[A + B] \times [C + D + E] \times [F + G]$$

Figure 5.7 Formula for a UK privately owned company, manufacturing packaging and other products

$$\text{Internal audit risk} = 20\,\frac{(A + 2B + 2C + 2D + 3E + F + 3G)}{n_1} \times \frac{(H + I + 2J + K + 2L)}{n_2}$$

$$\times \frac{(M + N + O + 3P + 2Q + 2R)}{n_3}$$

where:

At least one factor must be scored within each of the three sets of brackets.
Each factor scored is scored on a scale 1 to 5.
The score given to a factor is weighted by the weight shown.
Within a set of brackets the weighted factor scores are summed.
The sum of the contents of the SIZE brackets only is multiplied by 20.
The sum of each of the brackets is divided by n_1, n_2 or n_3 respectively.
n_1 is the sum of the weights of the SIZE factors scored
n_2 is 5 × the sum of the weights of the CONTROL factors scored.
n_3 is 5 × the sum of the weights of the AUDIT factors scored.

The maximum possible score for an auditable unit using this formula is 100.00 and the minimum score is 0.16.

and:

Size: A = Amount of capital employed
           B = Amount of capital to be employed
           C = Amount of working capital tied up
           D = Debt exposure
           E = Size of budget
           F = Total business exposure
           G = Turnover

Control: H = Budget variance
           I = Information
           J = Management and staff
           K = Operational risk inherent in this type of operation
           L = Standard of internal control

Audit: M = Effectiveness of external audit
           N = Extent of internal audit knowledge of the business
           O = Extent of language competence of internal audit staff
           P = Internal audit time criticality
           Q = Past effectiveness of internal audit
           R = Significance of past audit

204 Leading edge internal auditing

Figure 5.8 Formula for a specialised lubricants and chemicals marketing company

144 auditable units

Internal audit risk =

$$20\frac{(A + B + 3C + 3D + 3E)}{n_1} \times \frac{(3F + G + 3H + 2I + 2J)}{n_2} \times \frac{(3K + L + 2M + 2N)}{n_3}$$

where:

At least one factor must be scored within each of the three sets of brackets.
Each factor scored is scored on a scale 1 to 5.
The score given to a factor is weighted by the weight shown.
Within a set of brackets the weighted factor scores are summed.
The sum of the contents of the SIZE brackets only is multiplied by 20.
The sum of each of the brackets is divided by n_1, n_2 or n_3 respectively.
n_1 is the sum of the weights of the SIZE factors scored.
n_2 is 5 × the sum of the weights of the CONTROL factors scored.
n_3 is 5 × the sum of the weights of the AUDIT factors scored.

The maximum possible score for an auditable unit using this formula is 100.00 and the minimum score is 0.16

and:

Size:
- A = Number of employees
- B = Value of fixed assets
- C = Value of debtors
- D = Value of sales
- E = Value of stock

Control:
- F = Changes in computer systems since last visit
- G = Manufacturing capability
- H = Changes in senior management since last visit
- I = Number of days debtors
- J = Stock holding in days

Audit:
- K = Time since last review by consultancy and audit
- L = Number of outstanding recommendations
- M = Number of recommendations made by external auditors
- N = Number of recommendations made by consultancy and audit in last report

Figure 5.9 Formula for a manufacturer and distributor of brands of alcoholic beverages

Internal audit risk =

$$20 \frac{(12A + 3B + 12C + 5D)}{n_1} \times \frac{(5E + 7F + 3G + 3H)}{n_2} \times \frac{(I + J + K)}{n_3}$$

where

At least one factor must be scored within each of the three sets of brackets.
Each factor scored is scored on a scale 1 to 5.
The score given to a factor is weighted by the weight shown.
Within a set of brackets the weighted factor scores are summed.
The sum of the contents of the SIZE brackets only is multiplied by 20.
The sum of each of the brackets is divided by n_1, n_2 or n_3 respectively.
n_1 is the sum of the weights of the SIZE factors scored.
n_2 is 5 × the sum of the weights of the CONTROL factors scored.
n_3 is 5 × the sum of the weights of the AUDIT factors scored.

The maximum possible score for an auditable unit using this formula is 100.00 and the minimum score is 0.16

and:

Size: A = Gross turnover and expenditure
        B = Number of staff
        C = Potential impact on group
        D = Value of all assets and brands

Control: E = Business climate
        F = Concerns expressed by management
        G = Control rating from previous audit
        H = Experience and stability of management and staff

Audit: I = Effectiveness of other review agencies
        J = Length of time since last audit
        K = Special concerns of internal audit

scored as, for instance:

$$[4 + 2] \times [1 + 3 + 2] \times [1 + 5]$$

therefore:

$$[(4 + 2)/2] \times [(1 + 3 + 2)/(3 \times 5)] \times [(1 + 5)/(2 \times 5)].$$

The above example assumes that all factors are weighted equally. If they are not, as most likely should be the case and is so for the examples given in the figures to this chapter, the formula has a modified structure, as described below.

206 Leading edge internal auditing

Figure 5.10 Formula for a privately owned, diversified health care company, in diagnostics, orthopaedics, molecular medicine, therapeutics and biochemistry

Internal audit risk =

$$20 \frac{(3A + 10B + 7C + 8D + 5E)}{n_1} \times \frac{(10F + 6G + 8H + 7I)}{n_2} \times \frac{(10J + 7K + 4L + 7M)}{n_3}$$

where:

At least one factor must be scored within each of the three sets of brackets.
Each factor scored is scored on a scale 1 to 5.
The score given to a factor is weighted by the weight shown.
Within a set of brackets the weighted factor scores are summed.
The sum of the contents of the SIZE brackets only is multiplied by 20.
The sum of each of the brackets is divided by n_1, n_2 or n_3 respectively.
n_1 is the sum of the weights of the SIZE factors scored.
n_2 is 5 × the sum of the weights of the CONTROL factors scored.
n_3 is 5 × the sum of the weights of the AUDIT factors scored.

The maximum possible score for an auditable unit using this formula is 100.00 and the minimum score is 0.16

and:

Size: A = Headcount
           B = Sales
           C = Expenses
           D = Profitability (impact on group)
           E = Inventory

Control: F = Complexity of operations
           G = Business climate
           H = Management concerns
           I = Experience and stability of staff

Audit: J = Results of last audit
           K = Time since last audit
           L = Effectiveness of other review bodies
           M = Internal audit concerns

Figure 5.11 Formula for a personal finance subsidiary of a UK clearing bank

Internal audit risk =

$$20\frac{(A+4B+2C+4D+E)}{n_1} \times \frac{(4F+3G+4H+2I+2J+2K+L)}{n_2} \times \frac{(M+2N+5O)}{n_3}$$

where:

At least one factor must be scored within each of the three sets of brackets.
Each factor scored is scored on a scale 1 to 5.
The score given to a factor is weighted by the weight shown.
Within a set of brackets the weighted factor scores are summed.
The sum of the contents of the SIZE brackets only is multiplied by 20.
The sum of each of the brackets is divided by n_1, n_2 or n_3 respectively.
n_1 is the sum of the weights of the SIZE factors scored
n_2 is 5 × the sum of the weights of the CONTROL factors scored.
n_3 is 5 × the sum of the weights of the AUDIT factors scored.

The maximum possible score for an auditable unit using this formula is 100.00 and the minimum score is 0.16

and:

Size: A = Average transaction value
        B = Budget/authority to commit
        C = Number of payments exceeding £50,000
        D = Potential monetary loss/profit, and loss impact
        E = Turnover

Control: F = Adherence to system development standards
         G = Control rating from last audit
         H = Fraud susceptibility
         I = Other audit/scrutiny
         J = Reliance on third parties
         K = System robustness
         L = Technological complexity

Audit: M = Contractual audit requirements
        N = Cost of task
        O = Requests from management

The maximum possible score from this formula can be calculated as 5 and the minimum score as less than 1. Multiplying by 20 gives the formula a more convenient range:

Internal audit risk = $20[(4 + 2)/2] \times [(1 + 3 + 2)/(3 \times 5)] \times [(1 + 5)/(2 \times 5)]$.

Weighting factors

We can build more sophistication into the formula by providing for differing weights for the various factors within the formula. Comparative weights are permanently assigned to each factor within each set of brackets. Because of the way the arithmetic of the formula functions, the weighting comparisons have to be made only between the factors within the same set of brackets. Thus the 'control' factors are weighted against each other but not against the 'size' and the 'audit' factors, and similarly with the 'size' and 'audit' factors. In the above examples no more than three factors have to be compared against each other in order to arrive at relative weights. The relative weights are a matter of judgement, based on the auditors' assessment of the relative importance of each of the factors within the formula.

Three or four factors can be compared visually against each other, but if there are more factors within a single set of brackets it is important to ensure that all logical comparisons are made. For instance, six factors within a single set of brackets require that 15 comparisons are made before relative weights for those factors can be determined. Figure 5.12 shows an example of a matrix technique which ensures that all these comparisons are made. The user enters the matrix from the top and compares each factor in turn with each factor listed down the left side of the matrix, entering his or her judgement as to the relative weight. The reciprocal of this is entered in the other cell (below the diagonal line of 1s where the same two factors are compared, though in reverse order). As shown in Figure 5.12, summing the columns and the rows, dividing one by the other and taking the square root of the results produces the relative weights. The effect of this is that every factor has been compared separately with every other factor and the calculations performed on this data have 'averaged out' any discrepancies between the auditor's judgements. A technique like this is not necessary when only a small number of factors have to be compared against each other. With a larger number and without a matrix such as this, there would be a risk that the auditor would not compare every factor against every other factor before deciding upon their relative weights.

The mathematical proof of this matrix technique can be demonstrated by ensuring that the matrix cells after those in the first line are completed so that the entered numbers are arithmetically consistent with the numbers entered into the first line. If this is done, the calculation of the relative weights, making use of all

Figure 5.12 Matrix method of arriving at relative weights for factors

Chosen control factors		Weighting matrix (11 factors, A to K)											
		A	B	C	D	E	F	G	H	I	J	K	
Access control vulnerability	A	–	0.6	–	–	5	2	1.5	1.5	–	–	1.8	17.4
Data control	B	1.67	–	–	0.3	5	3	2	–	–	0.5	–	17.5
Dependence upon third parties	C	–	–	–	0.7	5	2	1.5	–	0.8	0.5	0.6	15.1
Development time constraints	D	–	3.33	1.43	–	5	3	2	–	–	–	2	21.8
Overall audit assignment control risk matrix score	E	0.2	0.2	0.2	0.2	–	0.4	0.25	0.6	0.2	0.3	0.3	3.9
Quality of direction and management	F	0.5	0.33	0.5	0.33	2.5	–	0.5	0.7	0.5	0.5	0.5	7.9
Quality and experience of technical staff	G	0.67	0.5	0.67	0.5	4	2	–	2	–	1.5	–	14.8
Relative requirement for control	H	0.67	–	–	–	1.67	1.43	0.5	–	0.7	–	–	11
Technical control risk	I	–	–	1.25	–	5	2	–	1.43	–	–	–	16.7
Vulnerability from outsider abuse	J	–	2	2	–	3.33	2	0.67	–	–	–	2	17
Vulnerability from staff	K	0.56	–	1.67	0.5	3.33	2	–	–	0.5	–	–	13.6
Weights		1	1	1	1	6	3	2	2	1	1	2	
Factor weighting (X/Y, rounded)		(A	+B	+C	+D	+E	+F	+G	+H	+I	+J	+K)	
Sum of columns		9.26	12	11.7	7.53	40.8	20.8	11.9	12.2	9.2	8.8	12.2	
Sum of columns divided by adjusted sum of rows		0.53	0.69	0.78	0.35	10.60	2.65	0.80	1.12	0.55	0.52	0.90	
Square root of above row figures		0.73	0.83	0.88	0.59	3.26	1.63	0.90	1.06	0.74	0.72	0.95	

(Note: last row (square roots) would correspond to row A if all data entered into the matrix had been arithmetically consistent with row A data) the numbers in the matrix, will produce weights which are identical to those entered into the first line.

Giving the factors different weights means that the structure of the formula described in the previous section has to be modified slightly. Instead of dividing out the 'size' part of the formula by the number of 'size' factors scored, the division should be by the sum of the weights of the factors scored. Instead of dividing out the 'control' and 'audit' parts of the formula by the number of factors scored in each part times 5, the division should be by the sum of the weights of the factors scored in each part times 5, thus:

Audit risk = Size factors × Control factors × Audit factors

$$[2A + 3B] \times [2A + B + 5C] \times [2A + B]$$

$$20[(4 + 2)/7] \times [(1 + 3 + 2)/(8 \times 5)] \times [(1 + 5)/(3 \times 5)].$$

Seeking consensus

A new formula should be tested against sample audits to check that it yields reasonable results. Senior general management should be consulted about these results and their general support obtained. The formula is likely to show some audits to be more important than had previously been thought, and vice versa. It needs to be determined whether this is a consequence of inappropriate functionality of the formula or indeed is due to quite valid but previously overlooked considerations.

Chapter summary

In Part A of this chapter we took the perspective that an internal audit is a *project* and needs to be managed as such. It is a project overlaid with particular behavioural qualities as well as with a number of activities which need to be managed sensitively and effectively. We have shown that key activities are those of preparing for the audit, making appropriate introductions, finding and documenting facts, testing for compliance, completing the assessment of internal control, assessing the impact of control weaknesses, reporting audit results, concluding the audit and subsequent follow up.

In addition to these principal activities, there are a number of more general activities which facilitate the orderly and successful undertaking of an audit assignment, and we have looked at a number of these matters.

In Part B, we showed how we can apply risk assessment to the planning ▶

of programmes of audits to be conducted in the future. In other words, we are dealt with the challenge of completing an audit needs assessment using risk analysis concepts. We explored the components of internal audit risk, and suggested an approach to modelling internal audit risk. Some of the factors which are likely to need to be taken into account will be quite subjective, but this does not invalidate their use – subjectivity is an inevitable concomitant of successful internal audit planning. In this chapter we also addressed the mechanics of audit risk formula design, the business of selectively weighting factors within an audit risk formula, and the need to endeavour to achieve consensus about audit risk formula design.

Principia

1. Internal audit resources should be applied to the different activities of the business in proportion to audit risk.

2. Internal audit risk is the risk of giving a misleading opinion about the quality of internal control, having regard to the significance of the business activity.

3. Internal audit risk is basically a combination of inherent and control factors.

4. For the internal auditor, inherent risk refers to 'how much' is at risk.

5. For the internal auditor, control risk refers to the quality of the system, or process.

6. Inevitably, internal auditors have to exercise judgement in determining audit risk: it cannot be assessed entirely objectively.

7. It is desirable to obtain the approval of senior management and the board to the basis that internal audit will use to determine how it will allocate its audit resources between audits.

8. Applying a formula or other similar approach to audit planning allows trends over time in audit coverage to be discerned.

Case 5.1 Supervising

(Extracted from *In Business* (1997) II 2.2.1, ICSA Publishing, Hemel Hempstead)

The case

The importance of supervisory skills

Sound supervisory skills are essential for effective management activity in large or small organisations. They are concerned with the day-to-day office business. They concern the key management process skills. Supervisors are managers whose major activities focus on people and their problems. All levels of management have supervisory functions, but the supervisor's major function is working with and through non-management employees to meet the needs of the employees and the objectives of the organisation. Basically, supervision entails getting the job done efficiently to the contracted standard and keeping everyone involved committed and contented. It is a highly sophisticated role that demands:

1. A positive attitude – essential if a supervisor is to be effective.
2. Strong discipline – staff expect realistically high standards.
3. Human skills – a high degree of sensitivity to the needs of others.
4. Attention to details – these must be carefully balanced so that a supervisor is able to fulfil his or her responsibilities to the company and to subordinates.

The role of the supervisor

The key tasks of a supervisor include:

1. supervising work;
2. supervising people;
3. supervising day-to-day activities.

Supervising work

This includes:

- planning;
- organising;
- controlling and co-ordinating;
- decision-making.

Supervising people

This involves:

- leadership skills;

- job design skills;
- motivational skills;
- communications skills.

Supervising day-to-day activities

Responsibilities include:

- contribution to the selection and recruitment process;
- key role in training and employee development;
- involvement in staff appraisal procedure;
- exercise of practical management skills such as giving instructions, introducing change and conducting meetings;
- maintaining discipline and morale;
- handling complaints and grievances.

Supervisory checklist

Supervisory responsibilities are broken down into eight major areas:

1. Understanding the organisation.
2. Planning and setting work schedules.
3. Determining performance requirements.
4. Improving work methods.
5. Developing staff.
6. Achieving work output.
7. Keeping the staff well motivated.
8. Improving self.

This checklist will give you an idea of how you are doing as a supervisor and help to point out areas where you might improve.

Consider

How well you supervise and manage, paying particular attention to the planning side of supervision and management. Use the checklist to identify your strengths and weaknesses. Remember, planning is about proposed short-term and long-term actions.

CHAPTER 6

Measuring internal audit performance

> What cannot be measured cannot be improved.
>
> (Anon.)

At a time when internal auditing is being challenged by outsourcing alternatives and by other methods of reviewing managerial effectiveness, it is particularly important to be able to measure its contribution to the enterprise's profitability. Standards which govern internal audit practice make this obligatory.

So here we take a hard look at performance measures for internal auditing – measures of inputs (economy), process (efficiency), and especially outputs (effectiveness). Appropriate specific measures are recommended. In doing this we will be identifying the key aspects of internal auditing which need to be focused upon in order to improve internal auditing's contribution to the enterprise's profitability.

We consider the difficulties of finding reliable measures of internal audit performance. We distinguish between qualitative and quantitative measures. We suggest a value-for-money approach to auditing internal audit performance.

Important aspects of this chapter are the place of the internal audit charter in securing effective internal audit performance, and the importance of audit independence to this end. We identify the categories of performance measures which may be used to evaluate internal audit performance and the strengths and weaknesses of each. We give advice on their interpretation. We place the measurement of internal audit in context with (a) the general business environment, (b) professional standards for internal auditing, and (c) good management practice on planning and control. Finally we present a particular approach to the use of performance measures in value for money auditing which may be applied to assessing internal auditing performance.

Placing internal audit in context

Historically, the growth of internal auditing as a business service has been counter-cyclical, though not uniformly so. By this we mean that in the past, internal auditing has developed most strongly during times of economic constraint. Either directors, managements and now regulators have considered that investment in internal auditing is particularly important in constrained times, as an antidote to the control risks sometimes associated with stringent cost cutting; or managements have turned their attention away from financial, accounting and operational control (to which internal audit can contribute) when extra profits have been more easily secured by burgeoning sales.

Whether or not internal audit prospers in constrained times, in such times it certainly behoves internal audit to be able to demonstrate that their activity is cost effective and is managed so as to maximise its cost effectiveness. Even in periods of growth, acute competition means that every penny that is spent has to be justified. Where internal auditing is not a mandatory requirement, by statute law or by regulation, there is added pressure for audit to be able to demonstrate its worth.[1]

There are indications that managements are now placing internal auditing under a microscope, with the intention of determining whether it pays its way. Internal auditing is a costly service to run. Large amounts of profits from sales are needed to resource even a modest internal audit function.

Market testing internal audit

Even where internal auditing is a mandatory requirement, the requirement for compulsory or voluntary competitive tendering makes internal auditing a prime candidate for market testing and contracting out.[2] Every activity of a business is a potential candidate to be outsourced unless it is regarded as 'core' to the business, or to be kept in-house for security reasons. Established in-house internal auditing functions find they are tendering competitively against firms of public accountants, consultants specialising in internal auditing and other in-house internal auditing functions who have been given the freedom to tender for external work. To win the contract these outside parties may be willing to bid at marginal cost, especially if they have surplus capacity at certain times of the year.

There are many arguments for and against an enterprise contracting out its internal auditing; these are summarised in Figures 6.1 and 6.2. One aspect that has been largely overlooked is that performance measures for internal audit are particularly important so as to inform the decision initially, so as to provide the means of establishing performance-related contracts for internal audit provision, and so as to be able to monitor its ongoing provision after the contract has been let.

Figure 6.1 Potential advantages of contracting out internal auditing

- The business can more readily vary its spend on internal auditing, according to what it can afford, from time to time.
- The contractor is motivated to perform well and can be held to account for that performance.
- The provider can be changed more easily.
- The service may be provided at a lower price.
- An external provider may have a wider understanding as to how other enterprises tackle similar business issues.
- An external provider may have more extensive audit support resources to draw upon.
- An external provider may be able to develop the enterprise's own staff.
- The actual and perceived independence of an external provider may be greater – leading to more confidence in the results of the audit work.

Figure 6.2 Potential advantages of in-house internal auditing provision

- A deeper grasp of the enterprise's affairs.
- A finer adjustment of internal audit emphasis to the enterprise's needs.
- 'On the spot' responsiveness to management and the board; better able to take on unplanned work.
- A training ground for future senior executives.
- Confidentiality.
- More likely to have a genuine *internal audit* orientation as distinct from an *external audit* orientation.
- Unable to 'walk away'.

With the bias being towards accepting lowest cost bids, it is particularly important to devise and use internal audit performance measures which focus upon *outputs* first, *process* second and *inputs* last – the categorisation followed in this chapter, though in reverse order. Each of these three is, of course, important. Senior general management and the board responsible for contracting-out decisions should ensure that this sort of internal audit performance monitoring is in place. In-house heads of internal audit can influence management and the board towards this and, in so doing, should be maximising their own opportunities for securing the future internal audit work for their in-house internal audit departments.

If management and the board allow decisions on letting contracts for internal audit work to be made on the basis of price alone, rather than value for money, they are acting irresponsibly. Decisions based on price alone betray a lack of commitment to the value of internal auditing – perhaps merely a resignation to the provision of a skeletal internal audit service to comply with statutory or regulatory obligations. Even in enterprises with acute cash flow problems, decisions made on price alone are unjustified, as it is especially important that such businesses maximise value.

Since (a) mandatory obligation to have internal auditing and (b) cash flow difficulties often come together within the public sector, it is within that sector that we are currently experiencing most pressure to contract out internal auditing on price grounds alone.

Understanding what internal auditing Standards require

The Standards of the Institute of Internal Auditors specify that the director of internal auditing should establish plans to carry out the responsibilities of the internal auditing unit, and that these plans should be consistent with the internal auditing unit's charter and with the goals of the organisation (Figure 6.3). In the context of measuring internal audit performance, they go on to say that the goals of the internal auditing unit should be capable of being established within specified operating plans and budgets and, to the extent possible, should be measurable and accompanied by measurement criteria and targeted dates of accomplishment.

These Standards also require a quality assurance programme to evaluate the

Figure 6.3   Standard on planning (IIA)

Specific Standard 520 Planning

The director of internal auditing should establish plans to carry out the responsibilities of the internal auditing department

Guideline 520.01

These plans should be consistent with the internal auditing department's charter and with the goals of the organisation.

Guideline 520.03

The goals of the internal auditing department should be capable of being established within specified operating plans and budgets and, to the extent possible, should be measurable. They should be accompanied by measurement criteria and targeted dates of accomplishment.

Figure 6.4 Specific Standard 560 Quality Assurance (IIA)

> The director of internal auditing should establish and maintain a quality assurance programme to evaluate the operations of the internal auditing department.
>
> **Guideline 560.01.3**
> A key criterion against which an internal auditing department should be measured is its charter.
>
> **Guideline 560.03**
> Internal reviews should be performed periodically by members of the internal auditing staff to appraise the quality of the audit work performed. These reviews should be performed in the same manner as any other internal audit.
>
> **Guideline 560.04**
> External reviews of the internal auditing department should be performed to appraise the quality of the department's operations. These reviews should be performed by qualified persons who are independent of the organisation ... at least once every three years [and] ... should express an opinion as to the department's compliance with the Standards.

operations of the internal auditing unit and this is elaborated in the statement that a key criterion against which an internal auditing unit should be measured is its charter (Figure 6.4). Quality assurance is seen as being secured by means of supervision, internal reviews and external reviews.

So it is clear that the Institute of Internal Auditors considers there should be performance measures of an internal auditing unit and that these should include an evaluation of compliance with the charter of the unit and also with the Standards of the Institute; they should also include a measurement of the achievement of target dates.

The UK's Consultative Committee of Accounting Bodies is less forthcoming. Their guidance to their members[3] merely says that 'The head of internal audit should establish arrangements to evaluate the performance of the internal audit unit. He (*sic*) may also prepare an annual report to management on the activity of the internal audit unit in which he (*sic*) gives an assessment of how effectively the objectives of the function have been met.'

Categorising internal audit performance measures

Measures of internal audit performance have tended to focus upon input and process, rather than output. Auditors will understand the association between

Figure 6.5 A model of input, process and output

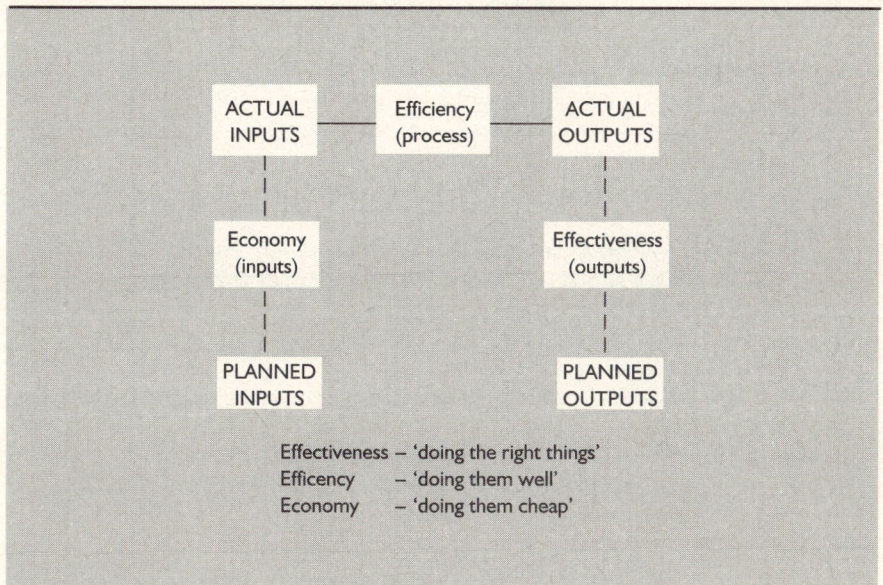

these three and economy, efficiency and effectiveness, respectively, as illustrated in Figure 6.5. The greatest challenge is how to develop a range of measures which throw light upon internal audit effectiveness (i.e. output measures).

Another way to categorise performance measures is according to whether they are quantitative or qualitative. We do not rely upon such a classification in this chapter, as in reality each performance measure can be conceived as being somewhere on a gradation between the extremes of objective (quantitative) and subjective (qualitative). An important characteristic of quantitative performance measures is that their measurement is objectively determined. Yet even in a very clear-cut case of a quantitative performance measure,[4] subjectivity is not avoided as the selection and design of that performance measure will have been based upon a judgement that it provided relevant guidance on relative internal audit performance, and the interpretation of the resulting data also will itself be very subjective. Soft, subjective measures are often given an aura of objectivity, so that they may be termed *quasi-quantitative*.[5]

Performance measures with a higher degree of objectivity than others are not necessarily the preferred ones to use: the criteria for selection of a performance measure should include a matching to the aspects of internal audit performance which are most important and which need to be monitored most.

Of crucial importance is determining which aspects of internal audit performance are most important and which most need to be monitored. Strictly speaking, an aspect of internal audit performance could be of first importance

Figure 6.6 Management satisfaction survey

Questions might include:
- How useful do you find internal audit?
- How appropriate have been the objectives and scope of internal audit's work in your area?
- How useful have been your discussions with audit *at the commencement* of the audit?
- How useful have been your discussions with audit *during* the audit?
- Were the auditors as open and communicative with you and your staff as you consider they should have been?
- Was the timing of the audit fieldwork satisfactory?
- Was the duration of the audit satisfactory?
- Were you satisfied with the time it took for audit to issue an agreed audit report?
- Do you consider the audit report to have been fair and balanced?
- Did you consider you had been fully consulted on matters which were included within the audit report?
- Did you find the audit report useful?

(Answers might be *excellent, satisfactory, barely adequate, unsatisfactory*.)

while not needing to be monitored so closely as other aspects – provided its achievement were assured, or, occasionally, if it were outside the scope of management to regulate its achievement.

Using our model of input, process and output, we now consider for each of these categories the most important aspects of performance as they relate to internal audit. Some measures of performance inform about more than one of these categories. For instance, the success of the internal auditing function in completing its planned programme of audits relates closely to whether the function has achieved its objectives (planned outputs), but it also gives potential insights as to whether the function has approached its work efficiently (process).

Another example of this overlap between categories of performance measure is the client satisfaction survey which provides data on the reputation of audit (Figure 6.6). To some extent this will result from the judgement that management has made about the professionalism of internal auditors they have observed in action (audit process); to some extent the answers will depend upon management's experience of the value of audit findings and recommendations (audit output). Some of the questions put to management in the survey will be targeted more to process than to output, and vice versa; but the impressions that management have about the professionalism of the audit process are likely to colour their answers to questions targeted at audit output; and their satisfaction with the audit output is likely to colour their impression of the audit process.

Measuring inputs

These performance measures throw light upon the economy with which the internal auditing activity is provided – whether by in-house provision or by external providers. Figure 6.7 suggests possible candidates for use as economy measures; those selected may need to be adapted if internal auditing is contracted out. For instance the 'number of auditors per 1,000 staff compared to the sector average' would require a conversion to full-time staff equivalents based upon the time that the outside consultants were spending in performing internal audit work. Data on the norms for each business sector are available from the impressive surveys of internal auditing conducted by The Institute of Internal Auditors.[6] A ratio of one internal auditor to every 50 or 100 total staff employed by the enterprise might be typical of financial institutions where tight control is an absolute priority, whereas 1:1,000 or 1:2,000 is more typical of large manufacturing companies, with civil engineering constructing firms even less thoroughly resourced with internal auditors – probably on account of other personnel, such as quantity surveyors, being engaged in quasi-internal auditing tasks.

In surveys of internal auditing practice we have found that the number of internal auditors tends to be more highly correlated with the total number of staff employed than with the size of the turnover, since we have also found that larger enterprises tend to achieve more turnover per member of staff employed.[7]

As a bald measure of economy, the number of auditors employed is useful, but there may still be diseconomies to be identified. Audit expenditure may be out of

Figure 6.7 *Input* **performance measures**

- Number of auditors per 1,000 staff compared to sector average.
- Levels of expenditure:
    — budget: actual;
    — cost per auditor day;
    — ratio of payroll to other costs;
    — comparison between audit sections;
    — comparison with previous periods.
- Allocation of productive time according to type of work (audit type; audit and non-audit work (such as firefighting), etc.).
- Extent to which audit staff are stretched.

control – either audit payroll expenditure or non-payroll costs. Some sections of the larger internal auditing unit may be more costly than others, perhaps without justification. Even where there is justification for differential costs between audit sections, this is useful information for management as it may point to possible opportunities to obtain better value for money in certain parts of the total audit programme than in other parts. Whether or not this is so will depend not just on cost considerations but the potential for audit effectiveness in the various parts of the total audit programme. So measures of economy must be interpreted together with measures of effectiveness (outputs) and efficiency (process) before appropriate management action can be determined.

We suggest amongst our input measures a measure of the extent to which audit staff are stretched. It is arguable that this should be categorised as an efficiency (process) measure. If audit staff are not being extended it is likely that the staff input is unduly costly. Ensuring that audit staff are extended is a matter of managing the audit function efficiently. If staff are extended they are likely to perform better and the effectiveness (outputs) of the audit function may be improved.

Internal auditing units are now frequently calculating the cost of each audit. Audit reports often highlight this figure. An increasing number of internal auditing functions are charging out the cost of the audit to the activity which has been audited. This practice encourages the auditors to perform well in order to keep the client satisfied. It also encourages the client to take the audit process more seriously, as the client is paying for it. It also more accurately reflects the total costs of running the different parts of the business.

Few management practices are entirely reasonable and the demerit of charging for audits conducted is that line management should not determine whether or not an audit is conducted, nor how much audit resource is allocated to the audit; since line management are not able to control the costs of auditing services, it is arguable that those costs should not be charged against their budgets.

Measuring processes

The emphasis with respect to process measures is the efficiency with which the internal audit activity functions. The efficiency analogy with an automobile is whether it runs as a well-oiled, well-maintained machine. This is distinct from the costs associated with running the automobile – which are matters of economy. It is also distinct from whether or not the automobile achieves the objectives set for it – such as luxury, prestige, speed, etc. – which is a matter of effectiveness. Of course these three overlap, as we have said before: a poorly maintained automobile is less likely to be effective, for instance.

Our model in Figure 6.5 shows that efficiency links economy with effectiveness. Perhaps a good overall measure of audit efficiency is therefore the average cost of each implemented audit recommendation.[8]

Figure 6.8 *Process performance measures*

- Training
- Professional activities
- Rotation of audit staff
- Extent of real responsibility – or is audit work specified in detail?
- Compliance with Standards
- Proportion of time which is productive
- Categorisation of productive time according to the stages of audit
- Target dates for various stages of an audit
- Time delay between end of fieldwork and issuance of final audit report
- Time spent on individual audits in comparison with planned time
- Comparison of time with results
- Time spent on total audits – in comparison with planned time
- Rate of completion on audits on schedule
- Reputation of audit (client satisfaction survey results)

Insight into the audit function's overall efficiency will come from exploring the achievement of target dates and the extent that audit management has been successful in maximising auditors' time actually spent conducting audits and, within that productive time, the way it has been allocated and supervised.

The audit client may also have some useful impressions about the professionalism of the audit approach which can be explored in a survey – see Figure 6.6. The main measure of professionalism of internal auditing is generally held to be The Standards for the Professional Practice of Internal Auditing issued by The Institute of Internal Auditors: performance measures can be devised to assess the extent to which an internal auditing function complies with these Standards. It should be pointed out that compliance requires commitment to them by the internal auditing function, but also needs support by senior general management and the board.

Measuring outputs

Here we are considering principally (a) whether or not internal audit achieves its objectives and, indeed, even (b) whether it achieves the right objectives. We suggest some output measures in Figure 6.10.

The Charter of the internal auditing function, as a statement of the distinctive rights and obligations of the audit function, is an important yardstick against which audit effectiveness or output should be measured. Certain elements of the Standards also relate to audit effectiveness as distinct from audit process.

Audit output is hard to measure. Internal auditors are knowledge workers

Figure 6.9 Implicit or explicit objectives of internal audit

- Reassurance to management that internal control is sound.
- Identifying non-compliance with a view to prevailing upon management to ensure future compliance.
- Identifying system weaknesses and developing recommendations for improvement.
- Persuading management to accept and implement successfully the audit recommendations for improvement.

Figure 6.10 *Output* performance measures

- Reporting success (see Figure 6.11).
- Cost savings achieved.
- Increased opportunities identified by audit.
- Completion of audit plan.
- Client satisfaction.
- Compliance with internal audit charter.
- Audit staff advancement.
- Occasions on which audit is consulted on systems changes.
- Level of requests for special audit assignments.

whose output is not always tangible. Knowledge workers conventionally issue reports, and internal auditors are no exception. Internal audit reports are a repository of information on audit output. Perhaps the principal objective on internal auditing is to reassure management that their systems of internal control are sound and, where they are not, to prevail upon management to implement measures which internal audit recommend to improve things in areas of weakness. Within this concept of internal auditing there are several implicit or explicit objectives (Figure 6.9).

The existence of an audit function with broad coverage provides a measure of reassurance to management and the board and the deterrent effect of internal audit may discourage future abuse. Perhaps the nearest we can get to measuring this type of audit effectiveness is to measure the planned coverage of internal audit and the extent to which internal audit succeeds in completing its planned programme of work.

An analysis of the findings in audit reports can measure the success of the internal auditing unit in identifying non-compliance with essential controls –

Figure 6.11 Internal audit reporting success

	Recommendations	Acceptances	Implementations	Successes
Number	1000	800	700	650
Losses	200	100	50	
Loss rate (%)	20	12.5	7.1	

perhaps comparing with the previous year, or comparing the success of different audit teams, or comparing the success of the audit function in certain areas of audit work compared to other areas.

With regard to identifying system weaknesses and developing recommendations for improvement and persuading management to accept and implement successfully the audit recommendations for improvement (Figure 6.9) a similar analysis of (a) past audit reports and (b) audit records of audit follow-up should allow a measurement similar to the example in Figure 6.11. Admittedly this is an inexact set of measures. It presumes, for instance, that success can be assessed: even where it can be assessed, the time delay is likely to be too great to make it a useful measure of internal audit performance. So it might be more practical to measure in accordance with Figure 6.11, but stopping short of trying to evaluate whether or not an implemented audit recommendation was successful.

It may be possible to attach money values to cost savings which follow management's acceptance and subsequent correction/implementation of audit findings and recommendations. It will never be possible, however, to account for the total value of the audit function to the business as a whole in terms of cost savings. The impact on costs of many accepted and implemented audit recommendations is indeterminable, as often we can never know what would have happened if management had not so acted. Nevertheless a historical record of known cost savings which have followed from audit work can give *one* indication of audit value for money. However, we should point out that it is human nature to overlook the additional costs which are often associated with internal audit outcomes. It is also human nature for the internal audit function to take credit for items suggested to the auditors by line staff, and it is certainly management and staff who should take the credit for successful implementation of audit recommendations. In measuring cost savings it is difficult to determine the length of time into the future that the audit department should compute the saving: the decision is arbitrary. For instance, if the audit department takes credit for savings over a 12-month period, this overlooks the fact that the business may continue to benefit from that audit finding indefinitely into the future. Despite these objections to measuring cost savings, doing so does have a place in the assessment of audit effectiveness.

Interpreting performance measures

Any performance measure may mislead if it is interpreted on its own. For instance, the number of internal auditors per 1,000 staff employed may show a very economic approach to internal auditing – but other measures may indicate that internal auditing is not very effective. Completion of all audits by their target dates may be at the expense of useful findings and recommendations being made in the audit reports. Measures of reporting success should be linked with measures of cost savings, time utilisation and the achievement of audit plans.

We also need to be cautious about placing too much confidence in our performance measures. It might be that they indicate a high degree of audit success and yet overlook important issues which bear upon internal audit effectiveness. Here we highlight just two possible issues of this sort.

First, *audit independence*. This is a prerequisite of successful internal auditing. Secondly, the *scope* of internal auditing work. Two quotations are helpful here:

> Whether or not audit is able to perform the full range of audit functions effectively and efficiently largely depends upon management attitude and support which is itself largely influenced by status and independence. The real sign of independence is that auditors are not impeded in their efforts to examine any area within the organisation whereas status often determines the significance attached to audit findings by management.[9]

> There is no persuasive reason why ... internal auditing should not [appraise operations generally, weighing actual results in the light of planned results]. Perhaps the only limiting factors are the ability to afford so broad an audit, the difficulty of obtaining people who can do a broad type of audit, and the very practical consideration that individuals may not like to be reported upon. While persons responsible for accounts and for the safeguarding of company assets have learnt to accept audit, those responsible for far more valuable things – the execution of plans, policies and procedures of a company – have not so readily learnt to accept the idea.[10]

Figure 6.12 highlights some of the issues which affect audit independence.

Integrating performance measures with good management practice

The performance measures we use to evaluate internal audit should harmonise with those which are applicable to the enterprise as a whole:

> The importance of the objectives identified for audit is that these should underpin an organisation's overall aims and objectives, so that audit's achievements aid the development of the organisation as a whole.[11]

Top management and the board should take the trouble to satisfy themselves

Figure 6.12 Factors affecting internal audit indepdendence

- Is internal audit organisationally distinct from any part of the enterprise in which it conducts audits?
- Does internal audit derive its authority from the board?
- Does internal audit have a direct working relationship with the audit committee of the board, and does the head of internal audit have a right of access to the chair of that committee?
- Does the head of internal audit have direct access to the chief executive, and does the chief executive receive reports on audit assignments from the head of audit?
- Does the head of audit have unrestricted access to the business's external auditors and to relevant regulatory authorities?
- Is the recognised scope of internal audit consistent with the resources allocated to it?
- Are there no operational areas or levels which are precluded from internal audit review?
- Does internal audit have unrestricted access to personnel and information?
- Is internal audit free of any responsibilities for conducting any operations other than independent reviews of internal control; and does internal audit avoid detailed involvement in systems design?
- Is it clearly *management*'s as distinct from *internal audit*'s, responsibility to accept and implement audit recommendations?
- Are the audit assignments conducted, and their timing, consistent with the assessment of the head of audit as to relative audit need?
- Is the content of audit reports entirely at the discretion of the head of audit?
- Is the organisational status of the internal auditing unit, and the executive seniority of the head of the audit and its staff, sufficient to underwrite the above requirements?
- Is it policy to staff the internal auditing unit with professionally competent and qualified personnel, and to require observance of the Code of Ethics and compliance with The Standards of the Institute of Internal Auditors?
- Is the assignment of auditors to particular audit assignments done with due regard to the need to maintain effective independence?
- Is there a charter which sets out the distinctive rights and obligations of the internal auditing unit which is consistent with the above needs and is generally understood throughout the enterprise?

that this is so. CIPFA suggests there are four fundamental questions to be asked of internal auditing without which performance measures for internal audit have little meaning (Figure 6.13).[12]

The Charter of the internal auditing unit is a device which assists greatly in enabling these four questions to be answered in the affirmative.

Figure 6.13 CIPFA's 'four fundamental questions' to be addressed by the audit committee, by management, by the head of internal audit, and by external audit

- Does internal audit have agreed and established goals?
- Is the work planned and resourced in such a way as to make achievement a realistic possibility?
- Does the achievement of these goals contribute to the attainment of the corporate objectives, i.e. establishing and maintaining internal control?
- Does internal audit achieve its defined goals?

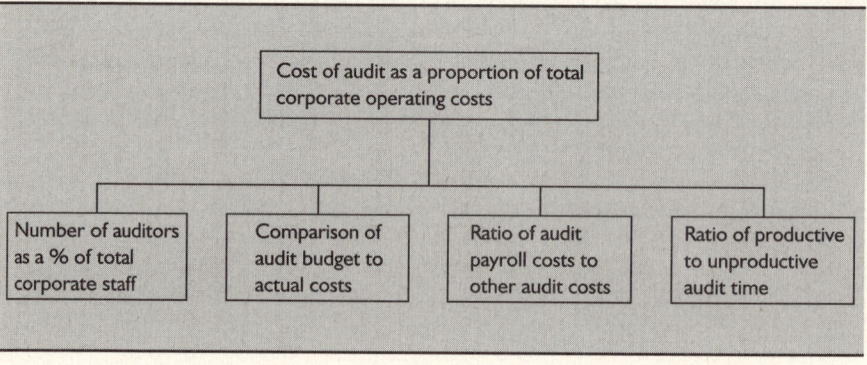

Figure 6.14 Economy (*inputs*) measures in the context of a value for money approach

Evaluating value for money from internal audit, using performance measures

In essence, value for money auditing endeavours to assess economy, efficiency and effectiveness making use of carefully chosen and carefully interpreted performance measures. So the approach we have taken in this paper is a value for money approach to evaluating the internal auditing function.

A refinement of the value for money audit approach is to organise the chosen performance measures into three hierarchies where the more junior levels of performance measures are intended to interpret the measurement of the more senior ones. The most senior measure in each hierarchy is intended to most accurately reflect the most important measure of economy (or efficiency, or effectiveness). Examples are given in Figures 6.14, 6.15 and 6.16.

Figure 6.15 Efficiency (*process*) measures in the context of a value for money approach

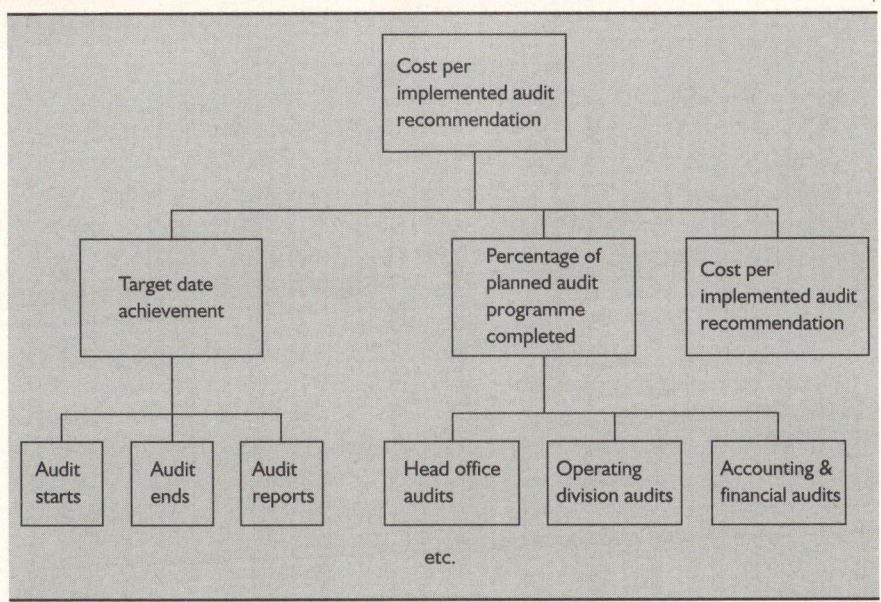

Figure 6.16 Effectiveness (*outputs*) measures in the context of a value for money approach

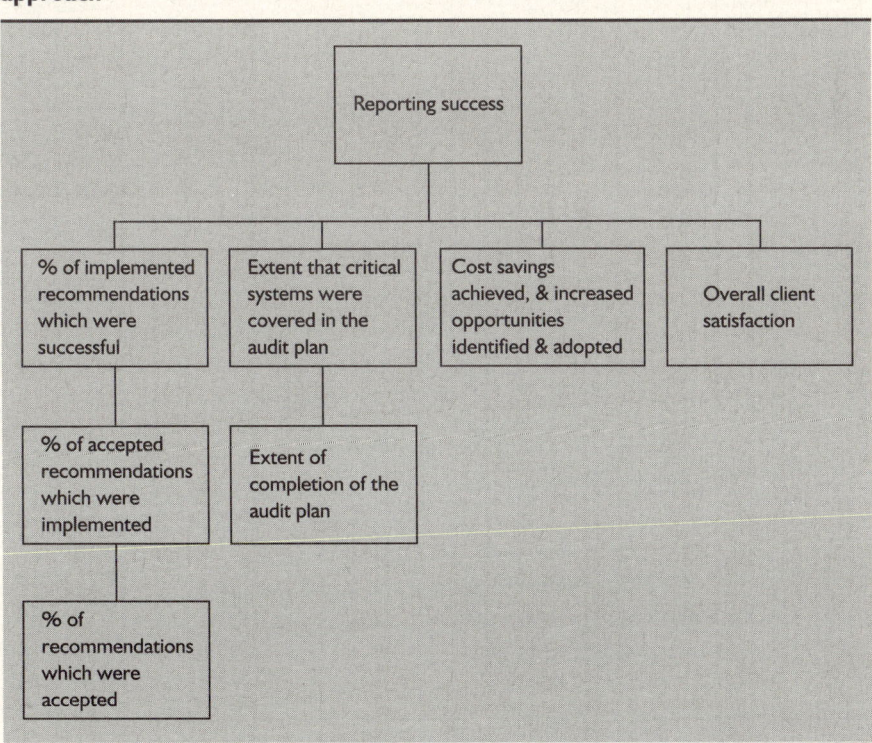

Chapter summary

Its is no longer sufficient for audit to view the historic reasons for its establishment as justification for its continued existence. Audit must and should be prepared to provide proof of its worth and value for money to the organisation as part of the organisation's continued growth.[13]

This chapter has sought to place internal audit in its broader economic context as a necessary prerequisite to the selection of appropriate methods to measure internal audit effectiveness. Being able to measure internal audit effectiveness is particularly important now that so much of internal auditing is being contracted out to outside providers of internal audit services. Internal auditing Standards contain helpful advice on assessing the quality of internal audit. We have shown that there are various categories of internal auditing performance measure, each of which has its place – input measures, process measures, and output measures. Measurements of internal audit performance are, however, only data to be interpreted with care – and then to be used to lead to better internal auditing performance.

Principia

1. Internal auditing is a costly service to run. Large amounts of profits from sales are needed to resource even a modest internal audit function.

2. Internal auditing is a prime candidate for market testing and contracting out.

3. If management and the board allow decisions on letting contracts for internal audit work to be made on *price* alone, rather than *value for money*, they are acting irresponsibly.

4. The goals of the internal auditing unit should be capable of being established within specified operating plans and budgets and, to the extent possible, should be measurable and accompanied by measurement criteria and targeted dates of accomplishment.

5. A key criterion against which an internal auditing unit should be measured is its charter.

6. Performance measures with a higher degree of objectivity than others are not necessarily the preferred ones to use: the criteria for selection of a performance measure should include a matching to the aspects of internal audit performance which are most important and which need to be monitored most.

▶

7. The client satisfaction survey provides data on the reputation of audit.
8. Performance measures can be devised to assess the extent to which an internal auditing function complies with Standards.
9. Audit output is hard to measure. Internal auditors are knowledge workers whose output is not always tangible.
10. Measures of reporting success should be linked with measures of cost savings, time utilisation and the achievement of audit plans.
11. The importance of the objectives identified for audit is that these should underpin an organisation's overall aims and objectives, so that audit's achievements aid the development of the organisation as a whole.
12. Value for money auditing endeavours to assess economy, efficiency and effectiveness making use of carefully chosen and carefully interpreted performance measures.

Notes

1. Chartered Institute of Public Finance and Accountancy (1992) *Measuring the Performance of Internal Audit*, p. 3.
2. The UK expression 'contracting out' is the equivalent to the US expression 'outsourcing'.
3. *Guidance for Internal Auditors*, Auditing Guideline 308 (London, Consultative Committee of Accounting Bodies, June 1990). In mid-1997 CIMA published an exposure draft of a much longer document, originally intended as an update of Guideline 308, though it is now uncertain as to what its status will be if and when it is released in final form. It now appears unlikely that it will be adopted by the Auditing Practices Board, which is shying away from acting as the arbiter of internal audit practice.
4. Such as, for instance, the elapse time between ending audit fieldwork and issuing the audit report. The decision to include this as one of the performance measures would be bound to be a matter of judgement; similarly there may be judgement involved in deciding the start and end points of the elapse time which is being measured. Judgement also has to be exercised in interpreting the resultant data – for instance, what elapse time is acceptable?
5. For instance, a satisfaction survey of internal audit clients, asking questions similar to those suggested in Figure 6.6, may be analysed numerically and trends compared over time or between different audit sections. The numeric presentation of the data tends to maks the high degree of subjectivity inherent within this performance measure.
6. See, for example, the *Survey of Internal Auditing in the United Kingdom & Eire*, 1995,

(Research Report No. 15, The Institute of Internal Auditors – UK) and similar international surveys with a US bias by IIA Inc.
7. A 1997 survey of internal auditing in large multinational manufacturing companies found that these companies employed one internal auditor for each 1,650 staff employed and that this had been stable since 1995. (Chambers, A.D. and Rand, G. (1997) *Survey of Internal Auditing in Health Care Companies*, Management Audit Limited.)
8. We evaluate this in more detail later in this chapter: 'Evaluating value for money from internal audit, using performance measures'.
9. Chartered Institute of Public Finance and Accountancy (1981) *Audit Occasional Paper No. 3: An Approach to the Measurement of the Performance of Internal Audit*.
10. Koontz, Harold and O'Donnell, Cyril (1976) *Management – A Systems and Contingency Analysis of Managerial Functions*, 6th edn (International Student Edition), McGraw-Hill, Tokyo, pp. 670–1.
11. CIPFA, *op. cit*, p. 2.
12. CIPFA, *op. cit*, p. 6.
13. CIPFA, *op. cit*, p. 1.

Case 6.1 Determination of appropriate internal audit resources

The case

The audit committee of the board has for some time been expressing concern about the level and quality of internal audit resources available to the enterprise. Certain non-executive directors on the audit committee think that the executive is not placing adequate stress upon internal audit. Over the past three years internal audit has been cut back as the business has downsized in response to declining turnover. Now the efforts of the executive are paying off and the company is expanding in terms of both turnover and new ventures. The executive is reluctant to increase fixed overheads to the level they were in 'the bad old days'. The executive reassures the audit committee that they are confident that internal audit coverage is sufficient in both quantity and quality. They offer that a senior executive should perform a special review of internal audit, reporting his conclusions to the audit committee; this senior executive fully understands the nature of internal auditing as he had, a few years before, been head of the enterprise's internal audit function.

What should the audit committee do?

Consider

The following solution:

The audit committee decided to accept the offer of the special review. In addition they indicated their intention to commission an external review of the internal audit function by someone, or a firm, competent to perform the review. While this might be the enterprise's external auditors, the committee was concerned that (a) they might not be sufficiently independent of the executive to be entirely objective, and (b) they might assess the quality of internal audit in terms of how useful internal audit was in meeting external audit objectives – which was not the point of the review. The audit committee decided to consult the Institute of Internal Auditors to properly resource this quality assurance review. The committee is particularly concerned that at a time of expansion, the enterprise's systems of internal control should be strong, and so an effective internal audit function is particularly needed at this time.

Case 6.2   Benchmarking

The case

The enterprise has been approached to be one of 15 participating in a benchmark study of internal auditing. For a variety of reasons they decided not to participate on this occasion, but used this opportunity to formulate their policy on participation in such a survey in the future.

Consider

The following solution:

This is what they decided:

- The enterprise does not compete with other enterprises on the strength of their internal audit function and so, in principle, there is no reason why internal audit should not be benchmarked.
- The most useful benchmarking of their internal audit will be against other internal audit functions in similar businesses of approximately similar size.
- They identified the following as being matters of particular interest to be gleaned from a benchmarking exercise:
  – comparative levels of internal audit resources (quantity and quality);
  – comparative practices with respect to outsourcing internal audit, control and risk self-assessment, etc.;
  – comparative costs of internal audit, distinguishing between payroll, travel and other costs;
  – comparative scope of internal audit programmes;
  – career profiles in internal audit;
  – best practice benchmarks in the cohort covered by the survey, etc.;
  – on cost grounds, being a relatively small business, they had a preference for utilising GAIN – the Institute of Internal Auditors' benchmarking service – rather than participating in a special exercise led by consultants.

Case 6.3 Measuring customer satisfaction

(Extracted from *In Business* (1997) D 23.7, ICSA Publishing, Hemel Hempstead)

The case

There are some pretty scientific ways of measuring customer satisfaction. Let's start with some unscientific ways, and call them the 'three Rs' of customer satisfaction. To remind you, these are:

(a) repeat business;
(b) deferrals;
(c) recommendations.

It depends upon the type of business you are in. Not too many house-holders make frequent purchases or repeat purchases of replacement windows. However, they may provide referrals or recommendations.

If we want to measure customer satisfaction, we can measure either what people do or what people say. To provide a parallel, what people say is the equivalent of an opinion poll before an election. What people do is the election result itself. As we know, the result is the reality. Wherever possible, measure what customers do, in preference to what they say.

Measuring what customers do

The three Rs give us some direction. If we track through all the steps of a typical customer engagement process, we may be able to identify opportunities to measure satisfaction.

(a) *Initial enquiries from a new customer* How did they hear about us? If someone has referred them to us, do we know who? What has worked in our customer engagement process? Do we remember to thank the person who made the recommendation?
(b) *Recommendations volunteered by existing customers* Do we have permission to use their name in the follow up? Do we thank them and keep them informed of the outcome? Do we ask for recommendations?
(c) *Customer buying patterns* Does the customer increase the value/frequency of their business with us? Do we start dealing with other contacts in that organisation? Do we see a trend in their approach?
(d) *Invitation to quote* How frequently are we invited to quote for business in our existing accounts? What is our 'win rate'?
(e) *Response to complaints/cancellations* Do we log all complaints and follow up afterwards? Do we have instances where supply contracts or orders are cancelled?

The following can be tracked on a monthly basis, if we collect the data:

(a) Number/value of sales leads.
(b) Source of leads by:

   (i) response to advertising/sales promotion;
   (ii) new enquiries from referrals/recommendations;
   (iii) additional business enquiries from existing customers;
   (iv) number of complaints/value of cancellations.

These may not all apply in every situation. However, we can plot the following ongoing business ratios on a monthly/quarterly basis to establish trends.

Value of response leads
Promotional response = Promotional spend.

By comparing with your advertising budget, sales budget, and other quarters, valuable information can be gained. Equally, tracking complaints/cancellations can be highly informative. The final piece of information of this particular jigsaw is to provide a consistent measure. As business expands, we need more leads to feed the situation. It is also important to legislate for growth in complaints. It is the ratio of complaints to existing customer business which is important. Finally, measuring is not enough. We have to react to the situation. Leads soon cool off if not followed up. Complaints become greater if ignored/unresolved. Now let's look at what people say.

What people say

Having established that actions speak louder than words, the words often help to explain the actions. There are two key areas here:

(a) The written word.
(b) The spoken word.

Customer satisfaction forms have become part of our lives, in hotels, restaurant chains, and car dealer service receptions. Many businesses get themselves into some amazing 'bear traps' over this. Here are a few key areas:

(a) Don't just ask for reactions, ask for background data. There are customers who are happy to pass a bored 5–10 minutes filling out your questionnaire. However, without any substantive questions to provide grounding, it may be a function of what kind of day or what kind of life they are having.
(b) Make it customer friendly. It may be easy to ask 100 questions in small print tick boxes which can be scanned into a computer. However, it may inhibit completion if you cannot get what you want in 10 ticks. You probably haven't thought about it.

(c) Provide free text. Ask why the customer feels this way or what they think would make the buying experience even better. Customers can be very frustrated if they are involved in a corporate interrogation rather than a two-way conversation.
(d) Circulate any questionnaires to your staff. Before inflicting them upon customers, ask your staff to complete the questionnaire (best at a meeting 10 minutes before the end of the day).
(e) Avoid tag-ons. That very earnest market researcher may want to know all about the demographics of the customers, but ruin the spontaneity and completion rate of the survey.
(f) Staff reward/recognition. Never never never reward/pay your staff upon what customers say. Staff have a way of encouraging customers to say the right things. This can lead to the surrealistic situation where a customer complaint is disbelieved because 'the customer satisfaction statistics say everything is OK'. It's like rewarding salespeople for the number of selling calls they make, not the business they produce. The worst-case scenario is where major issues are either not recognised or ignored because of a tendency for systems to deliver the answer people want to hear. Think of issues/complaints as icebergs. Ninety per cent of their substance is under the surface. Then think of the *Titanic*.
(g) Analysis/action. If you don't intend to use the information, don't collect it. Also, don't edit it according to your own value judgements. Ensure that you have a statistically valid methodology. Good or bad, share the information with staff and customers. Finally, do something with it.

Consider

1. List out all your customers, both internal and external to your internal audit unit and organisation.
2. How do the principles of achieving customer satisfaction through the selling and use of an organisation's products and services, as outlined in the case, apply to all your customers?
3. Create your own satisfaction measures for your internal auditing services. Develop processes to measure all your customers and all the services you provide.

CHAPTER 7

Reporting and progressing audit findings

> How audit findings should be communicated, orally and in writing. The follow-up of action by management on audit recommendations.
>
> Reports are the auditor's opportunity to get management's undivided attention. That is how auditors should regard reporting – as an opportunity, not dreary drudgery – a perfect occasion to show management how auditors can help.
>
> (Lawrence B. Sawyer (1996) *Sawyer's Internal Auditing*)
>
> Specific Standard 430 Communicating Results
>
> Internal Auditors should report the results of their audit work
>
> **Guideline 430.03**
>
> Reports should be objective, clear, concise, constructive and timely.
>
> (IIA)

Audit reports are *not* the end products of internal audits. One end product is reassurance to management and to the board, usually through its audit committee, that their systems of internal control are sound. Another is the communication of audit findings relating to weaknesses in internal control. Yet another is persuasive advice to management, which has the effect of correcting weaknesses in internal control.

As the written audit report is a very effective means of communicating and persuading to achieve these ends, it is used in almost every audit and on other occasions as well.

Communicating includes informing. An indication of audit reporting success is whether the intended messages are communicated clearly. Effective audit

238 Leading edge internal auditing

reporting also requires face-to-face communication: the written report is never an entirely satisfactory alternative to oral communication. The written audit report is also an invaluable source of record.

An internal audit can be an alienating process, and the phrase 'audit report' has an authoritarian ring to it. A key requisite of effective audit reporting is to ensure that the written audit report does not provoke a hostile response from those whom it is intended to persuade. Belittling line staff or line management is a sure way of alienating the readers. Readers should not lose face: if they do, then the objectives of audit reporting are unlikely to be achieved.

Understand the types of internal audit report

Internal auditors work on an assignment basis. Each audit assignment has a start and an end. The most common form of audit report is the *audit assignment report*, which follows the fieldwork of an audit assignment. Occasionally, a less formal memorandum may be more suitable if the scope of the audit is a very narrow targeted review, or if the auditors have no significant findings or recommendations and no other significant matters to be brought to management's attention.

Since management should usually be advised promptly of significant audit findings, *interim reports*, often oral or in informal memorandum form, are likely to be issued by auditors during long audits. See Figure 7.1.

Seriously adverse audit findings may require a later follow-up audit assignment, leading to a *follow-up audit report*.

Sometimes the results of audits with a broad scope will be best communicated on a need to know basis in more than one audit report, where responsibilities for different aspects of the operations under review are vested in more than one senior

Figure 7.1 Guidance on communicating results (IIA)

Guideline 430.01

... Interim reports may be written or oral and may be transmitted formally or informally.

SIAS No. 2 Communicating Results (430.01.1)

Interim reports may be used to communicate information which requires immediate attention, to communicate a change in audit scope for the activity under review, or to keep management informed of audit progress when audits extend over a long period. The use of interim reports does not diminish or eliminate the need for a final report.

manager. Senior managers do not need the burden of reading through material in audit reports which relates only to other managers' responsibilities, and it is usually preferable to keep the results of audit work reasonably confidential to those who need to know.

A barrier to communicating clearly is an unnecessary quantity of detail for the perceived needs of the reader. For this reason, many internal audit functions issue their assignment reports in two forms – a *summary audit assignment report* for the senior reader and a *detailed audit assignment report* for the more junior manager who needs to know the detail.

If only one form of audit report is written it should commence with 'the big picture' so that the busy reader has discretion as to whether he or she needs to study the detailed pages which follow. The contents of 'the big picture' will correspond to the contents of a summary audit assignment report.

Significant audit findings and recommendations relating to a number of audit assignments should be summarised in an *activity report* submitted to senior management and to the board or to the board's audit committee. Activity reports should also inform of any significant deviations from previously approved internal audit work schedules, staffing plans, and financial budgets, and the reasons for these deviations. See Figures 7.2 and 7.3.

The audit committee of the board is usually the most senior point within the business to whom internal audit reports directly. All those to whom internal audit reports need to be confident that the scope of internal audit coverage as well as the content of internal audit reports have not been unduly influenced by anyone at a more junior level. Internal audit should not subordinate its judgement on audit matters to that of others. If the scope of internal audit work or the content of internal audit reports had been unduly influenced in this way, then those to whom internal audit is reporting should have less confidence in the independence of internal audit, and thus less confidence in the objectivity of both the scope of internal audit coverage and also the contents of internal audit reports to them. This is perhaps the principal reason why the audit committee will pay particular attention to deviations from previously approved internal audit work schedules. It is also the reason why the audit committee will arrange to meet regularly with the head of internal audit when no other members of the executive are present. The audit committee itself is likely to be entirely non-executive, and certainly will be so if the composition of its membership is consistent with the best principles of corporate governance.

The activity report is a suitable medium to notify management and the board (a) whether the defined purpose, authority and responsibility of the internal auditing unit continues to be adequate, and (b) of the internal audit function's work, staffing and financial plans for the future: alternatively these matters can be covered in a separate *planning report*.

An annual *overall summary report on internal control* provided by internal audit will assist the audit committee to report its conclusions on the effectiveness of internal control to the board, and to frame the directors' annual report for

Figure 7.2   Internal audit organisational status and communication with the board (IIA)

Specific Standard 110 Organizational Status

The organisational status of the internal auditing department should be sufficient to permit the accomplishment of its audit responsibilities.

Guideline 110.01.6

The director of internal auditing should submit activity reports to management and to the board annually or more frequently as necessary. Activity reports should highlight significant audit findings and recommendations and should inform management and the board of any significant deviations from approved audit work schedules, staffing plans, and financial budgets, and the reasons for them.

SIAS No. 7 Communication with the Board of Directors (110.01.6.1–5)

Activity reports should be communicated, preferably in writing.

Significant audit findings are those conditions which, in the judgement of the director of internal auditing, could adversely affect the organisation. Significant audit findings may include conditions dealing with irregularities, illegal acts, errors, inefficiency, waste, ineffectiveness, conflicts of interest, and control weaknesses. After reviewing such findings with senior management, the director of internal auditing should communicate significant audit findings to the board, whether or not they have been satisfactorily resolved.

Management's responsibility is to make decisions on the appropriate action to be taken regarding significant audit findings. Senior management may decide to assume the risk of not correcting the reported condition because of cost or other considerations. The board should be informed of senior management's decision on all significant audit findings.

The director of internal auditing should consider whether it is appropriate to inform the board regarding previously reported, significant audit findings in those instances when senior management and the board assumed the risk of not correcting the reported condition. This may be necessary, particularly when there have been organisation, board, senior management, or other changes.

The reasons for significant deviations from approved audit work schedules, staffing plans, and financial budgets that may require explanation include:

a. Organisation and management changes.
b. Economic conditions.
c. Legal and regulatory requirements
d. Internal audit staff changes
e. Management requests
f. Expansion or reduction of audit scope as determined by the director of internal auditing

Figure 7.3 Internal audit purpose, authority and responsibilities (IIA)

Guideline 110.01.4

The purpose, authority, and responsibility of the internal auditing department should be defined in a formal written document (charter). The director should seek approval of the charter by senior management as well as acceptance by the board. The charter should (a) establish the department's position within the organisation; (b) authorise access to records, personnel, and physical properties relevant to the performance of audits; and (c) define the scope of internal auditing activities.

SIAS No. 7 (110.01.4.1)

The director of internal auditing should periodically assess whether the purpose, authority and responsibility, as defined in the charter, continue to be adequate to enable the internal auditing department to accomplish its objectives. The result of this periodic assessment should be communicated to senior management and the board.

Guideline 110.01.5

The director of internal auditing should submit annually to senior management for approval and to the board for its information a summary of the department's audit work schedule, staffing plan, and financial budget. The director should also submit all significant interim changes for approval and information. Audit work schedules, staffing plans, and financial budgets should inform senior management and the board of the scope of internal auditing work and of any limitations placed on that scope.

SIAS No. 7 (110.01.5.1–4)

The approved audit work schedule, staffing plan, and financial budget, along with all significant interim changes, should contain sufficient information to enable the board to ascertain whether the internal auditing department's objectives and plans support those of the organisation and the board. This information should be communicated, preferably in writing. A scope limitation is a restriction placed upon the internal auditing department that precludes the department from accomplishing its objectives and plans. Among other things, a scope limitation may restrict the:

a. Scope defined in the charter.
b. Department's access to records, personnel, and physical properties relevant to the performance of audits.
c. Approved audit work schedule.
d. Performance of necessary auditing procedures.
e. Approved staffing plan and financial budget.

A scope limitation along with its potential effect should be communicated, preferably in writing, to the board.

The director of internal auditing should consider whether it is appropriate to inform the board regarding scope limitations which were previously communicated to and accepted by the board. This may be necessary particularly when there have been organisation, board, senior management, or other changes.

Figure 7.4   Internal audit quality assurance (IIA)

> **Specific Standard 560 Quality Assurance**
> The director of internal auditing should establish and maintain a quality assurance programme to evaluate the operations of the internal auditing department.
>
> **Guidelines 560.03–04**
> *Internal reviews* should be performed periodically by members of the internal auditing staff to appraise the quality of the audit work performed. These reviews should be performed in the same manner as any other internal audit.
>
> *External reviews* of the internal auditing department should be performed to appraise the quality of the department's operations ... at least once every three years. On completion of the review, a formal, written report should be issued. The report should express an opinion as to the department's compliance with the Standards for the Professional Practice of Internal Auditing and, as appropriate, should include recommendations for improvement.

publication on internal control. As audit committees become more important in the total audit process, there is some indication of a tide of opinion suggesting that the chair of the audit committee should report publicly in the annual report of a business. Equally, some are suggesting that the published annual report should contain a report from the internal auditor and there are examples of this having been done.

In accordance with the guidelines to the Standards of The Institute of Internal Auditors, two special *internal audit quality assurance reports* are also to be prepared to notify the results of both the internal and the external reviews of the internal auditing unit. See Figure 7.4.

When an audit assignment report has been issued which is found to have included a significant error of fact or emphasis, an *assignment correction report* should be issued to correct the impression and the record. See Figure 7.5.

So the main types of internal audit reports may be as follows.

Reports on internal audit assignments

- Interim oral or written audit assignment reports during an extended audit.
- Informal audit memos issued during an audit.
- Audit assignment report(s) following conclusion of audit fieldwork – *either* (a) summary report(s) *and* (b) separate detailed report(s), *or* (c) comprehensive report(s) each commencing with a summary and followed by the detail.

Figure 7.5 Requirements of internal audit reports (IIA)

Guideline 430.03
Reports should be objective, clear, concise, constructive and timely.

SIAS No. 2 (430.01.1)
Objective reports are factual, unbiased, and free from distortion. Findings, conclusions, and recommendations should be included without prejudice.

a. If it is determined that a final audit report contains an error, the director of internal auditing should consider the need to issue an amended report which identifies the information being corrected. The amended audit report should be distributed to all individuals who received the audit report being corrected.
b. An 'error' is defined as an unintentional misstatement or omission of significant information in a final audit report.

- Informal audit memoranda at the conclusion of a narrowly targeted audit.
- Informal audit memoranda at the conclusion of audits without significant findings and recommendations.
- Assignment correction reports.
- Follow-up audit memos or audit reports.

Reports on the internal auditing unit

- Periodic assessments of the continued adequacy of the internal auditing unit's charter.
- The internal audit function's planning reports to management and the board.
- Activity reports to senior management and the board.
- Overall summary reports on internal control.
- Internal audit reports for publication.
- Reports on internal reviews of internal audit work done.
- Reports on external reviews of the internal audit function.

In addition, in many cases effective impact can be enhanced by using a covering note, or transmittal memorandum, to accompany the issuance of an audit report.

Tailor for the reader

Usually a report on an audit assignment should be addressed to one person only, even though it is likely to be copied to others. Audit reports other than assignment reports are more likely to be addressed to a number of people – such as to all members of the audit committee. Audit reports must be written for the person(s) to whom they are addressed. If the writer of the report keeps that person firmly in mind while writing the report this is likely to assist in ensuring that the report is tailored to the reader's needs. The better the addressee is known by the writer, the more likely it is that the report will be written in a suitable way to communicate with and to persuade this reader. If the addressee is not known by the writer, the writer should make enquiries of others as to the personality, background, experience, preferences and priorities of that person. To the extent that it is possible, this should also apply to those to whom the report will be copied, who also need to be properly informed and persuaded by the report.

It is always right to keep a report as simple as possible and this is particularly important if it is to be read by several people with varying backgrounds and interests. Jargon should be avoided at all times unless the writer is certain that the jargon is both familiar and acceptable to *all* the readers. Strange or unacceptable jargon impedes effective communication. Audit jargon in particular irritates and offends (words such as 'auditee', 'fieldwork', 'follow-up', etc.).

Understand the objectives of audit reports

There are general objectives of audit reports; and there are objectives which are specific to particular reports.

We have already seen that the main general objectives are to assist in informing and persuading the reader. Persuasion is not enough: the reader often needs to be galvanised into action and the report can help to achieve this. A measure of the internal audit function's productivity is whether it gets a 'sale' on every audit finding (or 'observation') and also on every audit recommendation (or 'point of action').

The Standards of The Institute of Internal Auditors place more stress on audit *findings* than upon audit *recommendations*. It is essential that those to whom internal audit addresses its audit reports accept the findings contained within them, since these relate to actual control weaknesses. If there is a disagreement on these findings this can usually be resolved by further work (either by internal audit or by management), since audit findings are usually factually based. There is more legitimate scope for disagreement on audit recommendations as these are matters of judgement. Management may decline to accept and implement an audit recommendation, preferring to carry the risk rather than incur the cost of change. Or it may occur to management that they will be able to solve the problem highlighted as an audit finding in an alternative and more effective way than that suggested in the associated audit recommendation(s). So, while internal auditors should always seek to make a 'sale' on every audit finding, it is not necessarily second best if audit fails to make a 'sale' on every audit recommendation.

Another general objective of audit reports is to project a consistent, professional image for the internal auditing unit. A poor report can seriously damage the reputation of the internal auditing unit. Factual errors are likely to discredit both the report and the internal auditing unit as a whole. Careless drafting, unprofessional language and poor presentation will mask valuable audit findings as well as spoiling the image of the internal auditing unit. A quality image for the internal auditing unit is important, as auditors will strive to live up to that image and management will assist in making this possible. In a real sense, the image of the internal auditing unit is its reality.

Audit reports also meet the general objective of recording the results of audit work. Apart from the recollections of those involved and the content of past audit working paper files (which will not be retained indefinitely[1]), the report is the only enduring information about what was achieved through the audit.

Every assignment report has its specific objectives to do with acceptance by management of (a) findings (or 'observations') of the audit and (b) the required action by management where appropriate. The report should emphasise the findings and action points which the auditors judge are most important.

Audit reports should never contain recommendations which would improve control but which would be impractical for management to implement. Audit reports should never contain recommendations which, if implemented, would be unlikely to assist management in the achievement of their objectives or in their avoidance of unwanted outcomes. So the internal auditor needs to be clear as to the potential benefits which would accrue from the implementation of audit recommendations.

Understand there are other ways to achieve the objectives of audit reports

The audit assignment report reinforces the messages of the audit. It is unwise to allow the report to reveal these issues for the first time. Material of sufficient importance to be included within an audit report is also of sufficient importance to be communicated promptly during the audit at the time the auditor, or the audit team, becomes aware of it. Provisional findings and points for action should be discussed with line management as they arise during the audit and may be put in writing at that time. If this is done, the final report will be much more acceptable to its readers. Discussing issues which arise during the course of the audit also provides a valuable means of testing the validity of emerging audit findings and recommendations. It also primes management as to what to expect in the audit report.

Special situations, such as that of suspected fraud, will require care in determining with whom the matter should be discussed during the course of the audit.

At the end of the fieldwork an exit meeting[2] should be held to review the results of the audit and to ensure that management's response has been given to all audit findings and points for action by management. This meeting is between the auditor in charge of the fieldwork and the line manager who heads the activity which has been the subject of the audit: each may be accompanied at the meeting by colleagues.

Use the Audit Summary Working Paper (ASWP) form

The ASWP form is a simple but powerful means of audit reporting *during* the audit. See Figure 7.6.

Select an appropriate reporting medium

As soon as the work has been completed on a topic within an audit, while it is fresh in the auditor's mind, the auditor completes the sections of this form which summarise the work done, the findings and the audit recommendations. Except where there is only one internal auditor in the function, discussion between audit colleagues may be needed – especially with regard to the audit findings and audit recommendations. It may be apparent that more audit work is needed before the findings and recommendations (if any) can be formulated.

The ASWP form, completed up to but not including the final section which allows for management's response to be added, is then routed as soon as it is available to appropriate line management for their consideration. Line management are thus kept in touch with progress during the audit and have the opportunity to consider the audit findings and recommendations as they are being developed. Line management are encouraged to complete the last section of the form and then to return it to the internal auditor or audit team before the end of the audit fieldwork.

The complete set of ASWPs prepared during the audit is sorted into subject sequence[3] and used as a convenient agenda for the exit meeting at the conclusion of the audit fieldwork. Where management's response has not already been appended to the ASWP, the exit meeting is used as an opportunity to obtain it. The auditors have then, in effect, discussed the draft audit report with management since the contents of these forms become the basis of the report. It is then straightforward to produce the final audit report promptly after the conclusion of the audit fieldwork.

As a word processed form, the cells of the ASWP expand automatically as data are added. Prepared on the auditor's notebook computer, the forms can be printed out smartly; and much of the text for the audit report has thereby been drafted during the audit fieldwork.[4]

In the past, audit reports have been issued on paper. Distribution in electronic form over the business's E-mail system is permissible if:

- it is accepted practice within the business for important internal management reports are issued in this form;

Figure 7.6 Audit summary working paper

AUDIT	PREPARED BY
SUBJECT	DATE
WORK DONE	
FINDING(S)/OBSERVATIONS(S) 1. 2. 3.	
QUANTIFIED RISK:	
RECOMMENDATIONS/ACTION TO BE TAKEN 1. 2. 3.	
MANAGEMENT RESPONSE	
RESPONSIBILITY	IMPLEMENTATION DATE

- issuance in this form does not impede the achievement of the objectives of the audit report – in particular, effective communication;
- due security and confidentiality can be achieved over the content.

Possibly one signed hard copy of the audit report should be kept on file in the audit department.

Develop a draft report for discussion

The contents of a final audit report should contain no significant surprises to most of those who read it. The draft report should be discussed with line management of the activity under review. This improves the likelihood of the final report being adopted. Discussion of the draft provides the following opportunities:

- to communicate the proposed report content orally;
- to persuade management where necessary of the approach taken in the proposed report;
- to confirm the accuracy of the factual material, including audit findings, to be contained within the report;
- to test the acceptability of proposed audit recommendations;
- to gauge management's general approval of the achieved coverage of the audit;
- to learn if any proposed wording inadvertently causes offence to management;
- to allow management's responses, together with agreed dates for corrective action, to be incorporated into the final audit report (Figure 7.7);
- to provide an opportunity for the auditors to make modifications to improve the acceptability of the final audit report;
- to prime management on what to expect in the final audit report, thereby increasing its acceptability;
- to provide management with the opportunity to commence taking the agreed actions which will be spelt out in the final audit report.

Using the ASWP approach ensures that draft findings and recommendations are discussed and most if not all of management's responses are obtained before the conclusion of the audit field visit. The ASWP approach also meets the requirement of giving management sight of the draft report before it is finalised and provides a mechanism for recording their responses. See Figure 7.8.

Whatever method is used, it is best that the draft is usually issued and discussed before the end of the fieldwork. Try to avoid issuing a draft report later than this and then awaiting management's responses in writing so that a final audit report can be issued even later – this leads to excessive delays in publishing the final audit report as well as losing the impact of an oral discussion of draft findings and recommendations towards the end of the fieldwork.

Figure 7.7 Discussion of internal audit conclusions and recommendations (IIA)

Guideline 430.02

Internal auditors should discuss conclusions and recommendations at appropriate levels of management before issuing final written reports.

SIAS No. 2 (430.02.1–2)

Discussion of conclusions and recommendations is usually accomplished during the course of the audit and/or at post-audit meetings (exit interviews). Another technique is the review of draft audit reports by management of the auditee. These discussions and reviews help ensure that there have been no misunderstandings or misinterpretations of fact by providing the opportunity for the auditee to clarify specific items and to express views of the findings, conclusions, and recommendations.

Although the level of participants in the discussions and reviews may vary by organisation and by the nature of the report, they will generally include those individuals who are knowledgeable of detailed operations and those who can authorise the implementation of corrective action.

Figure 7.8 Inclusion in reports of auditee's views (IIA)

Guideline 430.06

The auditee's views about audit conclusions or recommendations may be included in the audit report.

SIAS No. 2 (430.06.1)

As part of the internal auditor's discussions with the auditee, the internal auditor should try to obtain agreement on the results of the audit and on a plan of action to improve operations, as needed. If the internal auditor and auditee disagree about the audit results, the audit report may state both positions and the reasons for the disagreement. The auditee's written comments may be included as an appendix to the audit report. Alternatively, the auditee's views may be presented in the body of the report or in a cover letter.

Some drafting may remain to be done after the fieldwork has been completed. This is likely to relate to the introductory summary material, rather than to the detailed findings and recommendations. To the extent possible this should be drafted before the end of the fieldwork and seen and discussed with line management at that time. Only in exceptional cases should later first drafting of this material be allowed to delay issuance of the final audit report. Care needs to be taken to ensure that text drafted after the end of the fieldwork, and not seen by line management in draft form, is consistent with the sentiment discussed and agreed at the fieldwork exit meeting. Auditors should scrutinise the wording they use to ascertain there is no content unseen by line management which might inadvertently cause offence. For instance, emotive words should always be avoided.

As we have said, it should always be possible to come to agreement on factual matter. If management does not agree with the auditors on their factual findings, or are not entirely convinced, it should be possible to resolve this through further work either by the auditors or by management. While it is important to work for agreement on recommendations for action to be taken, these invariably involve judgement, and exceptionally it may be necessary to record in the final audit report a difference of viewpoint between internal audit and line management. It is more important that deficiencies are agreed and remedied by management – it is less important that management choose the particular means to do this which the auditors may have recommended.

Know which auditors should be involved

On large audits it is likely that the detailed parts of the audit report will be drafted by more than one person. The ASWP approach provides that the auditor who has completed a part of the audit is the auditor who, in consultation with his or her colleagues where appropriate, makes out the first four parts of the ASWP. Taken together, the ASWPs made out during an audit constitute the first draft of the detailed parts of the audit report. As part of a policy of 'empowerment' it is sound practice to devolve downwards the writing of audit reports as far as is expedient, and this is one way of doing so.

The section in the ASWP titled 'Quantified Risk' is a recent addition. It reflects the recent recognition that risk assessment is an essential component part of internal control. More and more managements are asking internal audit to express their findings in terms of quantified risk wherever possible. This makes it much easier for management to appreciate the relative importance of different findings, and to target their resources to where the perceived risks are greatest.

There is clearly a possibility of inconsistent styles emerging when drafting is done by more than one auditor. To overcome this, the summary sections at the commencement of the audit report may be drafted by one person who should review and amend the detailed sections drafted by other auditors, to achieve consistency of style. If the audit was conducted by a team, this task would usually be done by the team leader in charge of the fieldwork. Of course, where the audit is being conducted by one auditor only, that person will be responsible for drafting all sections of the audit report, and consistency of style is more readily achieved.

Figure 7.9 Signing internal audit reports (IIA)

> **Guideline 430.01**
> A signed, written report should be issued after the audit examination is completed.
>
> **SIAS No. 11 (430.01.3–.4)**
> The term 'signed' means that the authorised internal auditor's name should be manually signed in the report. Alternatively, the signature may appear on a cover letter.
> If audit reports are distributed by electronic means, a signed version of the report should be kept on file in the internal auditing department.

Figure 7.10 Reviewing internal audit reports (IIA)

> **Guideline 430.07**
> The director of internal auditing or designee should review and approve the final audit report before issuance.

It is preferable that the drafted audit report is then reviewed by an auditor who up to that point has not been involved in the audit or in writing the report. The purpose of this review is to raise editorial points and in particular to highlight ambiguities. This 'peer review' assists in ensuring that the report communicates clearly to readers without the knowledge and understanding which the field auditors acquired during their audit.

Either the director of internal auditing or, in the larger function, another audit manager with the former's delegated authority, should review and approve the drafted audit report which then becomes the final audit report. Where the report is issued in paper form it should be signed either by this person or by another designated by the director of internal auditing. See Figure 7.9.

Some internal auditing units (as a part of a policy of empowerment to improve motivation, commitment and fulfilment) follow the practice of audit reports being issued in the name of (or 'signed by') the auditor in charge of the fieldwork, while other internal auditing units require that *all* audit reports are signed by the director of internal auditing. See Figure 7.10.

Regardless of who signs the audit report, the names of the members of the audit team, the team leader and the audit manager should be associated with the formal record of the audit. They may appear in one of these places (Figure 7.11):

- printed on the cover sheet of the audit report;
- included in the Introduction section of the audit report;

Figure 7.11 Authorised report signatories (IIA)

> **SIAS No. 2 (430.01.3)**
> ... The internal auditor authorised to sign the report should be designated by the director of internal auditing.
>
> **SIAS No. 2 (430.07.1)**
> The director of internal auditing or a designee should approve and may sign all final reports. If specific circumstances warrant, consideration should be given to having the auditor-in-charge, supervisor, or lead auditor sign the report as a representative of the director of internal auditing.

- included in the covering note (or 'transmittal memorandum') which may accompany the issuance of an audit report.

Ensure appropriate circulation

Internal control is the responsibility of managers, and the monitoring of control arrangements is a necessary component part of internal control. Each senior line manager is likely to have responsibility for a number of activities, each of which may be under the control of more junior managers. Senior line managers can review the control of these activities for themselves but they usually find this is done more effectively if it is delegated to internal audit. So internal audit does what management would do if management had the time and know how.

It is consistent with this that audit reports should be addressed to the level of management which needs to know and is capable of ensuring that appropriate action is taken on the report.

It follows that the audit is primarily conducted for the 'boss' of the head of the activity which is being audited, and the audit report should be addressed to that person. It should be discussed in draft with line management of the activity which is being audited, including the head of that activity; their responses should be built into the final audit report and the report will also be copied to the head of that activity. See Figure 7.12.

It is best that audit reports on completed audit assignments are addressed to one person only and copied to as few additional people as is consistent with assisting in achieving effective communication of audit results. This preserves confidentiality and reduces the risk of line management losing face as a result of the audit. This will encourage line management and staff to participate more wholeheartedly during the audit process – which is necessary if auditing is to be effective and if audit reports are to be actioned effectively.

Figure 7.12 Circulation of audit reports

Addressed to:
- The manager(s) to whom the head of the audited activity reports.

Copied to:
- The head of the audited activity.
- The chief executive (who is the executive with overall responsibility for internal control).
- External audit.
- The director of internal auditing (as the departmental file copy).

The final decision on circulation should be that of the director of internal auditing or a member of audit staff who has the director's authority to make that decision. The decision should not be made by line management as this reduces internal audit independence and objectivity. Internal audit has a duty to ensure that audit findings are communicated to those who need to know.

Usually the distribution of audit reports should be disclosed. This can be done on the cover sheet of the report or in the cover note ('transmittal memorandum') which may accompany the report. Usually there should be no secret copies in circulation.

Audits with a broad scope may relate to a number of activities under the overall management of more than one senior line manager. Rather than address a single comprehensive report to all of these managers, more than one report may be produced so that each report includes only material relating to a single addressee's responsibilities.

External auditors have a right of access to all client information, and that includes internal audit reports. The charter for an internal auditing unit should grant authority to the director of internal auditing to disclose any audit findings, including the circulation of audit reports, to the external auditor. Circulating all audit reports to the external auditor makes it more straightforward for the director of internal auditing to ensure that sensitive findings are not excluded from the external auditor. On the other hand, the content of many internal audit reports is likely to be irrelevant to the external auditor and it may be inefficient routinely to send all reports to the external auditor.

Figure 7.13 sums up the circulation of the audit report.

Achieve appropriate timing

Audit reports are action documents. They are time-critical. They lose their impact if they are delayed. Delay may also invalidate their conclusions and thereby discredit the internal auditing unit.

Figure 7.13 Audit report distribution (IIA)

> **Guideline 430.07**
> The director of internal auditing or designee ... should decide to whom the report will be distributed.
>
> **SIAS No. 2 (430.07.2–.3)**
> Audit reports should be distributed to those members of the organisation who are able to ensure that audit results are given due consideration. This means that the report should go to those who are in a position to take corrective action or ensure that corrective action is taken. The final audit report should be distributed to management of the auditee. Higher-level members in the organisation may receive only a summary report. Reports may also be distributed to other interested or affected parties such as external auditors and the board.
>   Certain information may not be appropriate for disclosure to all report recipients because it is privileged, proprietary, or related to improper or illegal acts. Such information, however, may be disclosed in a separate report. If the conditions being reported involve senior management, report distribution should be to the board of the organisation.

Care should be taken to avoid standard methods which build in inevitable delay in the issuance of final audit reports and/or which take control of the timing away from the internal auditing unit. This occurs, for instance, when written responses to draft audit reports are awaited from line management before the final audit report can be produced and issued.[5] Suggested best practice is summarised in Figure 7.14.

Write balanced reports

It is very easy for an audit report to give the wrong overall impression. Most of the text rightly focuses on unsatisfactory findings even when the auditors have encountered an activity which is fundamentally under control, so the report may mislead management into concluding for themselves that a state of affairs is disastrous. On occasion, management may shield behind an audit report, using it to take unpopular action they were predisposed to take. For the audit process to be used in this way makes it harder for auditors to gain co-operation from line staff on future occasions. Certainly, the internal auditing unit should not encourage their reports to be misinterpreted and misused.

  Balance in an audit report is essential – not in the number of words, but in the

Reporting and Progressing Audit Findings 255

Figure 7.14 Getting audit reports out promptly

Ensure the following:
- Discuss with management audit findings as they are made during the audit.
- Draft the audit report before the conclusion of the audit fieldwork.
- Convene an exit meeting at the conclusion of the fieldwork to discuss with line management the audit findings and recommendations.
- Use the exit meeting as the final fieldwork opportunity to obtain management's responses – in particular their agreement to actions to be taken.
- Schedule adequate auditor time immediately after the fieldwork to finalise the audit report.
- Issue the final audit report within a target period (e.g. seven working days) of the completion of the fieldwork.

Guidelines on report writing style
- Present the report to the standard normally associated with an important internal management report (neither more flashy nor less impressive).
- Use a consistent appearance and style so as to promote the image of the internal auditing unit and to ensure that audit reports are instantly recognised as being audit reports.
- Consider standard forms, for instance a standard cover. Standard forms assist in maintaining consistency (as well as readability for those familiar with them).
- Make appropriate use of word processing capabilities to increase impact and improve readability.
- 'A picture can paint a thousand words.' High-quality, economically priced computer scanners make it feasible to include pictures in audit reports. Illustrations in words (i.e. examples) also make points more effectively than theoretical discussions. For instance, it is effective to illustrate a control weakness by describing an actual loss which has resulted.
- Be as concise as possible. This does not necessarily mean that the report will be brief.

emphasis of the audit report. The report should always contain an overall conclusion which should be balanced. For instance, it could read:

> In general we were very impressed by the quality of internal control with the exception that we are concerned as to the risk that the company may be paying for goods it does not receive ...

– providing an overall conclusion near the start of the report discourages the readers from drawing their own, perhaps unjustified, conclusions.

Balance can be achieved by concisely giving credit to line staff and management for their assistance during the audit and by acknowledging action already taken or agreed to remedy deficiencies.

The style of the report should emphasise the positive advantages of taking the

Figure 7.15   Balance in audit reports (IIA)

> **Guideline 430.05**
> Reports may ... acknowledge satisfactory performance and corrective action.
>
> **SIAS No. 2 (430.05.2)**
> Auditee accomplishments, in terms of improvements since the last audit or the establishment of a well-controlled operation, may be included in the audit report. This information may be necessary to fairly represent the existing conditions and to provide a proper perspective and appropriate balance to the audit report.

action which is recommended or has been agreed – rather than dwelling on the risks of not doing so.

To sum up, balance is achieved through:

- providing a balanced conclusion 'up front';
- giving due credit to line staff and management in the report;
- being positive: focusing on the advantages of change rather than on the risks of making no changes.

Draft reports effectively

It is often difficult to start writing a report. It may help to get it all down on paper (or keyed into a computer) as quickly as possible – and worry about style and readability later.

In exceptional cases, where it is not possible for the drafted report to be reviewed by another, the original writer should put it to one side for at least 24 hours and then read it through with a fresh mind. Making editing changes immediately after drafting a report almost invariably leads to overlooking desirable alterations.

The drafted report should be read through the eyes of the intended reader, asking: 'How is (are) the reader (or readers) going to react to this?'

Use an acceptable presentation style

First impressions are hard to change. An effective style of presentation for the audit report makes a good first impression and thereafter aids communication. Almost all managers have too much to read: attractive presentation makes reading more enjoyable and therefore more effective. Figure 7.16 gives some guidelines on report-writing style.

Figure 7.16 Rules for writing reports

Rule	The *wrong* way	The *right* way
Write in the way you talk	The functional area attributed its operational deficiencies to a lack of personnel resulting from budget limitations …	The department said it could not do the job because it could not afford staff …
Say exactly what you mean	The concept of a trade discount has ceased to exist.	The discount has ceased to be considered a trade discount.
	The accountant at headquarters serves in the same capacity for the branches.	The HQ accountant also serves as accountant for the branches.
Put words in their best order	The value has been determined for disposal purposes of these assets.	The value of these assets has been determined for disposal purposes.
Don't lose the subject	The policy provides as a maximum provision for replacement 25 per cent of the initial cost, and is adjusted in accordance with the inflation rate.	The policy is that provision for replacement is up to 25% of cost, adjusted for inflation.
Try to avoid splitting long phrases, and avoid subordinate clauses	These figures, which were net of allowances for depreciation, expenses, prepayments and the costs of other estimated services, were omitted.	These figures were omitted. They included allowances for depreciation, expenses, prepayments and the cost of other estimated services.
Put the weight of a sentence at the start or end of the sentence – the main points of impact. Try to avoid transitional words, but place them in the middle of a sentence if they have to be used.	However, it is not envisaged that a detailed study of the costings of every tender will be made.	Not every tender will be subject to a detailed study of costings, we envisage.

▶

Figure 7.16 Contd

Rule	The *wrong* way	The *right* way
Don't use the same word in two or more senses	We project that the results of this classification of project results ...	Because of this classification of project results, we forecast ...
Be positive	We do not believe the management accounts can be trusted.	We believe the management accounts cannot be trusted.
Avoid too much use of the passive	No response has been made by management.	Management has made no response.
Action words should act rather than be nouns	The elimination of the waste could be accomplished.	The waste could be eliminated.
Avoid meaningless 'it's'	It is thought by management ...	Management thinks ...
Avoid redundant words – use as few as necessary	During the course of our audit we noted that invoices are ...	Invoices are ...
	This surplus is after giving effect to deductions therefrom by reason of ...	This surplus is after deductions for ...
Don't repeat yourself	Numerous other products are produced or processed, in addition to the above items.	Numerous other items are produced.
Avoid jargon	We discussed this with the auditee.	We discussed this with management.

▶

Figure 7.16 Contd

Rule	The *wrong* way	The *right* way
Avoid posh language – keep it simple – use a short word rather than a long word	We engaged in an audit commensurate with staff availability.	We did the audit with available staff.
	modification	change
	initial	first
	optimum	best
	encounter	meet
	demonstrate	show
	aggregated	totalled
Avoid emotive language	audit findings	observations
	audit recommendations	points for action
	inflexible	firm
	obdurate	determined
	stubborn	strong
	pigheaded	decided
Avoid gender-specific language	The supplier should be required to sign in when he arrives.	Suppliers should be required to sign in when they arrive. or The supplier should be required to sign in on arrival

Use English well

The way something is written determines (a) whether and how it is understood by the reader, and (b) how the reader reacts to it. For audit reports the following rules should be followed.

Write clearly

The readers of audit reports are both short of time and weighed down by information overload. Auditors should not find it hard to accept that readers will rate a concise report which is easy to read much more highly than one which seeks

Figure 7.17 Essential attributes of audit reports (IIA)

> **Guideline 430.03**
> Reports should be objective, clear, concise, constructive, and timely.
>
> **SIAS No. 2 (430.03.2–5)**
> Clear reports are easily understood and logical. Clarity can be improved by avoiding unnecessary technical language and providing sufficient supportive information.
> Concise reports are to the point and avoid unnecessary detail. They express thoughts completely in the fewest possible words.
> Constructive reports are those which, as a result of their content and tone, help the auditee and the organisation and lead to improvements where needed.
> Timely reports are those which are issued without undue delay and enable prompt effective action.

to impress by its length and verbosity. Simple ideas do not need to be dressed up for effect. The reader will remember the message of the report if it has been communicated clearly, and will rate the report accordingly. See Figure 7.17.

A frequent reason for lack of clarity in expression within an audit report is a lack of real understanding about the issue – what is not clearly understood cannot be clearly expressed. However, what may be clearly understood need not be clearly expressed. A common failure is not to distinguish in reports clearly between (a) facts, (b) inferences drawn from the facts, and (c) opinions – the reader needs to know which of these is being expressed.

Be clear in audit reports about root causes. For instance, an avoidable loss noted during the audit may be an indication of a failure to comply with a control. A failure to comply with a control is likely to have a cause, and a more fundamental problem may lie behind that cause. Auditors should seek to identify the root causes and address these in their audit reports.

Clarity and impact is improved if the audit report uses language that management will relate to. For instance, rather than stress that 'goods received notes are not being matched with incoming invoices' it is better to stress that 'it is likely that management is paying for goods they do not receive'.

Clarity is also improved by use of short sentences and short words, and it is entirely misguided to think that these make a poor impression. The opposite of clarity is fog. The fog of a report can be expressed as the average number of words of three or more syllables in a sentence, i.e.:

$$\frac{\text{number of words with three or more syllables}}{\text{number of sentences}}.$$

Usually if this calculation is done for half a page of text within a report, the score is likely to be quite close to that for the report as a whole. Aim for a fog factor of 3.0 or lower.

Most famous speeches, written as much to be read as to be listened to, have very low fog factors. Churchill's speech in the House of Commons of 18 June 1940 is an example which conforms to the above rules to the extent possible for a brief text. It has a fog factor of 1.4. It is reproduced here with words of three or more syllables in **bold**:

> I expect the battle of Britain is about to begin. Upon this battle depends the **survival** of Christian **civilisation**. Upon it depends our own British life and the long **continuity** of our **institutions** and our Empire.
>
> The whole fury and might of the **enemy** must very soon be turned on us. Hitler knows that he will have to break us in this island or lose the war.
>
> If we can stand up to him all Europe will be free, and the life of the world may move forward into broad, sunlit uplands, but if we fail then the whole world, **including** the **United** States, and all that we have known and cared for, will sink into the abyss of a new dark age made more **sinister**, and perhaps more prolonged, by the lights of a **perverted** science.
>
> Let us therefore brace ourselves to our duty that if the British **Commonwealth** and Empire lasts for a thousand years men will say, This was their finest hour.

Lowering the fog factor can be achieved readily by dividing sentences into two or more sentences, and by using short rather than long words. Some long words may be unavoidable.

Document information available from word processing software can provide further information on comparative clarity, for instance:

- average word length;
- average words per sentence;
- maximum words per sentence.

Clarity also has to do with holding the reader's interest in other ways. A constructive and positive style – which emphasises opportunities for improvement rather than deficiencies – is looking at the business through the eyes of management who are there to achieve objectives, not merely to avoid mistakes. This style has much more natural interest.

Make sure structure and content are right

In the previous section we saw how proper use of English improves the clarity of reports. The structure of reports also has a profound bearing upon their clarity.

Many internal auditing units follow a general structure for their audit reports which corresponds to a fairly standard format. The first four sections may be

- (in the cover note to the addressee of the report) specify the requirement for the addressee to respond, and within a stipulated period.

Cover page

The cover can be used to hold, within a smartly pre-designed form, the following information – some of which may alternatively be included within the transmittal memorandum or within the report itself:

- indication of confidentiality and restricted circulation;
- indication that it is an audit report;
- title of audit;
- report reference number;
- report date;
- addressed to ...;
- copied to ...;
- prepared by ...;
- signed by ...;
- members of the audit team ....

Introduction

This will set the scene for the report. It *must* include:

- why the audit was conducted (i.e. the overall purpose of the audit);
- necessary contextual information.

It *may* include:

- reference to the date of the previous audit;
- the cost of the audit.

Objectives and scope

Purpose, objectives and scope cannot be neatly differentiated. The Introduction section contains a summary of purpose. Clearly, in general terms the objective of an audit is to achieve its purpose, but in this Objectives and Scope section, objectives should specify the control objectives contained within the scope of the audit, for instance:

- Was the audit limited to an investigation of controls which govern the reliability of accounting and financial information – for publication or for internal use by management?
- Did the audit cover controls over the safeguarding of assets?
- Did the audit cover controls over legal and regulatory compliance?
- Did the audit cover controls over the efficiency, effectiveness and economy of operational matters?

In this Objectives and Scope section, scope relates to breadth of the business activities over which the specified control objectives have been reviewed. Mention should be made of:

- Restrictions in scope of coverage. For instance, if it is an audit of payroll, it should be specified if one particular payroll was not included within the scope of the review. It is particularly important to indicate limitations of scope (and, on occasion, the reasons for those restrictions) so that the reader of the report does not obtain a false sense of reassurance of, for instance, (a) the extent to which the objectives of control have been considered, and (b) the breadth of the audit's coverage.
- The dates when the fieldwork took place.

Conclusion

The internal auditing unit's overall conclusion should relate directly to the objectives and scope of the audit.

Summary of main findings and recommendations (or 'Summary of main observations and actions to be taken')

The purpose of this section is to highlight the main points which are explored later in the Supporting Detail section, preferably taking only approximately a page to do so. The points in this section usefully can be cross-referenced to the Supporting Detail section. See Figure 7.20.

Supporting detail

This should be divided into sections according to subject, each section containing the following (which corresponds to the contents of the Audit Summary Working Paper form – see Figure 7.6) – preferably laid out clearly in this sequence, using these as sub-section titles:

- Subject.
- Work done. Be brief about the audit work done. Do not go into detail about this – too much detail can encourage the reader to enquire about the work done and dispute its appropriateness. This distracts the reader, consciously or unconsciously, from the more important findings and recommendations which the auditors need to communicate. It is up to the auditors to ensure that the quality of their work done is sufficient to support their findings and recommendations and it is not a matter which needs to be explained in the audit report.
- Findings (or 'Observations').
- Quantified risk.
- Recommendations (or 'Actions to be taken').

Figure 7.20 Recommendations in audit reports (IIA)

> **Guideline 430.05**
> Reports may include recommendations for potential improvements ....
>
> **SIAS No. 2 (430.05.1)**
> Recommendations are based on the internal auditor's findings and conclusions. They call for action to correct existing conditions or improve operations. Recommendations may suggest approaches to correcting or enhancing performance as a guide for management in achieving desired results. Recommendations may be general or specific. For example, under some circumstances, it may be desirable to recommend a general course of action and specific suggestions for implementation. In other circumstances, it may be appropriate only to suggest further investigation or study.

- Management response. This should include designated responsibility for implementation of agreed changes and agreed implementation dates. It may include an explanation as to why the weakness(es) exist or have existed.

Appendices

Relegate to appendices material which is necessary but which would distract the reader from grasping the argument in the Supporting Detail section, because it would represent a significant digression into excessive detail at that stage. See Figure 7.21

Present audit reports orally

Do not assume that the written audit report will achieve its impact without reinforcement. The close-out meeting at the end of the audit fieldwork is an opportunity to reinforce to line management at the field location, in advance of publication, the observations and points of action which will be contained in the audit report. The transmittal memorandum is another opportunity. Phone conversations at the time of issuance of the audit report, or shortly thereafter, are very valuable.

For a major audit, a carefully prepared and rehearsed oral presentation of the report to senior management is an excellent adjunct to issuing the report itself.

Follow up

Audit reports should be addressed to the level of management which needs to know and is capable of ensuring that appropriate action is taken on the report.

Figure 7.21   Follow-up (IIA)

Specific Standard 440 Following Up

Internal auditors should follow up to ascertain that appropriate action is taken on reported audit findings.

Guideline 440.01

Internal auditors should determine that corrective action was taken and is achieving the desired results, or that senior management or the board has assumed the risk of not taking corrective action on reported findings.

SIAS No. 13 (440.01.1–13)

Definition

Follow-up by internal auditors is defined as a process by which they determine the adequacy, effectiveness, and timeliness of actions taken by management on reported audit findings. Such findings also include relevant findings made by external auditors and others.

Responsibility

Responsibility for follow-up should be defined in the internal auditing department's written charter.

Management is responsible for deciding the appropriate action to be taken in response to reported audit findings. The director of internal auditing is responsible for assessing such management action for the timely resolution of the matters reported as audit findings. In deciding the extent of follow-up, internal auditors should consider procedures of a follow-up nature performed by others in the organisation.

As stated in Section 110.01.6(c) of the Standards, senior management may decide to assume the risk of not correcting the reported condition because of cost or other considerations. The board should be informed of senior management's decision on all significant audit findings.

Nature, timing and extent

The nature, timing, and extent of follow-up should be determined by the director of internal auditing. Factors which should be considered in determining appropriate follow-up procedures are:

a.   The significance of the reported finding.
b.   The degree of effort and cost needed to correct the reported condition.
c.   The risks that may occur should the corrective action fail.
d.   The complexity of the corrective action.
e.   The time period involved.

Certain reported findings may be so significant as to require immediate action by management. These conditions should be monitored by internal auditors until corrected because of the effect they may have on the organisation.

▶

Figure 7.21 Contd

There may also be instances where the director of internal auditing judges that management's oral or written response shows that action already taken is sufficient when weighed against the relative importance of the audit finding. On such occasions, follow-up may be performed as part of the next audit.

Internal auditors should ascertain that actions taken on audit findings remedy the underlying conditions.

Scheduling

The director of internal auditing is responsible for scheduling follow-up activities as part of developing audit work schedules. Scheduling of follow-up should be based on the risk and exposure involved, as well as the degree of difficulty and the significance of timing in implementing corrective action.

Process

The director of internal auditing should establish procedures to include the following:

a. A time frame within which management's response to the audit findings is required.
b. An evaluation of management's response.
c. A verification of the response (if appropriate).
d. A follow-up audit (if appropriate).
e. A reporting procedure that escalates unsatisfactory responses/actions, including the assumption of risk, to the appropriate levels of management.

Techniques

Techniques used to effectively accomplish follow-up include:

a. Addressing audit report findings to the appropriate levels of management responsible for taking corrective action.
b. Receiving and evaluating management responses to audit findings during the audit or within a reasonable time period after the report is issued. Responses are more useful if they include sufficient information for the director of internal auditing to evaluate the adequacy and timeliness of corrective action.
c. Receiving periodic updates from management in order to evaluate the status of management's efforts to correct previously reported conditions.
d. Receiving and evaluating reports from other organisational units assigned responsibility for procedures of a follow-up nature.
e. Reporting to senior management or the board on the status of responses to audit findings.

The person to whom the report is addressed is the person from whom the internal audit function should receive a formal reply. It is all too easy for auditors to walk away from an audit after the audit report has been issued, leaving management to accept and implement audit recommendations, or to fail to do so as the case may be. If line management become used to a lack of attention from the internal auditing unit after their issuance of an audit report, it becomes more likely that line management will lack the incentive to action responsibly the audit report. It is good practice for management's indication of acceptance of audit findings and recommendations, together with their undertakings with respect to implementation, to be incorporated into the audit report.

It is also good practice for there to be a formal, known requirement for a written response to the internal auditing unit from management to whom the report is addressed. This requirement might be for a response within a stipulated period from the date of issuance of the audit report. An indication that this is a requirement should be incorporated into the Introduction section of the audit report.

Follow-up on audit findings and recommendations is a shared responsibility between the internal auditing unit and line management. The internal auditing unit is responsible for ensuring that line management understands its responsibilities for action on receipt of an audit report. The internal auditing unit is also responsible to ensure, so far as is practical, that it knows the status of each audit recommendation. Usually it will suffice for audit to rely on the written response to the audit report from line management, or for internal audit to make enquiries of line management to ascertain the status of audit recommendations. On occasion, if the importance of the issues raised by the audit warrant it, or if internal audit has reservations about the reliability of management, follow-up audit visits may be conducted to confirm the status of audit recommendations. Since follow-up audit visits are time-consuming and often unpopular, they should be used sparingly.

The internal auditing unit is responsible to ensure that audit findings and recommendations are communicated to the appropriate level of management. When there has been a lack of satisfactory action by line management to whom audit findings and recommendations have been addressed, the internal auditing unit should consider whether more senior management (and ultimately the audit committee of the board) now need to be informed and, if so, inform them appropriately.

Line management is responsible for the management and control of their operations and therefore have the responsibility for following-up upon the receipt of audit reports. It is their responsibility to determine what action should be taken, to make arrangements for that action to be taken, to monitor the successful implementation of that action and to keep the internal auditing unit informed of progress.

Figure 7.22 Monitoring the status of audit recommendations

- Date first communicated to management.
- Date of audit report which contained the recommendation.
- Date management accepted the recommendation.
- Date by which management undertook to implement the recommendation.
- Date that recommendation was implemented.
- Date that the internal auditing unit confirmed satisfactory implementation.

Measure reporting success

Management may remedy an audit observation relating to a control weakness without necessarily following the recommendation the auditors made. Nevertheless, in this case the audit finding was accepted and a satisfactory response by management was implemented.

As a measure to maximise audit productivity, internal auditing units should maintain a schedule of the status of their audit recommendations, along the lines suggested in Figure 7.22. The target should be total acceptance of all audit findings (or 'observations') and timely implementation of all recommendations (or 'points for action').

Retain audit reports

Whereas the audit file of working papers current for this audit should be retained until the end of the next audit visit and then destroyed, a copy of past internal audit reports should be retained indefinitely, being archived when storage space becomes an issue.

Review audit reports

At intervals a sample – perhaps 10 per cent – of issued audit reports should be reviewed by a senior internal auditor and findings relating to reporting strengths and weaknesses discussed within the internal auditing unit with a view to implementing improvements where necessary. If the internal auditing unit comprises just one auditor it would be best that this review was conducted by someone independent of the internal auditing unit.

Chapter summary

Having read this chapter you should appreciate that there are differing kinds of internal audit reports, including reports on internal audit assignments and reports on the internal auditing unit itself. The chapter has sought to show how audit findings should be communicated – whether orally or in writing, or both. There may be appropriate means other than the written audit report to assist in the achievement of the objectives of internal audit reporting.

Advice has been offered on achieving a successful report writing style. To do this, audit reports need to be tailored for the specific reader(s), and the purposes of the audit report need to be clearly understood by its drafter. The need for, and the meaning of 'balance' in audit reports has been considered. Good use of written English has been explored.

The structure and content of audit reports needs to be appropriate to their objectives. In this context the roles have been explained of transmittal memoranda, cover pages, introductory sections, sections on objectives and scope, conclusions, summaries of main findings and recommendations, supporting detail, and appendices.

The generation of good internal audit reports on audit assignments may be facilitated in a number of ways, which are discussed in this chapter. These may include the use of Audit Summary Working Paper (ASWP) forms, careful selection of an appropriate reporting medium, developing and issuing draft reports for discussion, and determining appropriate circulation. Timing is also important.

We have shown why 'follow up' after issuance of audit reports is important as a shared responsibility of internal audit and management, and how this may be undertaken.

Other matters addressed in this chapter include the measurement of audit reporting success, the retention of audit reports, and the systematic review of issued internal audit reports.

Principia

1. The end product of internal auditing is reassurance that internal control arrangements are sound, or, where necessary persuasive advice to make internal control sound.

2. Audit reports are potentially an effective means of communication but they are not the end product of an audit and there are additional means of communication which the internal auditor should use.

▶

3. Audit reports are action documents – their publication should not be delayed.

4. Audit reports should be objective, clear, concise, constructive, and timely.

5. The most senior point to whom internal audit reports are addressed should be confident that internal audit has not subordinated its judgement to that of others – with respect either to the scope of audit work or to the content of audit reports.

6. On audit findings, there should be agreement between internal audit and responsible management because they are factual; as to audit recommendations, agreement may not always be forthcoming as they are matters of auditor judgement with which management may not always concur.

7. The image of the internal auditing unit is very close to the reality.

8. What is not clearly understood by the auditor cannot be clearly expressed by the auditor.

9. Audit follow-up is a responsibility shared between internal audit and those to whom internal audit reports are addressed.

Notes

1. Most internal auditing units will have two working paper files for each audit – a permanent audit file of schedules of continuing importance, and a current audit file of the schedules constructed during the course of a particular audit. An important part of the current audit file is the schedules which record the details of the audit tests conducted. The internal audit current audit file should be retained until the end of the following audit of the business activity as it will be useful to refer back to this file during the next audit. The permanent audit file evolves over time: as schedules are superseded they are transferred into the current audit file extant at that time. Correspondence and copies of past audit reports may be filed separately or within the permanent or current audit files depending upon their nature. Past audit reports should be retained indefinitely.

    External auditors, in view of the litigation risk, would retain their current audit files for at least six years.
2. Variously known as an exit meeting, close-out meeting, or wind-up meeting.
3. An alternative sequence for the agenda of the exit meeting would be by order of importance.
4. Standard Audit Programme Guides cover about 200 different business activities each of which might be an internal audit. They incorporate macros which, when invoked, (a) automatically generate an ASWP, and (b) organise all the ASWPs together in draft audit

report format. Standard Audit Programme Guides software work in WordPerfect, WORD, AmiPro or WordPro word processing software. Further details from Management Audit Limited: tel: +44 (0)1790 763350; fax: +44 (0)1790 763253; E-mail: ManagementAudit@compuserve.com

5. Although not recommended, where this practice is followed, a rule should be established that a written response to the audit report is required from the manager to whom it is addressed within a stipulated period – such as two weeks from the date of the report.

Case 7.1   Some rules for written communication

(Extracted from *In Business* (1997) II 2.9.2, ICSA Publishing, Hemel Hempstead.)

The case

Rule one: make it easy to read

Use short words and phrases, rather than elaborate sentences with many sub-clauses and polysyllabic words. We confuse 'insurance speak' with sophistication: using words like 'accomplish', 'acquiesce', 'cognisant' and 'supersede' rather than 'do', 'agree', 'aware' and 'replace' in a business communication doesn't demonstrate a wide command of the English language; it just creates a barrier between the reader and their understanding.

Rule two: make it easy to understand

Short, well-constructed sentences that use one word rather than three make communication clear and accessible. Avoid long paragraphs. Use bullet points or sub-headings where appropriate. Delete the verbiage and padding. If a word doesn't add meaning, take it out. For example, don't write this:

> The purpose of this letter is to provide an explanation of how we reached our decision to make the service available on an around the clock basis, and to see on a first hand basis the service in action please call my secretary on the above number and arrange a mutually convenient appointment for us to meet.

– when you could write this:

> This letter is to explain how we reached our decision to make the service available around the clock. To see it in action first hand, please call my secretary and arrange an appointment.

The same meaning with 24 fewer words.

Rule three: make it convincing

- Have facts not opinions.
- Use well-constructed, well-supported arguments.

- Offer a balance of views; anticipate objections and try to answer them in a positive, assertive way that supports your case.
- Don't ramble – stick to the point.
- Have a beginning, middle and end, and avoid repetitions.
- If it's a long document, have a summary at the beginning and one sentence summaries at the start of each new section.

Consider

How do your own internal audit reports compare and contrast with the above rules.

CHAPTER 8

Impact of information technology on internal auditing

> The use of information technology in internal audit is no longer an option; it is a necessity.
>
> (The IIA Research Foundation (1991) *Systems Audibility and Control*)

Using IT to improve audit service

Internal audit is the appraisal of the systems of internal control primarily on behalf of management and the board. Increasingly, enterprises' systems are IT-based. It follows that it can never be satisfactory for internal audit to assume that the IT systems of an enterprise are working satisfactorily: management is asking internal audit to provide them with that assurance. Internal audit assurance of this is achieved by ensuring that the internal audit scope covers each of the three following areas, which can be likened to a three-legged stool – remove any one leg and internal audit coverage becomes seriously inadequate:

- internal audit of the IT systems development process;
- internal audit of the IT facilities;
- internal audit of individual IT applications.

The internal auditor is likely to make use of audit software to facilitate effective internal auditing in each of the above three areas. Software, including electronic audit working papers, will also assist internal auditors to administer their audit projects to a higher standard.

Matching audit technology to management's technology

As a general rule, internal auditors can assume that their internal auditing will be inadequate unless they are making use of IT for audit purposes which is as sophisticated as the IT which management are utilising to run and control the business. This means, for instance, that if management is using on-line real-time data processing, a suitable audit response is for audit to be using on-line, real-time auditing.

This places a premium upon the importance of internal audit becoming involved at the design, development and implementation stages of IT systems and applications.[1] In part, this involvement is as internal control consultants – to ensure that IT systems are implemented with satisfactory internal control built in and to ensure that requisite audit software is built into the systems prior to implementation.

Being constructive as well as objective

Some auditors are concerned about their involvement at the development stages of an IT system or application. They feel this turns them into system designers. They worry that they thereby lose their independence, having become too close to the design characteristics of the new system. They are concerned that on a later occasion they will not be able to review the system with adequate objectivity, on account of their earlier involvement in its development. Perhaps this is an example where internal audit should not elevate the principle of independence above everything else. There is never such a state as total independence for anyone – and the internal auditor is no exception. Internal audit needs to preserve sufficient independence so that they can be reasonably objective in the conduct of their audit work and in the formulation and communication of their audit findings and recommendations. At the same time, internal audit should be a constructive service to management.

It is much more valuable for management to be advised of potential control weaknesses at the development stage of an IT application than to be confronted by the consequences of those design deficiencies at some point after implementation. This provides management with the opportunity to rectify the matter before the damage is done. It is easier for the internal auditor to win the argument at the development stage – when everything is fluid, and management as well as the project team are more open to suggestion. It will be harder to win the argument after implementation when the focus has moved away from the design characteristics of the new system and the project team has probably been disbanded. Making amendments to established systems is very costly and prone to error. Rectifying the consequences of breaches in internal control can also be extremely costly, time-consuming and prejudicial to efficient business operations.

Of course it is harder for internal audit to identify control problems at the design stage. They are likely to be self-evident after implementation. Yet, if internal auditors are experts in internal control, they should be willing to use that expertise when it is of most value to their clients, not just when it is easiest so to do. The whole point of professional expertise is that it can be applied in complex circumstances which require the exercise of considerable judgement. Even if internal audit cannot be confident as to what may be the right approaches to address internal control challenges, it should be possible for internal audit to raise the issues at the development stage, and to form a view as to the adequacy of the responses received from management and the project team. In other words, internal audit will know the questions to ask about internal control – even if they are not confident as to the answers. Raising the obvious issues can be very helpful, especially when the development of the new system is in the hands of IT specialists. The obvious questions for internal audit to ask might include:

- How are you ensuring that all data will enter the system – once only, on time and accurately?
- How are you protecting the system from unauthorised access?
- Are you defining for each item of data who may add, delete, amend or review that data, and then ensuring that activity is limited to this?
- Is there going to be adequate evidence after the event of all system activity?
- Have you identified and minimised the risks to continuity of processing, and made arrangements which will enable recovery in event of disruption?
- Have you avoided excessive dependence on key personnel?
- What arrangements have been made to ensure that user manuals and systems documentation will be adequate, available upon implementation, and kept up to date?

Internal auditors can guard against losing too much independence in the following ways when they give advice during systems development:

- Internal auditors may avoid formally becoming members of the IT project team. Their attendance at project team meetings may be clearly specified as being their capacity as internal auditors.
- Internal auditors may give advice on internal control at the development stage while making it clear that it is management's responsibility to decide whether to accept and implement their advice, and it is management's responsibility to handle the implementation of internal audit advice which they accept.
- Subsequent internal audit reviews of the same system *after* implementation may be made by a different auditor from the auditor, or audit team, who advised during the development phase. Where this is not possible, special care must be exercised by the auditor or audit team to ensure that they work objectively on the subsequent occasion, being open to the possibility that their earlier advice may not have been effective.

Management's responsibility for IT control

Care must also be taken to ensure that management and the project team are not tempted to abdicate their own responsibility for internal control within a new IT

Figure 8.1 Internal audit objectivity and involvement during systems development

> **IIA Standards for the Professional Practice of Internal Auditing: 120.03**
>
> The internal auditor's objectivity is not adversely affected when the auditor recommends standards of control for systems or reviews procedures before they are implemented. Designing, installing and operating systems are not audit functions. Also the drafting of procedures for systems is not an audit function. Performing such activities is presumed to impair audit objectivity.

system. It might be too easy for the view to prevail that, since internal audit is involved at the development stage, management can rely on internal audit's 'health check' to ensure that internal control will be effective in the new system. It is a sound practice for internal audit to establish with management, preferably in writing, that their involvement at the development stage does not diminish management's own responsibility to ensure that internal control will be effective.

Fundamentally, involvement by internal audit at the development stage does not break new ground for internal auditors. Internal auditors have always made recommendations in audit reports. There has always been a likely return visit by internal audit on a later occasion when the systems in place may reflect characteristics contained in earlier audit recommendations which management has accepted and implemented. So there has always been this challenge to continued internal audit objectivity on subsequent occasions. Bringing forward the initial internal audit review to the development stage of the system does not fundamentally alter anything. The Standards of the Institute of Internal Auditors address this issue (Figure 8.1).

Auditing the systems development process

Determining what is the audit universe of auditable units is one of the most challenging tasks facing an audit manager. Each auditable unit which corresponds to a business activity (such as production, sales accounting, etc.) readily suggests itself as a possible audit topic. Others are more easily overlooked. One of these may be the audit of the systems development process. In any business that is embarked upon major change, such as during business process re-engineering, it is likely that the internal audit function should audit the change process itself.

Whether or not this change process is well designed, with effective internal controls built in, will be a crucial determinant of whether the business makes its changes successfully. This is not the same audit as the audit of a particular project which applies the laid down 'rules' for implementing major change: what we are referring to here is the examination by internal audit of those rules themselves. These two audits overlap to the extent that the auditor's compliance testing during that audit of the change process will review particular change projects to determine whether the laid down change processes have been complied with.

Following a systems approach

As with other auditing, the internal auditor will follow a systems approach to the audit of the change process. In essence, the systems approach can be summed up as referring to an audit which sets about answering the following questions:

- What is the official, laid down system?
- Is it being complied with?
- Is it adequate?
- What might go wrong?
- Has it gone wrong?
- What is being done to prevent it going wrong?

Linking IT developments to the more general change processes of the business

Of course the design and implementation of an IT system or application represents change. It is change which needs to be governed by an effective system for handling IT design and implementation. Each time an IT system or application is designed, the quality of the resulting system will largely be dependent upon the quality of the standard procedures which govern IT developments as well as the extent to which they have been complied with. So the audit of the systems development process itself is an important audit to be conducted – especially so now that most business systems are strongly IT-based.

Here we take a bird's-eye view of the main issues which will feature in this audit. We look at the main activities involved in the development of a new IT system or application, some typical risks associated with these activities and suggested measures to guard against these risks.

Having good, laid down procedures

The business should have laid down procedures for handling the development of new IT-based systems. Without these, new systems will be developed to a variable standard of quality and in diverse ways which make difficult team working and subsequent system maintenance. In all businesses except the smallest, these should be documented to the extent that the nature of these procedures is apparent to all who need to be aware of them. The procedures should be kept up to date and there should be a process to ensure that this is so. One of the challenges is the orderly introduction of amendments to procedures: if procedures manuals are held on-line, then it is a relatively simple matter to ensure that all users have immediate access to any amended edition. When procedures have not been changed, there should be a process of reviewing them to ensure that they are still up-to-date and that no changes are needed. It should be clearly understood that it is the obligation of management and IT project teams to follow these procedures, and there needs to be evidence of management confirming that this is the case.

In this chapter we suggest that these are the main activities involved in the development of a new IT application, together with some of their associated pitfalls. Each of these should be reviewed in an internal audit of the systems development process.

Stressing the feasibility study ('project proposal')

First, there is the feasibility study. The perceived business need for a new or amended IT system needs to be investigated and the case needs to be made out. An IT solution may not necessarily be the answer to the challenge the business is facing. The feasibility study should be conducted by a team comprising IT and user personnel so that the practical business aspects as well as the technical IT issues are both taken on board. The feasibility study is a significant user of resources as, once the business challenge has been accurately defined, it may need to explore a number of different possible solutions which will need to be worked up within the feasibility study in considerable detail up to the level of an outline system specification. Anything less than this will be inadequate, as the feasibility study must recommend a fully costed solution with time-scales, resource requirements and alternatives spelt out in enough detail to be a basis for management to make a decision on whether to proceed and to bring into play the resource commitments which the project will entail. The feasibility study report should include predicted performance indicators for all the essential features of the system, such as response times, down times, volumes, file sizes, data rejection rates, etc.

It is best that the feasibility study report is presented in writing and with an oral and visual presentation. After full debate, management's written authorisation to proceed with the project is the signal to develop the project in detail. The system may need to be specially programmed, or it may use packaged software with or without program modifications. Even if no modifications are required to packaged software, a significant amount of skilled tailoring is likely to be needed to turn the package into useful software to meet the business need. Whatever the nature of the detailed specification which is required, it should be made in writing and each part of it should be approved by the project manager and by senior line management whose staff will be the users of the system.

Ensuring there is a steering committee

It is sound practice to have a standard rule to establish a project steering committee comprising technical IT representatives and key user personnel. It might meet fortnightly. Internal and (depending upon the nature of the system) external audit should be invited to send observers to steering committee meetings. This provides an important forum for internal audit to make a contribution at the development stage of the system. Its primary purpose is to act as a clearing house for the key design features which are being specified.

Documenting the system

Programmers develop the software working from the written, authorised detailed specifications. Modifications to those specifications should also be made in writing. This documentation becomes an essential part of the overall system documentation and it is essential that it is comprehensive, accurate and kept up to date. Many IT systems are eventually abandoned when their ongoing maintenance becomes impractical due largely to the disastrous state of system documentation.

Testing

Programmers have a responsibility to test their programs using test data they may design for themselves. When a programmer is satisfied that his or her program works according to specification, it is a good practice for the programmer to formally sign off the program. One programmer's coding should be desk checked by another, to encourage high standards of work and to reduce the risk of fraudulent or malicious routines being built into programs. Link testing a program module with the modules which interface with that program can also be a formal responsibility of the programmer: many programs work well on their own but fail when working in concert with other programs in a system, due principally to misconceptions about the form of linkages. As with documentation of the detailed system specification, so it is with program documentation: it is essential that it is comprehensive if the system is to be maintained successfully into the future. Hard copies of source program code should be maintained securely. Back-up copies of source programs should be made and kept securely at a remote location.

All of the programs in the system need to be brought together and tested in a comprehensive system test under the control of the project manager or the user department. It needs to test all of the features of the system using realistic volumes of data and values of data. It should be a test over several cycles of the system. It should include a test of occasional routines such as year-end or month-end routines. Care should be taken to ensure that all unusual conditions or data and all categories of invalid data and conditions are included within the test. Anything less than this is likely to be an incomplete test of the system, risking implementation of a defective system. Beyond the challenge of ensuring that the system is tested thoroughly, there is the challenge of ensuring that all untoward outputs from the test, and all untoward updating of computer-based files, are noticed. It is best that the results of the test are predetermined and then the actual results can be compared with what was expected. Much of this testing may be automated to achieve higher standards of reliability: test data can be generated by the computer, expected outputs determined by the computer and comparisons made between actual and expected outputs, using the computer to do this.

Developing user procedures

Often omitted is the timely development of user manuals describing for users the features of the new system and how they can be applied. Users need this manual before they go live with the new system – at that stage, even with the best of training, they will need to refer to the manual most frequently. The user manual should be available, at least in draft form, for training user personnel. We are all aware that we can learn about a new IT system better if we are able to refer to a user manual during our training. So the user manual's development should not be an afterthought for the project team; but often it is left until later, as the project team, up against time deadlines, focuses all its efforts into getting the software working. The right time to draft the user manual is during the development of the system itself, when all the functionality of the system is fresh in the minds of the project team: if this is not done there will be a serious risk of the user manual not referring at all to some of the features within the system – which thus become unavailable to users.

Converting files

Nested within an IT development project is usually another IT project, which may be as demanding as the development of the system itself. This is the preparation of the computer-based files which the system will require. This may be a conversion of an existing database into the format required by the new system, or it may be a matter of collecting data and entering it into the computer for the first time. Usually it is some of both of these. These data will be the 'standing' or 'permanent' data that the system will depend upon on an ongoing basis – names, addresses, account numbers, etc. The validity of these data is even more important than the validity of the much shorter-lived transaction data. The successful implementation of the new system will be in peril if the permanent data are inaccurate and incomplete, prior to implementation. They must be carefully checked. Where a conversion of data held formerly in a different format is involved, control totalling may assist in reconciling the old data with the new. Once loaded onto the computer, these data may have to be maintained as their values change before the new system goes live. So the scheduling of file creation and file conversion prior to implementation needs to be done very carefully. Some permanent data may not be available until just before switching over to the new IT system, but nevertheless need to be available to the new system, accurately and completely, as soon as they are implemented – this is likely to apply to carry-forward balances in accounts, to stock records, etc. So the data creation project may need to include a crash programme of data entry or data conversion just before going live with the new system. If implementation of the new system is to be phased, then the data creation programme will also have to be planned in a phased way.

Implementing new systems

Implementation can be a struggle. Possibly the new system has been promoted on the basis that fewer staff will be needed to run it, and, prior to implementation, the level of staff has been run down. During implementation it is likely that more rather than fewer staff will be needed. To some extent it is likely that the old system will run in parallel with the new for a while. Initially, even with the best training, the staff are likely to be slow in their use of the new system. So it is important that adequate resources have been planned for the implementation phase. Business partners may also need to be advised of the switch-over between the old and the new systems – both because of the dislocation upon their own systems and because of a possible degradation of turnaround time in the early stages of implementation.

Running the old system in parallel with the new allows comparison to be made between the two before the old system is dropped. But it is demanding on resources and demoralising upon staff if it goes on for too long. If the system has been thoroughly tested, then parallel running should not be necessary as an additional test of the new system. Parallel running also poses the question as to whether the output of the old or of the new system should be used. If the old system's output is used, then the carry-forward balances will need to be adjusted on the new system before switch-over takes place. Parallel running may be justified on a pilot implementation, but not indulged for the remaining implementation, which may be completed in phases of increasing size as confidence builds. Depending upon the nature of the system, complete implementation may have to be achieved almost overnight without any parallel running, in order to preserve business continuity.

Appraising implemented systems

Post project review should be regarded as an essential part of an IT system development. It entails a comparison of the performance of the new system with the promises made for it in the earlier feasibility study. It is a deterrent to extravagant claims being made for a proposed new system in order to get approval for its development. It provides an opportunity to determine how the new system is not performing up to specification – often a small amount of fine-tuning can rectify this. It helps the business to learn lessons for future IT system developments. Ideally this post-project review should not be conducted by any member of the project team, as independence is desirable. Neither, in theory, should it be the responsibility of internal audit to conduct this post-project review: it is an essential control and thus a management responsibility to resource. The internal audit role with respect to the post-project review, as with any other internal auditing, should be to review whether the procedure for post-project review is adequate and whether it is being applied effectively.

Post-project reviews can be repeated over time to check that the system is still performing up to standard.

At the development stage of the system, consideration should be given to the opportunities to build program coding into the system which monitors the performance of the system and reports to management on a timely basis significant trends as they develop over time and exceptions which occur on particular occasions. Rather similar coding may be built into the system to report matters of audit interest directly to the internal auditors.

Auditing IT facilities

Every IT application which uses a piece of computer equipment depends upon what we may call the 'IT facility controls' which are in place for that computer. This applies to PCs, mini-computers, mainframe computers, network and telecoms equipment, and so on. Similarly, IT applications depend upon effective control over the operating systems software in use, and over the shared databases which a number of IT applications may access. Because these controls often have a broad impact upon a large number of applications, they are sometimes termed 'general controls'. They should be the subject of review by internal audit. Here we consider some of the most important.

Information is perhaps the key resource of most modern enterprises. It needs to be safeguarded. A key to this is effective access control. This may be physical access control to IT equipment, or programmed access control, in the case of on-line systems. We need to consider whether we are effectively restricting use of computer equipment, and access to system documentation, software and computer media, only to those who need this in order to do their authorised work.

At the basic level of the office PC there should be discipline over the secure custody of electronic media and the physical control over computer use. In the case of the PC or the networked PC, much can be achieved by means of passwords and encryption, but care should be taken not to assume a degree of security for these techniques which may not in fact exist.

Use of a computer, access to software and access to computer files can all be restricted by means of password control. Of course, a password should not display when it is typed. Multiple attempts to break into a computer system by 'guessing' passwords should lead to that terminal being barred until a supervisor clears it again. The system should not permit the use of common words as passwords, nor those which have been used previously. The password controller function, which amongst other things issues new passwords to new members of staff, may be a better controlled function if it is shared between two people. Then the business avoids excessive dependence upon a single key member of staff, and the two members of staff act as a cross-check on each other to some extent. New passwords can be issued in two halves by two separate password controllers – so that no one person knows a new person's complete password. The system should require that a new password issued to a member of staff is changed by that member of staff as soon as it has been used once; and thereafter the system should require frequent changes of passwords. Staff should be discouraged from displaying their passwords in conspicuous places, and the disclosure of a password to a colleague, whether by informal delegation or in some other manner, should be treated as a disciplinary matter. It may not be necessary for a computer to hold a table of authorised passwords: instead the computer may hold a table of derivatives of the authorised passwords. Then if someone illegitimately obtains a display of this table it will not disclose to that person anyone's password. A terminal should log off after time out, so that another person cannot easily utilise a terminal logged on legitimately by another but then left unattended. Electronic 'time locks' can be arranged so that terminal access to an on-line system is only available to particular terminals during their recognised working hours. Terminal identities may be determined so that particular terminals are only allowed to access programs which they are legitimately entitled to use. The line link for data processing between a terminal and a central computer should be established only after the central computer has dialled back the remote terminal which is seeking access – as this reduces the risk of an unauthorised terminal masquerading as being an authorised terminal.

Now that businesses have so much IT equipment and software, physical custody becomes a major challenge. An inventory of equipment and software becomes important. There is a clear need for effective procedures to be in place and enforced to prevent the unauthorised, illegal use of software. Procedures need to be in place to reduce the risk of virus contamination or the export of viruses to the business partners of the enterprise. Internal audit may develop self-test internal control questionnaires for computer users to complete and return to internal audit. Internal audit may then be able to evaluate the quality of control and make informed decisions as to where it may be necessary to perform audit fieldwork; in this way, managers become more aware of IT control.

Of fundamental importance is the regular storage of back-up copies of all computer programs and data files in a separate secure location so that recovery can be made if the production versions become lost, damaged or destroyed.

Auditing individual IT applications

Each application is designed in a unique way. While all applications rely on the general controls, each also relies on a blend of unique user and programmed controls which are specific to the application alone. It is convenient to think of these as being controls over input, processing, computer files and output, though in practice the techniques which achieve these control effects tend to contribute to more than one of these at the same time. But the fact remains that there should be effective control of input, processing, files and output in every computer application.

- Input must be secure, accurate, complete, on time, entered once only and properly authorised.
- Processing must be accurate, complete, on time and authorised.
- Computer files must maintain their integrity and be kept securely.
- Output must be produced on time and distributed to authorised users only within a satisfactory timeframe.

Some of the control techniques which assist in achieving these objectives have already been discussed. A few more can be mentioned here.

Overall, manual accounting controls allow us to generate control totals outside the computer system which we can reconcile to totals produced by the computer software. Thus, for instance, we can double-check that the right number of pay-slips have been produced by a payroll system.

Check digit control assists in ensuring that numbers retain their validity and so, for instance, help to avoid updating incorrect records. Control over input forms may be facilitated by using prenumbered forms.

In the case of batched input data, input should be kept securely after it has been prepared and prior to its entry into the computer, so that none of its contents can be amended in an unauthorised way. Batch control can ensure that all data enter a computer system once only, completely and accurately in certain respects. With on-line data entry, batch control for at least some data will not be practical: we may endeavour to compensate for this control weakness by, for instance, reading back to the customer an on-line order that the customer is placing. On-line data entry has the advantage that many validity tests on the data being entered can be done at the data entry stage, when for instance the order is being placed.

Control totalling of computer-based data files is an essential way of checking their continued integrity. Of course the IT system can be programmed to do this, and to report exceptions for management review. Where data are assumed not to have changed, as with price list data for instance, they should nevertheless be periodically checked.

Consideration may need to be given to the degree of security associated with computer output. With on-line systems it is likely that output will only be available at the terminal which was authorised to request it. Paper-based output is more difficult to secure from prying eyes. Prenumbered computer output forms make it easier for us to account for every form: we called these 'accountable documents' but we should note that the control is worthless unless it is applied.

Using audit software

Internal audit is the review of the effectiveness of internal control. So in this chapter we have concentrated on how control may be achieved in IT-based systems. We now turn our attention to how internal auditors can use the computer to aid them in their audit work.

The most common use of computers for audit purposes is the use of audit interrogation packages such as ACL[2] or IDEA.[3] Both of these work on PCs. Other interrogation packages are available for use on mainframe and mini-computer systems. Audit interrogation packages allow the auditor to gather data of audit interest present on clients' computer files. All the auditor needs to be able to do is specify the structure in which the data are held on the computer file and specify the task or tasks that the auditor wishes the audit interrogation software to undertake. This can automate large quantities of internal audit work, as well as making the results more reliable. It can mean that the auditor no longer needs to depend on the results obtained through testing a small sample – the audit interrogation package can, for instance, look at every record on the file.

Audit interrogation packages depend upon the information being left behind on the computer file after processing. These packages are designed to perform readily a large number of tasks which auditors are likely to wish to conduct. Here are a few examples:

- select samples, at random or at intervals or in some other way, for further audit work (such as physical verification);
- select items which do not conform to the rules of the system – such as credit limits exceeded;
- select items which conform to rules but are of audit interest – such as large gains or losses on disposal of a fixed asset;
- re-performance of calculations, control totalling and analysis to tie-in to management accounts, etc.

The argument that the internal auditor should be able to rely on management's software for this sort of information is insufficient. First, management's software may not have been designed to do everything that the auditor wishes to do. Secondly, the internal auditor can use audit interrogation software to confirm that management's software is doing its job properly – a reassurance that management expects the internal auditor to give. Thirdly, using audit interrogation software might simply provide the most efficient way for the auditor to achieve a particular audit objective. It is important, however, that the auditor does not merely have a toolkit of techniques looking for problems. First, the auditor should know what is the audit objective. The auditor should use the most cost-effective way of achieving that objective.

Audit interrogation software allows several computer files to be compared against each other – for instance, one month-end customer file could be compared with the previous month's file to identify movements between the two dates, while additional files such as price list and stock files could also be referenced at the same time. Some internal auditors are now using audit interrogation software in data-matching exercises, looking for apparent fraud[4] by cross-relating two or more computer files from different IT systems, perhaps coming from different organisations.

In practice, the chief challenge is setting up a particular audit interrogation using an audit interrogation package. Thereafter it can be used again and again very easily, changing parameters from time to time to modify the questions being addressed.

Audit interrogation packages scrutinise what purports to be genuine data held on clients' computer files. If the data are found to be invalid or unusual, this may imply that the system's controls have not functioned properly. On the other hand, the test data method reviews the controls in the system to ascertain they are working properly. If the test data method finds that certain controls do not always function properly, this may indicate that there could be errors in the associated real data on the computer files. The integrated test facility is an example of the test data method whereby many or all of the IT systems of a business are developed with an integrated test facility built in. The auditor can devise dummy data to process through the system in order to check that unusual conditions or other conditions of audit interest are processed correctly by the system. Of course, great care must be taken to ensure that the auditor's dummy data are not confused by the system with real data. Since the system distinguishes dummy data from real data, it could be argued that the system may give special treatment to the auditor's data: however, in most cases which the auditor is investigating, this is unlikely.

One limitation of the test data method is that it only allows the auditor to explore the functioning of procedures of which the auditor is aware, or which he or she suspects. For instance, the presence of an asterisk in a particular input field might result in an illicit double payment; but it would be highly unlikely that the auditor would ever think of putting an asterisk in that particular field, so that illicit procedure would always remain untested by the test data method.

It can be argued that audit interrogation packages of this conventional type are yesterday's solution to yesterday's problem – even though they are quite powerful audit tools which many internal auditors, especially in small businesses, have yet to start using, let alone maximise the use of. Their principal limitation is that they are dependent on data left behind on the computer file after processing. A more powerful audit software approach would be audit software embedded into the systems which management are using, eavesdropping on processing in real time and recording the details of items of audit interest onto an auditor's computer file for later audit inspection. In effect, the auditor would be generating his or her own audit trail. We know of no proprietary package developed as embedded audit software though there are many examples where tools of this sort have been designed and embedded into particular in-house IT systems. This is another reason for the auditor to be involved at the development stage of a system – to ensure that audit requirements for embedded audit software are specified in time or, to make the same point more generally, to determine that the system will be auditable. It is too late to specify an embedded audit software requirement after the system has been designed and implemented.

Using software for audit administration

Just as managers and staff are now computer users and indeed computer operators and IT system designers, so internal auditors are becoming the same. Apart from software for audit interrogation purposes, internal auditors are now utilising electronic audit working papers as well as software for audit needs assessment and control evaluation. Flowcharting packages aid in audit documentation of systems. Project management software helps control the progress of audits and time-reporting software assists in accounting for the utilisation of internal audit resources.

> **Chapter summary**
>
> In this chapter we have examined how IT can be used by internal auditors to improve their service to the organisation and how IT impacts upon the scope of internal audit work. We have suggested that internal auditors need to have access to IT technology commensurate in sophistication to the IT technology that management is using – if internal audit is to be effective.
>
> It is always important not to dilute the responsibility of management for internal control, including for IT-based internal control. Nevertheless, it is constructive for internal audit to be involved in the development phase of IT systems and we have shown how this can be done without significantly jeopardising internal audit objectivity.
>
> In this chapter we explored how a comprehensive internal audit approach includes auditing the systems development process itself. IT developments can be linked to the more general change processes of the business. An effective IT development process requires good, laid-down procedures: this embraces the need for effective feasibility studies, effective project steering committees, thorough documentation of IT systems, comprehensive system testing, the timely development of sound user procedures, careful conversion files, and cautious implementation of new systems. All this should be followed by objective appraisal of newly implemented systems.
>
> Beyond this, the chapter explores the importance of auditing IT facilities ▶

and of auditing individual IT applications – and how these audits may be approached.

Of course, no chapter of this sort would be complete without a review of the use of audit software, including (a) what are generally termed 'computer assisted auditing techniques' ('CAATs') as well as (b) software for audit administration. As with line managers, internal auditors are now not just computer users, but also computer operators and even IT system designers (for audit purposes).

Principia

1. Management are unlikely to have effective control unless the IT technology (hardware and software) they are using for control purposes at least matches the sophistication of the technology they are using to perform the basic operations of the business.

2. Internal auditors are unlikely to audit effectively unless the IT technology (hardware and software) they are using for audit purposes at least matches the sophistication of the technology management is using to perform the basic operations of the business and achieve effective control over those operations.

3. The 'black box' approach of auditing around the computer is not a viable option for the internal auditor – even if, on occasion, it might be an option for the external auditor.

4. Audit interrogation software directly reviews the validity of corporate data and indirectly assesses the adequacy of internal controls: test data audit methodologies do the reverse, but audit interrogation software is often the more effective internal audit tool because it is so powerful.

5. A comprehensive approach to IT auditing by the internal auditor is like a three-legged stool. It comprises the audit of (a) the systems development process, (b) the general IT facilities, and (c) individual applications. Remove one of these legs and the audit scope becomes unstable.

6. Just as managers have become computer users, computer operators and IT systems designers, so must internal auditors.

7. Some businesses have too much data but too little information: some have too much information but too little analysis: some have too much analysis but too few decisions based upon that analysis: others have too many decisions but too little action to implement those decisions: others have enough or too much action but not enough control over their actions.

Notes

1. In this chapter 'system' is used to refer to one or more associated computer applications and the hardware and users required to run these applications. We use the word 'application' to refer to a discrete business activity which utilises the computer – such as payroll, sales accounting, etc.
2. ACL: Audit Command Language, obtainable in the UK from Alan Livesey of DATA Services Ltd: tel: 44 (0)1634 672277.
3. IDEA: Interactive Data Extraction and Analysis, obtainable in the UK from AuditWare Systems Ltd, The Old Sawmills, Neville Estate Yard, Bridge Road, Bridge Green, Tunbridge Wells, Kent TN3 9JR: tel: +44 (0)1892 512348.
4. An example of this would be multiple student grant applications made by one student masquerading as living in several different local authority areas.

Case 8.1 Use of interrogation software

The case

During the course of an audit of a computerised sales accounting system, the internal audit team realised that they should test to see whether (a) some new customers' orders were being processed and despatched before their new accounts had been authorised, (b) some invoices were showing incorrect volume discounts, (c) some customers were exceeding their credit limits, and (d) some accounts were overdue. In addition, the team needed to quantify the scale of any of these unwanted happenings. The computer system that management were using gave abundant printed output and also had comprehensive on-line enquiry functionality.

The team put their heads together to work out the most cost effective way of solving this audit challenge.

Consider

The following solution:

The team decided to use their own interrogation software to conduct a 100 per cent test for each of (a), (b), (c) and (d). This required a number of the company's computer files to be on-line when the auditors used their interrogation software – including the customer master files, orders files, invoice files and the price list file.

By opting for this solution, the auditors avoided having to rely on the results of testing a small sample only. They also avoided reliance upon management's software giving the auditors correct answers – indeed their audit interrogation was a useful way of confirming the reliability of management's software. They also created a software audit approach which they could use readily on other occasions.

Case 8.2　Effective audit use of portable computers

The case

Three of a small internal audit function of four professional staff spend their time travelling the world auditing their business's operating units and agencies. The Head of Internal Audit and her staff are dedicated to high standards of work and understand that an essential part of this is effective supervision of internal audit work done, and that evidence of supervision should be contained within the internal audit files. But it is impractical for the Head of Internal Audit to visit field locations while internal audits are being conducted.

Consider

The following solution:

The field internal auditors have been issued with notebook computers weighing about 4lb (1.8 kg). Each of these computers has a single PCMCIA card which allows transmission of data via a GSM phone or a conventional landline phone, and it also functions as a network card. Each computer has facsimile software which allows secure binary file transfer. Almost wherever the auditors are in the world, they are able to transmit their audit files to the head of internal audit, who reviews them by displaying them on her screen and typing in audit points before transmitting the necessary data back to the field auditors. Generally they use the company's Intranet for this purpose, the working papers being an attachment to an E-mail transmission. They always make sure their files are transmitted in encrypted form. Sometimes they use the Internet, but they are concerned about its security and the uncertainty as to whether and when a transmission arrives. When their company's Intranet is not available to them they prefer to use their fax software, sending their audit files as binary file attachments to a fax, in encrypted form: that way they know when it has arrived.

The audit manager is not altogether enamoured by this new development which her progressive staff have forced upon her. It means that she no longer has an excuse for not reviewing the working papers of her field auditors. Her field auditors have also found that a good time to get her attention is to transmit their audit working files to her over the weekend, asking for her comments to be transmitted back to them before Monday morning.

Case 8.3　Best practice internal audit involvement with information technology

(Extracted from Ridley (1997), *BRACE 2*, published by The Housing Association Forum, using the Systems Auditability and Control® (SAC) framework (1991), published by The IIA Research Foundation.)

The case

Brace 2 framework

Audit and control environment

Ensuring that an adequate audit and control environment is in place is the responsibility of management. (SAC Executive Summary 1–17)

Selected benchmark

The need for joint planning and working partnerships between executives, line managers, users and IT specialists.

Clear and appropriate allocation of responsibilities for all aspects of IT development and use.

Top managers who understand what IT can do for a business *and* what is involved in successfully implementing and managing change.

Champions to drive multi-functional projects and influential *sponsors* to see that they are given the appropriate priority and attention.

Encouragement of entrepreneurial risk-taking, subject to realistic benefit assessment which avoids stifling initiative or letting investments proceed without business goals being clearly defined.

An effective strategic planning process.

Co-ordinated education, training and personnel policies.

Continuous measurement of the effectiveness and performance of IT.
(Amdahl Executive Institute, 1990)

Using information technology in internal auditing

The use of information technology in internal audit is no longer an option; it is a necessity. (SAC Executive Summary 1–19)

Selected benchmark

Advancements in information technology and the reliance of organisations on information systems continue to provide significant challenges to management and internal auditors. In order to function effectively, all internal auditors require increased skills in information systems and technology. Today's internal audit departments are addressing these challenges through the following:

- integration of internal audit and information skills;
- staffing approaches that include 'borrowing' specialists from the functional organisation and 'tours of duty' in internal audit;
- a focus on training and certifications.

Managing computer resources

The function of managing resources is to provide, operate and maintain the hardware and systems software platforms that support the processing of application systems. (SAC Executive Summary 1–20)

Selected benchmark

Specific operating procedures, defined policies or standards should be established for governing such elements as:

- departmental and individual responsibilities;
- staff policies (including training, disciplinary procedures, etc.);
- safety and security;
- Data Protection Act implications;
- operations and workflow;
- programming standards;
- system development standards;
- documentation standards;
- machine room best practice;
- access control and logical security policy;
- contingency planning in the event of disaster;
- software change control;
- service levels and user support facilities;
- authorisations;
- accounting policy.

(Chambers/Rand, 1994)

Managing information and developing systems

...the concepts of systems planning, information management and systems development and maintenance. (SAC Executive Summary 1–21)

Selected benchmark

A clearly defined information systems and technology strategy is a prerequisite for any organisation seeking to ensure effective IT acquisition procedures. Organisations have a wide range of options for satisfying their IT requirements, ranging from large central mainframe installations to a plethora of personal microcomputers. Similarly, the modes of operation may range from simple batch processing through to on-line enquiry, transaction processing and other interactive operations.

The choice of options, however, should be dictated by the needs and resources of the organisation: what is acquired should satisfy existing and anticipated business needs and be within the capability of the organisation to resource and utilise

...The strategy should be regularly reviewed to reflect changing requirements. (CIPFA Computer Audit Guidelines, 1994)

Business systems

Business systems fall into two categories:

- Core application systems common to most organisations (e.g., human resources, financial systems).
- Industry-specific systems (e.g., electronic funds transfer, insurance claims, computer-integrated manufacturing, public utility customer service systems, and retail merchandise planning).

(SAC Executive Summary 1–21)

Selected benchmark

The leading edge of IT is now its use in strategic information systems ... The following categorisation of IT systems is a strategic continuum, progressing through to the most advanced strategic systems ...:

Administrative and accounting systems – *using IT to perform routine clerical tasks*

Operational systems – *using IT to automate the processes of the enterprise*

Personal systems – *making managers not just computer users but computer operators and possibly system developers*

Expert systems – *embedding professional expertise in IT systems as a tool for less professional personnel to use effectively*

Co-operative systems – *tying suppliers and customers to the business*

Strategic systems – *competitive advantage through imaginative application of IT.*

(Chambers and Rand, 1994)

End-user and departmental computing

Applications that users acquire, develop, maintain and operate outside the traditional information systems arena present a new set of risks, controls, and audit considerations. (SAC Executive Summary 1–22)

Selected benchmark

We have devised ... key steps for an organisation to consider in successfully implementing end-user computing (EUC):

1. Benchmark EUC ....
2. Formalise planning, budgeting, billing and evaluation processes.
3. Organise EUC resources to satisfy documented client needs.
4. Enlist user participation for EUC policy development.
5. Create procurement guidelines which promote fast response, but ensure that products foster connectivity and inter-operability.

6. Provide sufficient education and training.
7. Guide application development strategies and create an application warehouse.
8. Promote relational subject databases to facilitate query processing yielding satisfactory data integrity.
9. Treat computer networks as strategic assets which enable fast, group decisions to be completed.
10. Maintain tight data security to promote confidence in the data extracted for analyses and reports.
11. Promote adequate physical security to protect the hardware, software and data.
12. Create extended audit programs for compliance and substantive testing when material financial or operational risks are identified.

(Rittenberg/Senn/Bariff, 1990)

Emerging technologies

... the emergence of local area networks, database management systems, and powerful microcomputers: ... (SAC Executive Summary 1–26)

Selected benchmark

The future promises constant change ... including imaging, cooperative processing and knowledge based systems. Many of the risks and controls will not be new. The methods by which controls are implemented, however, may be different. The techniques auditors may use to assess the effectiveness of and compliance with controls may require additional technical knowledge and skill. Today's internal auditors must be prepared for the future and must remain apprised of emerging technologies.

(SAC, 1991)

Telecommunications

Complex and sophisticated networks now support critical business operations. ... As a result of this increased dependence on telecommunications, organisations face new risks and control challenges. (SAC Executive Summary 1–23)

Selected benchmark

Controls to mitigate such risks, include:

- Sound network planning and design practices.
- Physical and logical access controls, including encryption and protection of audit trails and logs.
- Message verification procedures, including header/trailer records, parity checking and sequence number verification.

Impact of IT on internal auditing 297

- Segregation of duties and management review of exceptions.
- Contingency procedures.
- Management of vendor relationships.

(SAC, 1991).

Security

Adequate security measures are necessary to protect the integrity, confidentiality, and availability of data and systems resources. (SAC Executive Summary 1–24)

Selected benchmark

There are a number of areas which are critical for the successful implementation of a security strategy and which are necessary if a department is to have confidence that secure systems are in place or being developed. These areas include:

(a) emphasising a coherent security infrastructure with clearly defined roles and responsibilities;
(b) the development and maintenance of appropriate security criteria and methodologies. These include the internationally agreed Information Technology Security Evaluation Criteria (ITSEC);
(c) the implementation of central and local security monitoring practices in developing and live systems; and
(d) the development of a comprehensive security training programme which meets the needs of both specialist security and generalist information systems staff.

(Government Information Systems Manual, 1993)

Contingency planning

The principal objective of contingency planning is to ensure that an organisation can continue critical operations in the event of an interruption in information systems processing. (SAC Executive Summary 1–24)

Selected benchmark

The way forward: better business protection

Do a self-audit check on your own company . . .

. . . think beyond the superficial.

Identify and assign a monetary value to business critical information.

Prioritise your organisation's critical processes and key business information by agreement with the head of each business department, and do the same at department level. Identify what you need to have in place in the event of an emergency which will allow those critical processes to operate effectively, e.g. data back up, alternative equipment and facilities, and additional expertise.

Put the issue of business continuity on the agenda of the next board meeting. Gain commitment for positive action.

Ensure that all employees are informed and the key people are involved at all relevant stages. Examine potential sources of interruption which could lead to losses, e.g. do your PCs all have anti-virus software installed? Are your employees fully trained?

Get a measurement system in place to record events, losses, mistakes and lessons learnt. This ensures continuous improvement.

Integrate business recovery planning into quality assurance and general business developments.

(IBM/Cranfield School of Management, 1996)

Consider

Each of the benchmarks and identify current gaps in your own use and audit of information technology. Use the following benchmark guide.

Action should be taken to establish a benchmarking team from those with interest and/or responsibility for internal auditing in your organisation. The team should include at least one main internal audit customer. Then take the following six steps.

STEP 1 Determine the features of your internal audit function to be benchmarked. Do not choose too many – no more than five at first. Use the research results as a guide.

STEP 2 Agree what influences there are on your features: consider both internal and external influences. Use these influences to improve your benchmarks.

Before proceeding, identify the internal and external influences which determine how IT is used in your organisation. See influences at the following five levels, all of which interact one with the other. Study how these levels influence IT in your organisation and internal auditing service:

- professional institutes;
- regulators;
- industry/sector associations;
- internal audit networks;
- your organisation and internal audit customers.

Agree measures for each of your benchmarks. The right measures are important. Test how appropriate they are by trying to link them into your team's vision of excellent and superior internal audit. If the link is not strong, change your measure.

STEP 3 Use your measures to identify and agree 'current gaps' between your practices and chosen benchmarks.

STEP 4 Analyse your 'current gaps'. Look for causes where you do not already match your benchmark's level of service. Consider structure, processes, delegated responsibilities, competencies, resources etc. Agree what actions need to be taken to achieve best practice; over what time span and how they will be measured. Promote and publish your key measures.

STEP 5 Continuously follow-up achievement of your benchmarks. Celebrate success.

STEP 6 Start your next five features!

Case 8.4 Information Technology glossary

(Extracted from *In Business* (1997) A13.8, ICSA Publishing, Hemel Hempstead.)

Anti-virus software Software designed to detect and often eliminate computer viruses from an information system.

Application controls Specific controls unique to each computerised application.

Application software Programs written for a specific business application in order to perform functions specified by end users.

Application software package Set of prewritten, precoded, application software programs that are commercially available for sale or lease.

Applications portability The ability to operate the same software on different hardware platforms.

Archie A tool for locating data on the Internet that performs key word searches.

ASCII American Standard Code for Information Interchange. A seven- or eight-bit binary code used in data transmission.

Attribute Piece of information describing a particular entity.

Bit A binary digit representing the smallest unit of data in a computer system.

Browser A software tool that supports graphics and hyperlinks and is needed to navigate the Web.

Bugs Program code defects or errors.

Byte A string of bits, usually eight, used to store one number or character in a computer system.

CD-Rom Compact disc read-only memory. Used for imaging, reference and database applications with massive amounts of data and for multimedia.

Database Collection of data organised to service many applications at the same time by organising data so that they appear to be in one location.

Decision-support system (DSS) Computer systems at the management level of an organisation that combine data and sophisticated analytical models to support decision-making.

Desktop publishing Technology that produces professional quality documents combining output from word processors with design, graphics, and special layout features.

Digital image processing Technology that converts documents and graphic images into computerised form so that they can be stored, processed and accessed by computer systems.

Digital scanners Input devices that translate images such as pictures or documents into digital form for processing.

DOS Operating system for 16-bit microcomputers based on the IBM Personal Computer standard.

Electronic data interchange (EDI) Direct computer-to-computer exchange between two organisations of standard business transaction documents.

Electronic mail The computer-to-computer exchange of messages.

Executive Support Systems (ESS) Information systems at the strategic level of an organisation designed to address unstructured decision making through advanced graphics and communications.

Expert system Knowledge-intensive computer program that captures the expertise of a human in limited domains of knowledge.

File A grouping of characters into a word, group of words, or complete number.

File server Computer in a network that stores various programs and data-files for users of the network. Determines access and availability in the network.

Gateway Communications processor that connects dissimilar networks by providing the translation from one protocol to another.

Gopher A character-oriented tool for locating data on the Internet.

Graphical user interface The part of an operating system that users interact with that uses graphic icons and the computer mouse to issue commands and make selections.

Hard disk Magnetic disk resembling a thin steel platter with an iron oxide coating, used in large computer systems and in many microcomputers.

Information superhighway High-speed digital telecommunications networks that are national or worldwide in scope and accessible by the general public.

Information system Interrelated components that collect, process, store and disseminate information to support decision-making, control, analysis and visualisation in an organisation.

Input The capture or collection of raw data for processing in an information system.

Integrated software package A software package that provides two or more applications, such as spreadsheets and word processing, providing for easy transfer of data between them.

Intellectual property Intangible property created by individuals or corporations

which is subject to protections under trade secret, copyright and patent law.
Internet An international network of networks connecting over 20 million people from 100 countries; it is the largest information superhighway in the world.
Local area network (LAN) Telecommunications network that requires its own dedicated channels and that encompasses a limited distance, usually one building.
Mainframe Largest category of computer, classified as having over 50 megabytes to over 1 gigabyte of RAM.
Management information systems (MIS) Computer systems that support the monitoring, controlling, decision-making and administrative activities of middle managers.
Megabyte Approximately 1 million bytes.
Modem Device for translating digital signals into analog signals, and vice versa.
Multimedia Technologies that facilitate the integration of two or more types of media such as text, graphics, sound, voice, full-motion video or animation into a computer-based application.
On-line processing A method of processing information in which transactions are entered directly into the computer system and processed immediately.
Operating system The system software that manages and controls the activities of the computer.
Server Satisfies some or all of the user's request for data and/or functionality such as storing or processing shared data and controlling access to shared databases.
Software The detailed instructions that control the operation of a computer system.
Software package A prewritten precoded, commercially available set of programs that eliminates the need to write software programs for certain functions.
Spreadsheet Software displaying data in a grid of columns and rows, with the capability of easily recalculating numerical data.
Voice mail System for digitising a spoken message and transmitting it over a network.
Wide area network (WAN) Telecommunications network that spans a large geographical distance.
Windows A graphical user interface shell that runs in conjunction with the DOS microcomputer operating system. Supports multitasking and some form of networking.
World Wide Web A set of standards for storing, retrieving, formatting and displaying information using a client/server architecture, graphical user interfaces, and a hypertext language that enables dynamic links to other documents.

Consider

1. Understand the information technology words and terms in the glossary.
2. Keep the glossary up to date by adding new words and their definitions, such as:
   - virtuality;
   - intranet;
   - CAATS;
   - contingency planning;
   - computer security;
   - passwords;
   etc.

CHAPTER 9

Internal auditing working with the board

> We hold the view that corporate governance is very much about adding value. Companies and other enterprises with a professional and positive attitude to governance are stronger and have a greater record of achievement.
>
> (Bain and Band (1996) *Winning Ways Through Corporate Governance*)

Boards of directors have always had a duty to determine policy and overall strategy, then to monitor performance and finally to ensure that corrective measures are taken, where it becomes apparent that either policy or its implementation is at fault. Since internal control provides reasonable assurance of the achievement of corporate objectives, it follows that the board is responsible for internal control. Of course, internal audit is a process of independently appraising the effectiveness of internal control. Internal audit therefore is a valuable service to the board.

Day-to-day responsibility for internal control is vested in management; by 'internal control', we mean 'management control'. The expression differentiates management control from 'external control', which is control over the business and its board as exercised by the stakeholders in the business – shareholders, creditors, etc. The concept of external accountability, control and audit are encapsulated neatly in the classic quotation which we reproduce in Figure 9.1. So, internal audit provides a day-to-day service to management as well as a service to the board.

Understanding responsibility for internal control

At this stage we would do well to remind ourselves of certain definitions. The most helpful definition of internal control is COSO's, given in Figure 9.2, which firmly

Figure 9.1 The spirit of external control

> Without audit, no accountability; without accountability, no control; and if there is no control, where is the seat of power? ... great issues often come to light only because of scrupulous verification of details.
> (Professor W.J.M. MacKenzie in the foreword to E.L. Normanton (1966) *The Accountability and Audit of Governments*, Manchester University Press, Manchester; and Frederick A. Prager, New York)
>
> The equivalent sentiment for internal control might read:
>
> Without internal audit, no monitoring; without monitoring, no internal control; and if there is no internal control, where is the seat of power? ... great issues often come to light only because of scrupulous verification of detail.

Figure 9.2 COSO's 1992 definition of internal control

> Internal control is broadly defined as a process, effected by an entity's board of directors, management and other personnel, designed to provide reasonable assurance regarding the achievement of objectives in the following categories:
>
> - effectiveness and efficiency of operations;
> - reliability of financial reporting;
> - compliance with applicable laws and regulations.

places internal control as the essential mechanism for the achievement of overall objectives, which is the responsibility of the board. Rutteman, the UK equivalent of COSO, starts by saying: 'The board is ultimately responsible for the system of internal control used in the company or group and for monitoring its effectiveness. It will normally delegate the detailed design and operation of the system and some of the monitoring procedures.'

Of course, delegation does not mean abdication: delegation requires reporting and supervision. As the monitoring of internal control is, at least in part, delegated by the board to internal audit, the board will require there to be in place a satisfactory system of reporting to the board by internal audit, and a satisfactory mechanism for the board to monitor the performance of internal audit itself.

Figure 9.3 The Rutteman 1994 definition of internal control and internal financial control

---

Internal control

The whole system of controls, financial and otherwise, established in order to provide reasonable assurance of:

(a) effective and efficient operations;
(b) internal financial control; and
(c) compliance with laws and regulations.

Internal financial control

The internal controls established in order to provide reasonable assurance of:

(a) the safeguarding of assets against unauthorised use or disposition; and
(b) the maintenance of proper accounting records and the reliability of financial information used within the business or for publication.'

Defining internal control

Rutteman defines internal control in a very similar way to COSO (Figure 9.3). The Institute of Internal Auditors' Standards continue with a fivefold classification of the objectives of internal control (Figure 9.4); indeed the COSO and Rutteman classifications are not identical, as Rutteman includes 'the safeguarding of assets' as a part of internal financial control, whereas COSO classifies the safeguarding of assets as part of internal control, as it contributes to the effectiveness and efficiency of operations. Each of these different ways of classifying internal control in essence covers the same ground.

Reporting publicly on internal control

Both the COSO (US) and the Rutteman (UK) guidance were developed for directors confronted by the challenge of reporting publicly on the effectiveness of internal control within their annual report. The implementation of this reporting practice is having very significant effects upon the relationships between internal audit and boards of directors, as we see later in this chapter.

In the event, in the US the Securities and Exchange Commission, repeating their stance of the late 1970s in the wake of the US Foreign Corrupt Practices Act

Figure 9.4 The Institute of Internal Auditors' definition of internal control

Internal control is a process within an organisation designed to provide reasonable assurance regarding the achievement of the following primary objectives:

- The reliability and integrity of information.
- Compliance with policies, plans, procedures, laws, and regulations.
- The safeguarding of assets.
- The economical and efficient use of resources.
- The accomplishment of established objectives and goals for operations or programs.

(1995 Glossary, and 1978 Standard 300.05; the bullet points are retained from the 1978 Standards; the preamble is of 1995 vintage, borrowing phraseology from COSO.)

(1977), backed off from making a directors' public internal control report mandatory, though the COSO guidance is usually followed by those US enterprises which do publish such a report – and well over 50 per cent of the largest US corporations do. In the US the published report on internal control is typically in the name of the CEO and the CFO, it is restricted to internal financial control as of the year end date, and internal financial control is itself limited to control as it contributes to the reliability of published financial statements, excluding financial information used within the business.

We should stress that developments in public reporting on internal control are not just a 'large corporation' issue. The UK requirements are currently mandatory for all UK listed companies but are being interpreted as an aspect of good corporate governance for many other types of enterprise – large and small. For instance, many unlisted companies, charities, housing associations, organisations within the NHS, Training and Enterprise Councils and the like are now in the process of implementing measures to report publicly on internal control.

In the UK it is a Stock Exchange listing requirement that listed companies disclose within their annual report any aspects of the Cadbury Code of Best Practice with which they do not comply, giving reasons for non-compliance. One item in the Code is that 'the board should establish an audit committee of at least 3 non-executive directors with written terms of reference which deal with its authority and duties'. Another item in the Code is that 'The directors should report on the effectiveness of the company's system of internal control'. It was this latter item which awaited the Rutteman guidance prior to implementation in 1995. Strictly speaking, UK listed companies do not have to publish a directors' internal control report but, if they do not, they must draw attention in their annual report to the absence of such a report, giving an explanation for its absence. The effect of this is that virtually all UK-listed companies do publish a directors' internal control report. Rutteman came to their rescue by ameliorating the perceived rather harsh stipulations of the Cadbury Code.

Deciding the scope of the directors' internal control report

Following Rutteman, directors may restrict the scope of their published internal control reports to internal *financial* control only, though Rutteman does encourage them to broaden the scope of their internal control reports to cover the other objectives of internal control – 'effective and efficient operations' and 'compliance with laws and regulations' (Figure 9.3). Unlike COSO, the Rutteman guidance defines internal financial control as including (a) the controls which contribute to the reliability of financial information used within the business, as well as (b) that for publication, and also embraces (c) the controls which contribute to the safeguarding of assets. Rutteman also requires that the directors' internal control report covers the whole of the period being reported upon, rather than being a report on internal control as of the year end date only.

Rutteman also allows that directors may disclose within their public report on internal control their opinion about the effectiveness of internal control, although Rutteman does not specifically encourage them to do so, and certainly does not insist upon it. This was a response to expressions of concern about the intended meaning of 'effectiveness' and anxieties that statements of this sort could be held against directors if they subsequently proved to be misguided. The minimum internal control reporting requirements are set out in Figure 9.5. Note that directors need only disclose that they have reviewed the effectiveness of their system of internal financial control; they need not disclose the results of that review. Strictly speaking they only need to review it and are not required even to draw any conclusions from that review either for public dissemination or for internal use only.

Despite the absence of any imposed obligations to do so, some companies are reporting their directors' opinion on the effectiveness of internal control with a broader scope than just internal *financial* control. When they do so, at present their external auditors restrict themselves to reporting on the directors' internal control report[1] only to the extent of its minimum compliance with Rutteman (Figure 9.5), and even then, the external auditors' reports are negative assurance reports only.

Understanding the mission of the audit committee

In Figure 9.6 we summarise the mission of an audit committee. Generally a board will entrust to its audit committee the consideration of internal control, although

Figure 9.5 Public reporting on internal control – minimum Rutteman requirements for the content of the report

The statement should contain as a minimum:

(a) acknowledgement by the directors that they are responsible for the company's system of internal financial control;
(b) explanation that such a system can provide only reasonable and not absolute assurance against material misstatement or loss;
(c) description of the key procedures that the directors have established and which are designed to provide effective internal financial control;
(d) confirmation that the directors (or a board committee) have reviewed the effectiveness of the system of internal financial control.

Where weaknesses in internal financial control have resulted in material losses, contingencies or uncertainties which require disclosure in the financial statements or in the auditors' report, the directors should:

(a) describe what corrective action has been taken or is intended to be taken; or
(b) explain why no changes are considered necessary.

Figure 9.6 The four duties of an audit committee

Primary duties

- To ensure that published financial information can safely go out in the board's name.
- To ensure that the board responsibly discharges its overall responsibility for internal control.

Secondary duties

- On behalf of the board, to ensure that the business has in place satisfactory arrangements for external audit.
- On behalf of the board, to ensure that the business has in place satisfactory arrangements for the monitoring of internal control, which is likely to include an internal audit function.

internal control remains the responsibility of the board as a whole. Most large businesses and an increasing number of smaller ones now have audit committees as standing committees of the board. We are unaware of available data relating to the smaller business: Figure 9.7 shows the recent position with respect to the larger company.

Figure 9.7 Data on audit committees (from the June 1995 *Price Waterhouse Corporate Register*, published by Hemmington Scott)

	Number of companies with audit committee	Average size of audit commitee	Average number of non-executive directors	Number of audit committees without executive members
FTSE 100 companies	100	4.24	4.05	92
Mid-250 companies	245	3.95	3.53	207

In some smaller businesses and also in various public or quasi-public-sector enterprises, the audit committee comprises executive as well as non-executive directors, whereas the Cadbury model is that it should be entirely non-executive, with executives and others in attendance at the discretion of the chair of the committee for certain agenda items. In these businesses the audit committee might have other responsibilities which would now be regarded as incompatible with the core audit committee role. These extra responsibilities might include approval of financial decisions and consideration of executive remuneration – which ideally should be the responsibility of the board itself or of a finance and a remuneration committee of the board, respectively.

Interfacing internal audit with the audit committee

While we address here the interfaces of internal audit with the audit committee, rather similar liaison is likely to be appropriate between internal audit and other monitoring functions within the business – such as the compliance function where this exists. Internal audit may interface with the audit committee with respect to each of the responsibilities of the audit committee (Figure 9.6). In practice, internal audit usually plays only a small role with regard to the reliability of financial information for publication – such role as it does play here is likely to be through informing the audit committee of internal control issues which may impact upon the reliability of financial statements. Internal audit may play a more significant role in assisting the audit committee to discharge its responsibility to ensure that the enterprise has an appropriate external audit service. The audit committee may ask internal audit to evaluate the quality of external audit provision. Primarily the interface between internal audit and the audit committee will relate to the other two responsibilities of the audit committee – to evaluate internal control, and to evaluate the quality of internal audit provision.

Acting as secretary to the audit committee

Sometimes the head of internal audit acts as the secretary to the audit committee, but this too is unsound. The committee needs to take an objective view of the quality of internal audit and the professionalism of the head of internal audit. It will be harder for the committee to do this if the head of internal audit does, in effect, control its agendas and minutes and needs to be present, ideally for every moment of every committee meeting. Being a main board committee, the secretarial arrangements for the audit committee should be similar to those for the board itself.

Locking in the audit committee with the head of internal audit

Yet the head of internal audit does need a close relationship with the chair of the audit committee. The terms of reference of the internal audit function should empower the head of internal audit to communicate with the chair of the audit committee directly: this should include direct access between audit committee meetings and the opportunity to ensure that matters of internal audit concern become agenda items at audit committee meetings, where appropriate. While internal auditing Standards advise only that 'independence is enhanced when the board concurs in the appointment or removal of the director of the internal auditing department',[2] we would say that the terms of reference of the audit committee should stipulate that management should seek the prior approval of the audit committee to the appointment or dismissal of the head of internal audit.

A wise chair of the audit committee will arrange to spend time with the enterprise's internal auditors between audit committee meetings. Perhaps half a day spent within the internal audit department once or twice a year should suffice. This provides a different, effective opportunity to learn about internal audit concerns. It also 'breaks the ice', making it easier for the head of internal audit and his or her colleagues to approach the chair of the audit committee directly and without trepidation.

Reporting to the audit committee on audit work done

In a routine way, one item on the agenda of most audit committee meetings will be to receive from the head of internal audit a report on internal audit work completed since the last audit committee meeting. Although Cadbury suggests that an audit committee should meet at least twice a year, most audit committees meet more frequently than that, and four meetings at least per year are not unusual. This report from internal audit is likely to be a summary of the conclusions and main findings and recommendations of all internal audits completed since the last audit committee meeting. It may include interim summary reports on audits in progress.

Most audit committees do not wish to see the detailed audit reports on audit assignments except in special cases, as this is likely to be too much text for audit committee members to master. Some audit committees follow the practice of nominating one of their members to 'shadow' the finance director and another (or the same member) to 'shadow' the head of internal audit. In this case the 'shadow' is likely to receive on behalf of the audit committee a copy of each detailed internal audit report.

Meeting privately with the head of internal audit

As Cadbury recommends with respect to the external auditor, it is sound practice for the audit committee to take time to meet the head of internal audit without any other members of the executive being present. This is often easiest to arrange if it takes place at the end of each meeting. This gives the head of internal audit the opportunity to be more frank about difficult issues, but the audit committee should always be on their guard for indications that the head of internal audit is uneasy about making full disclosure of a matter, perhaps due to anxiety about possible reactions and consequences with regard to his or her executive colleagues.

Accounting for internal audit progress against plan

The regular reporting by the head of internal audit to the audit committee will also account for internal audit progress against plan. In particular the audit committee will want to understand clearly what planned audit assignments have not been conducted as planned and the reasons for this. It could be that internal audit is being diverted away from its planned programme of audits previously agreed with top management and the audit committee – either because management wishes certain areas to be left alone, or because management is 'borrowing' internal audit for non-internal audit work. Or it could be that internal audit is under establishment levels. Whatever the reason it is a matter of concern to the audit committee as it relates to the adequacy of internal audit coverage.

Ensuring the audit committee can rely on internal audit objectivity

In practice, the audit committee is likely to be the most senior point within the business to whom internal audit reports. One way of defining internal auditor independence is to say that the most senior point within the enterprise to whom internal audit reports should be confident that internal audit has not subordinated its judgement to that of anyone or any body at a more junior level within the business. If internal audit judgement has, or may have been, subordinated, then the audit committee can no longer rely on the reports that internal audit submits to it. Subordination of judgement may occur, for instance, in the following circumstances:

- The planned programme of audits is not as internal audit would have intended, having been modified by management.
- One or more internal audits were cancelled or deferred at the insistence of management, against the better judgement of internal audit.
- Management prevented internal audit from obtaining access to information or explanations which internal audit considered necessary for the satisfactory completion of audit work.
- The content of audit reports, and of their summaries through to the audit committee, has been unduly influenced by management.

Approving the planned programme of internal audits

To complete the circle, if the audit committee is to review the audits conducted against the planned programme, it follows that the audit committee should have an interest in approving the planned programme in the first place. In the interests of internal audit independence it is desirable that the head of internal audit determines the audits which will be conducted and their timing. Of course, he or she will listen to management and to the audit committee and will endeavour to take on board their advice without distorting internal audit coverage away from what internal audit considers it should be. But it is reasonable that management and the audit committee should scrutinise and approve the planned programme of future internal audits – and thereafter monitor its achievement.

Internal audit should be prepared for the audit committee to challenge the basis upon which internal audit draws up its planned programme of future audits. The committee will want assurance that internal audit coverage corresponds to relative degrees of business and control risk. We discussed risk-based audit planning in Chapter 5. It is preferable to arrive at a basis for planning programmes of audits, agreed between internal audit, management and the audit committee, and for internal audit then to be given the freedom to apply that basis without interference, as this contributes to the effective independence of internal audit and thus to the reliance that can be placed upon internal audit by those to whom internal audit reports.

Undertaking special assignments for the audit committee

Internal audit also should be prepared for the possibility that on occasion, the audit committee may commission assignments to be conducted directly on the committee's behalf by internal audit.

Assisting in developing an internal control report for publication

At the commencement of this chapter we considered the responsibility of directors to report publicly on internal control. Whether or not the directors opt for the minimal content which may be contained in such reports (Figure 9.5), this should not determine the scope of their interest in internal control. Directors are responsible for all aspects of internal control, not just internal financial control (Figures 9.2 and 9.3). They may decide not to disclose their opinion on internal control *effectiveness* but they should surely form an opinion thereon at least for internal purposes. So we recommend that the audit committee's purview of internal control, on the directors' behalf, should cover all aspects of internal control and should lead to the audit committee's communication to the board of the committee's opinion as to whether internal control is effective. The process which the audit committee follows to arrive at its internal control report to the board should be carefully documented, and this is especially important, to support retrospectively the sentiment expressed in the directors' published reports on internal control.

Overall summary opinions on internal control by internal audit

In Figure 9.8 we provide a pro forma of a systematic approach which the audit committee may take to its consideration of the effectiveness of internal control. Space does not allow us to go into this in detail. Here we just highlight the overall summary report on internal control to the audit committee from internal audit. If the audit committee, comprising only non-executive directors meeting as a committee about four times a year, is now expected to reassure the board as to the effectiveness of all aspects of internal control over the whole year under review and also taking account of the period of time between the year end and the publication of the annual report, then it is reasonable for the audit committee to ask internal audit, who are likely to have been at work through the entire year, to provide to the audit committee a similar statement of assurance. In the past, internal auditors have been content to audit on a long-term cycle basis. If, in the past, internal audit has been expressing opinions on internal control to the audit committee, these opinions have usually been qualified with respect to the scope of internal audit coverage. Now, the following example parody of an internal audit opinion on internal control is no longer adequate:

> Internal audit works to a three-year cycle and some of this year's internal audits were conducted early in the year. But on the assumptions (a) that what internal audit has not examined this year is as well controlled as what we have examined, and (b) what internal audit examined early in the year has not changed since – then internal audit is reasonably confident that internal control is effective.

The audit committee will expect an unlimited scope opinion from internal audit about the effectiveness of all aspects of internal control. We suggest a wording

Figure 9.8   Audit committees formally reporting on internal control[3]

After the year end, but shortly before finalising the annual report, the audit committee should meet to conclude its consideration of internal control. Because of the tight deadlines at this time of the year, as much preparatory work as possible should have been done at earlier audit committee meetings. The scope may be limited to internal *financial* control.

The committee's formal review of internal control should be systematic, having inputs, process and outputs. Enterprises have considerable discretion in their approach which is likely to make use of some of the following.

Inputs (i.e. evidence on internal control for the committee to consider[4])

- Intelligence gathered as board members during the year.
- A report from the Executive on the key procedures which are designed to provide effective internal control.
- The committee's assessment of the effectiveness of internal audit.
- Reports from internal audit on scheduled audits performed.
- Reports on special reviews commissioned by the committee from internal audit or others.
- Internal audit's overall summary opinion on internal control.
- The overall results of a control self assessment process.
- Confirmation that key line managers are clear as to their objectives.[5]
- Letters of representation ('comfort letters') on internal control from line management.
- The external auditors' management letter.
- A losses report from the CEO or FD.
- An executive report on any material developments since the b/s date and the present.
- The Executive's proposed wording of the internal control report for publication.

Process

- Ensure adequate committee time (half a day?) and enough advance notice to prepare and study agenda papers.
- Bring forward to mid-year meetings as much as possible of the committee's consideration of internal control, away from the y/e deadlines and allowing more time for any necessary remedial action.
- Review all evidence (*Inputs*, above) in committee.
- Take oral advice from management, internal and external audit and others in attendance.
- Draw conclusions as a committee.

▶

Figure 9.8 Contd

Outputs

For transmission to the board prior to going to print with the annual report

- Endorsement of the key control procedures (Rutteman says these are for the *directors* to have established) as being satisfactory.
- Committee opinion on internal (financial) control effectiveness – whether for publication or for internal use only.
- Committee's proposed draft internal control report for publication.
- Any Committee concerns about internal control of sufficient importance for the board.

For transmission to senior executive management

- Outstanding committee concerns about internal control.
- The committee's required revisions of approach for the future.

---

for such an opinion in Figure 9.9. The revision of internal audit approach to be able to give such an opinion may comprise the following, amongst other measures:

- a risk-based method of audit planning;
- risk-based methods of internal control evaluation;
- internal audit use of letters of representation on internal control from key line managers (Figure 9.10);
- internal audit consideration of the effectiveness of the enterprise's programme of control and risk self-assessment;
- follow-up audits where necessary towards the end of the year to confirm the status of systems audited earlier in the year.

Assessing the effectiveness of internal control

COSO's five components of internal control have been adopted by Rutteman as the criteria for assessing internal control effectiveness. We summarise these in Figure 9.11. Of course, these are more to do with the internal control process than with its outcomes. Clearly, both should be examined in an assessment of internal control effectiveness: if the outcome includes a major fraud, for instance, then it is unlikely that it could be said that internal control had been effective.

Figure 9.9 Internal audit's overall summary opinion on internal control effectiveness

To: The Board of Directors, ABC Company

or

The Audit Committee, ABC Company

We have completed the programme of internal auditing coverage of internal control at the ABC Company for the year ended 19xx. The internal auditing work was performed in accordance with Standards for the Professional Practice of Internal Auditing and included such tests and appraisals of the competent policies, procedures, systems and processes as we considered necessary for the company and its business units.

The study and evaluation were made using the criteria for effective internal control developed by [cite criteria, for example those established in the Rutteman Report. In the instance of the Rutteman criteria, a broad definition of the term internal control as the whole system of controls, financial and otherwise, established in order to provide reasonable assurance of:

- effective and efficient operations;
- internal financial control; and
- compliance with laws and regulations.]

The scope of our coverage included (a) consideration of presentations made by the chief financial officer and other senior members of management regarding the design and operation of the internal control structure, (b) relevant work performed by X and Y, the independent accounting firm retained by the ABC company to perform the annual examination of ABC's financial statements, and (c) the performance of such internal audits of the internal control structure throughout the company as we considered necessary.

[Optional: Because of inherent limitations in the overall effectiveness in any system of internal control and the necessarily limited nature of the study and evaluation we designed and completed, it is conceivable that deficiencies may have existed during 19xx that were not detected and that errors, omissions or irregularities may have resulted which were not detected and corrected. Moreover, any internal control structure may be circumvented by actions of those members of management whose position and authority permit unrestricted freedom to act.]

In our opinion, the internal control structure in effect during 19xx conformed to and complied with the internal control criteria [such as Rutteman] in all material aspects. Specifically, the policies, procedures, systems and processes were designed and operated in order to achieve:

- effective and efficient operations;
- reliable financial reports;[6]
- compliance with laws and regulations.

Montague Smithers
Head of Internal Audit

Figure 9.10 Letter of representation on internal control (sometimes known as a 'comfort letter'; a related concept is the 'accounting declaration')

From: A Line Manager

To: Internal Audit, or to:

   Line Manager immediately senior (copy Internal Audit), or to:

   The Audit Committee (copy Internal Audit) in the case of the most senior executive management

Re.:   Representations on internal control

Date:
_____

I confirm that the objectives I am responsible for achieving are clearly defined and understood. I acknowledge that the development and maintenance of effective internal control to provide reasonable assurance of the achievement of these objectives are amongst my key managerial responsibilities. I am confident I understand what this entails and have been given the necessary authority to achieve these outcomes.

Having monitored achievement of my objectives and the functioning of the internal control arrangements in place within my area of responsibilities I consider that throughout 19xx internal control has been adequate to provide reasonable assurance of effective and efficient operations, of internal financial control, and of compliance with laws and regulations; and that these arrangements have been complied with in all material respects throughout this period.

I have communicated to my staff the essential elements of an effective system of internal control and have ensured that (a) they are aware of their responsibilities especially in areas of potential critical risk and (b) they have been empowered to operate appropriate control procedures effectively.

All staff within my area of responsibility, at all levels, have been appraised of their duty to report upwards unresolved matters of concern about internal control and to deal expeditiously and effectively with such matters reported to them. In reporting upwards, staff have been empowered, without risk of victimisation, to bypass intermediate levels of management where they consider this to be necessary. I have taken appropriate steps to confirm that no matters remain unresolved as a result of this process. All such matters drawn to my personal attention by staff have been dealt with to my satisfaction.

No findings or recommendations relating to internal control made by internal or external audit or by others remain outstanding.

I have considered whether significant changes have been made to business practices in my area of responsibility which may have weakened internal control and believe that this is not the case. Furthermore our plans for future change have been appraised in the context of their internal control impact and I believe these issues have been addressed satisfactorily.

I am unaware of any weaknesses in control or irregularities in accounting practice which should be drawn to your attention.

Figure 9.11   Criteria for assessing internal control effectiveness[7]

Control environment

Covers matters such as the example and policies set by the board; the organisation structure and delegation of authority arrangements; and a professional approach to financial reporting.

Identification and evaluation of risks and control objectives

Now acknowledging that the evaluation of risk is an essential part of an effective system of internal control, since controls need to be commensurate with relative risk.

Information and communication

No system of internal control is adequate unless there is appropriate information and communication. This includes, *inter alia*, availability of performance indicators, and quality information systems.

Control procedures

All the specific activities which exist, or should exist, for a control purpose.

Monitoring and corrective action

Now, the monitoring of internal control (by internal audit and/or in other ways) is clearly acknowledged as an essential part of an effective system of internal control.

On the other hand, there may have been no unwanted outcomes yet the system of internal control may be very unsatisfactory – even though its weaknesses may not yet have been exploited, by accident or intention.

Any careful appraisal of these five 'components' (or 'criteria') of internal control will go a long way towards being able to express an opinion about the effectiveness of all aspects of internal control, not just internal financial control. This is because these components act upon operational efficiency and effectiveness and upon compliance with laws and regulations as well as acting upon the objectives of internal financial control. As an example, a code of business conduct (which belongs to the 'control environment' component of internal control, will contribute to reliable financial reporting, to safeguarding assets, to complying with laws and regulations and to operational efficiency and effectiveness. So internal audit and the audit committee, if they are to come to an opinion about internal financial control effectiveness, will find themselves well on the way to coming to an opinion about the effectiveness of internal control in *all* its aspects.

Chapter summary

In this chapter we have explored the board's responsibility for internal control and how internal audit may assist the board to discharge its responsibilities in this regard. The pivotal role of the audit committee has been explained. We addressed the issue of directors' public reports on internal control and the determination of the scope and content of these reports, together with the approach which may be taken to determine the effectiveness of internal control and to report thereon. We have shown how the internal audit function can assist the board, through its audit committee, in the consideration of internal control effectiveness and in the development of internal control reports for publication. One requirement may be that internal audit furnishes the audit committee of the board with internal audit's overall summary opinion on internal control and in this chapter we considered the implications of this developing requirement.

Constructive, appropriate participation by, and reporting to, audit committee meetings by internal audit is essential, and in this chapter we explored how this may be achieved. We considered the appropriate interface of internal audit with the audit committee together with whether the head of internal audit should act as the secretary to the audit committee. We suggested ways in which the relationship between internal audit and the audit committee can be enhanced. The different ways in which internal audit should report and account to the audit committee were examined, including reporting to the audit committee on audit work done, meeting privately with the audit committee, securing committee approval of planned programmes of internal audits, and accounting to the committee for internal audit progress against plan.

From the audit committee's perspective, it is important that the committee can rely upon internal audit objectivity, so we touched on the practical implications of this, as well as upon the issue of internal audit undertaking special assignments directly on behalf of the audit committee.

Principia

1. The board has overall responsibility for the effectiveness of all aspects of internal control.

▶

2. Internal audit should serve the board and all of management.

3. An enterprise should ensure that its internal audit function has unrestricted access to the audit committee of the board.

4. The appointment, dismissal or transfer of the head of internal audit should have prior approval of the audit committee.

5. Internal audit should not subordinate its judgement on audit matters to that of others.

6. Internal audit should arrange its programme of work so that it is able to provide the board, through its audit committee, with an annual, overall summary opinion on the effectiveness of internal control.

References

Cadbury, A. (1992) *Report of the Committee on the Financial Aspects of Corporate Governance*, Gee, London.

Chambers, A.D. (1995) 'Reporting on Internal Control', *Professional Briefing Note No. 8*, Institute of Internal Auditors, London.

Committee of Sponsoring Organisations of the Treadway Commission – 'COSO' (1992) *Internal Control – Integrated Framework*, AICPA, New York, USA.

Institute of Internal Auditors (1995) *Standards for the Professional Practice of Internal Auditing*, IIA Inc, Altamonte Springs, Florida, USA.

Working Group on Internal Control – 'The Rutteman Working Group' (1994) *Internal Control and Financial Reporting – Guidance for Directors of Listed Companies Registered in the UK*, ICAEW, London.

Notes

1. Cadbury stipulated that the directors' internal control report was one of the aspects of compliance with the Cadbury Code which should be reviewed and reported upon by the external auditors.
2. Standard 110.01.3 (1995) (Institute of Internal Auditors Inc., Altamonte Springs, Florida, USA).
3. This appeared in its original form in Chambers (1995).
4. For the UK, in general these inputs should relate to the period under review. The US guidance envisages that the published report on internal control will relate only to control in place *as of the year end date*, whereas Rutteman requires (§9) that:

    The directors' statement should cover the period of the financial statements and should also take account of material developments between the balance sheet date and the date upon which the financial statements are signed.

5. Contemporary definitions of internal control (COSO and Rutteman) acknowledge that internal control is intended to provide reasonable assurance of the achievement of objectives. It follows that to assess whether internal control has been effective, management should be clear as to their objectives and whether they have been achieved. Failure to achieve objectives might not be a consequence of defective internal control; for instance it may be due to external events. Succeeding in achieving objectives might not be a consequence of effective internal control since control weaknesses might not have been exploited. So it is wise to consider both the extent to which objectives have been achieved as well as to the framework of internal control in coming to an opinion on the effectiveness of internal control. The Rutteman focus is (inappropriately) almost exclusively on the latter – implying that the internal control processes themselves are the criteria for assessing internal control effectiveness with no regard to whether objectives have been achieved. COSO is more balanced.
6. Note, in the UK the Rutteman requirement includes in addition to reports for publication, those which are used internally.
7. While Rutteman calls these the criteria for assessing internal control effectiveness, COSO defines them as the five essential components of any effective system of internal control. COSO uses slightly different words as labels for these five components/criteria. Readers are recommended to consult the 'Rutteman Report' for more detail on these five criteria, and the 'COSO Report' provides much more detail.

Case 9.1   Terms of reference for the audit committee

The case

The head of internal audit was asked to draft the terms of reference for the company's new audit committee. He obtained outside advice from a specialist firm of consultants. Ultimately, the board adopted the following terms of reference for the audit committee.

Audit Committee terms of reference

1. Constitution

1.1   At a meeting held at [location] on [date] the Board of Directors of [Company name] resolved to establish a standing Committee of the Board without executive responsibilities, to be known as the Audit Committee, in accordance with these Terms of Reference which were adopted.

2. Membership

2.1   The membership of the Committee shall be appointed by the Board from amongst the non-executive Directors of the company and shall consist of a minimum of three members, the majority of whom shall be independent of the company. A quorum shall be three members.

2.2   The duties and responsibilities of a member of the Audit Committee are in addition to those set out for a member of the Board of Directors.

2.3   The Chair of the Committee, who shall not be the Chair of the Company, shall be appointed by the Board by formal Board resolution.

3.   Attendance at meetings

3.1   The Chief Financial Officer, the Head of Internal Audit and a representative of the independent accountant shall normally attend meetings. All other Board members and the Chief Executive Officer shall also normally have the right to attend.

3.2   The Chair of the Committee may instruct any officer or employee of the company to attend any meeting and provide pertinent information as necessary.

3.3   At the request of the Chair any executive in attendance may be required to leave the meeting.

3.4   At least once a year, the Committee shall meet with the Head of Internal Audit and the independent accountants respectively, without the presence of executive management to discuss any matters that either the Committee or these two believe should be discussed privately.

3.5   The Company Secretary shall be the secretary of the Committee.

4.   Frequency of meetings

4.1   Meetings shall be held at least three times yearly or more frequently as circumstances require.

4.2   The Committee Chair shall convene a meeting upon request of any Committee member who considers it necessary.

4.3   Whenever possible Committee meetings shall be scheduled to allow for adequate time for Committee business, and so that they can be reported promptly and effectively to the Board.

5.   Authority

5.1   The Committee is authorised by the Board to investigate any activity it deems appropriate. It is authorised to seek any information from any officer or employee of the company all of whom are directed to co-operate with any request made by the Committee.

5.2   The Committee is authorised to engage any firm of accountants, lawyers or other professionals as the Committee sees fit to provide independent council and advice and to assist in any review or investigation on such matters as the Committee deems appropriate.

5.3 The Head of Internal Audit reports functionally to the Chair of the Audit Committee (and administratively to the Chief Executive Officer).

6. Duties

The duties of the Committee shall be to:

General

6.1 To ensure that there is an open avenue of communication between the internal auditors, the independent accountants and the Board of Directors.

6.2 Review annually and, if necessary propose for formal Board adoption, amendments to the Committee's Terms of Reference.

6.3 Consider, in consultation with the independent accountants and the Head of Internal Audit, the audit plans and scope of the independent accountants and internal auditors, ensuring that co-ordination of audit effort is maximised.

Financial statements

6.4 Review with management and the independent accountants at the completion of the annual examination:

a. The company's annual financial statements and related footnotes.
b. The independent accountants' audit of the financial statements and report thereon.
c. Any significant changes which have been required in the independent accountants' audit plan.
d. Any significant difficulties or disputes with management encountered during the course of the audit.
e. Other matters related to the conduct of the audit which are to be communicated to the Committee under generally accepted auditing standards.

Internal control

6.5 Enquire of management, the Head of Internal Audit, and the independent accountants about significant risks or exposures and evaluate the steps taken to minimise such risk to the company.

6.6 Consider and review with management and the Head of Internal Audit significant findings during the year and management's responses thereto.

6.7 Consider and review with the independent accountants and the Head of Internal Audit:

a. The adequacy of the company's systems of internal control including computerised information systems controls and security.

b. Any related significant findings and recommendations of the independent accountants and of the internal auditors, together with management's responses thereto.
c. The contents of the independent accountants' Management Letter, together with management's responses thereto.

External audit

6.8 Recommend to the Board of Directors the independent accountants to be appointed and their compensation; review and approve the scope and quality of their work, and their discharge or resignation.

6.9 Consider with management and the independent accountants the rationale for employing audit firms other than the principal independent accountants.

Internal audit

6.10 Review and approve, where possible in advance of the event, the appointment, replacement, re-assignment, or dismissal of the Head of Internal Audit.

6.11 Receive periodic reports on the quality of internal audit as required by the *Standards for the Professional Practice of Internal Auditing*, which standards the Committee will enjoin and enable Internal Audit to observe.

6.12 Consider and review with management and the Head of Internal Audit:

a. Any difficulties encountered in the course of internal audits, and any restrictions placed on internal audit scope of work or access to required information or personnel.
b. The audit plan of future audits to be conducted.
c. The internal auditing department's budget and staffing.
d. Any changes which have been required in the previously approved audit plan.
e. The internal audit department's Charter.

7. Reporting

7.1 The Chair of the Committee shall report on Committee business to the Board of Directors with such recommendations as the Committee may deem appropriate.

7.2 The Committee shall recommend approval of the annual report and accounts to the Board of Directors.

7.3 After due consideration, the Committee will propose to the Board of Directors the wording of internal control reports for publication.

7.4 The Secretary shall distribute copies of the minutes of meetings of the Committee to all members of the Board of Directors, and the minutes shall be an agenda paper of the next Board meeting.

Consider

1. How the above terms of reference compare with those for your own audit committee.
2. How they can be improved.

Case 9.2 Timing and content of audit committee meetings

The case

The Head of Internal Audit was asked to advise the audit committee on the timing and content of their meetings. The company year end is 31 December. It is a small listed company.

The solution

This is the essence of the advice which the Head of Internal Audit developed:

> At a minimum the committee will need to meet four times a year. We are showing the agenda for the February meeting as dealing, *inter alia*, with the financial statements for publication as well as with the assessment of the effectiveness of internal control. With two heavy items like this it is likely that one will be dealt with inadequately unless adequate committee time is safeguarded. Accordingly we are suggesting a full day meeting but an alternative would be two separate meetings at approximately the same time during February. Further meetings should be arranged as required.
>
> In each case we recommend that the audit committee's meeting is scheduled 8–10 days before the associated board meeting so that its draft minutes may be tabled at the board meeting and spoken to by the chair of the audit committee.
>
> These are the meetings we suggest, together with their principal agenda items:

1. July (8–10 days before the associated board)

.1 Interim results
.2 Summary reports on internal audit work done.
 .1 Including internal audit time alone with the committee.

2. November (8–10 days before the associated board meeting)

.1 Summary reports on internal audit work done
 .1 Including internal auditor time alone with the committee.
.2 Discussion and approval of the internal audit plan of work to be conducted in the coming financial year.

3 February (likely to be a full day's meeting, ideally about 8 days before the associated board)

.1 Final results
   .1 Including external auditor time alone with the committee.
.2 Review of internal control
   .1 External auditor's draft management letter
      .1 Including committee time alone with the external auditor.
   .2 Summary reports on internal audit work done.
      .1 Including committee time alone with the internal auditor.
   .3 Committee's review of internal audit's overall summary opinion on internal control.
   .4 Committee's consideration of the Executive's Losses Report
   .5 Formulation and adoption of the committee's opinion of the effectiveness of internal control over the year under review, and their draft internal control report for publication (both for communication to the board).

   etc.

.3 Committee's recommendation, for transmittal to the board, on the appointment of the external auditors for the current year's audit.

4. April, May or June (8–10 days before the associated board meeting)

.1 Consideration of planned external audit approach.
.2 Preliminary review of whether to consider appointing alternative external auditors for the *following* financial year.
.3 Summary reports on internal audit work done.
   .1 Including committee time alone with the internal auditor.
.4 Receive a report on an external quality assurance review of the internal audit function (once every three years).
.5 Committee conclusions on the present and planned future adequacy of the internal audit function.
   .1 Including time *without* the internal auditor being present.

Consider

1. How this calendar and the agendas compare with those for the audit committee in your own organisation.
2. How the calendar and agendas can be improved.

Case 9.3 Implementing a control and risk self-assessment programme

The case

Organisation X is a young but large, growing and progressive housing association with 180 staff. It is committed to developing a 'no blame', participative and empowered management culture. It sees the distinction between 'management' and 'other' personnel as being more a matter of the content of the activity than of the status of the staff involved. It has embarked upon a process of cultural change designed to achieve a genuinely people-focused, empowered enterprise with excellent communications, motivated and fulfilled members of staff, and exemplary customer care.

It has been decided that a programme of control and risk self-assessment will be an ideal opportunity to give substance to this programme of cultural change. It has invited an external consultant to advise on this programme. The consultant has visited X and prepared the following proposal.

Proposal

We believe it is important that X applies its changed culture widely and deeply so that it is given a real opportunity to take root permanently in a practical way. By the completion of this proposed programme of CRSA, all or most staff in Organisation X will have experienced and participated in the cultural change in a quite profound way.

To a large extent CRSA naturally applies the principles which are at the heart of this change process: CRSA was born in the mid to late 1980s out of an empowerment programme within a major Canadian-based multinational oil company.

The particular approach to CRSA which we are proposing further exploits the participative, communicative, 'no blame' attributes of X's corporate style, for instance by the use of anonymous voting.

Our proposed CRSA project has the following components, though, of course, these are subject to discussion and appropriate amendment. We have worked on the basis that the planning and development work should be completed within two months and that the programme, in particular the workshops, will commence towards the end of September 1997.

Initial determination of the workshop groups

Our intention is to work with internal audit and to 'divide' X into what will be a number of CRSA workshop groups. There should be one workshop group for each activity which is important to X. This means there is likely to be one workshop group for each functional area ('department', 'section', etc.) which exists within X. Additionally there is likely to be one workshop group for each key business process which cuts across structural sections – such as, for instance, managing the development and launch of new products and services. There is also likely to be one workshop group for each corporate service activity – including, most likely, one for the board, one for each of the board's committees, one for the Personnel function and one for internal audit etc. There may be a place for further workshop groups which combine X staff with the staff of business partners or with other people – where key activities involve collaboration with others. There may be a case to duplicate an activity in a second workshop group if the number of involved staff makes this feasible and desirable in a particular case.

At present we are working on the assumption that no workshop group will comprise more than 16 participants plus one or two facilitators, but most workshop groups are likely to be considerably smaller – say six to eight people. Sometimes appropriate membership of a workshop group may include staff from outside the activity who have an interest in it – this would be the case for the workshop group on internal audit, for instance.

The facilitators would be either or both of (a) consultant staff and/or (b) internal audit staff.

Determination of the CRSA scope

At present we propose that each of the workshops should address two sets of issues, as follows. While these sets are not entirely mutually exclusive they both need to be explored by each workshop group in order to maximise the value which will flow from the CRSA process. Set 2 flows naturally from Set 1.

Set 1: The general questions for assessing the effectiveness of internal control. By addressing these questions there will emerge action plans for improvement.

Set 2: Identification and prioritisation of the issues specific to the workshop group, as follows:

- the work objectives of the group;
- how these objectives are likely to change;
- the risks the group faces (of not achieving objectives, or of unwanted outcomes);
- how these risks are likely to change;
- the controls in place to meet these risks;
- the effectiveness of these controls – for current and future risks;
- new measures to be taken to address risk and maximise opportunity to achieve objectives;
- action plans for improvement;

- determination of technology to be used in the CRSA workgroups.

We suggest we should pursue a choice between two options, with a strong preference for the second (for the reasons given).

Option 1: Uses Method 1 only
A development of Standard Audit Programme Guides methodology (a) to assist in steering each workshop through consideration of the issues in Sets 1 and 2 (above), and (b) to document workshop discussion and decisions.

Option 2: Combines Method 1 with Method 2
Some features of the SAPG approach of Method 1 plus anonymous voting and report preparation. Anonymous voting offers the following advantages:
- democratic;
- avoids expressions of judgement which are influenced by fear of offending other workshop members or incurring their displeasure;
- enjoyable – a great motivator;
- immediate scoring – with ranges of responses immediately clear;
- speeds up the workshop, better for maintaining participant interest;
- allows exploration in greater depth within given time; reduces required duration of workshops;
- promotes the development of consensus – breaks through any log jams in a non-threatening way.

We estimate that Option 2 workshops facilitated by anonymous voting will typically require a short working day – probably a 10am start, ending at 4pm. We consider the intensity of participant workshops would make a longer workshop day too demanding: Option 1 would thus require a similar timeframe in Day 1, followed by a half day on the following day to round off the workshop.

Development of the technology

The SAPG component will require some consultancy time in consultation with internal audit.

CRSA training sessions for X staff

We propose that four one-day CRSA training sessions should be run for X staff in collaboration with internal audit. They will cover the following:
- What is the meaning of 'internal control'?
- What is the meaning of 'risk'?

- What do we mean by 'control and risk self-assessment'?
- How will CRSA work in X?
- What are the next steps?

The workshops

These will be held at X and are likely to commence late in September 1997. At this stage, for pricing purposes, we are assuming:

- there will be 20 workshops concluding in July 1998;
- each workshop will take the short working day referred to above.

Following a workshop, half a day of consulting time will be allocated to post-workshop activity which will entail:

- ensuring the workshop documentation is complete;
- ensuring that action plans are understood and agreed.

Consider

(Refer also to Chapter 2 when considering your responses to the case.)

1. Further aspects to be decided by X are:

- membership of each workshop group – hierarchical, mixed levels, cross functional, etc.;
- sequence in which the workshop groups will be staged – top-down, bottom-up, mixed;
- scheduled dates for the workshop groups – intervals between workshops and follow-ups;
- whether it is intended to cover all of X in one year, and thereafter treat CRSA as an annual programme.

2. Prepare the advice you will give for the self-assessment methods for your own organisation, including use of any or all of the following:

- use of organisation visions and mission statements;
- use of function key objectives;
- design and issue of control assessment questionnaires;
- use of routine monitoring and inspection results;
- implementation of new internal checks;
- use of existing control charts and other measures;
- implementation of special observations or investigations;
- use of internal audit or other audit results;
- new audit programmes.

Case 9.4 Control risk assessment – defining a new vision

(Reprinted with permission from The IIA Inc., *CSA Sentinel*, No. 1, 1997.)

The case

Tim J. Leech and Bruce McQuaig of MCS Control Training and Design have developed a 'new vision' of control and quality management. Leech and McCuaig describe their Control and Risk Self-assessment (CRSA) model as 'a process that allows work groups to identify or refine the business/quality objectives that they should be fulfilling, while assessing the adequacy of the controls in place to meet those objectives.' CRSA is further described as 'a team-driven business process that organisations around the world are using to refine visions, analyse the current reality, and improve the quality of all business processes.'

Organisations that are moving to the new vision of control and quality management must understand the elements in their environments that may affect implementation. In the information (in this case), Leech provides a framework for looking at the traditional and the new, and the barriers and impediments that may deter implementation of CRSA.

Historical/traditional

- Assign duties/supervise staff.
- Policy/rule driven.
- Limited employee participation and training.
- Narrow stakeholder focus.
- Auditors and other specialists are the primary control analysts/reporters.

In the historical/traditional environment:

- management and staff are responsible for complying with prescribed methods and procedures;
- management and staff receive limited training on control and quality assessment and design;
- auditors, consultants, and other specialists are regarded as the experts on control and quality systems and design;
- outside specialists are often called in to analyse areas where concerns and/or problems exist;
- the personnel who do the work are often not directly responsible for selecting the controls used to help assure that their business and quality objectives are achieved;
- candidness and full disclosure on the current state of control and risk is not encouraged and often is discouraged and punished;

- fear and blame are sometimes utilised as strategies when problems surface;
- Internal control and total quality/continuous improvement are not integrated programmes or concepts.

The New Vision

- Empowered, accountable employees.
- Culture of continuous improvement and learning.
- Extensive employee participation and training.
- Broad stakeholder focus.
- Staff at all levels, in all functions, are the primary control analysts and reporters.

In the new environment:

- management and staff are accountable for designing and maintaining control systems that provide the desired level of assurance regarding the achievement of business and quality objectives;
- management and staff are provided with control assessment and design skills that are adequate for proper fulfilment of their responsibility to assess and report to officers, the board, and others on the current status of control, quality and risk;
- consensus at all levels on relevant business and quality objectives is a primary goal;
- candid disclosure of the state of control and the risks being accepted by the unit or organisation is encouraged and rewarded;
- accountability for business and quality objectives exists and is accepted by staff at all levels and in all functions. Employees at all levels are responsible for finding new and better ways to improve and optimise control portfolios so that achievement of organisational objectives is advanced;
- employees at all levels and in all functions continually reassess the adequacy and appropriateness of control choices and make adjustments when new information emerges regarding risk status, prioritisation of objectives, and the control options available;
- control and quality management are considered to be synonymous and are fully integrated programmes/concepts.

A New Vision – barriers and impediments

Management and staff

Some of the most common barriers and impediments that challenge organisations striving to actualise the New Vision include the following:

- Control and quality self-assessment is often not recognised or acknowledged by senior management as a core competency for all staff, at all levels, an in all functions.
- Regular self-assessment of control and quality management frameworks and/or systems by staff in all areas of an organisation is not considered in most organisations to be a core business process. Unless regular formalised team-driven self-assessment is viewed as a standard business process on a par with other annual processes such as budgeting and performance appraisal, the commitment necessary to sustain long-term improvement often disappears.
- Some managers fear and resist the new accountabilities that come with the new vision and are upset with the perceived reduction in power and responsibility.
- A small percentage of employees are comfortable in rule and policy driven environments. They are comfortable with the fact that they are not expected, or required, to continuously learn and improve, or to take responsibility for regularly assessing and reporting on business/quality objectives, control design, or residual risk status.
- There are currently a limited number of qualified trainers and facilitators with the knowledge, skills, and willingness to teach assessment and design skills to work teams. Most training to date on control and quality analysis and reporting has been focused at auditors. Many auditors do not see it as their role to teach these skills to their clients. Some are not well-suited to teach and/or facilitate team-driven self-assessment.
- Many senior managers have not recognised that control management and quality management are synonymous terms that should be managed and reported on by the responsible work teams. They have also not fully endorsed the view that quality includes not only product quality and/or customer service, but also cost control, regulatory compliance, fraud prevention, safety, and other key business/quality areas.

Auditors

When auditors are asked whether their organisations are, or should be, striving to actualise the concepts embodied in the New Vision, more than 95 per cent state that they either 'agree' or 'strongly agree'. Experience suggests, however, that many auditors are impeding, not accelerating, their organisation's progress toward the New Vision. The following points may help to explain this contradiction.

- Auditors have been conditioned to believe that it is they who hold primary responsibility for assessing and reporting directly on the status of control and quality management. Most of the audit profession's standards and training courses have been established in accordance with this direct review and report role paradigm.

- Auditors are comfortable with the role of being the primary control/quality assessors and reporters. This is compounded by the fact that most officers and directors see assessment and reporting on control and quality management to be audit's job – not the job of the work teams responsible for the objectives.
- Although some auditors accept the benefits and advantages of the New Vision, they lack the conviction and selling skills necessary to convince senior management that a self-assessment approach would better meet the needs of all stakeholders. This situation sometimes persists even after these auditors have acknowledged that the New Vision of control and quality management is likely to out-perform dramatically the Historical/Traditional approach on most relevant evaluation and success criteria.
- Many organisations use a narrow definition of internal control focused on financial reporting and control. Regulators and professional accounting organisations foster and promote narrow definitions of internal control. This often convinces staff that control and quality management have little in common.
- The idea of having management and staff self-assess and report on their current control and quality status is a new concept that has not been promoted by regulators or quality standards boards.

Consider

1. How does the new vision for CSRA apply in your organisation?
2. Are your internal audit staff CSRA 'traditional' or 'visionary'?
3. Are you integrating quality and control into your CSRA?

Case 9.5 Tomorrow's company: the role of business in a changing world

(Extracted from *In Business* (1997) II 1.9.3, ICSA Publishing, Hemel Hempstead.)

The case

In January 1993, the Royal Society of Arts (RSA) brought together senior executives from 25 of the United Kingdom's top businesses under the leadership of Sir Anthony Cleaver, chairman of IBM United Kingdom Limited, to develop a shared vision of tomorrow's company.

In parallel with the corporate support, the RSA established an Inquiry Network of some 500 persons drawn from Fellows and other interested individuals. The aim of the exercise was practical, and to stimulate thoughts about how to maintain business performance in a world that was becoming not only more comprehensive, but also increasingly critical and vigilant of business standards. An interim report was published in February 1994 reflecting the inquiry's thinking at the end of the first year.

The report was made available to more than 8,000 business leaders and opinion formers, including participants to conferences held in Leeds, Newcastle and Exeter. In addition to the consulting process, additional information was obtained from interviews with chairmen and chief executives, as well as from market research.

The final report opens with an executive summary which sets out the case for change, then presents the inquiry's vision, outlines the inclusive approach and concludes with making it happen. The case for change opens with the view that there are too few world-class companies in the United Kingdom and too few being developed. Supporting data are provided for this claim along with some reasons. Change, it is claimed, is being brought about through globalisation, new employment patterns and organisational structures, environmental issues and the decline in defence. The section concludes with the hypothesis that the rules of competiveness are being rewritten with the result that people and relationships are the key to sustainable success.

The inquiry's vision moves from the exclusive importance of shareholders' interests to one based on partnership, teamwork, shared values and shared goals. It is proposed tomorrow's company will be one adopting an inclusive approach as a route to sustainable success.

With the inclusive approach:

(a) Purpose and values will be communicated.
(b) A unique success model will be developed.
(c) A positive value will be placed on relationships.
(d) A good relationship will be established with all stakeholders while maintaining a strong licence to operate.

The inclusive approach is applied to a number of topics, covering:

- leadership;
- an approach to people;
- an approach to investment needs and to society.

The key headings under leadership include:

(a) A clear understanding of directors' duties.
(b) A new language for business success.
(c) A measurement system that is consistent with purpose and values, while bringing reporting into line with the recommendations from Cadbury 1, etc.

The key headings under people include:

(a) Tomorrow's company will anticipate changes in employment patterns.
(b) Tomorrow's company will motivate individuals.
(c) Tomorrow's company will maintain a flexible organisational structure while participating in exploring the future of work.

The investing community can help in two ways:

(a) By making it a priority for investors and those who advise them to apply the inclusiveness test to their investments.
(b) By making it a priority for institutions to adopt an inclusive approach to ensure their competitive position is not weakened by adversarial behaviour.

The role for company leaders is to:

(a) Develop community partnerships.
(b) Work with government to manage the competitive agenda.
(c) Improve business representation and networking structures.
(d) Enhance supply chain performance.
(e) Clear the way for the growth of small businesses.

In conclusion, the inquiry considers how to make it happen. It sets out four agendas covering directors, managers, pension fund managers, pension fund trustees and actuaries, accountants and auditors, and lastly learners and educators – including individuals and parents, schools and careers advisers, management educators.

The RSA can be contacted at 8 John Adam Street, London WC2N 6EZ: tel: 0171 839 1641. In addition to the report, there is a summary of 'what the papers say'.

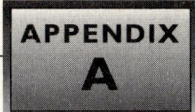

APPENDIX A

Glossary of terms

(A definition of words and terms used in this book. Those with references are extracted from the glossary published by The IIA with its Standards for the Professional Practice of Internal Auditing, 1996.)

Activity reports of the internal auditing department highlight significant audit findings and recommendations and inform senior management and the board of any significant deviations from approved audit work schedules, staffing plans, and financial budgets, and the reasons for them. (1 10.01.6)

Adequate control is present if management has planned and organised (designed) in a manner which provides reasonable assurance that the organisation's objectives and goals will be achieved efficiently and economically. (300.02.4)

Analytical auditing procedures are performed by studying and comparing relationships among both financial and nonfinancial information. The application of analytical auditing procedures is based on the premise that, in the absence of known conditions to the contrary, relationships among information may reasonably be expected to exist and continue. Examples of contrary conditions include unusual or nonrecurring transactions or events; accounting, organisational, operational, environmental, and technological changes; inefficiencies; ineffectiveness; errors; irregularities, or illegal acts. (420.01.1b and c)

Appreciation means the ability to recognise the existence of problems or potential problems and to determine the further research to be undertaken or the assistance to be obtained. (250.01.4)

Audit objectives are broad statements developed by internal auditors and define intended audit accomplishments. (410.01.1a)

Audit procedures are the tasks the internal auditor undertakes for collecting, analysing, interpreting, and documenting information during an audit. Audit procedures are the means to attain audit objectives. (410.01.1a)

Audit programme is a document which lists the audit procedures to be followed during an audit. The audit programme also states the objectives of the audit. (410.01.6a)

Audit report is a signed, written document which presents the purpose, scope, and results of the audit. Results of the audit may include findings, conclusions (opinions), and recommendations. (430.01, 430.04 and 430.04.5)

Audit scope refers to the activities covered by an internal audit. Audit scope includes, where appropriate:
- audit objectives;
- nature and extent of auditing procedures performed;
- time period audited;
- related activities not audited in order to delineate the boundaries of the audit. (430.04.4)

Audit work schedules include (a) what activities are to be audited; (b) when they will be audited; and (c) the estimated time required, taking into account the scope of the audit work planned and the nature and extent of audit work performed by others. (520.04)

Audit working papers record the information obtained, the analyses made, and conclusions reached during an audit. Audit working papers support the bases for the findings and recommendations to be reported. (420.01.5 and 420.01.5c)

Auditable activities consist of those subjects, units, or systems which are capable of being defined and evaluated. Auditable activities may include:
- policies, procedures, and practices;
- cost centres, profit centres, and investment centres;
- general ledger account balances;
- information systems (manual and computerised);
- major contracts and programmes;
- organisational units such as product or service lines;
- functions such as electronic data processing, purchasing, marketing, production, finance, accounting, and human resources;
- transaction systems for activities such as sales, collection, purchasing, disbursement, inventory and cost accounting, production, treasury, payroll, and capital assets;
- financial statements;
- laws and regulations. (520.04.5)

Auditee includes any individual, unit, or activity of the organisation that is audited.

Authorisation implies that the authorising authority has verified and validated that the activity or transaction conforms with established policies and procedures. (300.03.2a)

Authorising includes initiating or granting permission to perform activities or transactions. (300.03.2a)

Board includes boards of directors, audit committees of such boards, heads of agencies or legislative bodies to whom internal auditors report, boards of governors or trustees of nonprofit organisations, and any other designated governing bodies of organisations.

Cause is the reason for the difference between the expected and actual conditions (why the difference exists). (430.04.7c)

Charter of the internal auditing department is a formal written document which defines the department's purpose, authority, and responsibility. The charter should (a) establish the department's position within the organisation; (b) authorise access to records, personnel, and physical properties relevant to the performance of audits; and (c) define the scope of internal auditing activities. (110.01.4)

Code of ethics of The Institute of Internal Auditors (IIA) sets forth standards of conduct for members of The IIA and Certified Internal Auditors to effectively discharge their responsibilities. The Code of Ethics calls for high standards of honesty, objectivity, diligence, and loyalty. (240.01)

Conclusions (opinions) are the internal auditor's evaluations of the effects of the findings on the activities reviewed. Conclusions usually put the findings in perspective based upon their overall implications. (430.04.8)

Condition is the factual evidence which the internal auditor found in the course of the examination (what does exist). (430.04.7b)

Conflicts of interest refers to any relationship which is or appears to be not in the best interest of the organisation. A conflict of interest would prejudice an individual's ability to carry out their duties and responsibilities objectively. (280.01)

Control is any action taken by management to enhance the likelihood that established objectives and goals will be achieved. Management plans, organises, and directs the performance of sufficient actions to provide reasonable assurance that objectives and goals will be achieved. Thus, control is the result of proper planning, organising, and directing by management. (300.06)

Control environment refers to the attitude and actions of the board and management regarding the significance of control within the organisation. The control environment provides the discipline and structure for the achievement of the primary objectives of the system of internal control. The control environment includes the following elements:
- integrity and ethical values;
- management's philosophy and operating style;
- organisational structure;
- assignment of authority and responsibility;
- human resource policies and practices;
- competence of personnel. (300.07.4)

Cost-benefit relationship means that the potential loss associated with any exposure or risk is weighed against the cost to control it. (300.02.5)

Criteria are the standards, measures, or expectations used in making an evaluation and/or verification (what should exist). (430.04.7a)

Detective controls are actions taken to detect and correct undesirable events which have occurred. (300.06.1)

Directing involves, in addition to accomplishing objectives and planned activities, authorising and monitoring performance, periodically comparing actual with planned performance, and documenting these activities to provide additional assurance that systems operate as planned. (300.03.2)

Directive controls are actions taken to cause or encourage a desirable event to occur. (300.06.1)

Director of internal auditing (Director) identifies the top position in an internal auditing department. The term also includes such titles as General Auditor, Chief Internal Auditor, Chief Audit Executive, and Inspector General.

Due professional care calls for the application of the care and skill expected of a reasonably prudent and competent internal auditor in the same or similar circumstances. Due professional care is exercised when internal audits are performed in accordance with the Standards for the Professional Practice of Internal Auditing. The exercise of due professional care requires that:

- internal auditors be independent of the activities they audit;
- internal audits be performed by those persons who collectively possess the necessary knowledge, skills, and disciplines to conduct the audit properly;
- audit work be planned and supervised;
- audit reports be objective, clear, concise, constructive, and timely;
- internal auditors follow up on reported audit findings to ascertain that appropriate action was taken. (280.01)

Economical performance accomplishes objectives and goals at a cost commensurate with the risk. (300.02.7)

Effect is the risk or exposure the auditee organisation and/or others encounter because the condition is not the same as the criteria (the impact of the difference). (430.04.7d)

Effective control is present when management directs systems in such a manner as to provide reasonable assurance that the organisation's objectives and goals will be achieved. (300.03.1)

Efficient performance accomplishes objectives and goals in an accurate and timely fashion with minimal use of resources. (300.02.6)

Error as it relates to internal audit reports is an unintentional misstatement or omission of significant information in a final audit report. (430.03.1b)

External auditors are audit professionals who perform independent annual audits of an organisation's financial statements.

External reviews of the internal auditing department are performed to appraise the quality of the department's operations. External reviews should be performed by qualified persons who are independent of the organisation and who do not have either a real or apparent conflict of interest. (560.04)

Findings are pertinent statements of fact. Audit findings emerge by a process of comparing what should be with what is. (430.04.6 and .7)

Flowchart is a representation, primarily through the use of symbols, of the sequence of activities in a system (process, operation, function, or activity). (420.01.5d)

Follow-up by internal auditors is defined as a process by which they determine the adequacy, effectiveness, and timeliness of actions taken by management on reported audit findings. Such findings also include relevant findings made by external auditors and others. (440.01.1)

Formal internal reviews are periodic self-assessments of the internal auditing department to appraise the quality of the audit work performed. These reviews generally are performed by a team or an individual selected by the director of internal auditing. (560.03.1)

Fraud encompasses an array of irregularities and illegal acts characterised by intentional deception. (280.01.1)

Goals are specific objectives of specific systems and may be otherwise referred to as operating or programme objectives or goals, operating standards, performance levels, targets, or expected results. (300.02.2)

Guidelines are suitable means of meeting the General and Specific Standards for the Professional Practice of Internal Auditing. (Introduction)

Illegal acts refers to violations of laws and governmental regulations. (280.01.1)

Independence allows internal auditors to carry out their work freely and objectively. This concept requires that internal auditors be independent of the activities they audit. Independence is achieved through organisational status and objectivity. (100.01)

Information is data the internal auditor obtains during an audit to provide a sound basis for audit findings and recommendations. Information should be sufficient, competent, relevant, and useful. (420.01.2)

Internal auditing is an independent appraisal function established within an organisation to examine and evaluate its activities as a service to the organisation. The objective of internal auditing is to assist members of the organisation in the effective discharge of their responsibilities. To this end, internal auditing furnishes them with analyses, appraisals, recommendations, counsel, and information concerning the activities reviewed. The audit objective includes promoting effective control at reasonable cost.

Internal auditing department includes any unit or activity within an organisation which performs internal auditing functions.

Internal auditor is an individual within an organisation's internal auditing department who is assigned the responsibility of performing internal auditing functions.

Internal control is a process within an organisation designed to provide reasonable assurance regarding the achievement of the following primary objectives:

- the reliability and integrity of information;
- compliance with policies, plans, procedures, laws, and regulations;
- the safeguarding of assets;
- the economical and efficient use of resources;
- the accomplishment of established objectives and goals for operations or programmes. (300.05)

Irregularity refers to the intentional misstatement or omission of significant information in accounting records, financial statements, other reports, documents or records. Irregularities include (a) fraudulent financial reporting which renders financial statements misleading and (b) misappropriation of assets. Irregularities involve:

- falsification or alteration of accounting or other records and supporting documents;
- intentional misapplication of accounting principles;
- misrepresentation or intentional omission of events, transactions, or other significant information. (280.01.1)

Management includes those individuals with responsibilities for setting and/or achieving the organisation's objectives.

Monitoring encompasses supervising, observing, and testing activities and appropriately reporting to responsible individuals. Monitoring provides an ongoing verification of progress toward achievement of objectives and goals. (300.03.2b)

Objectives are the broadest statements of what the organisation chooses to accomplish. (300.02.1)

Objectivity is an independent mental attitude which requires internal auditors to perform audits in such a manner that they have an honest belief in their work product and that no significant quality compromises are made. Objectivity requires internal auditors not to subordinate their judgement on audit matters to that of others. (120.01 and .02)

Operations refers to the recurring activities of an organisation directed toward producing a product or rendering a service. Such activities may include, but are not limited to, marketing, sales, production, purchasing, human resources, finance and accounting, and governmental assistance. (350.01.1)

Preventive controls are actions taken to deter undesirable event from occurring. (300.06.1)

Proficiency means the ability to apply knowledge to situations likely to be encountered and to deal with them without extensive recourse to technical research and assistance. (250.01.1)

Programmes refers to special purpose activities of an organisation. Such activities include, but are not limited to, the raising of capital, sale of a facility, fund-raising campaigns, new product or service introduction campaigns, capital expenditures, and special purpose government grants. (350.01.2)

Purpose statements in audit reports describe the audit objectives and may, where necessary, inform the reader why the audit was conducted and what it was expected to achieve. (430.04.3)

Quality assurance is a programme by which the director of internal auditing evaluates the operations of the internal auditing department. The purpose of the quality assurance programme is to provide reasonable assurance that internal auditing work conforms with the Standards for the Professional Practice of Internal Auditing, the internal auditing department's charter, and other applicable standards. The quality assurance programme should include the following elements:

- supervision;
- internal reviews;
- external reviews. (560.01)

Ratio analysis is the study of financial condition and performance through ratios derived from items in the financial statements or from other financial or nonfinancial information. (420.01.1h)

Reasonableness test is a comparison of an estimated amount, calculated by the use of relevant financial and nonfinancial information, with a recorded amount. (420.01.1h)

Recommendations are actions the internal auditor believes necessary to correct existing conditions or improve operations. (430.05.1)

Regression analysis is a mathematical procedure which is used to determine and measure the predictive relationship between one variable (dependent variable) and one or more other variables (independent variable). (420.01.1h)

Risk is the probability that an event or action may adversely affect the organisation or activity under audit. (410.01.1b and 520.04.2)

Risk assessment is a systematic process for assessing and integrating professional judgements about probable adverse conditions and/or events. The risk assessment process should provide a means of organising and integrating professional judgements for development of the audit work schedule. (520.04.10)

Risk factors are the criteria used to identify the relative significance of, and likelihood that, conditions and/or events may occur that could adversely affect the organisation. (520.04.6)

Scope limitation is a restriction placed upon the internal auditing department that precludes the department from accomplishing its objectives and plans. Among other things, a scope limitation may restrict the:

- scope defined in the charter;
- department's access to records, personnel, and physical properties relevant to the performance of audits;
- approved audit work schedule;
- performance of necessary auditing procedures;
- approved staffing plan and financial budget. (110.01.5b)

Senior management refers to those individuals to whom the director of internal auditing is responsible.

Significant is the level of importance or magnitude assigned to an item event, information, or problem by the internal auditor.

Significant audit findings are those conditions which, in the judgement of the director of internal auditing, could adversely affect the organisation. Significant audit findings may include conditions dealing with irregularities, illegal acts, errors, inefficiency, waste, ineffectiveness, conflicts of interest, and control weaknesses. (110.01.6b)

Standards for the Professional Practice of Internal Auditing (the Standards) are the criteria by which the operations of an internal auditing department are evaluated and measured. They are intended to represent the practice of internal auditing as it should be.

Statement of Responsibilities of Internal Auditing is a document which presents in summary form the:

- objective and scope of internal auditing;
- responsibility and authority of the internal auditing department;
- independence of internal auditors.

Supervision is a continuing process, beginning with planning and ending with the conclusion of the audit assignment. Supervision includes:

- providing suitable instructions to subordinates at the outset of the audit and approving the audit programme;
- seeing that the approved audit programme is carried out unless deviations are both justified and authorised;
- determining that audit working papers adequately support the audit findings, conclusions, and reports;
- making sure that audit reports are accurate, objective, clear, concise, constructive, and timely;
- determining that audit objectives are being met. (230.01 and .02)

Survey is a process for gathering information, without detailed verification, on the activity being examined. The main purposes are to:

- understand the activity under review;

- identify significant areas warranting special emphasis;
- obtain information for use in performing the audit;
- determine whether further auditing is necessary. (410.01.5a)

System (process, operation, function, or activity) is an arrangement, a set, or a collection of concepts, parts, activities, and/ or people that are connected or interrelated to achieve objectives and goals. (This definition applies to both manual and automated systems.) A system may also be a collection of subsystems operating together for a common objective or goal. (300.02.3)

Trend analysis is the analysis of the changes in a given item of information over a period of time. (420.01.1h)

Understanding means the ability to apply broad knowledge to situations likely to be encountered, to recognise significant deviations, and to be able to carry out the research necessary to arrive at reasonable solutions. (250.01.3)

APPENDIX B

The Institute of Internal Auditors Code of Ethics

Purpose

A distinguishing mark of a profession is acceptance by its members of responsibility to the interests of those it serves. Members of The Institute of Internal Auditors (Members) and Certified Internal Auditors (CIAs) must maintain high standards of conduct in order to effectively discharge this responsibility. The Institute of Internal Auditors (Institute) adopts the Code of Ethics for Members and CIAs.

Applicability

This Code of Ethics is applicable to all Members and CIAs. Membership in The Institute and acceptance of the 'Certified Internal Auditor' designation are voluntary actions. By acceptance, Members and CIAs assume an obligation of self-discipline above and beyond the requirements of laws and regulations.

The standards of conduct set forth in this Code of Ethics provide basic principles in the practice of internal auditing. Members and CIAs should realise that their individual judgement is required in the application of these principles.

CIAs shall use the 'Certified Internal Auditor' designation with discretion and in a dignified manner, fully aware of what the designation denotes. The designation shall also be used in a manner consistent with all statutory requirements.

Members who are judged by the Board of Directors of The Institute to be in violation of the standards of conduct of the Code of Ethics shall be subject to forfeiture of their membership in the Institute. CIAs who are similarly judged also shall be subject to forfeiture of the 'Certified Internal Auditor' designation.

Standards of conduct

I. Members and CIAs shall exercise honesty, objectivity, and diligence in the performance of their duties and responsibilities.

II. Members and CIAs shall exhibit loyalty in all matters pertaining to the affairs of their organisation or to whomever they may be rendering service. However, Members and CIAs shall not knowingly be a party to any illegal or improper activity.

III. Members and CIAs shall not knowingly engage in acts or activities which are discreditable to the profession of internal auditing or to their organisation.

IV. Members and CIAs shall refrain from entering into any activity which may be in conflict with the interest of their organisation or which would prejudice their ability to carry out objectively their duties and responsibilities.

V. Members and CIAs shall not accept anything of value from an employee, client, customer, supplier, or business associate of their organisation which would impair or be presumed to impair their professional judgment.

VI. Members and CIAs shall undertake only those services which they can reasonably expect to complete with professional competence.

VII. Members and CIAs shall adopt suitable means to comply with the Standards for the Professional Practice of Internal Auditing.

VIII. Members and CIAs shall be prudent in the use of information acquired in the course of their duties. They shall not use confidential information for any personal gain nor in any manner which would be contrary to law or detrimental to the welfare of their organisation.

IX. Members and CIAs, when reporting on the results of their work, shall reveal all material facts known to them which, if not revealed, could either distort reports of operations under review or conceal unlawful practices.

X. Members and CIAs shall continually strive for improvements in their proficiency, and in the effectiveness and quality of their service.

XI. Members and CIAs, in the practice of their profession, shall be ever mindful of their obligation to maintain the high standards of competence, morality, and dignity promulgated by The Institute. Members shall abide by the Bylaws and uphold the objectives of The Institute.

Adopted by Board of Directors, July 1988.

APPENDIX C

The Institute of Internal Auditors Statement of Responsibilities of Internal Auditing

The purpose of this statement is to provide in summary form a general understanding of the responsibilities of internal auditing. For more specific guidance, readers should refer to the Standards for the Professional Practice of Internal Auditing.

Objective and scope

Internal auditing is an independent appraisal function established within an organisation to examine and evaluate its activities as a service to the organisation. The objective of internal auditing is to assist members of the organisation in the effective discharge of their responsibilities. To this end, internal auditing furnishes them with analyses, appraisals, recommendations, counsel, and information concerning the activities reviewed. The audit objective includes promoting effective control at reasonable cost. The members of the organisation assisted by internal auditing include those in management and the board of directors.

The scope of internal auditing should encompass the examination and evaluation of the adequacy and effectiveness of the organisation's system of internal control and the quality of performance in carrying out assigned responsibilities. Internal auditors should:

- review the reliability and integrity of financial and operating information and the means used to identify, measure, classify, and report such information;
- review the systems established to ensure compliance with those policies, plans, procedures, laws, and regulations which could have a significant impact on operations and reports, and should determine whether the organisation is in compliance;
- review the means of safeguarding assets and, as appropriate, verify the existence of such assets;
- appraise the economy and efficiency with which resources are employed;

- review operations or programmes to ascertain whether results are consistent with established objectives and goals and whether the operations or programmes are being carried out as planned.

Responsibility and authority

The internal auditing department is an integral part of the organisation and functions under the policies established by management and the board. The purpose, authority, and responsibility of the internal auditing department should be defined in a formal written document (charter). The director of internal auditing should seek approval of the charter by senior management as well as acceptance by the board. The charter should make clear the purposes of the internal auditing department, specify the unrestricted scope of its work, and declare that auditors are to have no authority or responsibility for the activities they audit.

Throughout the world, internal auditing is performed in diverse environments and within organisations which vary in purpose, size, and structure. In addition, the laws and customs within various countries differ from one another. These differences may affect the practice of internal auditing in each environment. The implementation of the Standards for the Professional Practice of Internal Auditing, therefore, will be governed by the environment in which the internal auditing department carries out its assigned responsibilities. Compliance with the concepts enunciated by the Standards for the Professional Practice of Internal Auditing is essential before the responsibilities of internal auditors can be met. As stated in the Code of Ethics, members of The Institute of Internal Auditors, Inc. and Certified Internal Auditors shall adopt suitable means to comply with the Standards for the Professional Practice of Internal Auditing.

Independence

Internal auditors should be independent of the activities they audit. Internal auditors are independent when they can carry out their work freely and objectively. Independence permits internal auditors to render the impartial and unbiased judgments essential to the proper conduct of audits. It is achieved through organisational status and objectivity.

The organisational status of the internal auditing department should be sufficient to permit the accomplishment of its audit responsibilities. The director of the internal auditing department should be responsible to an individual in the organisation with sufficient authority to promote independence and to ensure a broad audit coverage, adequate consideration of audit reports, and appropriate action on audit recommendations.

Objectivity is an independent mental attitude which internal auditors should maintain in performing audits. Internal auditors are not to subordinate their judgment on audit matters to that of others. Designing, installing, and operating systems are not audit functions. Also, the drafting of procedures for systems is not an audit function. Performing such activities is presumed to impair audit objectivity.

The Statement of Responsibilities of Internal Auditing was originally issued by The Institute of Internal Auditors in 1947. The current Statement, revised in 1990, embodies the concepts previously established and includes such changes as are deemed advisable in light of the present status of the profession.

APPENDIX D

The Institute of Internal Auditors Summary of General and Specific Standards for the Professional Practice of Internal Auditing

100 Indepedence – Internal auditors should be independent of the activities they audit

110 Organisational Status – The organisational status of the internal auditing department should be sufficient to permit the accomplishment of its audit responsibilities.
120 Objectivity – Internal auditors should be objective in performing audits.

200 Professional proficiency – Internal audits should be performed with proficiency and due professional care

The Internal Auditing Department

210 Staffing – The internal auditing department should provide assurance that the technical proficiency and educational background of internal auditors are appropriate for the audits to be performed.
220 Knowledge, Skills, and Disciplines – The internal auditing department should possess or should obtain the knowledge, skills, and disciplines needed to carry out its audit responsibilities.
230 Supervision – The internal auditing department should provide assurance that internal audits are properly supervised.

The Internal auditor

240 Compliance with Standards of Conduct – Internal auditors should comply with professional standards of conduct.

250 Knowledge, Skills, and Disciplines – Internal auditors should possess the knowledge, skills, and disciplines essential to the performance of internal audits.
260 Human Relations and Communications – Internal auditors should be skilled in dealing with people and in communicating effectively.
270 Continuing Education – Internal auditors should maintain their technical competence through continuing education.
280 Due Professional Care – Internal auditors should exercise due professional care in performing internal audits.

300 Scope of work – The scope of internal auditing should encompass the examination and evaluation of the adequacy and effectiveness of the organisation's system of internal control and the quality of performance in carrying out assigned responsibilities

310 Reliability and Integrity of Information – Internal auditors should review the reliability and integrity of financial and operating information and the means used to identify, measure, classify, and report such information.
320 Compliance with Policies, Plans, Procedures, Laws, and Regulations – Internal auditors should review the systems established to ensure compliance with those policies, plans, procedures, laws, and regulations which could have a significant impact on operations and reports and should determine whether the organisation is in compliance.
330 Safeguarding of Assets – Internal auditors should review the means of safeguarding assets and, as appropriate, verify the existence of such assets.
340 Economical and Efficient Use of Resources – Internal auditors should appraise the economy and efficiency with which resources are employed.
350 Accomplishment of Established Objectives and Goals for Operations or Programmes – Internal auditors should review operations or programmes to ascertain whether results are consistent with established objectives and goals and whether the operations or programmes are being carried out as planned.

400 Performance of audit work – Audit work should include planning the audit, examining and evaluating information, communicating results, and following up

410 Planning the Audit – Internal auditors should plan each audit.
420 Examining and Evaluating Information – Internal auditors should collect, analyse, interpret, and document information to support audit results.
430 Communicating Results – Internal auditors should report the results of their audit work.
440 Following Up – Internal auditors should follow up to ascertain that appropriate action is taken on reported audit findings.

500 Management of the internal auditing department – The director of internal auditing should properly manage the internal auditing department

510 Purpose, Authority, and Responsibility – The director of internal auditing should have a statement of purpose, authority, and responsibility for the internal auditing department.

520 Planning – The director of internal auditing should establish plans to carry out the responsibilities of the internal auditing department.

530 Policies and Procedures – The director of internal auditing should provide written policies and procedures to guide the audit staff.

540 Personnel Management and Development – The director of internal auditing should establish a programme for selecting and developing the human resources of the internal auditing department.

550 External Auditors – The director of internal auditing should coordinate internal and external audit efforts.

560 Quality Assurance – The director of internal auditing should establish and maintain a quality assurance programme to evaluate the operations of the internal auditing department.

APPENDIX E

Sample charter for small internal auditing departments

Example Company, Inc. internal auditing department charter

Introduction

The purpose of this charter is to establish the internal auditing department's position within this organisation, authorise its access to records, personnel, and physical properties relevant to the performance of audits, and to define the scope of internal auditing activities.

Nature of internal auditing

Internal auditing is an independent appraisal activity established within an organisation to examine and evaluate its activities as a service to the organisation. It is a control that functions by examining the adequacy and effectiveness of other controls.

Objective of internal auditing

The objective of internal auditing is to assist members of the organisation in the effective discharge of their responsibilities. To this end, internal auditing furnishes them with analyses, appraisals, recommendations, counsel, and information concerning the activities reviewed. The auditing objective includes promoting effective control at reasonable cost.

Scope of internal auditing

The scope of internal auditing encompasses the examination and evaluation of the adequacy and effectiveness of the organisation's system of internal control and the quality of performance in carrying out assigned responsibilities. The scope of internal auditing includes:

- reviewing the reliability and integrity of financial and operating information and the means used to identify, measure, classify, and report such information;
- reviewing the systems established to ensure compliance with those policies, plans, procedures, laws, and regulations that could have a significant impact on operations and reports, and determining whether the organisation is in compliance;
- reviewing the means of safeguarding assets from various types of losses such as those resulting from theft, fire, improper or illegal activities, and exposure to the elements and, as appropriate, verifying the existence of such assets;
- appraising the economy and efficiency with which resources are employed;
- reviewing operations or programmes to ascertain whether results are consistent with established objectives and goals and whether the operations or programmes are being carried out as planned.

Responsibilities and authority of internal auditing

The lead auditor is assigned the responsibility for carrying out an internal auditing programme as previously described. This responsibility includes co-ordinating internal auditing activities with the organisation's external auditors and others so as to best achieve the auditing objectives and those of the organisation.

In carrying out this mission, the lead auditor is given access to all records, personnel, and physical properties relevant to the performance of audits. Any instances in which records, personnel, or physical properties relevant to an audit are not made available to the lead auditor upon his or her request will be reported to the CEO and the Board of Directors (or designated subcommittee).

The lead auditor will report directly to the CEO with direct access to the Board of Directors or designated subcommittee (audit committee). The lead auditor will submit annually to the CEO for approval and to the Board of Directors (or its designated subcommittee) for its information a summary of the department's audit work schedule, staffing plan, and financial budget.

The lead auditor, upon the completion of an audit, will discuss the audit findings with the member of management responsible for the area audited. A written report of the audit findings and the manager's response will be sent to the CEO within 30 days of the audit's completion (with a copy to the chairman of the audit committee). Follow-up procedures will vary depending on the severity of the audit findings, but will be within one year at the latest.

Fraud

Deterrence of fraud is the responsibility of management. The internal auditing department is responsible for examining and evaluating the adequacy and the effectiveness of actions taken by management to fulfill this obligation.

Internal auditors should have sufficient knowledge of fraud to be able to identify indicators that fraud might have occurred. If significant control weaknesses are detected, additional tests conducted by internal auditors should include tests directed toward the identification of other indicators of fraud.

Internal auditors are not expected to have knowledge equivalent to that of a person whose primary responsibility is to detect and investigate fraud. Also, auditing procedures alone, even when carried out with due professional care, do not guarantee that fraud will be detected.

The internal auditing department will assist in the investigation of fraud in order to: (1) determine if controls need to be implemented or strengthened, (2) design audit tests to help disclose the existence of similar frauds in the future, and (3) help meet the internal auditor's responsibility to maintain sufficient knowledge of fraud.

A written report will be issued at the conclusion of the investigation. It will include all findings, conclusions, recommendations, and corrective action taken.

Performance standards

Internal audits will be performed according to organisational policy, the Standards as issued by The IIA, and good business sense.

Signature..
   Chief Executive Officer,
   Example Company, Inc.

Date..........................

Signature..
   Chairman of Audit Committee

Date..........................

APPENDIX F

Sample code of business conduct

(Reprinted from The IIA-UK Statement *Reporting on Internal Control*, 1995.)

XYZ Limited

XYZ is a major multinational corporation whose business partners range from governments and multinationals through to small suppliers, and whose ultimate customers are the many individuals who rely on the quality of our products for their well-being. So it is appropriate that we are seen to operate responsibly and with ethical integrity in our business conduct and in our corporate governance – to a standard which would usually be associated with the major public, listed companies who are so often our competitors – and we should avoid even the suggestion of impropriety. This should be so even when the law is permissive. In principle, there should be no risk to our local or international reputation if any details about our business affairs were to become public knowledge. At all times our business must be conducted honestly and scrupulously, free of deception and fraud.

To these ends, this Code provides detailed guidance on the application to issues of business conduct of the policies outlined in XYZ's Statement of Corporate Principles. A separate Code of Ethical Conduct applies those policies to scientific and ethical issues in particular – as they impact upon personnel, customers and the environment.

Copies of the three documents are available at all locations to all staff – from regional and country managers, divisional and business unit heads. They are also available through internal audit locally or at Group level, from whom guidance on interpretation and application may be sought by staff.

This document has been approved by the Executive Committee and adopted by the Board of XYZ. The Executive Committee reviews annually the Code's appropriateness and effectiveness. As part of this review, line managers annually are required to formally monitor their and their staff's performance in observing the requirements of this Code within their areas of responsibility and, where judged appropriate, to develop initiatives to provide reasonable assurance of future compliance.

The Board places particular importance upon timely actions to be taken whenever necessary to identify, contain and eliminate illegal acts.

A fundamental principle of the way XYZ conducts its business affairs is that applicable laws and regulations are to be scrupulously observed at all times. Practical difficulties may arise in many cases, such as when there are conflicts between the law of different countries, when local business custom and practice is inconsistent with local law or when there is ambiguity as to the legal position. Any case of actual or prospective non-compliance with law should be raised urgently with management and, if material, with the Group Chief Executive.

The XYZ person responsible should endeavour to ensure that equivalent standards to those set out in this Code are followed in companies in which XYZ has an interest but does not have control and also in those businesses with whom XYZ has contractual relationships. Where they are not, the XYZ person responsible should refer the matter upwards within XYZ.

The Board of XYZ regards it as the duty of every individual employed by or acting for XYZ to follow all the requirements of this Code. Any proposed action which appears to be in breach of any requirement of this Code should not be progressed without full disclosure to and prior approval of the Group Chief Executive or as delegated to the Group Financial Controller or the Group Director of Internal Audit. Appropriate behaviour by individuals which is in compliance with this Code and also specifically approved departures from this Code will be supported by the company under the principle of collective responsibility.

Your duty to comply with this Code includes a duty both to yourself and to XYZ to raise any concerns you may have on any matter of business conduct which appears to be a violation of this Code and in which you are actively involved. In addition you have a right to raise similar concerns about the conduct of others even where you are not directly involved. Usually you should first raise a matter of concern with your line manager and you should do so at the earliest opportunity. At your discretion you may raise your concerns directly with senior management, with local internal audit or with the Group Director of Internal Audit and you should do so where an issue remains unresolved to your satisfaction after you have consulted your immediate management about it.

Conflicts of interest

Directors and employees of XYZ are responsible to avoid any real or apparent conflict between their own personal interests and those of XYZ. This may be at risk with respect to:

- dealings with suppliers, customers and other parties doing, or seeking to do, business with XYZ;
- transactions in securities of XYZ or of any company with whom XYZ has or is likely to have a business relationship;
- acceptance of outside positions whether or not for a fee.

In appropriate circumstances XYZ encourages its directors and staff to be active outside the company.

XYZ's assets and other resources should not be used for any purpose other than for XYZ's business. They are not to be used for personal gain. These resources include but are not limited to staff time, materials, property, plant, equipment, cash, software, trade secrets and confidential information.

In cases of doubt, an employee should discuss the matter with his or her manager.

Business gifts, favours and entertainment

XYZ operates in many host countries of the world with widely differing laws, regulations, customs and business practices. As a multinational XYZ is expected by its host in each case to conform to local societal norms and values whether enshrined in their laws, regulations, customs or business practices. Ethical dilemmas abound and have to be managed in harmony with the requirements of this Code.

By way of illustration, these may be some of the dilemmas:

- inconsistency between different applicable laws within one country;
- inconsistency between the laws of different countries involved in a transaction;
- inconsistency between law on the one hand and customs and practice on the other hand;
- an opportunity to achieve a considerable social good (such as by successfully marketing an effective pharmaceutical product) but only at an ethical cost (such as by making a facilitating payment);
- the difficulty of distinguishing convincingly between on the one hand facilitating payments which may in some circumstances be permissible (to facilitate a legal right which might otherwise be withheld or delayed) and bribes which should not be permissible even when legal (to influence a business decision or gain an unfair commercial advantage which is not a right);
- at what level a payment becomes extravagant.

As a general rule, XYZ does not encourage the practice of giving or receiving gifts, even those of nominal value. Employees should use their best endeavours to ensure so far as is possible that commercial criteria, rather than the influence of gifts, favours or entertainment, best serve XYZ's business interests and their ongoing maintenance.

In determining whether any given or received business gift, favour and/or entertainment is permissible under this Code each occurrence (and all connected ones taken together) are required to pass all of the following tests unless a requirement is specifically waived by the Group Chief Executive or his or her delegatee. These tests should also be applied equally to gifts etc. made indirectly by another party such as by an agent using funds which could be construed as having originated in XYZ.

The tests:

- it could not be interpreted reasonably as an improper inducement;
- it is necessary;
- it would be considered nominal or moderate, and neither extravagant nor too frequent;
- it would be considered appropriate to the business responsibilities of the individual concerned;
- in the case of a gift etc. received, it would be capable of reciprocation as a normal business expense;
- unless of nominal value, there is appropriate prior specific approval usually of regional management;
- it is properly recorded, whether given or received;
- the Group Financial Controller and the Group Director of Internal Audit have both been made fully aware of it beforehand;
- it is lawful and ethical.

Confidentiality

All of XYZ's employees and contractors have a general duty to ensure that all XYZ's data and information which they encounter is handled with discretion. XYZ personnel are not permitted to use confidential price sensitive information or to engage in other ways with competitors or others to fix the market price for products. XYZ's information (whether technical, commercial, financial, personnel or other) must not be disclosed so as to place XYZ at a potential or actual commercial disadvantage, or for the benefit of another party who is not entitled to receive it. Employees and contractors must ensure they act so as not to jeopardise (a) the rights of staff and others under privacy legislation and (b) the responsibilities and restrictions which apply to XYZ under data protection and other legislation.

Internal control

All businesses and projects owned, managed or controlled by XYZ must maintain an adequate system of internal control which is in accordance with XYZ's control policies. Management and staff are responsible to ensure that, within their respective areas of responsibility, necessary arrangements at acceptable cost are in place and are complied with to give reasonable assurance that the objectives of internal control are met. These objectives include:

- the achievement of business objectives efficiently and economically;
- the reliability of information used internally and for external reporting;
- the safeguarding of corporate resources;
- compliance with laws, regulations and policies of the company.

The necessary arrangements comprise proper attention to the following:

- the control environment;
- information and communication;
- risk analysis;
- control activities or procedures;
- monitoring.

All incidents involving a breakdown of control leading to any actual or potential losses should be reported upwards immediately to management and to internal audit. For companies in which XYZ has an interest but does not have control, the XYZ person responsible should endeavour to ensure that equivalent standards are applied, and should refer the matter upwards within XYZ when they are not.

Operational and accounting records

Responsible staff must ensure that all the operational records and books of account of the business represent a reliable, truthful, accurate, complete and up-to-date picture in compliance with prescribed corporate procedures and external standards and regulations; and that they are suitable to be a basis for informed management decisions. The prompt recording and proper description of operations and of accounting transactions is a duty of responsible staff. Falsification of records and books is strictly prohibited. No secret or unrecorded bank accounts, funds of money or other assets are to be established or maintained; no liabilities should knowingly go unrecorded or unprovided for; and there should be no off-books transactions.

Relationships with suppliers

It is as important for XYZ to secure satisfactorily its sources of supply as it is for XYZ to achieve and maintain market penetration. To this end, the viability and well-being of XYZ's suppliers must be a key concern of XYZ's management and staff. Employees have a duty to ensure that XYZ observes the terms of purchase orders and contracts – including the payment of suppliers according to agreed payment terms.

While it is appropriate that due weight be given to the quality of past service to XYZ rendered by a supplier, the placing of an order for goods or services should always be demonstrably defensible on commercial grounds, and as a general principle XYZ's employees should be active in seeking new sources of supply. Excessive dependence upon particular sources of supply should be avoided whenever possible.

Political activities and contributions

XYZ recognises that a healthy political climate is, in the long term, an essential attribute of a prosperous and stable society as well as a key ingredient for the long term success of XYZ, whose mission is to improve the quality of life of ordinary people through the responsible application of its expertise. XYZ acknowledges that a healthy political climate depends in part upon adequate funding of the political process, upon there being active participation by many in the political process, and upon open and well informed debate on societal issues. XYZ Group companies are authorised to make political donations in the countries where they operate in so far as the objective is to facilitate a healthy political process by contributing to the adequacy of funding, by raising the level of participation or by enhancing the quality of informed debate on issues related to the XYZ business – but only to the extent that such contributions are:

- entirely lawful;
- in the public domain;
- modest in amount and not disproportionate in size to local conditions and to XYZ's public profile;
- not designed to prejudice political or commercial outcomes;
- properly recorded in the accounting records;
- authorised in advance by the appropriate Managing Director.

XYZ has an enlightened self interest in communicating information and views on issues of public concern which have an important impact upon the XYZ business: management should be active in looking for appropriate opportunities to do so. The information and views so communicated must be relevant, reliable and responsible.

XYZ strives to be a good employer with regard to individual staff who are actively involved in politics. Accordingly XYZ management should facilitate and not unnecessarily impede the process when individual XYZ staff exercise their legal rights to become actively involved in local or national politics. In turn, staff who are politically active, or minded to become so, should be candid with their XYZ management so that management are best able to be co-operative and difficulties are more likely to be avoided. Staff so involved have an obligation to XYZ to weigh carefully their obligations to XYZ when actual or potential conflicts of interest arise – in their use of time, in campaigning on issues of relevance to the XYZ business, and so on. Employees engaging in political activity do so as private individuals and not as representatives of XYZ.

Conduct towards employees

XYZ is committed to its employees. An underlying principle is to maximise the extent to which all employees have the opportunity to achieve their personal potential through their work with XYZ. XYZ believes that it succeeds through the dedication of all its employees. Their motivated involvement, work satisfaction and security are high priorities. In part, this depends upon the implementation of appropriate commercial policies so that employees share in the company's success; in part upon policies which relate to health and safety. Apart from the inalienable right of every person to their personal dignity, practices which intentionally or unintendedly infringe upon personal dignity are likely to interfere with an individual's work performance.

In the conduct of his or her business responsibilities every XYZ employee is expected to apply the principle of equal opportunity in employment. No member of staff shall discriminate so that another member of staff (or a member of staff of a contractor, supplier or customer) is victimised or less favourably treated than another on grounds of race, colour, marital status, religion, sex, sexual orientation, ethnic or national origin, or legal political activity. Treatment shall at all times be fair in terms of compensation, job security, work experiences, recognition of achievement and opportunities for advancement.

Staff shall be recruited for their relevant aptitudes, skills, experience and ability; and their advancement shall be on the same grounds according to the opportunities available within XYZ.

Employment practices including recruitment practices, contract terms and working conditions shall be sensitive to the culture of the country concerned so as to ensure that company conduct does not contribute to unacceptable social tensions or malaise. At the same time, care must always be taken to ensure so far as is reasonably possible (a) that no harm occurs to those whose services the company employs while they are engaged in work-related activity, and (b) that the equal opportunity principles outlined in the preceding two paragraphs are applied.

XYZ seeks to ensure that employees have and exhibit mutual respect for each other at all times – both at work and also at business-related functions. XYZ staff are expected to behave in this way towards other employees, contractors, suppliers and customers. Harassment is unacceptable. Discrimination – in action, writing or through remarks – is a form of harassment. Unwelcome verbal and physical advances and derogatory remarks are other forms of harassment. It is a duty of all XYZ employees to ensure that their behaviour at no time contributes towards the creation of an intimidating, offensive or hostile work environment. For staff to identify with XYZ and for XYZ to benefit most from the potential within its staff, the approach to their staff of XYZ's managers and supervisors must be as open and candid as possible. Staff also must be made to feel that they can communicate upwards without formality, rebuff, rancour or victimisation. While not abdicating their personal responsibility, managers should delegate downwards to as great an extent as possible so as to empower and develop their staff. Rigid hierarchical styles of management should be discouraged and staff may address any issues directly above the level of their immediate supervisor if they judge this to be appropriate.

Conduct by people acting on XYZ's behalf

In the introduction to this Code I indicated that the XYZ person responsible should endeavour to ensure that equivalent standards to those set out in this Code are followed in companies in which XYZ has an interest but does not have control, and also in those businesses with whom XYZ has contractual relationships. I also stated that it is the policy of the Board of XYZ that those employed by or acting for XYZ should follow all the requirements of this Code. For instance, contractors working on behalf of XYZ must ensure they act in accordance with this Code with respect to confidentiality, conflicts of interest, the making and receiving of gifts and with respect to their and their employees' conduct towards XYZ's employees and towards those whom the contractors employ on XYZ's business.

It is not accepted that management and staff of XYZ circumvent their obligations under this Code by deputing unacceptable practices to intermediaries acting directly or indirectly on XYZ's behalf so that XYZ may achieve a desired end while endeavouring to avoid any opprobrium.

Conduct in the community, and charitable contributions

XYZ accepts that it has community obligations where it does business. We have a general duty to avoid conduct prejudicial to the best interests of the communities where we do business. We have a positive duty as well as a self-interest, as corporate citizens committed within our business to improving the well-being of individuals, to use our best endeavours to enhance community life. Apart from altruistic motivations which are important, we believe that a positive approach to our community relations is in the best long term interests of our company, of those who work within it, and of our present and future customers.

Staff are asked to assist XYZ to be proactive in searching out appropriate opportunities to contribute positively to community affairs and staff will be encouraged by XYZ to do likewise as individuals. Our contributions may be in leadership by initiating or steering community projects; they may be supportive in terms of donations of facilities, equipment, materials, time or cash.

To avoid waste, our community support should be targeted to improving economic or social well-being in demonstrable ways with a particular emphasis upon improving the quality of life of ordinary people. In nature and scale our support should be appropriate in each community while bearing favourable comparison with other companies of similar standing. Our support should be consistent with XYZ's business interests and corporate image, and should have a clear potential to enhance both of these.

Customer relations and product quality

XYZ has no future unless it continues to satisfy customer needs in a competitive environment characterised by rapid technological advances. The company acknowledges the primacy of the following principles which it expects its staff, as of duty, to apply consistently in practice and to encourage those who supply our ultimate customers to do likewise:

- we strive to ensure that the specifications of our products meet or exceed customer requirements at economical price;
- we strive to provide services which are excellent value for money and are delivered courteously and with sensitivity to our clients' requirements;
- we endeavour in all circumstances to ensure that all information about our products and services is reliable and a sufficient basis for fully informed customer decision making;
- we will be truthful and not misleading in our public relations, marketing and advertising;
- we are committed to satisfying enquiries, complaints and suggestions thoroughly and promptly;
- we are committed to meeting or exceeding all statutory requirements with regard to our products and services as well as to their marketing, sale, distribution and subsequent after-sales support.

Grievance procedures

Every XYZ operating unit must have in place and comply with suitable procedures to ensure that the concerns of staff on any issue related to this Code are considered promptly and thoroughly, and that remedial action is taken where appropriate.

Please use your best endeavours to bring this code appropriately to the attention of all personnel, to all new employees, to our business partners and contractors as well as their staff and to any others with whom we are associated or do business with.

(Chairman's signature)

APPENDIX G

Key issues in common business activities

In the space of this appendix, it is not possible to be exhaustive. We have selected just 15 of the most important business activities, and for each we show what we consider to be amongst the main issues which need to be addressed. We express these issues as statements, depending upon the user to interpret their significance and applicability in particular cases. They are intended to be useful in suggesting avenues to be addressed.

Readers who need more detail might like to refer to the computer-based Standard Audit Programme Guides (SAPGs) by Management Audit (see Appendix I), which cover in much more detail approximately 200 business activities, as well as having other functionality. Some of the content of this Appendix has been extracted, with appropriate modifications, from parts of the SAPG product.

Here, we address, in summary form:

1. the board;
2. planning;
3. management information;
4. marketing;
5. sales;
6. purchasing;
7. production;
8. stores/warehousing;
9. distribution;
10. personnel and pensions;
11. payroll;
12. treasury and cash;
13. accounts receivable;
14. fixed assets;
15. accounts payable.

I. The board

1.1 Its constitution and organisation should address its responsibilities effectively.

1.2 Its membership should be suitable to the needs of the business.
1.3 There should not be excessive concentration of power at the top of the business.
1.4 The board's business, and that of its committees, must be conducted efficiently and effectively.
1.5 Total compensation packages of executive and non-executive directors should be appropriate.
1.6 The board must have a means of ensuring that earlier formal resolutions it has taken are recalled as being board policy until rescinded or replaced.
1.7 The board must ensure that it is in control of the business.
1.8 The board is responsible for (a) overall policy and for (b) corporate governance.
1.9 The board's directors need adequate access to information and advice.
1.10 The directors need to understand their, and the board's, legal responsibilities.
1.11 There should be a schedule of matters reserved to the board for its decision.
1.12 Formal delegation of authority guidelines should be established and approved by the board.
1.13 The board should approve a corporate *Code of Business Conduct*, or similar.

2. Planning

2.1 There must be appropriate processes in place to ensure the business develops in an effective manner.
2.2 Objectives and goals must be established, authorised and communicated for the main business operations, and management must be assured they are up-to-date and appropriate.
2.3 Effective mechanisms must be in place to plan for the achievement of authorised objectives.
2.4 There must be mechanisms to identify and evaluate new business opportunities and the potential for competitive advantage.
2.5 Data used for planning purposes must be sufficiently accurate, relevant and up-to-date.
2.6 All plans need to be fully assessed, costed and authorised prior to implementation.
2.7 Responsibilities for implementing plans must be adequately defined and allocated.
2.8 There will need to be arrangements to avoid management wasting time and resources on unrealistic or uneconomic plans.
2.9 Plans should be subject to adequate monitoring to ensure effective implementation.

2.10 Implementation delays and problems need to be promptly identified and resolved.
2.11 Management must make sure that staff are fully involved and consulted during planning.

3. Management information

3.1 There needs to be a clear association between (a) the *objectives* of management, and (b) the information available to management – so that the latter can inform management of their progress in achieving the former.
3.2 Some businesses have plentiful *data* but too little *information* derived from that data; others have plentiful information but too little *analysis* performed on that information; others have plentiful analysis but too little *decision*; others have too little *action* following decisions. Is the balance right?
3.3 Applicable *external* information (e.g. about the market) needs to be available – as well as internally generated information about business performance.
3.4 There must be satisfactory security over the collection, processing, retention and disposal of information.
3.5 Data protection principles should be complied with, with regard to personal data.
3.6 The business should consider the scope to develop strategic information systems (targeted at suppliers and/or staff and customers) so as to achieve a competitive advantage by reducing costs and/or improving service and reliability.
3.7 Responsibility for management information should be formally assigned to one or more managers who is/are formally responsible for appraising its *quality* and *utilisation*.
3.8 Information must be *timely* – produced and distributed promptly at the most appropriate intervals from up-to-date data.
3.9 Information must be clearly and reliably dated with no risk of out-of-date reports being used as if current.
3.10 Information, especially personal information, should not be retained longer than necessary.
3.11 Information must be *complete* enough to meet the operational needs of managers. It must adequately inform as a basis for necessary management action.
3.12 Adequate information must be appropriately available to cover *all* operational areas of the business.
3.13 Information needs to be *accurate* enough to be used reliably by management.
3.14 Management reports must be *consistent* (a) between each edition, and (b) between different reports which relate to associated issues.
3.15 *Cut-off* should be handled reliably (for instance, to ensure mutual

consistency between a number of related reports or items of information).
3.16 *Clarity* in management reports is important. For instance, they should be (a) clearly titled, dated and captioned, and (b) attractive, unambiguous and easy to use.
3.17 Management reports should be *concise* without being too brief. Proper use should be made of reporting by exception only.
3.18 All management information should be *relevant* to the business and to those who receive it (who should fully appreciate its purpose).
3.19 Management information must be satisfactorily and promptly *acted upon* by those who receive it.
3.20 Exception reports should be followed up.
3.21 An inventory should be maintained of confidential and sensitive corporate information, and the handling and issuance of this information should be subject to proper authorisation controls.
3.22 There should be satisfactory access controls to (a) the site, (b) the buildings, (c) departmental information stores, and (d) computers.
3.23 Data needs to be adequately secure while being transmitted (e.g. by making use of encryption).

4. Marketing

4.1 Management needs to define and authorise strategic business objectives.
4.2 There must be mechanisms to check that all product developments are consistent with strategic business objectives.
4.3 Management should establish, authorise and implement documented procedures for the development and evolution of all product ranges.
4.4 Management needs assurance that their product plans remain adequate, appropriate, viable, etc.
4.5 Mechanisms are needed to ensure that the product design and specification stages are effectively conducted so as to avoid problems and repercussions during later development stages (i.e. production or cost implications).
4.6 All the appropriate and relevant recognised quality and performance standards have to be in the product development process.
4.7 Market research will be necessary to establish that a product has a viable market, etc.
4.8 Management needs assurance that all the relevant issues are addressed to ensure the most appropriate launch of the eventual product.
4.9 There should be appropriate processes to ensure that all the resources required to undertake a development are accurately identified, costed, justified and authorised.
4.10 All product developments require good project management to achieve (a) coordination of all affected functions to ensure achievement of development objectives; (b) definition of key stages of the project and the monitoring of

progress; and (c) authorisation and control of all project resources and costs.
4.11 Measures are needed to ensure that new or modified products are subject to extensive, adequate and appropriate testing (including any sector specific or specialist product testing requirements).
4.12 The launch of new products needs to be adequately planned and coordinated (i.e. in terms of supporting promotion, adequacy of stocks, etc.).
4.13 Actual sales of new products must be monitored in order to ensure that the overall business objectives are achieved.
4.14 Management needs accurate and up-to-date awareness of market trends, customer needs and competitor activities as the basis for their own planning and decision making.
4.15 Steps must be taken to ensure that customer requirements are identified and effectively addressed.
4.16 Management will need to correlate market research findings with product development, promotional and sales activities.
4.17 All market research activities need to be accurately costed, and justified as being worthwhile and authorised.
4.18 Management needs assurance that promotional activities and advertising are appropriately targeted and offer value for money.
4.19 Potential new markets and opportunities to differentiate products will need to be identified.
4.20 On-going measures are required to ensure that products continue to match the required performance, quality and price criteria.
4.21 New and prototype products/services will need realistic market testing before full launch, with the results carefully measured and utilised.
4.22 Management needs assurance that market research data is accurate and reliable.
4.23 A planned approach to advertising and promotion must be agreed, authorised and implemented.
4.24 Management needs assurance that advertising and promotional expenditure are adequately targeted, budgeted, effectively used and fully accounted for.
4.25 There must be mechanisms to prevent expenditure on unauthorised advertising and promotional schemes.
4.26 The engagement of external advertising agencies, creative consultants, and marketing companies should be subject to adequate assessment, justification and authorisation.
4.27 Management needs assurance that the organisation is only paying for actual advertising and promotional activities.
4.28 Measures are required to ensure that all advertising and promotional activities are lawful, accurate and project a positive corporate image.
4.29 Budgets must be established and actual expenditure monitored against budget.

4.30 Precautions are needed to prevent unauthorised access to or leakage of advertising and promotional plans.
4.31 Management must ensure that promotional activities are adequately defined, authorised, proficiently conducted and adequately resourced.
4.32 Measures are needed to ensure that sales, marketing and promotional staff are well informed about the products and present a positive corporate image.
4.33 All sponsorship deals should be subject to a written agreement, and monitored to confirm that all the prescribed obligations have been satisfactorily discharged.
4.34 Documented pricing and discount policies should be authorised and implemented, and based upon established profit margins, etc.
4.35 Steps should be taken to ensure that prices remain competitive, profitable and sustainable.
4.36 Management needs assurance that the correct prices and discounts are always applied to invoices (with mechanisms in place to detect and report any unauthorised variations).
4.37 Management needs assurance that product costing information is accurate, complete, and reliable as the basis for determining prices.
4.38 Measures are needed to ensure that changes to prices and discount structures are justified, authorised and correctly applied.
4.39 When applicable management needs to take into account the effects of taxation (i.e. VAT or sales tax), duty and any prevailing price constraints when determining pricing levels.

5. Sales

5.1 Sales activities need to be in accordance with defined and authorised strategies and quotas.
5.2 Measures must be in place to ensure that current and potential customers are identified and that customer data is accurately maintained up-to-date.
5.3 Management needs assurance that adequate (and justifiable) sales staff are provided and that they are suitably trained and knowledgeable about the company products.
5.4 Sales staff workloads need to be allocated appropriately (e.g. through defined territories or specific customer allocations) and management needs to measure and monitor performance (i.e. for leads and confirmed sales).
5.5 Mechanisms are needed to ensure that all orders fully comply with company pricing, discounting and credit policies.
5.6 Measures should be applied to ensure that customers are financially stable and reliable and that unsuitable customers are not accepted.
5.7 Credit limits should be set for individual customers, and be subject to a higher level of authority prior to orders being accepted.
5.8 Management needs assurance that all order data is accurately captured,

conforms to company policies, and is accurately reflected through delivery and invoice accounting.

5.9 Mechanisms must be in place to confirm the accuracy and validity of sales staff expenses, commissions, bonuses, etc.

5.10 Management need to be aware of the actual costs associated with maintaining the sales force, and this data should be related to budgets and required levels of sales activities as a means of determining the effectiveness of sales activities.

5.11 Appropriate staff should be engaged in following up delinquent accounts and resolving customer complaints (and management needs assurance that such actions are effectively conducted).

5.12 Management needs assurance that all the administrative and regulatory requirements of export sales are correctly fulfilled.

5.13 Management must ensure that projected sales targets are accurately and realistically determined.

5.14 The establishment of sales targets/quotas and any subsequent amendment should be subject to suitable authorisation (and this should be evidenced).

5.15 Management should maintain adequate records of historical sales trends, volumes, etc. as the basis for sales planning (and be sure of the accuracy and validity of such data).

5.16 Management must ensure that all actual sales data is accurately and completed captured.

5.17 Management needs assurance that they are provided with accurate and up-to-date sales performance statistics.

5.18 Prompt action must be taken to detect and react to sales performance shortcomings, etc.

5.19 Management should determine and justify the staffing establishment of the sales function so as to avoid either under or over-staffing.

5.20 Management needs to ensure that sales staff are adequately trained and knowledgeable about company products and terms of business.

6. Purchasing

6.1 Authorised and documented purchasing policies and procedures should be developed, implemented, and adequately communicated to all affected parties.

6.2 Management must be assured that all purchase orders are justified, authorised, within budget and accounted for within the correct accounting period.

6.3 Mechanisms are needed to prevent the invalid, unauthorised and fraudulent use of official orders.

6.4 Management should ensure that adequate and appropriate supplies are obtained to sustain the required business activities.

6.5 Management needs to ensure that goods and services are always obtained at the most economical and fair price.
6.6 Management needs assurance that all suppliers are stable, reliable, and capable of meeting the organisation's needs at the optimum price.
6.7 There must be suitable processes to ensure that supplies are to the required standard, specification and quality.
6.8 Mechanisms are needed to ensure that all goods are received on time and that overdue deliveries are identified and progressed.
6.9 Management needs confidence that all purchases are correctly reflected in the stock control and accounting records.
6.10 There should be processes to ensure that all purchasing activities fully comply with all the relevant legislation and regulations.

7. Production

7.1 Management needs to be confident that production and manufacturing requirements are accurately defined and suitably authorised.
7.2 Mechanisms are required to ensure that authorised production/manufacturing requirements are effectively communicated to all affected parties, and that suitable plans are agreed and implemented to meet the defined obligations.
7.3 Processes are needed to ensure that all the required resources and facilities (i.e. materials, staff, machines, knowledge, etc.) are available to meet the required production obligations.
7.4 Management needs assurance that actual progress and use of production facilities are effectively monitored and that problems, shortfalls and delays would be promptly detected and corrected.
7.5 There should be measures to ensure that the required quantity of products is actually manufactured and accounted for.
7.6 Management needs to be confident that the items produced conform to the required quality standards, and defect rates are effectively monitored.
7.7 Management must take measures to minimise and avoid disruption of production caused by machine breakdown, poorly experienced staff, and absence of raw materials and components.
7.8 The utilisation of all resources (materials and workforce) should be fully accounted for and waste be promptly identified and appropriate action taken.
7.9 Management must be kept informed of overall production performance and efficiency, and there should be evidence of corrective action being taken to address shortcomings, etc.
7.10 Mechanisms are needed to ensure that compliance with all the prevailing legislation and regulations is confirmed.

8. Stores/warehousing

8.1 Storage requirements must be projected accurately and planned for.
8.2 Geographical location of warehouses should be appropriate with regard to distribution efficiency and economy and customer needs.
8.3 Storage locations (e.g. bins, bays, etc.) need to be clearly identified.
8.4 Warehousing facilities must protect goods from damage and deterioration.
8.5 Warehousing facilities must protect goods from theft and pilferage.
8.6 Unauthorised access to warehouses should be prevented.
8.7 All stock issues, deliveries and transfers must be valid, authorised and correctly executed.
8.8 Goods (especially hazardous materials) must be stored safely and in accordance with established regulations and good practice.
8.9 Staff must be adequately trained to handle goods.
8.10 Appropriate handling devices (trolleys, pallets, forklift trucks, cranes, etc.) should be utilised in cost effective ways.
8.11 Relevant regulations and legislation must be observed.
8.12 Management should decide on adequate, up-to-date and relevant insurance cover – for both goods (*in situ* or in transit) and storage facilities.

9. Distribution

9.1 Distribution arrangements must be adequate, efficient and able to cater for current and future demands.
9.2 There must be adequate and timely liaison and information flow between the sales, production, stock control, distribution and transport functions in order to ensure that customer demands are fulfilled.
9.3 Management must be assured that the most appropriate, efficient and cost effective distribution and transport options are utilised.
9.4 Only correctly constituted and valid consignments should be actioned, and these must be accurately reflected in the relevant accounting systems.
9.5 External distribution and transport contract arrangements should be appropriate, authorised and regularly monitored for quality, performance and value for money.
9.6 External contractors' charges must be valid and authorised, with mechanisms to prevent the payment of invalid or erroneous charges.
9.7 Are adequate precautions taken to protect goods in intermediate storage and transit from damage and loss?
9.8 Deliveries should be undertaken in the required timescale, and agreed and signed for.
9.9 Discrepancies on delivery should be identified, documented, investigated and resolved.
9.10 Management needs assurance that the delivery vehicle fleet is appropriate, adequate and is operated efficiently and legally.

10. Personnel, and pensions

10.1 Documented policies should be established for staff recruitment, training, remuneration, performance appraisal, and disciplinary matters.

10.2 Compliance with employment regulations and laws must be assured.

10.3 Standard remuneration scales and employment conditions should generally be implemented, and management need to be aware of staff engagements which fall outside these standards.

10.4 Management needs to be sure that all staff recruitment and appointments are warranted and authorised.

10.5 There must be an accurate contract of employment for all staff appointments.

10.6 There should be a satisfactory approach to 'manpower' and succession planning.

10.7 Current and future skill requirements must be determined and action taken so that staff are developed to meet these requirements.

10.8 Management need assurance that all training and staff development activities are justified, authorised and appropriately targeted.

10.9 Management need assurance that pension scheme(s) are correctly established, and operated; and comply with the legislation and good practice.

10.10 Management and pension fund trustees need to be confident that all pension funds are kept separate from company activities and are fully and accurately accounted for.

10.11 The pension fund should be subject to regular scrutiny by suitably qualified external auditors.

10.12 Processes should be in place to ensure that all payments from the fund are valid, authorised, correctly calculated, paid over to bona fide persons, and fully accounted for.

10.13 Management needs assurance that the operations of any other schemes (e.g. executive share option schemes) comply with the current legislation and are properly accounted for.

10.14 Management needs ways to confirm that staff are performing at appropriate levels and standards.

10.15 The performance of staff must be assessed against realistic and measurable factors and objectives.

10.16 Staff appraisal and disciplinary procedures must comply with the current legislation, and with best practice.

10.17 Management need grounds to be confident that cases of persistent absenteeism or serious misconduct would be detected and appropriately dealt with.

10.18 Management needs grounds to be confident that they have identified and adequately addressed all the Health & Safety risks and hazards within the organisation.

10.19 There must be processes in place to ensure that staff are fully aware of workplace risks, correctly utilise safety equipment and generally protect themselves.
10.20 Sufficient and appropriate safety equipment must be provided and measures taken to ensure that it is in working order.
10.21 Sufficient fire prevention and protection systems should be provided and regularly tested.
10.22 Adequate first aid, medical, hygiene and cleanliness facilities must be provided.
10.23 Management needs ground to be confident that all hazardous materials are safely, correctly and securely stored.
10.24 The basis for communicating with the workforce and their representatives must be clearly established, endorsed and communicated.
10.25 Suitably experienced and qualified staff, familiar with negotiation and other relevant techniques, should have responsibility for dealing with labour relations.
10.26 Management needs assurance that all company vehicle purchases and allocations are authorised, in accordance with the current policy, and are correctly treated in the accounts.
10.27 There must be suitable processes to ensure that all vehicles are operated legally and in accordance with all the relevant regulations.
10.28 Management must exercise satisfactory control over fuel and running costs, so that only justified, appropriate and authorised costs are accounted for.

11. Payroll

11.1 There must be sufficient measures to prevent payroll payments being made to invalid or unauthorised persons.
11.2 Payroll sums must be calculated correctly, and disbursed securely and on time.
11.3 Tax and deductions must be calculated accurately and disbursed securely.
11.4 Measures must exist to ensure that management is provided with accurate payroll cost data on a regular basis to support their decision making, etc.
11.5 Management needs assurance that all payroll transactions are correctly reflected in the accounting system in the proper accounting period.

12. Treasury and Cash

12.1 There should be written policies governing Treasury operations, authorised transaction types, financial limits, etc.
12.2 Treasury function objectives should be established and communicated.

12.3 Treasury procedures should be established and applied.
12.4 Policies and procedures should be consistent with each other in all respects.
12.5 The Treasury function should be monitored independently, adequately and on a timely basis.
12.6 Treasury personnel must be adequately trained.
12.7 Support facilities (hardware, software, on-line services, etc.) should be adequate to support an effective Treasury function. Treasury staff need adequate, accurate, relevant and timely data to support their decision making and trading activities.
12.8 Working capital requirements must be defined, communicated, monitored and controlled.
12.9 Relevant laws and regulations must be observed.
12.10 All Treasury transactions must be supported by accurate documentation, authorisation, and effective audit trails.
12.11 All Treasury transactions and fund movements must be correctly recorded, accurately accounted for, reported to management in a clear and timely way.
12.12 Management need to be able to confirm that all Treasury transactions are of an approved type and within the established limits for individual transactions; and management needs to do this.
12.13 All maturing funds/investments, income and interest receipts must be identified, recorded, correctly handled and correctly accounted for.
12.14 Management must be aware of all active corporate bank accounts, their purpose, and current details.
12.15 Corporate bank accounts should be established only at the request of senior management for a defined and authorised purpose which should be evidenced.
12.16 There should be mechanisms to prevent the unauthorised set up and operation of bank accounts.
12.17 Banking arrangements should be optimised in terms of account type, transaction levels, interest payable on balances, levels of charges, etc. The arrangements generally should maximise the return on surplus cash balances.
12.18 Management need assurance that all banking transactions are accurate, complete, and authorised.
12.19 There should be written procedures governing the setting up and use of banking facilities; and these should be applied.
12.20 Management need mechanisms to ensure that they are aware on a timely basis of overdraft situations. Overdraft arrangements should be negotiated and authorised in advance of requirements.
12.21 Realistic cheque signing mandates should be established and unauthorised members of staff should not be able to raise cheques drawn against corporate accounts.

12.22 Management should ensure that *all* bank accounts are taken into account within the Treasury function.
12.23 Management should ensure that only authorised bank loans and financing arrangements are set up.
12.24 All petty cash floats must be known, accounted for, and controlled.
12.25 There should be clear policies and procedures for recording, authorising and processing petty cash and expense claims.

13. Accounts receivable

13.1 Management need to ensure that all goods delivered and services performed are identified and duly invoiced to customers.
13.2 Steps should be taken to avoid trading with financially unstable or unsuitable customers, except where the risk is appropriately controlled.
13.3 There should be procedures to ensure that all required invoices are correctly raised using the appropriate prices and discounts, and that they are recorded, dispatched, and accounted for within the accounting system.
13.4 Management needs grounds to be confident that all customer remittances are correctly identified, recorded and accounted for.
13.5 Management needs adequate, timely and accurate information on potential and actual debt cases to enable them to react promptly.
13.6 Overdue accounts should be promptly identified and effectively progressed.

14. Fixed assets

14.1 Management should implement an authorised policy governing capital acquisitions and expenditure which is subject to review and update.
14.2 Management must ensure that all capital expenditure is properly authorised.
14.3 Management should ensure that all fixed assets are identifiable and correctly reflected in the accounts.
14.4 Fixed assets should be subject to regular verification.
14.5 Management must establish and implement a depreciation and accounting treatment policy for assets which (a) reflects current, permitted accounting practices, and (b) matches accounting charges to the accounting periods which benefit from the assets.
14.6 Depreciation must be calculated accurately and accurately reflected in the accounts.
14.7 Fixed assets should be secured satisfactorily against loss or damage.
14.8 Asset disposals and write offs should be authorised and be in the best interests of the business.
14.9 Where appropriate, fixed assets should be adequately insured.

14.10 Management will need to ensure that suitable reserves are made for the replacement of key fixed assets.

15. Accounts payable

15.1 Management needs to establish arrangements which ensure that only valid invoices are paid where the goods and services have been correctly and fully received.
15.2 There should be mechanisms to prevent the payment of inaccurately priced/calculated or duplicated invoices.
15.3 All invoices should be authorised prior to payment – unless suitable alternative controls exist to recover inappropriate payments.
15.4 There must be satisfactory processes to ensure that the values of paid accounts and outstanding invoice liabilities are accurately and completely reflected in the accounting system.

APPENDIX H

Principia for leading edge internal auditing

1. Principia for leading edge internal auditing values

1. Understanding the history and development of internal auditing is the foundation for creating a vision for its future.
2. Internal auditing is developing as a spectrum of unrestricted traditional, new and leading edge activities, across all organisations of all sizes, in all sectors.
3. Best practice internal auditing and good management practices use the same quality measures of planning, doing, checking and action.
4. Many of the attributes demonstrated by internal auditors, and valued most by management, are the same attributes recommended in codes of best practice for external auditors.
5. Seeking best practice internal auditing is a continuous learning process.
6. Professional internal auditors critically understand today's and tomorrow's management principles and practices.
7. To be successful, internal auditing must attract and satisfy talented people.
8. Internal auditing objectivity and independence are its most important assets.
9. Co-ordination of all audit work in an organisation strengthens its objectivity and independence.
10. Imagination and confidence are the keys to innovative internal auditing.

2. Principia for leading edge control experts

1. Internal auditors should always be seen as control experts.
2. Planning, organising, directing and monitoring are essential parts of all control activities.
3. Divisions of responsibilities are a key control mechanism.
4. Financial, social, quality and environmental control objectives are international issues, across all supply chains, in all sectors.
5. Control embraces all aspects of governance, including ethics, equality, honesty, caring and sustaining.

6. Creating integrated control frameworks in an organisation provides an understanding of their strengths and weaknesses.
7. Understanding how fraud is perpetrated is key to its prevention and detection.
8. The best internal auditors review control in the past and present, and accurately forecast the future.
9. Internal auditing should contribute to the reliability and integrity of all management reports and statements on control.
10. Control self-assessment by managers is essential for all aspects of management, and auditing.

3. Principia for marketing internal auditing

1. Success of modern internal auditing lies in how it is researched and developed, and then promoted in the organisation market place.
2. Innovation and understanding its customers' needs are the keys to how internal auditing should be sold throughout the audit process.
3. Internal auditing vision and mission statements must be exciting.
4. Measures of internal auditing performance must be linked to its customers' and organisation's objectives.
5. Audit committee's should strengthen internal auditing objectivity and independence.
6. Internal audit charters must be based on professional standards and a code of ethics.
7. Use superlatives to reinforce internal audit staff and market their services.
8. Internal auditing procedures and documents are an essential part of marketing internal auditing quality.
9. Benchmark internal audit marketing with the marketing of other services, within and outside the organisation it serves.
10. Market internal auditing as a contribution to your organisation's quality improvement programmes.

4. Principia for internal audit teams

1. Successful internal audit teams in an organisation's web of teams are everything.
2. Look for features of excellence in internal audit team work.
3. Use team concepts to encourage change, quality and innovation in the internal audit unit and organisation it serves.
4. Learn to recognise applaud and reward achievement by internal audit teams.
5. Audit recommendations are best when they are created by a successful team.

5. Principia for audit planning

1. Internal audit resources should be applied to the different activities of the business in proportion to audit risk.
2. Internal audit risk is the risk of giving a misleading opinion about the quality of internal control, having regard to the significance of the business activity.
3. Internal audit risk is basically a combination of inherent and control factors.
4. For the internal auditor, inherent risk refers to 'how much' is at risk.
5. For the internal auditor, control risk refers to the quality of the system, or process.
6. Inevitably, internal auditors have to exercise judgement in determining audit risk: it cannot be assessed entirely objectively.
7. It is desirable to obtain the approval of senior management and the board to the basis that internal audit will use to determine how it will allocate its audit resources between audits.
8. Applying a formula or other similar approach to audit planning allows trends over time in audit coverage to be discerned.

6. Principia for measuring internal audit performance

1. Internal auditing is a costly service to run. Large amounts of profits from sales are needed to resource even a modest internal audit function.
2. Internal auditing is a prime candidate for market testing and contracting out.
3. If management and the board allow decisions on letting contracts for internal audit work to be made on *price* alone, rather than *value for money*, they are acting irresponsibly.
4. The goals of the internal auditing unit should be capable of being established within specified operating plans and budgets and, to the extent possible, should be measurable and accompanied by measurement criteria and targeted dates of accomplishment.
5. A key criterion against which an internal auditing unit should be measured is its charter.
6. Performance measures with a higher degree of objectivity than others are not necessarily the preferred ones to use: the criteria for selection of a performance measure should include a matching to the aspects of internal audit performance which are most important and which need to be monitored most.
7. The client satisfaction survey provides data on the reputation of audit.
8. Performance measures can be devised to assess the extent to which an internal auditing function complies with Standards.

9. Audit output is hard to measure. Internal auditors are knowledge workers whose output is not always tangible.
10. Measures of reporting success should be linked with measures of cost savings, time utilisation and the achievement of audit plans.
11. The importance of the objectives identified for audit is that these should underpin an organisation's overall aims and objectives, so that audit's achievements aid the development of the organisation as a whole.
12. Value for money auditing endeavours to assess economy, efficiency and effectiveness making use of carefully chosen and carefully interpreted performance measures.

7. Principia for reporting and progressing audit findings

1. The end product of internal auditing is reassurance that internal control arrangements are sound, or, where necessary persuasive advice to make internal control sound.
2. Audit reports are potentially an effective means of communication but they are not the end product of an audit and there are additional means of communication which the internal auditor should use.
3. Audit reports are action documents – their publication should not be delayed.
4. Audit reports should be objective, clear, concise, constructive, and timely.
5. The most senior point to whom internal audit reports, should be confident that internal audit has not subordinated its judgement to that of others – with respect either to the scope of audit work or to the content of audit reports.
6. On audit findings, there should be agreement between internal audit and responsible management because they are factual; as to audit recommendations agreement may not always be forthcoming as they are matters of auditor judgement with which management may not always concur.
7. The image of the internal auditing unit is very close to the reality.
8. What is not clearly understood by the auditor cannot be clearly expressed by the auditor.
9. Audit follow-up is a responsibility shared between internal audit and those to whom internal audit reports are addressed.

8. Principia for impact of information technology on internal auditing

1. Management are unlikely to have effective control unless the IT technology (hardware and software) they are using for control purposes at least matches the sophistication of the technology they are using to perform the basic operations of the business.
2. Internal auditors are unlikely to audit effectively unless the IT technology (hardware and software) they are using for audit purposes at least matches

the sophistication of the technology management is using to perform the basic operations of the business and achieve effective control over those operations.
3. The 'black box' approach of auditing around the computer is not a viable option for the internal auditor – even if, on occasion, it might be an option for the external auditor.
4. Audit interrogation software directly reviews the validity of corporate data and indirectly assesses the adequacy of internal controls: test data audit methodologies do the reverse, but audit interrogation software is often the more effective internal audit tool, because it is so powerful.
5. A comprehensive approach to IT, auditing by the internal auditor is like a three-legged stool. It comprises the audit of (a) the systems development process, (b) the general IT facilities, and (c) individual applications. Remove one of these legs and the audit scope becomes unstable.
6. Just as managers have become computer users, computer operators and IT systems designers, so must internal auditors.
7. Some businesses have too much data but too little information: some have too much information but too little analysis: some have too much analysis but too few decisions based upon that analysis: others have too many decisions but too little action to implement those decisions: others have enough or too much action but not enough control over their actions.

9. Principia for internal auditing working with the board

1. The board has overall responsibility for the effectiveness of all aspects of internal control.
2. Internal audit should serve the board and all of management.
3. An enterprise should ensure that its internal audit function has unrestricted access to the audit committee of the board.
4. The appointment, dismissal or transfer of the head of internal audit should have prior approval of the audit committee.
5. Internal audit should not subordinate its judgement on audit matters to that of others.
6. Internal audit should arrange its programme of work so that it is able to provide the board, through its audit committee, with an annual, overall summary opinion on the effectiveness of internal control.

APPENDIX 1

List of organisations that can be contacted

The Audit Faculty, The Institute of Chartered Accountants in England and Wales

PO Box 433, Moorgate Place, London EC2P 2BJ, UK

The Audit Faculty is the main focus in The ICAEW for all Chartered Accountants working in the areas of external and internal audit. It is a centre of excellence and an authoritative voice on matters relating to the auditing profession. It provides services to its members and makes representations to Government in the UK, the EU Commission, and other authorities.

Audit Policy and Advice, Financial Management Reporting and Audit Directorate

H.M. Treasury, 2nd Floor, Allington Towers, 19 Allington Street, London SW1E 5EB, UK

Responsible for setting the internal audit standards and promoting best practice in internal audit for central government auditors and associated bodies.

British Deming Association

The Old George Brewery, Rollerstone Street, Salisbury, Wiltshire SP1 1DX, UK

The British Deming Association is dedicated to holistic management practice based on the technique of W. Edwards Deming and bringing meaning back into people's working lives. Its principal aims are:
- to promote a greater awareness and understanding – particularly among top management – of the importance of Dr Deming's philosophy to the individual business, the national economy and society in general;
- to help people adopt the Deming approach to further The objectives of their own organisations;

- to provide members with a forum for study and exchange of appropriate information and experience;
- to form a supportive network with links to The Edwards Deming Institute in the USA and other national and international authorities.

The British Quality Foundation

Vigilant House, 120 Wilton Road, Victoria, London SW1V 1JZ, UK

The British Quality Foundation was set up in November 1992 with the aim of enhancing the performance and effectiveness of all types of organisations in the UK through the promotion of Total Quality management. It introduced the UK Quality Award as a means of identifying rewarding and publicising outstanding organisations to become the role models for Total Quality management. the award scheme and the underlying model, provide a framework for all organisations to assess themselves to identify areas for improvement and, ultimately, to bring them up to the level of the best organisations.

The Chartered Institute of Chartered Secretaries and Administrators

16 Park Crescent, London W1N 4AH, UK

ICSA promotes the advancement of efficient administration of commerce, industry and public affairs by the continued development of the study and practice of secretaryship and administration of companies and other bodies. Its objectives are:

- to qualify people as Chartered Secretaries in accordance with a comprehensive and relevant scheme of examination, practical experience and continuing professional development;
- to set and promulgate the highest standards of propriety and best practice in the Profession;
- to raise the profile of the Profession through an increased awareness of the contribution made by Chartered Secretaries in all types of organisation;
- to provide high quality support in secretaryship to both organisations and individuals.

The Chartered Institute of Public Finance and Accountancy

3 Robert Street, London WC2N 6BH, UK

The leading professional accountancy body for public services, whether in the public or private sectors. It provides education and training in accountancy and financial management, and sets and monitors professional standards. Its professional qualification is supported by a range of products and services.

Department of Trade and Industry

Contact: DTI regional offices

'Managing into the 1990s programme' is part of the DTI's Enterprise Initiative. This programme is supported by literature, practical advice and videos on free loan, dealing with quality improvement policies, ISO 9000-Quality Systems and the concept of Total Quality Management (TQM).

The European Confederation of Institutes of Internal Auditors

Contact: The Institute of Internal Auditors – UK

The ECIIA was founded in 1982 by a number of European National institutes, which represents 19 European Nations, plus Israel, and is the voice for internal auditing in Europe. Many of its members are affiliated to The IIA.

The European Foundation for Quality Management

Brussels Representative Office, Avenue des Pléiades 19, 1200 Brussels, Belgium

The European Foundation for Quality Management has a membership of over 440 European organisations, all of whom recognise the role of quality in improving efficiency, effectiveness and achieving business excellence. The EFQM is committed to promoting quality as the fundamental process for continuous improvement of the organisation.

The Housing Association Internal Audit Forum

Contact: Kelsey Beswick Network Housing Association Ltd., Network House, 10–12 Neeld Parade, Wembley Hill Road, Wembley, Middlesex HA9 6QU, UK

The Housing Association Internal Audit Forum(HAIAF) provides independent advice to housing associations on all internal audit matters. Established in 1990, HAIAF has grown as a group, currently comprising 120 members, providing a support network of auditors with a range of specialist skills. The forum's main objective is to create a centre of excellence in its field by producing good practice guides for use by auditors and as reference for other managers and audit committee members.

The Institute of Chartered Accountants of Scotland

27 Queen Street, Edinburgh EH2 1LA, UK

Published controversial proposals in 1993, on auditing into the 21st century, in particular the future of internal auditing and its relationships with external auditing.

The Institute of Internal Auditors Inc.

249 Maitland Avenue, Altamonte Springs, Florida 32701-4201, USA

The IIA's mission is to be the primary international associate, organised on a worldwide basis, dedicated to the promotion and development of the practice of internal auditing. The IIA is committed to providing, on an international scale, comprehensive professional development activities, standards for the practice of internal auditing and certification; researching, disseminating, and promoting to its members and to the public throughout the world knowledge and information concerning internal auditing, internal control, and related subjects; establishing meetings worldwide in order to educate members and others as to the practice of internal auditing as it exists in various countries throughout the world; bringing together internal auditors from all countries to share information and experiences in internal auditing and promoting education in the field of internal auditing. Its services to members and others includes quality assurance reviews, global benchmarking, certification programmes, control self-assessment advice, training, research and publications.

The Institute of Internal Auditors Research Foundation

249 Maitland Avenue, Altamonte Springs, Florida 32701-4201, USA

A nonprofit organisation devoted to assisting auditors in understanding, addressing, and overcoming the daily challenges they face in the workplace. Providing valuable research to the profession of internal auditing for more than 20 years. The IIARF continually informs professionals of the latest auditing and control trends. The IIARF accomplishes its objectives by researching, disseminating, and promoting knowledge and information about internal auditing, internal control and related subjects. The IIARF has published more than 100 reports on a wide variety of subjects, ranging from information systems technology and business management to the impact of business process reengineering on internal auditing.

The Institute of Internal Auditors – UK

13 Abbeville Mews, 88 Clapham Park Road, London SW4 7BX, UK

The IIA-UK is the primary body in the UK and Ireland representing, promoting and developing the professional practice of internal auditing and is a major contributor to the development of internal auditing worldwide. The IIA-UK is affiliated to The IIA.

The Institute of Management

Management House, Cottingham Road, Corby, Northants NN17 1TT, UK

Promotes the development, exercise and recognition of professional management.

Management Audit Limited

Water Mill, Moat Lane, Old Bolingbroke, Spilsby, Lincolnshire PE23 4EU, UK

Management Audit is a progressive internal auditing consultancy in corporate governance and advice on internal auditing – with an international reputation and clients across the world. Products include software, training material and auditing guides.

MCS Control Training and Design Inc.

Mississauga, Ontario, Canada

World leaders in control design training and work team driven control and risk self-assessment (CRSA). Creator of the Historical/Traditional and New Vision concepts of CRSA.

National Institute of Standards and Technology

Administration Building – Room A537, Gaithersburg, Maryland 20899, USA

USA responsibility for The Malcolm Baldrige National Quality Award is assigned to the Department of Commerce. The MBNQA is an annual award to recognise US companies that excel in quality management and quality achievement. NIST, an agency of the Department's Technology Administration, manages the award programme. NIST's goals are to aid US industry through research and services. Much of NIST's work relates directly to quality and quality-related requirements in technology development and technology utilisation.

National Society for Quality through Teamwork (NSQT)

2 Castle Street, Salisbury SP1 1BB, UK

The NSQT is an independent voluntary membership organisation dedicated to helping UK organisations to develop a culture in which everyone is involved in managing and improving their own processes and works together in teams to improve the service to customers. Since its launch in 1982 by 20 founder companies, the NSQT has developed into the UK's leading authority on achieving Quality through Teamwork, with more than 400 member organisations today. The NSQT organises a programme of regional meetings and site visits designed to promote best practice, and its annual conference is the largest teamwork conference in Europe. Its team of dedicated trainers actively facilitate management and workplace teams to achieve their aims.

Quality Audit Division, The American Society for Quality Control

611 East Wisconsin Avenue, PO Box 3005, Milwaukee, Wisconsin 53201-3005, USA

Supports auditors and other stakeholders by defining and promoting auditing as a management tool to achieve continuous improvement, effective communication, and increased customer satisfaction. It defines and publishes standards of quality auditing applicable to all business and industries. It has a programme for Quality Auditor certification.

South Bank Business School, South Bank University

103 Borough Road, London SE1 0AA, UK

The SBBS is one of the largest business schools in the UK. It is one of a few universities in the UK teaching and researching professional internal auditing. It has been teaching internal auditing since 1980 and provides internal auditing electives at undergraduate level. It has recently established review courses for The IIA Certified Internal Auditor (CIA®) learning programme. These are held twice each year linked to students' study plans and the CIA examinations in May and November.

Training and Enterprise Councils

Contact your local area TEC

TEC's will provide advice and guidance on the national Investors in People Standard. Investors in People adds teeth to quality programmes, motivates people, satisfies customers and builds an organisation's reputation. Achieving the Standard means a commitment at the top of an organisation to benchmark and measure to each of its requirements.

Index

Accessibility 93
Accountability 63, 64
Accounting records 361
Accounts payable 379
Accounts receivable 378
ACT motif 115
Activity report 239
Added value 3–51, 134, 148, 153–6
Advisory group 138
American Institute of Certified Public Accountants 60
American Society for Quality Control, Quality Audit Division 390
Analytical approach 112
Appointments 70
Approach dictionary 180–1
Arthur Andersen 52
Attributes of world-class internal auditing 15
Audit Commission 94, 95
Audit committee 22, 117–19, 307–10
　and head of internal audit 310
　and internal audit 309
　and internal control 314–15
　duties of 308
　reporting on audit work done 310
　secretary 310
　status 118
　terms of reference 321–4
　theory 118–19
　timing and content of meetings 325
Audit Faculty (ICAEW) 56, 385
Audit project, psychology 186–8
Auditing News 28
Auditing Practices Board (APB) 16
Auditing Practices Board Statement (SAS 500) 4
Auditing Practices Committee of CCAB Limited 61
Auditors' Code 16, 18
　see also Code

Authorisation 54
Authority 55, 188, 241, 349

Bellamy, A.M. 30
Benchmarking 12–13, 31–6, 106, 233, 293–7
Best practice 136–7
　achieving xxxi
　benchmarking (BPB) 12
　codes 68
　internal auditing 30–7
Beta test 49–50
Board of directors 68, 303–36, 366–7, 384
　communication with 240
　working with 303–36
Brace 1 106
Brace 2 293–8
Brainstorming 48, 155
British Deming Association 385
British Quality Foundation 386
Business activities, key issues 366–79
Business ethics. *See* Ethical issues
Business excellence, POCL 179–80
Business gifts, favours and entertainment 359–60
Business role in changing world 334–6
Business systems 295

Cadbury Code of Best Practice 306–7, 309–11
Cadbury Committe 61, 63, 102–3
Cadbury Report on the Financial Aspects of Corporate Governance. *See* Cadbury Committee
Canadian Institute of Chartered Accountants 62, 66
Capability 66
Cash handling 376–8
Certified Internal Auditor (CIA) 40
　examinations 53
Characteristics, teamwork 155

391

392 Index

Chartered Institute of Chartered Secretaries and Administrators 386
Chartered Institute of Public Finance and Accountancy (CIPFA) 6, 62, 65, 227, 386
Charters 91–9, 119–21, 125–9, 186, 223, 227, 386
Chief internal auditor 37
Choice 92, 93
Citizen's Charter 91–9
Classification 54
Client relationships 158
CoCo study 62
Code of business conduct 357–65
Code of conduct 55, 70
Code of ethics xxix, 346–7
Code of practice 68, 306–7
Colour 143
Commitment 66
Committee of Sponsoring Organisations of the Treadway Commission. See COSO
Committee on the Financial Aspects of Corporate Governance. See Cadbury Committee
Communications 157
Community obligations 364
Competency framework for internal auditors (CFIA) 20
Competition 129–31
Compliance 147–8, 175
 testing for 190
Compliance auditor 145–6
Composition 143
Computer networks 157
Confidentiality 360
Conflict in teamwork 164
Conflicts of interest 358–9
Continuous improvement 112, 127, 156, 162
Contract staff 130
Contracting out vs. in-house internal auditing 216
Control 72–3, 175
 assessment 190
 defining 57–65
 post–1990 definition 61
 pre–1990s definition 60
Control and risk self-assessment (CRSA) programme 327
 defining a new vision 331
Control environment, top-down review of 85–91
Control experts 52, 53, 380–1
Control frameworks, criteria 66–7

Control objectives 65–9
Control overview, case study 82–3
Control Self-Assessment Centre 78
Control strengths 108
Control systems, effectiveness assessment 54
Control weaknesses 109–10, 190
Corporate governance 63, 72–3, 87–8, 102–3, 165
 defining 57–65
 standards in public services 65
Corporate level involvement 39
COSO 61, 62, 303–6, 315, 321
Creativity 54, 115, 142, 143, 165
Criminal, thinking like a 74
CSA Qualification 78
Customer focus 112, 127, 134
Customer needs and job specifications 121–2
Customer relations 364–5
Customer retention 89–90
Customer satisfaction, measuring 234–6
Customers as suppliers 161

Delegation of authority 55
Delphi study 30–7
Department of Trade and Industry (DTI) 387
Design quality 153–82
Detailed audit assignment report 239
Development 173–7
Director of internal audit 88, 90
Discrimination 76, 93
Distribution arrangements 374
Documentation 123, 130
 information technology (IT) 281

Eastman Kodak Company 154, 155
Easycall Limited 85–91
Economy 175
Education 173–7
Effectiveness 13–14, 54, 175
Efficiency 54, 175
Efficiency measures and value for money 229
Employees, conduct towards 362–3
Employment regulations 55
Empowerment 76
End products 237
Enlightenment 76
Environment 175
Environmental issues 76
Equality 175
Ernst & Young 6
Ernst & Young International 157
Ethical issues xxix, 73, 76, 175, 346–7

European Confederation of Institutes of Internal Auditors (ECIIA) 387
European Foundation for Quality Management 387
Excellence in teamwork 162–3, 180
Excitement in internal auditing 123–5, 142–4
Executive directors 68
External control 304
External review overview 87

Fabrizius, Michael P. 28
Fact finding and documenting 190
Findings 244
First Report of the Committee on Standards in Public Life 64
Fixed assets 378–9
Flexibility 54
Follow-up
  audit report 238
  audit visit 191–2
Foreign Corrupt Practices Act 1977 305–6
Fraud check-list 75
Fraud prevention 74, 88–9, 137
Future, understanding the importance of 75–6

GAIN benchmarks 12
Garitte, Jean-Pierre xxiv, 29
Glossary of terms 299–301, 337–45
Governance. *See* Corporate governance
Government Internal Audit Manual (GIAM) 136–7
Grievance procedures 365

Head of internal audit
  and audit committee 310
  meeting with 311
Her Majesty's Inspectorate of Schools 97
Honesty 64
Housing Association Internal Audit Forum (HAIAF) 102, 387
Housing associations (HA) 100–7

ICAEW 1994 61
ICAEW Audit Faculty 56, 385
IIA Educator 20
IIA Standards 38, 92, 93, 119, 124, 127, 130, 159, 162, 192, 217–18, 244, 278
  General 100 – Independence 160
  General 200 – Professional proficiency 160
  General 300 – Scope of work 160
  General 400 – Performance of audit work 160
  General 500 – Management of the internal audit department 160
  Guidelines 520.01 217
  Guidelines 520.03 217
  Guidelines 560.01.03 217
  Guidelines 560.03 218
  Guidelines 560.04 218
  Specific 520 – Planning 217
Imagination 115
In Search of Excellence 57, 151
Independence 21–3, 31, 226, 227, 349, 351
Information availability 93
Information technology (IT) xxxi, 275–302, 383–4
  appraising implemented systems 283–4
  auditing applications 286
  auditing facilities 284–5
  auditors' concerns 276–7
  best practice involvement with 292–9
  contingency planning 297–8
  converting files 282–3
  developing user procedures 282
  documentation 281
  feasibility study 280
  glossary 299–301
  implementing new systems 283
  interrogation software 291
  management's responsibility for control 277–8
  security 297
  software 287–9
  steering committee 281
  testing 281–2
  use to improve audit service 275
In-house internal auditing vs. contracting out 216
Innovation 23–4, 54, 115
  in teamwork 163–5
Inputs
  in performance measures 216, 221–2
  model 219
  performance measures 221–2
Inspectorate of Constabulary 96
Institute of Business Ethics 73
Institute of Chartered Accountants in England and Wales (ICAEW) 5, 61, 62, 385
  Audit Faculty 56
  see also ICAEW
Institute of Chartered Accountants of Scotland 387
Institute of Internal Auditors (IIA) 4, 19, 38, 60, 388

394 Index

Institute of Internal Auditors (*contd*)
  Research Foundation 20, 388
  Statement of Responsibilites of Internal
    Auditing xxxi
  see also IIA Standards
Institute of Internal Auditors – UK (IIA-UK)
  53, 55, 61, 63, 388
  MIIA professional level examinations 42,
    63
  PIIA practitioner level examinations 41
  qualifications 41–7
Institute of Management 389
Integrity 63, 64
Interim reports 238
Interlocking teams 154, 157–8
Internal audit unit
  quality measure for 126
  reports on 243
  services provided by 24
Internal auditing
  1987 37
  1997 28–30
  activities 188–9, 192–3
  analysis 7
  and audit committee 309
  and consultancy 106
  assignments 242
  audit scale 143
  audit scope 34, 226, 352
  Audit Summary Working Paper (ASWP)
    form 246–8
  audit technology, matching to management's
    technology 275–6
  charter 104
  communicating results 237–8
  communication with board of directors 240
  definition xxxi
  evidence of 5–6
  fieldwork 191
  function 37, 88
    worldwide 135
  history and development 3–5
  implicit or explicit objectives 224
  leading edge xxxi, 3–51
  modern xxix–xxxiv
  needs assessment 192–213
    subjective judgements in 201–2
  overall summary opinions 313
  placing in context 215
  planned programme 312
  planning 185–213, 367–8, 382
  planning and conducting 185–92

  policy and advice 136–8, 180, 385
  preparation 189
  principles and practices xxix, 380–4
  professionalism in 32
  progress against plan 311
  recommendations 187
  reports 191, 237–73, 383
    and controls 69
    authorised report signatories 252
    balance 256–8
    circulation of 252–3
    communicating results 262
    content 263
    cover page 264
    distribution 254
    draft report 248–50
    drafting 250
    effective drafting 256
    essential attributes of 260
    follow up 266–9
    measuring success 270
    medium selection 246
    objectives 244–5, 245–6
    objectives and scope 264–5
    oral presentation 266
    planning 239
    presentation style 256
      recommendations 266, 270
    requirements 243
    reviewing 251, 270
    rules for writing 257–61
    signing 251
    structure and content 261
    success 225, 237
    summary of main findings and
      recommendations 265
    summary reports 262
    timing of 253–4
    transmittal memorandum 262–4
    types of 238
    writing style 256–8
  responsibilities xxxi
  risk 193–4
    components 195
    modelling 194–5
  risk formula 195–210
    mechanics of design 202–8
    scoring scale for audit factors 199
    scoring scale for control factors 198
    scoring scale for size factors 197
    seeking consensus 210
    weighting factors 208–10

vision of 11
working papers 192
Internal Auditor 14
Internal control 303–5, 360–1
   and audit committee 314–15
   definition 303, 305, 306
   directors' report 307
   effectiveness 315–19
   letter of representation on 317
   overall summary opinions 313
   public reporting 308
   report 313
   reporting publicly 305
   structures 57
Internal financial control 103, 305, 307
International standards xxix
Introductions 189
ISO 9000 125, 127–30

Job descriptions 138–41
   lead auditor 138
   staff auditor 139–40
Job specifications 125–9
   and customer needs 121–2
Job vacancies 23
   notices of 121–2
Johnson, Howard J. 30
Johnson, Thomas A. 29

Key Result Areas (KRAs) 170
Knowledge 142–3
Kodak 169–70

Language skills 134
Leadership 64
Leading edge
   adding value through professionalism 16–19
   internal auditing xxxi, 3–51
   values of small internal audit unit 13–14
League tables of performance 95
Learning 67
Letter of comfort 77, 317
Letter of representation on internal control 77, 317
Line 142
Link management 72–3
Local authority audit 94
Local authority services 95

Management 353
   defining 57–65

Management Audit Limited 389
Management control xxx, 52–110
Management information 368–9
Management leadership 112
Management of internal auditing 36
Management perceptions of internal audit value 56
Management principles and practices xxx
   and performance measures integration 226
Management satisfaction survey 220
Manager's role in teamwork 173–7
Manuals 123, 125–9
Market testing 215–17
Marketing 111–52, 369–71, 381
   academic vs. practical 151
   exciting internal auditing pictures 123–5
   internal audit 104–6
   linkage to bottom line 151–2
   objective and independent 117–19
   overview 150–2
   quality issues 125–9
Mautz and Sharaf's postulates of auditing 10
MCS Control Training and Design Inc. 389
Meetings 192
Mission 135
Modelling 50
Modern internal auditing xxix–xxxiv
Monitoring 67, 71
   performance 219–20

National Audit Office 94, 137
National Federation of Housing Associations (NFHA) 101
National Housing Federation (NHF) 101
National Institute of Standards and Technology 389
National Society for Quality through Teamwork (NSQT) 155, 389–90
Network Housing Assciation Limited (NHA) 100–7
New internal audit 8
New offering opportunities 47–50
New product process 49
Newton, Sir Isaac xx
NHS audit 95
Nolan Committee on Standards in Public Life 64, 70
Non-executive directors 68
Nonfinancial audit findings 39

Objectives 54, 66, 85
Objectivity 21–3, 31, 38–9, 64, 311–12

Office of the Auditor General of Canada 15
Openness 63, 64, 70, 93
Operational records 361
Organisational status 240
Organisational structures 55
Outputs
　model 219
　performance measures 216, 223–5
Outside resistance to internal auditor 146–7
Outsourcing 130
　advantages and disadvantages 131
Overall summary report on internal control 239

Partners in business achievement 106
Payroll measures 376
Pensions 375–6
Performance 72–3, 352
　evaluation form 140–1
　league tables of 95
　monitoring 219–20
　teamwork 163
Performance measures 214–36, 382–3
　categorising 218–21
　inputs 216, 221–2
　integrating with good management practice 226
　interpreting 226
　outputs 216, 223–5
　process 216, 222–3
　value for money 228
Performance of internal auditing 3
Personnel 375–6
Perspective 143
Planning. See Audit planning
Police 96
Political activities 362
Portable computers 292
Post Office Counters Ltd (POCL) 177–82
　business excellence 179–80
　difficulties experienced 178–9
　early years 177–8
　initial progress 178
Postulates of auditing 10
Price vs. value for money 217
Price Waterhouse Corporate Register 309
Principia 25–6, 80, 132–3, 165, 211, 230–1, 271–2, 290, 319–20
Prisons Inspectorate 96
Proactive small internal audit unit xxix
Problem-solving opportunities 48
Problem-solving partners 164

Problem-solving process 159–61
Process
　management 180
　model 219
　performance measures 216, 222–3
Product launching 50
Product quality 364–5
Production and manufacturing requirements 373
Professional examinations 40–7
Professional practice 278, 351–3
Professional proficiency 351
Professional standards 119–21
Professionalism 159, 220
　adding leading edge through 16–19
Professionalism in internal auditing 32
Progress reports 192
Project work 186
Promotion criteria 111–12
Psychology, audit project 186–8
Public life, principles of 64
Public purse protection 136–8
Public services, corporate governance standards in 65
Purchasing policies and procedures 372–3
Purpose 241

Quality
　in products and services 73
　of public services 92
Quality-associated missions 116
Quality assurance 127, 130, 218, 242
　programme 217
　reports 242
Quality Audit Division, American Society for Quality Control 390
Quality leadership process 154
Quality management 149, 159
Quality measure for the internal audit unit 126
Quality policy 130
Quality programme 149–50, 156
Quality promotion 112–14
Quality rules 112–13
Quality system 127
Quality systems 159
Quasi-quantitative measures 219

Recommendations 162–3, 239, 244, 249
Recruitment and training 55
Recycling opportunities 48
Refining 50

Reliability 175
Reporting on Internal Control 63
Representation letters 77
Resource availability 232–3
Responsibilities 241, 303–4, 348–50
   division of 54
Responsibilities of internal auditing xxxi
Retail company, case study 83–5
Retention of customers 89–90
Reviewing, audit reports 251
Risk assessment 77, 185
Risk components, synonyms of 194
Risk implications 99–100
   see also Internal audit risk
Role conflict 187–8
Royal Society of Arts (RSA) 334
Rudloff, Robert W. Jr. 29
Rules and regulations 71
Russell fraud check-list 75–6
Rutteman Report 304, 305, 307, 308, 315, 321

Safeguards 54
Sales activities 371–2
School standards 97
Screening 49
Securities and Exchange Commission 305
Security 54, 175, 297
Segregation 54
Selection 173–7
Self-assessment 77–9
Self-reporting 77–9
Self-supervising teams 156
Selflessness 64
Sentinel 78
Serafini, Richard M. 29
Seven S Framework 57–8
Shaping 49
Shareholders 85
Skills 58
Small internal audit unit xxix
   leading edge values 13–14
   proactive xxix
SMART programme 178
Social services 97–8
Social Services Inspectorate 97
Software for audit administration 287, 289
South Bank Business School, South Bank University 390
Special assignments 312
Staff dimension 58
Staff recruitment and development xxx

Stakeholders 71, 73
Standards. *See* IIA Standards
Statement of responsibilities 348–50
Storage requirements 374
Strategic partnerships 130
Strategy 16, 58
Strengths 86
Structure 58
Style 58
Subscription fraud 89
Substantiation 54
Success 175
   teamwork 168, 172
Summary audit assignment report 239
Superordinate goals 57, 58
Supervision 192, 212–13
   importance of supervisory skills 212
   role of supervisor 212–13
Supplier-process-customer chain 127
Supplier relationships 361
Supply chain teams 159
Systems auditor 145
Systems changes 58
Systems development 145, 278–84

Talented people 19–21
Teaching managers to self-assess and report on responsibility and control 77–9
Team learning 156
Teamwork 112, 127, 153–6, 381
   achievements 162
   characteristics 155
   composition of team 167
   conflict 164
   control 167
   effectiveness 154–8
   excellence 162-3, 180
   IIA Standards 159
   innovation 163–5
   manager's role in 172
   performance 163
   popularity 166
   success 168, 172
   technology in 157–8
   working across boundaries 168
   working context 166
Teamwork relationship 158
Technology
   in teamwork 157–8
   needs to understand the challenges and impact of xxxi
Telecommunications 157, 296

Testing 50
Time span 56, 75–6
Tone 142–3
Top management support 3
Top-down review of control environment 85–91
Total quality management (TQM) 73, 125, 144–50
Traditional audit work 8
Training 149–50, 155, 156
Training and Enterprise Councils (TECs) 390
Treadway Commission 14
Treasury Officer of Accounts (TOA) team 137
Treasury operations 117, 137–8, 376–8

UK Consultative Committee of Accounting Bodies 218

Value for money 92
  and efficiency measures 229
  economy (inputs) measures 228
  performance measures 228
  vs. price 217
Video conferencing 157
Vision 125–9, 134, 174, 175
Vision 115–17, xxx
Vision of internal auditing 11

Warehousing facilities 374
Weaknesses 86–7
Whistleblowing 70
Work undertaken by internal audit units 8
Workshop groups 327
World-class internal auditing, key attributes 52
Worldwide internal audit function 135
Written communication rules 273